Abby Mandel's Cuisinart® Classroom

Cuisinart Cooking Club, Inc., Publisher
Greenwich, Connecticut

1817

HARPER & ROW, PUBLISHERS, New York
Cambridge, Philadelphia, San Francisco, London,
Mexico City, São Paulo, Singapore, Sydney

With enormous gratitude to the thousands of enthusiastic students, my fellow cooks, who have helped me to refine my teaching and writing techniques through hundreds of classes.

And with appreciation to my loyal, resilient staff, who have supported me in this effort and smiled through tastings until I was satisfied — even when that involved 30 chocolate cakes, 25 pita breads, and all the Mandarin pancakes that 50 pounds of flour can make!

My special thanks to Patricia Dailey, who cheerfully saw me through the countless dozens of eggs required for testing the recipes for the second edition, and to my editor, Ruth McElheny, for the dedication and respect for accuracy that have made a significant contribution to this book.

Edited by Ruth S. McElheny

Design by Catherine N. Goulet

Photography direction by Lora Koenig and Pamela Stewart

Photography by Jeffrey Weir

Front cover photograph by Fredric Stein

The cover photograph shows Abby Mandel with a selection of dishes made by her new technique for beating egg whites: Raspberry Chiffon (page 298), Chocolate Torte (page 294), and Fresh Strawberry Cake Roll (page 302).

ISBN: 0-06-091182-4
Library of Congress Catalog Card Number: 83-47567

Cuisinart® is a registered trademark of Cuisinarts, Inc. Greenwich, Connecticut
Sixth Printing, May, 1984

Contents

Preface

If I ever doubted my conviction that the food processor is rapidly becoming the most convenient and widely used appliance in the American kitchen, those doubts disappeared when 65,000 copies of the first edition of this book sold in little more than a year.

Versatile, easy to use and easy to maintain, food processors contribute to better health by encouraging home preparation of foods once storebought, from bread to ground meat and peanut butter to baby food. And most important, they contribute to our pleasure at the table by effortlessly handling all the time-consuming tasks that accompany preparation of fine food: chopping, slicing, shredding, mixing, puréeing and kneading.

The rapid sale of the first edition gives me a chance to share with you in this revision some newly developed recipes using egg whites beaten in the food processor — a feat assumed impossible until recently.

To the 230 recipes of the original edition, I have added 23 entirely new recipes and revised a number of others to incorporate my new technique for beating egg whites.

Until now, use of beaten egg whites seemed so complicated and unpredictable to many cooks that they didn't even try to enter one of the most rewarding domains of cookery. Thanks to the food processor, a skill thought unattainable becomes simple, bringing a whole new dimension to your cooking. Let's go to work!

Clockwise from bottom: Spinach Pasta with Scallions and Tomatoes, page 103; Carrot, Prune and Raisin Cake, page 211; Mushroom Mayonnaise, page 270; Crudités, page 3; Caraway Pumpernickel Bread, page 183; Serving Plate, with Roast Beef Slices.

Welcome to My Classroom!_____

Since 1975 I have taught over 500 Machine Cuisine® classes to thousands of students. This book contains more than 250 recipes that my students and I have enjoyed.

I teach because I want to make others as excited about cooking as I am. In my classes, there's food everywhere — seafood sizzling in sauté pans, enough fruits and vegetables to stock a small farm stand, loaves of bread in the oven, homemade pasta drying on the counters, tart shells ready to be filled. While I teach, the blades of my food processor whirl, as entrées, vegetables, salads, doughs, pastries and desserts take shape. I answer students' questions as I work. They never wait to ask a question, knowing that later they'll be too busy eating to remember it.

Each two-hour class is planned as a feast — not only so the students can enjoy a variety of tastes, but also so I can emphasize how the food processor allows them to prepare more than they thought possible in so little time. I mix and knead bread dough, arrange beautifully garnished main courses, add a quick sauce and make dessert, completing all the tedious preparation tasks in minutes.

I acquired my first food processor at a Smith College benefit bazaar in 1973, because Julia Child praised it during her cooking demonstration at that event. I bought one partly because the profit went to my alma mater, little realizing how much that purchase would contribute to my future education!

Although I had always loved to cook, I had no professional aspirations. As a housewife with three children, I assumed I could never acquire the skills of a trained chef. But once I started cooking with the food processor, I realized the machine would allow me to try things that I had neither time nor patience for before. I worked my way through the equivalent of a professional apprenticeship, because the machine was there to do the cutting, slicing, shredding, mixing, puréeing and kneading — all the tasks that previously took hours. The consistently reliable and attractive results spurred my imagination. Whether I wanted an exquisite garnish of julienne-cut vegetables or a crusty loaf of French bread, the machine provided almost instant "arm power".

With the food processor I became both a teacher and a dedicated student. I am still studying and learning, usually at home, where I develop recipes for my classes as well as for my weekly newspaper column and the monthly food processor feature I write for *Bon Appetit* magazine. But two or three times a year I go to Europe, where I have had the good fortune to work with some of the world's greatest chefs. No small part of my learning process takes place in the Machine Cuisine® classroom, however, where students challenge me continually with their cooking needs and problems.

I want to give my students more than explanations of individual recipes. To engage them in the creative process of cooking and to share the opportunities that the food processor opened for me, I try to teach cooking principles and food processor techniques simultaneously. Despite its compact size and its resemblance to other counter-top appliances, the food processor is unlike any of them: it is a general-purpose, versatile appliance. Unlike a mixer with attachments that take time to change (and to wash), the food processor lets you shift instantly from slicing fruit to making pastry, from making pizza dough to slicing sausage or shredding cheese. It won't automatically make you a great cook, but it will help you make the most of your culinary talent and inventiveness.

This book reflects my teaching goals. The recipes give detailed cooking information and explain food processor techniques needed to ensure completely successful results. In my classroom, I do not divide lessons into "beginner" and "advanced" levels, and I have not done so here. Explicit food processor directions make such distinctions irrelevant. You can make a mousse or a sherbet just as easily as you whip together a simple dip. Some recipes call for more steps than others, but none of them requires complex skills. I am confident that you can open this book to any dish that tempts you and prepare it perfectly on your first try.

The recipes in this book do not call for exotic or special ingredients. Why save time on food preparation only to squander it shopping? Because of the wide variation in seasonal produce, I encourage substitutions. The easiest and most accurate way to substitute dry ingredients is by weight: if you have a kitchen scale (and you should!), you can conveniently substitute an equal weight of one vegetable, fruit or type of flour for another.

I don't think you should have to flip back and forth between recipes and instructions, so I have described essential techniques as explicitly as possible in each recipe. If you have not used the food processor before, you should read your instruction manual carefully to become familiar with the manufacturer's recommendations.

My recipes have been developed and tested in a standard-size Cuisinart® food processor with a conventional feed tube. But I own every other brand of food processor on the market and have retested recipes in them, just to make sure that each recipe will work no matter which machine you use. Although all the food processors perform adequately, some have stronger motors than others. You are most likely to notice the discrepancy when you try to knead stiff doughs: if your machine slows down, indicating that it can't handle the whole recipe, divide the dough in half, process it in two batches and combine the batches by hand.

I have experienced the impact of the food processor revolution thousands of times — in my own cooking, in my students' accomplishments, and in the kitchens of professional chefs. One recent development I find especially noteworthy is the Cuisinart® expanded feed tube, which allows you to make larger slices and eliminates much of the trimming once needed to fit such foods as whole oranges, tomatoes and onions into the conventional feed tube. The expanded feed tube has done away with my "soup bag" — the scraps I used to save from food that had to be cut to fit the feed tube.

Recent surveys show that people buy more food processors than any other appliance. Manufacturers have encouraged this trend and responded to it by providing vastly improved instruction manuals. I no longer feel that I have to explain the basic parts of a machine or to describe which parts to use for chopping meat, shredding vegetables or kneading dough. So I list here only those processor pointers that you may not find, or may overlook in the manuals. Then we can get on with the real revolution — the fresher, more interesting and more imaginative fare that everyone can enjoy, thanks to the food processor!

Here are notes from my Machine Cuisine® classroom about the most common problems and errors. Keep them in mind when converting your own recipes for the food processor or when devising variations on the recipes in this book.

1. **Think through the preparation sequence and you will rarely have to wipe out the work bowl between steps of a recipe. Parsley, garlic and shallots can only be chopped effectively in a clean bowl, so process them before other ingredients, even if you are reserving them for later use.**

2. **A good general rule is to process the hardest ingredients first, leaving liquids until last. (The procedure for making cakes is an exception; see the note on cakes below.)**

3. **When chopping, do not put large pieces of food in the work bowl. Cut large food to be chopped into 1-inch pieces, smaller foods (such as a single onion) into quarters.**

4. **Mince garlic cloves or shallots by dropping them through the feed tube with the machine running.**

5. **Do not try to chop ingredients by continuous processing. To retain control over texture, turn the machine on and off and check contents of work bowl after each "off" turn.**

6. Don't attempt to chop too much food at one time. With smaller batches, you have more control. The exception is parsley, which you can chop by the bowlful as long as you remove the stems.

7. To chop ingredients with high water content, such as celery, green peppers and cucumbers, first slice them, then insert the metal blade and chop them in small batches.

8. To make even slices and shreds, regulate pressure on the pusher according to texture of the food — firm for hard foods like carrots, medium for zucchini, light for mushrooms and so on. Always use light pressure for cheese.

9. Do not mash potatoes with the metal blade. Shred first, add milk and butter, then process briefly with metal blade.

10. When puréeing vegetables for soup, don't process them with all the liquid. Drain the vegetables and purée them without any liquid. Then add 1/2 cup of the liquid and stir the resulting mixture back into the broth.

11. When adapting yeast bread recipes to the food processor, don't add all the flour until the dough has massed together. You can then determine how much more flour is necessary, eliminating the risk of tough, dry dough.

12. Do not cream the butter and sugar for cake batters. First process the eggs and sugar, then add the butter.

13. Add dry ingredients to a cake batter last. Turn the machine on and off just until the flour disappears. Don't use the method of alternating liquid and dry ingredients.

14. Process confectioners sugar with the metal blade to remove lumps before you add other frosting ingredients.

15. Do not process pastry dough until it forms a ball; stop processing as soon as it starts to mass together.

16. Who says you can't beat egg whites in a food processor? Turn to page 273 to find out how.

Always remember that many, many recipes in other cookbooks can be prepared more easily and quickly with the help of a food processor, but the sequence of dealing with ingredients will often be very different from that described in the original recipe. When adapting a recipe for the food processor, consult the notes above, then read similar recipes in this book. Review the sequence in which ingredients are processed. This will guide you in processing the ingredients of your own recipes.

Note: Because parsley weighs so little in small quantities, it is difficult to specify weight. We measured it in cups and fractions of cups, which should always be loosely packed.

Menu Suggestions

Brunch
Oranges Orientale
Omelets with Onion Filling
Sausage Patties
Hazelnut Apple Cake

Formal Brunch
Gazpacho Bloody Mary
Poached Fish with
　Cucumber Caper Sauce
Pasta Primavera
Fruit Lovers' Platter
Caramel Nut Rolls

Summer Luncheon
Parsnip and Spinach Soup
Eleven Layer Salad
Basic French Bread
Chocolate Mousse

Picnic
Sliced Rare Beef, Mushroom
　Mayonnaise
Pumpernickel Bread
Spinach Pasta with Scallion
　and Tomato Topping
Crudités
Carrot, Prune and
　Raisin Cake

Italian Picnic
Sicilian Caponata
Turkey Tonnato
Sliced Tomatoes with Basil
　Vinaigrette
Wheat Germ Bread with
　Spinach Filling
Mocha Fudge Cake
Fresh Fruit

Cocktail Party
Smoked Salmon Pâté
Curried Chicken and
　Almond Canapés
Fruit-Glazed Ribs
Poached Scallops with
　Tomato Vinaigrette
Leek and Mushroom Quiche
Crudités with
　Blue Cheese Dip

Informal Barbecue
Feta Cheese Ball
Herbed Barbecued Turkey
Corn on the Cob
Zucchini Flan
Festive Coleslaw
Maple Walnut Cake

Formal Barbecue
Cheese Puffs (*Gougères*)
Barbecued Duck with
　Apricot Glaze
Rice with Vegetables
Orange, Avocado and
　Jerusalem Artichoke Salad
Lemon Saxon Pudding

Informal Italian Buffet
Antipasto Platter
Herb French Bread
Osso Bucco
Fresh Spinach Pasta
Orange Cake Ring

Dinner Buffet
Shrimp and Vegetable
　Mousse Mosaic
Sliced Beef, Madeira Sauce
Fresh Spinach Cannelloni
Herb French Bread
Mixed Green Salad with
　Creamy Parsley Dressing
Tartlets/Zested Strawberries

Dinner
Mussels Vinaigrette
Chicken Breasts with
　Scallions and Pistachios
Egg Noodles
Red Pepper and Water
　Chestnut Salad
Berries Supreme

Middle Eastern Dinner
Crudités with Spinach Dip
　Mimosa
Turkish Meat Casserole
Whole Wheat Pita Bread
Greek Salad
Coffee Nut Mousse

Mediterranean Dinner
Italian Salad in Marinated
　Artichokes
Chicken Provençal
Herb Pasta
Garlic Cheese Bread
Biscuit Tortoni with Fresh
　Strawberries

Chinese Dinner
Shrimp Egg Rolls
Stir-Fried Sesame Lemon
　Chicken
Asparagus Fried Rice
Broccoli, Mushroom and
　Bean Sprout Salad
Caramelized Orange
　Custard

Shellfish Dinner
Celery Egg-Drop Soup
Crab Stir-Fry
Clam Pilaf
Pineapple Sherbet

Formal Dinner
Scallop Mousse
Boneless Leg of Lamb with
　Mushroom Stuffing
Lacy Potato Pancakes
Layered Spinach, Carrot
　and Parsnip Purée
Mixed Green Salad with
　Herb Vinaigrette Dressing
French Almond Tarts

Formal Dinner with Fish
Onion Tart
Broiled Fish Fillets with
　Ginger and Lime Sauce
Stir-Fried Broccoli, Celery
　and Water Chestnuts
Mushroom Risotto
Raspberry and Apple
　Sherbet with *Tuiles*

Mexican Supper
Guacamole
Chili and Cornmeal Pie
Fresh Orange Tart

Appetizers

Appetizers

Crudités
Herbed Blue Cheese Dip
Spinach Dip Mimosa
Eggplant Caviar
Guacamole
Feta Cheese Ball with Radish Shreds
Curried Chicken and Almond Canapés
Fruit-Glazed Ribs with Orange Slices
Mussels Vinaigrette
Shrimp Egg Rolls
Marinated Scallops with Pimiento
Sicilian Caponata
Oysters Midas
Smoked Salmon Pâté with Mustard Watercress Sauce
Scallop Mousse with Scallop Hollandaise Sauce
Cheese Puffs (*Gougères*)
Onion Tart
Leek and Mushroom Quiche
Antipasto Platter

What is an appetizer? An hors d'oeuvre? A first course? It is whatever, and as much as, you want it to be — whether sit-down formal or finger-food fun!

For me, the best part of cooking is creating different experiences. I like the quiet intimacy of a beautiful French dinner no less than the all-out party mood of a heaping buffet. I know that a wonderful dinner will give any group of people something in common and that an unusual menu will help a shy guest enter the conversation. So I choose appetizers accordingly — to set the tone and the pace for the rest of the evening.

Sometimes I compose a fabulous spread of nothing but appetizers — an informal assortment of many little choices and flavor combinations. The theme might be Italian, with an antipasto selection of Caponata, Mussels Vinaigrette, White Bean and Tuna Salad, lots of colorful vegetable salads and plenty of Garlic Cheese Bread. Or there might be no theme at all, just an abundance of the kind of delicious morsels that you can't get enough of — like Shrimp Egg Rolls and Fruit Glazed Ribs, or Crudités with several dips and slices of Smoked Salmon Pâté, or Leek and Mushroom Quiche. At other times, a subtler approach is definitely called for; then I signal the mood as soon as guests are seated, with the glorious mussel-studded Scallop Mousse or the sublime luxury of Oysters Midas.

Onion Tart, page 22.

More than anything else, I want my students to be versatile, to be unafraid of meeting any occasion. So I have tried to suggest the scope of possibilities with the recipes in this chapter. There are Shrimp Egg Rolls or Fruit Glazed Ribs for a Chinese dinner, a fantastically light Onion Tart for French elegance, Guacamole for a Mexican party and Cheese Puffs (*Gougères*) for delicate cocktail nibbling. But I can't see any reason not to begin a French dinner with South American Scallops Seviche or to overlook Curried Chicken Almond Canapés for a backyard barbecue. If you think in terms of presenting a sequence of tastes and textures, you won't feel bound by conventional menu combinations. Nor do you have to stick with the recipes in this chapter. There are dozens of other dishes in this book that I often serve in appetizer-size portions, ranging from Moo Shu Chicken, Mediterranean Pizza and Poached Scallops with Tomato Vinaigrette to most of the pastas and salads. By the same token, the quiches and fish pâtés included in this section make excellent entrées for a luncheon or brunch.

To understand my enthusiasm for all kinds of appetizers, you have to realize how much work the food processor eliminates. It used to take more time to prepare all those little party tidbits than it did to compose the most elaborate main course. But the machine reduces many steps to a single process. There's very little difference in preparation time, for example, between the recipes for Herbed Blue Cheese Dip and the festive Feta Cheese Ball with Radish Shreds. The same puréeing technique used with the cheeses is the basis for Smoked Salmon Pâté and Scallop Mousse. These exquisite first courses used to be beyond the skills and patience of most home cooks, but now they're only slightly more time-consuming than a dip. Once you have produced perfect vegetable slices and made pastry with the food processor, you can feel free to choose crudités or quiche for openers according to what's most appropriate rather than what's simplest. You might even consider the quiche more convenient because it can be made ahead and frozen.

When I entertain, I look for two special qualities in the recipes. One is colorful presentation: Everything should look terrific! The other is what I call the "countdown" factor: The menu should be do-able in stages, with some parts completed a day or two in advance. These appetizers are the kind of fare I look to for impressive beginnings and unhurried hostessing. They are either very fast or sure to hold up in the refrigerator. And they are as vividly tempting as the sunny egg garnish for Spinach Dip Mimosa, the accent of orange slices for Fruit Glazed Ribs, and the beautiful contrast of peach-colored Smoked Salmon Pâté with pale green Watercress Mustard Sauce.

Make a selection of vegetables from the list, keeping in mind a need for contrast in color and texture.

Carrots, peeled and cut into pieces to fit the feed tube horizontally

Turnips or kohlrabi, peeled and halved if necessary to fit the feed tube

Cucumber, unpeeled, scored, halved if necessary to fit the feed tube, and cut into lengths to fit the feed tube

Beets, scrubbed or peeled

Large mushrooms, stems cut flat

Zucchini, unpeeled, scored, and cut into lengths to fit the feed tube

Broccoli, with flowerets removed and stems peeled and cut into lengths to fit the feed tube

Cherry tomatoes

Lettuce leaves

Medium Slicing Disc or French-Fry Disc: Slice the vegetables, applying light, medium or firm pressure on the pusher depending on the hardness of the vegetable. Carrots, turnips, beets, broccoli stems and kohlrabi require firm pressure; cucumber and zucchini require medium pressure; mushrooms require light pressure. (The turnips, beets, zucchini and kohlrabi can be processed with the medium slicing disc or the French-fry disc, but the other vegetables must be sliced.) Serve the *Crudités* with Artichoke Dill Mayonnaise, Guacamole, Eggplant Caviar, Herbed Bleu Cheese Dip, Pimiento Mayonnaise, Watercress Sauce or Spinach Dip Mimosa. Recipes for all of these are in the book and can be found in an Index.

1 small garlic clove, peeled
1 large scallion (1 ounce, 30g), including the green top, cut into 1-inch (2.5 cm) pieces
1/4 cup (6 cl) parsley leaves
8 ounces (225g) cream cheese, at room temperature, cut into 3 pieces
2 ounces (55g) blue cheese, at room temperature
1/4 cup (6 cl) sour cream
2 teaspoons Worcestershire sauce or Five Spice Marinade (available in Chinese food sections)
1/2 teaspoon dried dill weed

Metal Blade: With the machine running, mince the garlic by dropping it through the feed tube. Add the scallion and parsley, and mince them by turning the machine on and off. Add the cream cheese and blue cheese and process for 5 seconds. Add remaining ingredients and process for 2 seconds. Refrigerate in an airtight container for several hours, or overnight. Serve with *Crudités* (see Index) or chips.

Makes 1-1/2 cups (35 cl).

Variation

Thinned with milk or cream, this dip can be transformed into a delightful salad dressing.

For fewer calories, substitute Michel Guérard's *Fromage Blanc* for the sour cream.

10 ounces (285g) fresh spinach, including the stems, washed
1 large egg, hard-boiled and peeled
1 small onion (1 ounce, 30g), peeled and quartered
1/4 cup (6 cl) parsley leaves
4 anchovies, rinsed and patted dry with paper towels
2 tablespoons lemon juice
1 tablespoon white wine vinegar
1/4 cup (6 cl) Basic Mayonnaise (see Index)
1 teaspoon seasoning salt
1 cup (24 cl) sour cream or 1 cup *Fromage Blanc* Michel Guérard (see Index)

Place the spinach, with only the water clinging to its leaves, in an enameled or stainless steel saucepan. Cook, uncovered, over moderately high heat, turning it once or twice with a wooden spoon, until it is wilted. Transfer the spinach to a colander and hold it under cold running water until it is completely cool. Drain it well and wrap it in a kitchen towel, squeezing out as much moisture as possible.

Metal Blade: Chop the egg white coarsely by turning the machine on and off about 6 times, and reserve it. Process the egg yolk for 2 seconds, or until it is finely riced, and reserve it. Mince the onion by turning the machine on and off about 4 times. Add the spinach and the remaining ingredients, except the sour cream. Process the mixture until it is well blended, stopping the machine once to scrape down the sides of the work bowl. Add the sour cream and combine it by turning the machine on and off a couple of times. Add salt and pepper to taste. Transfer to a serving dish and refrigerate it, covered, until serving time. To serve, garnish the dip with an outer ring of the reserved egg white and a center of the reserved egg yolk. Serve it with *Crudités* (see Index), potato chips, or pita bread, buttered, sprinkled with sesame seed, and toasted in the oven.

Makes 1-1/2 to 2 cups (35 to 47 cl).

Spinach Dip Mimosa, with *Crudités* (see page 3)

Here is a versatile dip that is also delicious on hamburgers or ground lamb patties.

1 large eggplant
(1 pound, 455g),
unpeeled and trimmed
1 cup (24 cl) parsley
leaves
1 large garlic clove,
peeled
1 small piece of onion
(1/2 ounce, 14g), peeled
1/2 cup (12 cl) Basic
Mayonnaise (see
Index)
1/2 teaspoon dried basil
1/2 teaspoon dried
oregano
1/2 teaspoon dried dill
weed
2 teaspoons lemon juice
1 teaspoon salt
Freshly ground pepper

Preheat the oven to 350°F. (175°C.).

Bake the eggplant on a baking sheet for 50 minutes, or until it is completely softened. Let it cool and cut it into quarters.

Metal Blade: Mince the parsley by turning the machine on and off. With the machine running, mince the garlic and onion by dropping them through the feed tube. Add the eggplant and purée the mixture, stopping the machine once to scrape down the sides of the bowl. Add the remaining ingredients. Process the mixture for 5 seconds and correct the seasoning. Transfer the dip to a crock, cover it and refrigerate.

Serve with toasted pita bread, crackers, or *Crudités* (see Index).

Makes 2 cups (47 cl).

Guacamole

Usually served as a dip for *Crudités* and tortilla chips, this is also wonderful with hamburgers, tacos or a mixed vegetable salad.

1/4 cup (6 cl) parsley
    leaves
1 small piece of onion
    (1/2 ounce, 15g), peeled
1 ripe avocado
    (8 ounces, 225g),
    peeled, halved, pitted
    and cut into cubes
1 strip bacon, cooked
    crisp, drained and
    crumbled
2 teaspoons lime juice
2 drops Tabasco sauce
2 tablespoons Basic
    Mayonnaise (see
    Index)
1 small tomato
    (4 ounces, 115g),
    peeled, seeded and
    quartered
1/4 teaspoon salt

Metal Blade: Mince the parsley by turning the machine on and off. Set it aside. With the machine running, mince the onion by dropping it through the feed tube. Add the avocado, bacon, lime juice, Tabasco sauce and mayonnaise and combine the mixture, turning the machine on and off about 4 times. Then purée the mixture for 10 seconds, stopping once to scrape down the sides of the bowl. Add one tomato and the salt and turn the machine on and off about 6 times to chop the tomato.

Transfer the mixture to a serving bowl and garnish it with the chopped parsley. Serve with *Crudités* (see Index) or tortilla chips.

Makes 1-1/4 cups, (30 cl).

A fresh and flavorful version of an old friend.

Cheese

- 1 garlic clove, peeled
- 3 medium scallions (1-1/2 ounces total, 45g, including green tops, cut into 1-inch (2.5 cm) lengths
- 2 8-ounce packages (455g total) cream cheese, at room temperature, each cut into 4 pieces
- 8 ounces (225g) Feta cheese, at room temperature, cut into 4 pieces
- 3 tablespoons sour cream
- 1-1/2 teaspoons dried dill
- 1 teaspoon dried oregano
- 1/2 teaspoon freshly ground black pepper
  Salt

Metal Blade: With the machine running, mince the garlic by dropping it through the feed tube. Add the scallions to the bowl and process the mixture for 3 seconds. Add remaining ingredients, except the salt, and combine by turning the machine on and off about 6 times. Then process for 20 seconds, stopping once to scrape down the sides of the bowl. Add salt to taste and adjust other seasonings, if necessary. Spoon the mixture into a 3-cup (70 cl) bowl lined with plastic wrap. Cover it and refrigerate.

Garnish

- 1/4 cup (6 cl) parsley leaves
- 10 large radishes (5 ounces total, 140g), trimmed

Metal Blade: Mince the parsley by turning the machine on and off about 10 times. Set it aside for the garnish.

Medium Shredding Disc: Shred the radishes, using medium pressure, and transfer them to a sheet of wax paper. The radishes must be shredded only a few hours before serving.

Shape the cheese mixture into a ball and roll it in the radishes, sprinkling on any remaining shreds of radishes. Put a sheet of plastic wrap over the ball and press the radish shreds into the cheese ball. Transfer the ball to a serving plate and garnish it with the reserved parsley.

This can be served with slices of raw zucchini, cucumber, kohlrabi, turnips or beets or with toasted pita bread.

Makes about 3 cups (70 cl).

Curried Chicken and Almond Canapés

These canapés make an elegant cocktail accompaniment, and are especially delicious made with toasted rounds of homemade *Pain de Mie* loaves (see Index).

1/3 cup (8 cl) chopped blanched almonds
2 large shallots (1 ounce total, 30g)
1/4 cup (6 cl) parsley leaves
3 ounces (85g) Monterey Jack cheese, chilled
4 ounces (115g) boned cooked chicken
1 cup (24 cl) Basic Mayonnaise (see Index)
1-1/2 teaspoons curry powder
2 teaspoons fresh lemon juice
2 drops of Tabasco sauce
1/2 teaspoon salt
Freshly ground pepper
72 thinly sliced rounds, each 1-1/2 inches in diameter, or 36 thinly sliced bread ovals, each 2-1/2 inches in diameter
Sliced blanched almonds

Metal Blade: Process the chopped almonds, shallots, and parsley leaves in the work bowl for 5 seconds and leave the mixture in the bowl.

Shredding Disc: Shred the cheese, using light pressure, and leave it in the bowl.

Metal Blade: Add the chicken, combine it with the other ingredients by turning the machine on and off about 6 times, and process the mixture for 2 seconds. Add the remaining ingredients except the bread rounds. Process the mixture for 5 seconds, and correct the seasoning. The spread will keep, refrigerated in an airtight container, for 1 to 2 days.

Preheat the oven to 500°F. (260°C.).

Toast the bread rounds or ovals or sauté them in butter on 1 side, until they are golden brown. Put 1-1/2 teaspoons of the spread on each toast round, or 1 tablespoon on each oval, mounding it toward the center. Top each canapé with an almond slice and place them on a baking sheet. Bake the canapés for 5 to 8 minutes, or until they are lightly colored and sizzling.

Makes 72 round or 36 oval canapés.

Variations

1. Substitute 1 cup (4 ounces, 115g) chopped cooked turkey for the chicken.

2. Add 1 tablespoon of mango chutney to the spread.

3. Use the spread on open-faced sandwiches. Butter 1 side of each slice of bread and put a single layer of thinly sliced tomato, sprinkled with salt and pepper, or apple on top. Cover the tomato or apple with a 1/4-inch layer of the spread and bake the sandwiches as described previously.

When prepared this way, the meat stays moist and fat-free, though coated with a crusty glaze that is both delicious and attractive.

Ribs _____

4 quarts (3.8 l) water
3 large onions (about 1 pound total, 455g), peeled and halved
4 large garlic cloves, halved
2 tablespoons salt
2 pounds (910g) spare ribs (choose baby back ribs and have the butcher split the racks in half lengthwise)

Bring the water to a boil in a large kettle with the onions, garlic and salt. Add the ribs and simmer them, uncovered, for 25 minutes. While they are simmering, prepare the glaze as described below.

Drain the ribs well and put them in a container just large enough to hold them. While they are hot, pour the hot glaze over them. Cover them and refrigerate for 24 hours, basting occasionally with the glaze.

Glaze _____

2 medium garlic cloves, peeled
3/4 cup sugar (5 ounces, 145g)
4 strips of orange zest, about 1/2 x 3 inches (1.25 x 7.5 cm), removed with a vegetable peeler
1 5-ounce (140g) can unsweetened pineapple chunks, drained
2 tablespoons frozen orange juice concentrate
3/4 cup (18 cl) cider vinegar
1/4 cup plus 2 tablespoons (11 cl) dark soy sauce
3/4 teaspoon dry mustard
3/4 teaspoon ground ginger
1/4 cup (6 cl) Scotch whiskey

Metal Blade: With the machine running, mince the garlic by dropping it through the feed tube. Leave it in the work bowl. Add the sugar and orange zest; process until the zest is finely minced, and transfer the mixture to a 4-quart saucepan.

Process the pineapple until it is puréed — about 2 seconds — scraping down the sides of the bowl as necessary.

Add the pineapple purée and all the remaining glaze ingredients except the whiskey to the saucepan containing the orange mixture. Allow the mixture to simmer for 5 minutes, then add the whiskey and simmer for 2 minutes longer.

Wipe out the work bowl with a paper towel, and preheat the oven to 400°F. (205°C.).

Garnish

1 seedless eating
  orange, scored and cut
  flat at ends
  Parsley sprigs

Medium Slicing Disc: Slice the orange, using firm pressure. (If it doesn't fit in the feed tube, cut it in half.)

Place the ribs in a foil-lined roasting pan or jelly-roll pan that holds them in a single layer. Pour over them any glaze left in the container and place them in the oven. After 25 minutes, turn them and brush them with glaze. Bake for 5 to 10 minutes more, or until they are dark brown.

Separate the ribs and arrange them in a shallow dish, garnished with orange slices and parsley sprigs.

Makes 8 servings.

Mussels Vinaigrette

24 large fresh mussels
   (2 pounds, 910g)
 2 tablespoons salt
   Dry white wine or
   water to measure 1
   inch (2.5 cm) in the
   kettle
 1 large garlic clove,
   peeled
2/3 cup (16 cl) parsley
   leaves
1/3 cup (8 cl) Basic
   Vinaigrette (see Index)
 1 small onion (2 ounces,
   55g), peeled and ends
   cut flat
 2 small lemons, scored
   and ends cut flat
1/2 teaspoon salt
   Freshly ground pepper

Wash the mussels under cold running water, discarding any that are open, and let them soak for 30 minutes in cold water with 2 tablespoons salt.

Drain the mussels, and scrub them by rubbing one against the other to remove the beards and dirt. Put them in a kettle with the wine or water. Cook them, covered, over high heat for 6 to 8 minutes, turning them with a large spoon after 3 minutes. Discard any that do not open. Drain the mussels, and transfer them to a large bowl.

Metal Blade: With the machine running, mince the garlic by dropping it through the feed tube. Add the parsley, and mince it by turning the machine on and off. Add the Basic Vinaigrette and process the mixture for 1 second. Set it aside.

Medium Slicing Disc: Slice the onion and lemons, using firm pressure.

Add the vinaigrette mixture, the onion slices, and half the lemon slices to the hot mussels. Add salt and pepper to taste and refrigerate the mussels, turning them several times, for 6 hours or overnight. Let the mussels stand at room temperature for at least 30 minutes before serving. Drain them, leaving them in the shells. Arrange them on a platter, and garnish them with the remaining lemon slices.

Makes 4 to 6 servings.

These Egg Rolls look their best when they are sliced to show their bright green filling. Prepare the cabbage a day in advance to guarantee its proper texture.

1 large Chinese celery cabbage (14 ounces, 400g), including the greens
6 large scallions (4 ounces, 115g total), including the green tops, cut into thirds
8 water chestnuts
1-1/2 cups (35 cl) cooked shrimp (about 12 ounces, 340g)
2 tablespoons peanut butter
1 tablespoon sesame oil
1 tablespoon light soy sauce
Salt to taste
10 egg roll wrappers
1 large egg, lightly beaten

The day before assembling the egg rolls, prepare the filling.

Medium Slicing Disc: Slice the celery cabbage, using medium pressure. Cook the sliced celery cabbage for 30 seconds in 6 quarts of boiling water with 2 tablespoons salt. Remove it to a colander and hold it under cold running water until it is cold to the touch. Drain the cabbage and wrap it in towels to absorb as much moisture as possible. Change the towels as they become saturated. Refrigerate the cabbage in the towels overnight, then put it in a large mixing bowl.

As the following ingredients are processed, transfer them from the work bowl to the mixing bowl with the cabbage.

Medium Slicing Disc: Place the scallions in the feed tube vertically and slice them, using light pressure.

Metal Blade: Chop the water chestnuts coarsely by turning the machine on and off.

Chop the shrimp coarsely by turning the machine on and off about 3 times. Add it to the mixing bowl. In a small bowl mix the peanut butter, sesame oil, light soy sauce and salt and add the mixture to the other ingredients. Use your hands to combine this mixture and adjust the seasoning. (This filling should be well seasoned.)

Makes 2-1/2 cups (60 cl) filling.

Assembly _____

It is important to roll each cylinder tightly if you plan to serve the Egg Rolls sliced. For each Egg Roll, use your hands to shape about 3 tablespoons of filling into a firm cylinder about 4 inches (10 cm) long and 1 inch (2.5 cm) in diameter. Lay the cylinder of filling diagonally across the lower middle of a wrapper and roll the lower flap tightly over the filling, leaving the upper triangle of the wrapper exposed. Bring the 2 side flaps securely across the cylinder, making sure there are no unnecessary wrinkles and no looseness in the wrapper. Brush the open wrapper triangle with lightly beaten egg and roll it smoothly into a neat tight package. Repeat the procedure with the remaining filling and wrappers.

Add oil to a depth of 3 inches (7.5 cm) to a wok or deep fryer. Heat the oil to 375°F. (190°C.), or until a piece of scallion sizzles when dropped into the oil. Deep-fry 3 egg rolls at a time for 2 minutes, or until they are golden brown. Transfer them with a slotted spoon to a platter lined with a double thickness of paper towels. The egg rolls can be refrigerated, wrapped in paper towels. For very crispy Egg Rolls, deep-fry them again before serving until they are dark brown. Drain them on paper towels and serve them immediately. The Egg Rolls can also be reheated for 10 minutes in a 450°F. (230°C.) oven that has not been preheated. Use a serrated knife or a very sharp knife to slice the Egg Rolls.

Makes 10 Egg Rolls or 40 1-inch (2.5 cm) slices.

Marinated Scallops with Pimiento

1-1/2 pounds (680g) bay scallops or sea scallops, rinsed and drained
1 small garlic clove, peeled
1/2 cup (12 cl) parsley leaves
8 large scallions (4 ounces total, 115g), including the green tops, cut into thirds
2-ounce (55g) jar pimientos, rinsed and drained
3 strips of lime zest, about 1/4 x 2 inches (3/4 x 5 cm) removed with a vegetable peeler
1/2 cup (12 cl) lime juice
1/2 cup (12 cl) water
1/4 cup (6 cl) oil, preferably safflower
2 drops Tabasco sauce
1/2 teaspoon dried dill weed
1 teaspoon salt
1/2 teaspoon freshly ground pepper
2 bunches of watercress

Quarter the scallops if they are large, and put them in a 1-1/2-quart (142 cl) glass bowl or plastic bag.

Metal Blade: With the machine running, mince the garlic by dropping it through the feed tube. Add the parsley, and turn the machine on and off until it is minced. Leave mixture in the work bowl.

Medium Slicing Disc: Wedge the scallions into the feed tube vertically and slice them, using light pressure. Cut the pimiento into 1/2-inch-long julienne strips. Add the pimientos and the mixture in the work bowl to the scallops. Add the remaining ingredients except the watercress, and toss the mixture gently but thoroughly. Refrigerate, covered, for at least 6 hours or overnight.

To serve, arrange watercress leaves on a serving plate. Drain the scallops, and place them in the center of the plate. Sprinkle them with salt and pepper.

Makes 6 to 8 servings.

Sicilian Caponata

Despite its many ingredients, *Caponata* is surprisingly easy to prepare. Use it alone as a relish, or serve it as a spread on Pita Bread (see Index), rounds of *Pain de Mie* (see Index) or Cumin Light Rye Bread (see Index).

1 large eggplant (about 1 pound, 455g), unpeeled, trimmed and cut to fit feed tube
2 teaspoons salt
2 small zucchini (1/2 pound total, 225g), washed and cut into feed-tube lengths
1 large tomato (1/2 pound, 225g), peeled and seeded
3 celery ribs (6 ounces total, 170g), including leaves, with strings removed
1 large green pepper (1/2 pound, 225g), seeded and cut into uniform rectangles
9 large mushrooms (1/2 pound, 225g), trimmed — optional
1/2 cup parsley leaves
2 garlic cloves, peeled
1 small onion (3 ounces, 85g), peeled
4 tablespoons oil
1 6-ounce (170g) can pitted black olives, drained
1/4 cup (6 cl) capers, drained
1/4 cup (6 cl) tomato paste
1-1/2 tablespoons sugar
1/2 cup plus 2 tablespoons (17 cl) red wine vinegar
1/2 cup (12 cl) water
2 teaspoons dried oregano
2 teaspoons dried basil
1 teaspoon anchovy paste
Salt
Freshly ground pepper

French-fry Disc or Medium Slicing Disc: Process the eggplant, using medium pressure, and put it in a colander placed over a bowl or paper towels. Sprinkle it with salt and let it drain for 30 minutes.

Insert the zucchini in the feed tube vertically and process, using medium pressure. Remove it from the bowl; set it aside. Process the tomato, using light pressure; set it aside.

Medium Slicing Disc: Insert the celery in the feed tube vertically and slice it, using medium pressure. Leave it in the bowl. Slice the green pepper, using medium pressure on the pusher, and leave it in the bowl. Slice the mushrooms, using light pressure. Remove all the vegetables from the work bowl and set them aside. Wipe the bowl with a paper towel.

Metal Blade: Put the parsley in the work bowl and mince it by turning the machine on and off abut 6 times. Remove it and set it aside for a garnish.

With the machine running, mince the garlic by dropping it through the feed tube. Leave it in the work bowl. Add the onion to the minced garlic and turn the machine on and off just until it is coarsely chopped.

Heat the oil in a large skillet. When it is hot, add the onion and garlic and sauté them over moderate heat until soft but not brown — about 5 minutes.

Rinse the eggplant to remove the salt, pat it dry with paper towels, and add it to the onion mixture. Cover and cook over moderately high heat for 4 minutes, shaking the pan occasionally to prevent the vegetables from sticking to it. Add all the prepared vegetables to the hot eggplant and combine gently with a rubber spatula.

Mix the remaining ingredients in a small bowl and pour them over the combined vegetables. Heat for about 2 minutes over moderately high heat, taking care not to overcook.

Transfer the *Caponata* to a serving dish and garnish it with the minced parsley. Serve hot, cold or at room temperature.

Makes 7 cups (1.6 l).

Without the watercress, this dish is identical to the *belons au champagne* served by Chef Gérard Rouillard at La Marée in Paris. It is one of the spectacular recipes that has earned the restaurant two stars in the Guide Michelin and Rouillard, his title of *Meilleur Ouvrier de France*, 1979. For a magnificent combination serve the oysters with chilled champagne.

24 fresh oysters, each with a half shell, scrubbed
2/3 cup (16 cl) oyster liquid or clam broth
1/2 cup (12 cl) dry champagne or Chablis
2 large shallots (1 ounce, 30g total)
Pinch of cayenne
1/2 cup (12 cl) *Crème Fraîche* (see Index)
1 recipe Hollandaise Sauce (see Index)
Salt
Freshly ground black pepper
1 small bunch watercress (2 ounces total, 55g), stems trimmed

In a 2-quart (190 cl) saucepan, poach the oysters in their liquid or clam broth, and the champagne or chablis over moderately low heat only until they are plumped. Do not allow the liquid to boil. With a slotted spoon, transfer the oysters to a plate.

Metal Blade: With the machine running, drop the shallots through the feed tube and process until they are finely chopped. Add the shallots and cayenne to the liquid in the saucepan. Reduce the liquid over high heat to 1/4 cup (6 cl). Add the *Crème Fraîche*; heat the mixture thoroughly and set it aside.

Make the Hollandaise Sauce and leave it in the work bowl. With the machine running, pour the heated cream mixture through the feed tube very slowly. Taste and adjust the seasoning as desired. (Oysters require generous seasoning.) The sauce can be kept in a double-boiler over warm, but not boiling, water.

Arrange the oyster shells on a baking sheet and preheat the broiler.

On each shell, arrange several watercress leaves. Spoon 1 teaspoon of the sauce over greens on each shell and top with an oyster. Nap the oysters with additional sauce and place them 6 inches (15 cm) from the heat. Broil for 2 to 3 minutes, or until the sauce is lightly browned, watching them carefully to prevent burning. Serve immediately.

Makes 8 servings.

Smoked Salmon Pâté with Mustard Watercress Sauce

This pâté, with its delicate smoky flavor, is among the most popular appetizers I've taught and yet it is very easy to make.

Pâté

- 1 large bunch watercress (3-1/2 ounces, 100g), stems removed
- 1 small onion (1 ounce, 30g), peeled and quartered
- 4 ounces (115g) Nova Scotia smoked salmon (not lox)
- 12 ounces (340g) fresh salmon fillets, skinned and cut into 1-inch (2.5 cm) cubes
- 2 teaspoons dried dill
- 2 teaspoons fresh lemon juice
- 1/2 teaspoon white pepper
- 1/2 teaspoon salt
- 1-1/4 cups (30 cl) heavy cream, chilled
- 2 large eggs

Preheat the oven to 250°F. (120°C.) and adjust a rack to the middle of the oven. Butter a narrow terrine with a 4-cup (9 dl) capacity; line the bottom with a generously buttered sheet of parchment paper.

Select several perfect watercress leaves and arrange them decoratively on the buttered parchment paper. Plunge the remaining watercress leaves in boiling water for 15 seconds and then plunge them immediately into cold water. Drain the leaves, squeeze them dry in a towel and reserve them.

Metal Blade: With the machine running, mince the onion by dropping it through the feed tube. Add the smoked and fresh salmon, dill, lemon juice, pepper and salt, and combine the mixture by turning the machine on and off about 8 times. Process the mixture for about 1 minute or until it is puréed. Scrape down the sides of the work bowl. With the machine running, add the cream in a slow steady stream through the feed tube. Do not add it faster than it can become incorporated in the salmon mixture. Add the eggs and process the mixture for 30 seconds. Transfer all but about 1/3 cup (80 ml) of the salmon mixture to a mixing bowl. Add the watercress to the mixture remaining in the work bowl and process the mixture until it is puréed, stopping the machine once to scrape down the sides of the bowl.

Spoon 1/4 of the salmon mixture into the prepared terrine, spreading it evenly to cover the bottom. Cut through it with a knife and bang the terrine on the counter twice to remove any air bubbles. Spoon the watercress mixture in a stripe down the center. Add the remaining salmon mixture along the sides and over the watercress stripe. Smooth the surface with a spatula and bang the terrine on the counter again. Cover the terrine with a sheet of buttered parchment paper, buttered side down, and bake the pâté in the preheated oven for 15 minutes. Reduce the temperature to 225°F. (110°C.) and bake the pâté for 25 minutes more, or until it is firm. Do not overcook. Remove the pâté from the oven and let it stand for 5 minutes. Invert the pâté onto a platter and serve it warm with Watercress Hollandaise (see Index), or at room temperature with Watercress Mustard Sauce. The pâté can also be refrigerated once it has cooled, and served cold.

Makes 12 servings.

Sauce

- 1 small bunch watercress (1 ounce, 30g), including stems
- 1/4 cup (6 cl) Dijon mustard
- 1 large egg yolk
- 1 teaspoon salt
  Freshly ground black pepper
- 1 cup (24 cl) safflower or vegetable oil
- 2 tablespoons evaporated milk or sour cream
- 2 teaspoons fresh lemon juice

Variations

Metal Blade: Put the watercress, mustard and egg yolk in the work bowl and process the mixture for 5 seconds, or until it is puréed, stopping the machine once to scrape down the sides of the bowl. Add the salt and pepper. With the machine running, drizzle the oil through the feed tube, adding it only as the purée thickens. If the purée is slow to thicken, process it without the addition of oil until it thickens. When all the oil has been added, pour the evaporated milk through the feed tube with the machine running. If using sour cream, add it to the work bowl, combining it by turning the machine on and off several times. Add the lemon juice. Process the sauce for 2 seconds, and adjust the seasoning. This sauce can be made a day in advance and kept refrigerated with an airtight cover.

Makes 1-1/4 cups (30 cl).

1. Substitute 12 ounces (340g) of fresh skinned trout fillets for the fresh salmon and use the same amount of Nova Scotia smoked salmon. The result is equally delicious, but doesn't have the delicate pale peach color.

2. Substitute a total of 16 ounces (455g) of fresh skinned trout fillets and 1/4 teaspoon of liquid smoke flavoring for both the fresh and the smoked salmon.

Smoked Salmon Paté with Mustard Watercress Sauce

A truly delectable mousse. I am especially fond of the version with mussels tucked into the center. They make a beautiful pattern in each slice of mousse as well as providing a savory additional flavor.

Mousse _____

16 fresh mussels (optional)
4 large shallots (2 ounces, 55g total), peeled and halved
Dry white wine or water to measure 1/2 inch in the pan
1 thin slice of bread (1 ounce, 30g), crust removed
1-1/2 cups (35 cl) heavy cream, chilled
1 lemon, scored and ends cut flat
2/3 cup (16 cl) parsley leaves
2 tablespoons dry vermouth or dry white wine
1 pound sea scallops
2 large eggs
1-1/2 teaspoons salt
1/2 teaspoon Tabasco sauce
1/4 teaspoon freshly grated nutmeg
Freshly ground white pepper
Parsley sprigs

Preheat the oven to 250°F. (120°C.) and lightly oil a 6-cup ring mold or loaf pan.

Wash the mussels under cold running water, discarding any that are open. Let them soak for 30 minutes in cold water with 1 tablespoon salt. Drain the mussels and scrub them by rubbing one against the other to remove the beards and dirt. Put the mussels in a large saucepan with 2 of the shallots and the wine or water. Cook them, covered, over high heat, stirring once, for about 5 minutes, or until the shells open. Discard any mussels that do not open and refrigerate 1/4 cup (6 cl) of the mussel cooking liquid. Remove the mussels from their shells and put them in a bowl with the remaining mussel cooking liquid.

Soak the bread in enough heavy cream to cover it. When it has absorbed as much liquid as it can, transfer it to a dish with a slotted spoon. Return any remaining cream to the refrigerator for later use.

Medium Slicing Disc: Slice the lemon, using firm pressure, and reserve it for a garnish.

Metal Blade: Mince the parsley by turning the machine on and off. Remove it from the work bowl and set it aside.

With the machine running, mince the two remaining shallots by dropping them through the feed tube. Transfer them to a small saucepan. Add the vermouth or dry white wine and cook the mixture over high heat until the liquid has almost evaporated. Return the shallot mixture to the work bowl, add the reserved bread and the scallops and combine the mixture by turning the machine on and off about 5 times. Then process the mixture for about 5 seconds, or until it is puréed. Scrape down the sides of the bowl. With the machine running, pour in all the heavy cream very slowly, making sure it is incorporated into the mixture as it is added. Add the eggs, the reserved 1/4 cup (6 cl) of mussel cooking liquid, the reserved minced parsley, except 1 tablespoon to be used for garnish, and the salt, Tabasco, nutmeg and pepper. Process the mixture for 10 seconds.

Spoon half the mousse into the prepared pan, spreading it evenly, and bang the pan on the counter once or twice to remove any air bubbles. Remove the mussels from the liquid with a slotted spoon, pat them dry on paper towels, and arrange them evenly over the mousse. Spoon in the remaining mousse, spreading it evenly, and bang the pan on the counter 2 more times. Cover the pan with a sheet of buttered parchment paper or wax paper, buttered side down, and bake the mousse in the preheated oven for 15 minutes. Reduce the temperature to 225°F. (110°C.) and bake for 35 to 40 minutes more, or until the mousse is firm. Do not overcook.

Prepare the Scallop Hollandaise Sauce while the mousse is baking.

Remove the mousse from the oven and let it stand for 5 minutes. Invert the mousse onto a platter and spoon the sauce sparingly over it. Serve the remaining sauce in a separate dish. Sprinkle the reserved minced parsley over the mousse and garnish the platter with parsley sprigs and the reserved lemon slices.

Makes 8 to 10 servings.

Sauce

- 1/4 cup (6 cl) parsley leaves
- 2 large shallots (1 ounce, 30g), peeled
- 2 tablespoons water
- 2 tablespoons butter
- 8 ounces (225g) bay or sea scallops
- 2 tablespoons dry vermouth or dry white wine
- 1 large egg yolk
- 1 teaspoon warm water
- 1/4 teaspoon dry mustard
- 1/2 teaspoon salt
  Pinch of white pepper
- 1 stick plus 2 tablespoons unsalted butter (5 ounces, 140g)

Metal Blade: Mince the parsley, turning the machine on and off about 6 times, and reserve it. With the machine running, mince the shallots by dropping them through the feed tube. Cook the shallots in the water and butter until they are soft and the water has evaporated. Slice the scallops in half horizontally and add them to the pan with the shallots. Pour in the vermouth or wine and cook the mixture just until the scallops turn opaque. This mixture can be prepared in advance and set aside.

To process the one egg yolk effectively, carefully prop a 2-inch (5 cm) book underneath the back of the machine so the egg yolk will accumulate in the front of the bowl. Put the egg yolk, warm water, mustard, salt and pepper into the work bowl and process the mixture for 1 minute. Heat the butter until it bubbles and with the machine running, drizzle it through the feed tube. Process until the sauce thickens. Combine the hollandaise and the scallop mixture in the top of a double boiler and heat gently over warm water.

Makes 1-3/4 cups (41 cl).

Note: If serving the Scallop Mousse cold, use the Scallop Mustard Mayonnaise (see Index) as the sauce.

These *Gougères* — without the scallions — are served at the three-star restaurant Taillevent in Paris. They have a spongy center and can be served plain or stuffed. If handled properly, they will taste fresh even after being frozen and reheated.

Glaze

1 large egg
1/2 teaspoon salt

Dough

2 scallions (1 ounce, 30g), including green tops, cut into 2-inch (5 cm) pieces
4 ounces (115g) imported *Gruyère* cheese, rind removed and at room temperature
2/3 cup (16 cl) water
1/3 cup (8 cl) milk
1 stick unsalted butter
1-1/4 teaspoons salt
Freshly ground pepper
1/2 teaspoon freshly grated nutmeg
1 cup unbleached all-purpose flour (5 ounces, 140g)
4 large eggs
2 tablespoons cold milk

Have ready two lightly buttered baking sheets.

Metal Blade: Process the egg and salt for 2 seconds. Reserve this mixture for the glaze and wipe out the bowl.

With the machine running, mince the scallions by dropping them through the feed tube. Leave them in the work bowl.

Shredding Disc: Shred the cheese, using light pressure. Leave it in the work bowl.

Metal Blade: Incorporate the cheese and scallions by turning the machine on and off about 4 times. Set the mixture aside and wipe out the bowl with a paper towel.

In a saucepan, bring the water, milk, butter and seasonings to a boil, stirring the mixture to melt the butter. Remove the pan from the heat. Beat in the flour with a wooden spoon for 1 minute, or until the mixture is well combined and leaves the sides of the pan. Then cook the mixture over moderate heat for 2 minutes, stirring occasionally.

Preheat the oven to 400°F. (205°C.) and place a rack in the lower half of the oven.

With the metal blade still in place, process the hot flour mixture (*panade*) with the eggs for 30 seconds, stopping once to scrape down the sides of the bowl, or until the eggs are completely incorporated and the mixture very thick and smooth. Add the cold milk and process for 7 seconds. Add the reserved scallions and cheese, and process all ingredients for 5 seconds.

Sprinkle the prepared baking sheets with water, then shake off excess.

Spoon the pastry mixture into a 16-inch (41 cm) pastry bag fitted with a 3/4-inch (2 cm) tube. Pipe the pastry onto the sheets in 1-1/4-inch (3 cm) rounds, cutting it from the tube with a knife if necessary.

Brush on the reserved egg glaze with a feather brush, smoothing the tops of the pastry puffs. Avoid dripping the glaze onto the baking sheets. Bake the puffs for 22 to 24 minutes, or until they are well browned. Transfer them to racks to cool.

Makes 40 puffs.

Note: Once cooled, unstuffed puffs can be frozen on baking sheets. After they are frozen, they can be packed in airtight freezer bags and returned to the freezer. The puffs should be reheated at 300°F. (150°C.) for 10 minutes, without first being thawed.

Variations

1. For Herbed Cheese Puffs, substitute 2 tablespoons of parsley sprigs and 1 teaspoon of dried dill for the scallions.

2. For Bacon Cheese Puffs, substitute 2 strips of bacon, cooked crisp, drained and crumbled, 2 drops of Tabasco sauce, and 1 teaspoon of Dijon-style mustard for the scallions.

3. For Olive-Stuffed Cheese Puffs, make a slit in the side of each puff and insert a small pimiento-stuffed olive.

An unusually delicate tart, served at Frédy Girardet's Restaurant Girardet in Crissier, Switzerland. Although Crissier is a small out-of-the-way village, many noted food critics consider Girardet's restaurant to be better than any restaurant in France.

2 large Spanish onions (1 pound total, 455g), peeled and cut to fit the feed tube
3 tablespoons unsalted butter
1-1/2 ounces (45g) slab bacon, cut into fine julienne strips
6 large eggs
1 cup (24 cl) heavy cream
1/4 cup (6 cl) milk
1/2 teaspoon freshly grated nutmeg
1-1/4 teaspoons salt
Freshly ground white pepper
Prebaked warm 11-inch (28 cm) Rich Butter Pastry Shell (see Index)

Medium Slicing Disc: Slice the onions, using medium pressure. In a large skillet melt the butter, add the onions and cover them with wax paper. Cook over moderate heat for 10 minutes. Remove the wax paper and cook over moderately low heat for 20 minutes more, or until they are completely softened but not browned.

Preheat the oven to 300°F. (180°C.) and place the rack in the middle of the oven.

Brown the bacon in a skillet and transfer it while still soft to paper towels.

Metal Blade: Process the eggs by turning the machine on and off about 3 times. Add the cream, milk, and seasonings, and combine the ingredients by turning the machine on and off about 3 times. Transfer the egg mixture to a large bowl. Stir in the onions and bacon. Taste and correct seasoning, if required. Ladle the mixture into the pastry shell, which should be warm. (The heat of the pan coagulates the egg in the mixture, preventing any leaks through the crust.) Fill only to 1/8 inch (0.3 cm) from the top. Bake the tart for 55 to 60 minutes or until it is browned and puffy. Transfer it to a rack and let it stand for 10 minutes before serving.

Makes 8 to 12 servings.

Variations

3 large leeks (14 ounces total, 400g), including the green tops
6 tablespoons unsalted butter (3 ounces, 85g)
3/4 cup (18 cl) finely diced ham
2 tablespoons peeled, seeded and diced tomato
2 tablespoons minced parsley leaves

1. To add color, sprinkle 1-1/2 teaspoons fresh basil, cut into fine julienne, and 2 tablespoons peeled, seeded and diced tomato over tart before cooking and press into surface.

2. Substitute this leek, ham and tomato mixture for the onions.

Preheat the oven to 325°F. (160°C.) and adjust the rack to the middle of the oven.

Mince the leeks with the metal blade and sauté them in the butter over moderately high heat for 15 minutes. Stir the leeks and ham into the egg mixture made as described in the master recipe. Ladle the mixture into the shell and sprinkle it with the tomato and parsley. Bake in a 325°F. (160°C.) oven for 40 minutes, or until it is lightly browned.

The bright green of the leek makes this quiche a vivid presentation.

6 large mushrooms (4 ounces total, 115g), trimmed
1 large leek (8 ounces, 225g), including the green top, split lengthwise, washed, and cut into 4-inch (10 cm) lengths
3 tablespoons butter
1 tablespoon oil
1 tablespoon flour
6 ounces (170g) Swiss cheese, chilled
2 tablespoons parsley leaves
4 large eggs
1-1/3 cups (31 cl) half-and-half or light cream
1 teaspoon salt
Freshly ground pepper
1 teaspoon dried oregano
Prebaked 11-inch (28 cm) Parsley Pastry Shell (see Index)

Preheat the oven to 375°F. (190°C.).

Medium Slicing Disc: Slice the mushrooms, using light pressure, and set them aside. Wedge the leek into the feed tube vertically and slice it, using medium pressure. Heat the butter and oil in a skillet and sauté the leeks over moderately high heat until they are softened. Stir in the flour and warm it, but do not let it cook. Remove the skillet from the heat. Stir the mushrooms into the leek mixture.

Shredding Disc: Shred the cheese, using light pressure, and set it aside.

Metal Blade: Mince the parsley by turning the machine on and off. Remove it and set it aside.

Mix the eggs by turning the machine on and off about 4 times. Add the half-and-half or cream, and combine by turning the machine on and off about twice. Pour the egg mixture into a large bowl and blend in the leek mixture, the cheese, and the salt and pepper. Pour the mixture into the pre-baked pastry shell, filling the shell only to 1/8 inch (0.3 cm) from the top. Sprinkle the top with the oregano and reserved parsley and bake for 40 minutes, or until the top is well colored. Transfer the quiche to a rack and let it stand for 15 minutes before serving. It can also be served at room temperature.

Makes 6 to 8 servings.

Note: This quiche can be frozen, but I prefer to freeze the cooled, prebaked crust separately and ladle in the filling just before baking. The filling can be prepared a day in advance and kept refrigerated. If you choose to freeze the quiche already baked, this particular crust will hold up better than most. The baked quiche should be removed from the pan, allowed to cool on a rack, and frozen on a baking sheet. After it is frozen it should be well wrapped in foil. To reheat, unwrap it and place it, still frozen, in the original pan. Bake it for 25 minutes or until it is heated through, in a 375°F. (190°C.) oven that has not been preheated.

Variation

The quiche filling can be baked without a crust in a well-buttered shallow 4-cup (95 cl) baking dish. Sprinkle the bottom of the dish with 1/4 cup (6 cl) of the shredded Swiss cheese. Ladle the filling over the cheese and bake as described in the master recipe.

For a large party this platter of *hors d'oeuvre* provides a spectacular array of colors, tastes, and textures. With a fresh loaf of crusty bread and a bottle of Chianti, it makes a terrific supper. Although I love having all the selections, a few will suffice for a small group.

Mussels Vinaigrette

Mushroom, Watercress and Red Pepper Salad

White Beans with Tuna

Radish, Scallion and Swiss Cheese Salad

Carrot, Turnip and Zucchini Salad

Eggplant and Pepperoni Salad

Italian Salad in Marinated Artichokes

Black Olives

Cherry tomatoes with greens

Scallions, including the green tops, trimmed

Stuffed Anchovies (available in flat tins)

Prepare all or several of the recipes and arrange them decoratively on large platters. Recipes are in this book; you will find the page number for each in the Index.

Antipasto Platter

Soups

Soups

Parsnip and Spinach Soup
Spring Vegetable Soup
Bouillabaisse with Sauce Rouille
Celery Egg-Drop Soup
Gazpacho
Dilled Cucumber Soup
Zucchini and Tomato Soup
Vegetable Beef Soup

Kettles of calories simmering on the back burner? Stomach-weighting cauldrons of reduced stock and starch? Not in my kitchen, not nowadays! The hearty soups of yesterday were doubtless grand affairs, but my tastes run to lighter things.

Lively colors, fresh garnishes and velvety textures distinguish my soups. None of my recipes calls for eggs, flour or cream. That eliminates the guesswork required to combine those ingredients with hot broth for classic bisques and cream soups. The only thickeners I use are pure vegetable purées — a food processor *tour de force*. Machine-puréed vegetables contribute both flavor essence and satisfying consistency. So count on fewer steps, fewer calories, less expense and the unusual treat of unmuddled taste.

Purée-thickened soups freeze beautifully. And all but the main-course Bouillabaisse and Vegetable Beef Soup can be served hot or chilled. Ladle them into mugs either way for a portable first course in the living room or on the porch.

Another advantage of my soup formula is that it accommodates whatever the garden or market yields. Master the basic proportions of vegetables to broth detailed in the Parsnip and Spinach Soup and its variations and you'll soon create your own blends. Asparagus, broccoli, potatoes and even avocados come to mind as possible substitutes for the parsnips and spinach. But use your own imagination and whatever bumper crops or leftover vegetables you have. Don't add salt and pepper until the very end, especially when using canned broth, which tends to be oversalted. Each vegetable will require a different amount of seasoning to complement its natural mineral content. A recipe for homemade broth, a true money-saver, is in the chapter on Basic Recipes.

The two main-course soups are one-pot meals at their best. The bouillabaisse boasts the inimitable fragrance of the south of France — a perfume of tomatoes, onion, garlic, saffron and orange. And the Vegetable Beef Soup is an old-time bowlful of all good things.

Bouillabaisse with Sauce Rouille, page 28.

A fresh vegetable soup that is wonderfully flavorful and low in calories. When making the easy variations, use a basic formula of 2-1/2 cups (60 cl) of vegetable purée to 6 cups (1.4 l) of broth.

5 large parsnips
(1 pound total, 455g),
unpeeled, trimmed
and cut into lengths to
fit the feed tube
1 large Spanish onion
(7 ounces, 200g),
peeled and cut into
wedges
1 small celery rib with
leaves, (1 ounce, 30g),
strings removed
5 to 6 cups (1.2 to 1.4 l)
chicken broth
2 cups (47 cl) spinach,
including the stems
(1/4 pound, 115g)
1/2 teaspoon freshly
grated nutmeg
Salt
Freshly ground pepper

Medium Slicing Disc: Slice the parsnips, onion and celery, using firm pressure. Transfer the vegetables to a 4-quart (3.8 l) kettle and add 5 cups (1.2 l) of chicken broth. Cover the kettle and bring the broth to a boil. Reduce the heat and simmer the mixture for 25 minutes.

Metal Blade: Transfer the vegetables to the work bowl with a slotted spoon. Add 1/2 cup (12 cl) of the liquid and purée the mixture for 1 minute, or until it is smooth. Scrape down the sides of the bowl, add the spinach, and process the mixture for 30 seconds. Stir the mixture into the broth, add the nutmeg, and salt and pepper to taste. Heat the soup, stirring in the remaining broth if it is too thick. Serve the soup hot or chilled.

Makes 6 cups (1.4 l).

Variations _____

1. For Carrot and Spinach Soup, use these vegetables in addition to the spinach: 1 small onion (3 ounces, 85g), 1 pound (455g) parsnips, and 1/2 pound (225g) carrots. Process the spinach with the purée just before serving and garnish the soup with 1/3 cup (8 cl) minced parsley.

2. For Mushroom and Parsnip Soup, use these vegetables in addition to the spinach: 9 large mushrooms (1/2 pound, 225g), with 3 reserved for garnish, 1 small onion (3 ounces, 85g), and 1 pound (455g) parsnips. Simmer them in 5 cups (1.2 l) of beef broth and purée, processing the spinach with the purée just before serving. Garnish the soup with the reserved mushrooms, thinly sliced.

3. A vegetable soup made from the basic formula of 2-1/2 cups (60 cl) of any cooked vegetable purée and 6 cups (1.4 l) of well flavored broth is an excellent use for leftover vegetables. The recipe can be halved to accommodate lesser amounts.

Note: All these soups can be frozen and served hot or chilled.

My favorite fresh vegetable soup — delicately flavored and beautiful with its crisp garnish.

1/4 cup (6 cl) parsley leaves
1 large onion (5 ounces, 140g), peeled and quartered
2 large celery ribs (6 ounces total, 170g), strings removed
1/2 pound (225g) asparagus, tips cut off and reserved, and stems peeled
1 large leek (6 ounces, 170g), white part only, split and washed
1 large parsnip (5 ounces, 140g), unpeeled and trimmed
1 wedge of iceberg lettuce (6 ounces, 170g)
2 garlic cloves, peeled
7 to 8 cups (170 to 190 cl) chicken broth
1 cup (24 cl) frozen small peas, thawed, at room temperature
1 teaspoon dried dillweed
Salt
Freshly ground pepper
Freshly grated nutmeg
4 large mushrooms (3 ounces total, 85g), trimmed and sides cut flat
4 ounces (115g) green beans, trimmed
1 large carrot (3 ounces, 85g), grooved vertically with a stripper and cut into 4-inch (10 cm) lengths
1 small turnip (3 ounces, 85g), peeled
1 small zucchini (3 ounces, 85g), cut into 4-inch (10 cm) lengths

Metal Blade: Mince the parsley by turning the machine on and off, and reserve it.

Medium Slicing Disc: Slice the onion, celery, asparagus stems, leek, parsnip and lettuce, using medium pressure. Transfer the vegetables to a kettle with the garlic and 7 cups (170 cl) of broth. Cover the kettle and bring the broth to a boil. Simmer the mixture for 40 minutes.

Metal Blade: Transfer the vegetables to the work bowl with a slotted spoon and purée them for 20 seconds, stopping the machine once to scrape down the sides of the bowl. Add 3/4 cup (18 cl) of peas and process the mixture for 5 seconds. Stir the purée into the broth. Add the dill, and season to taste with salt, pepper, and nutmeg. Stir in the remaining broth if the soup is too thick.

Medium Slicing Disc: Place the mushrooms in the feed tube, flat sides down and slice them, using light pressure. Reserve the mushrooms. Place the beans in the feed tube vertically and slice them, using medium pressure. Slice the carrots, using firm pressure.

French-Fry Disc or Medium Slicing Disc: Cut the turnips and zucchini with the French-fry disc, using medium pressure. If you do not have a French-fry disc, use the medium slicing disc and a double-slicing technique to make julienne strips. First slice the turnips and zucchini, using medium pressure. Then remove the slices from the work bowl and insert as many slices as you can into the feed tube, wedging them tightly so they will hold. It is sometimes easier to wedge them into the tube from the bottom. Slice the vegetables again, using medium pressure, to produce julienne strips. Repeat the process with any remaining slices.

Twenty minutes before serving, bring the soup to a boil and add the reserved asparagus tips and all the processed vegetables except the mushrooms. Simmer the soup for 12 minutes, then add the mushrooms and the remaining peas. Simmer the soup for 3 minutes longer and correct the seasoning. Serve the soup hot or cold, garnished with parsley.

Makes 8 to 9 cups (190 to 213 cl).

Note: This soup can be frozen after it is puréed, before the processed vegetables are added. Reheat the soup thoroughly and proceed with the recipe.

This bouillabaisse is light and fragrant, in the tradition of the new French cooking. I prefer this delicate version, but you may want to make its flavor more robust by adding a spoonful of *Sauce Rouille*.

Bouillabaisse

- 1 large leek (1/2 pound, 225g), split, washed, very dark green end trimmed, and cut into 2-inch (5 cm) pieces
- 1/2 cup (12 cl) parsley leaves
- 5 large garlic cloves, peeled
- 2 large onions (10 ounces total, 285g), peeled and quartered
- 2 tablespoons olive oil
- 4 large tomatoes (2-3/4 pounds total, 795g), peeled, seeded and quartered
- 1/4 teaspoon sugar
- 3 cups (70 cl) bottled clam juice or Fish Stock (see Index)
- 1 cup (24 cl) dry white wine or dry vermouth
- 1 cup (24 cl) water
- 2 strips of orange zest, removed with a vegetable peeler
  Pinch of cayenne
  Pinch of saffron threads
  Bouquet garni containing 6 parsley sprigs, 1 bay leaf, and 1/4 teaspoon fennel seed
- 1 teaspoon dried basil
- 1 teaspoon dried thyme
- 16 mussels
- 1 tablespoon salt
- 1 pound (455g) monkfish fillets, cut into serving portions

Medium Slicing Disc: Slice the leek, using medium pressure. Remove the slices and separate the dark green slices from the rest.

Metal Blade: Mince the parsley by·turning the machine on and off. Remove it and set it aside.

With the machine running, mince the garlic by dropping it through the feed tube. Add the onions and chop them by turning the machine on and off. Heat the olive oil in a large kettle and cook the garlic and onion over moderate heat until they are soft but not brown.

Add the white and light green slices of leek to the kettle and cook the mixture for 10 more minutes, or until the leek is softened.

With the metal blade still in place, chop the tomatoes coarsely by turning the machine on and off. Add them to the kettle with the sugar and simmer the mixture for 5 minutes. Add all the remaining ingredients, except the mussels, salt, and fish. Cover and simmer the mixture for 30 minutes. Strain the broth into a bowl, remove and discard the *bouquet garni* and 1 strip of orange zest. Transfer the vegetable mixture to the work bowl of the food processor, with the metal blade in place.

Process the vegetable mixture with 1/2 cup (12 cl) of the broth for 30 seconds, or until it is puréed, stopping the machine once to scrape down the sides of the bowl. Return the mixture to the kettle with the remainder of the broth.

Add enough salt and pepper, bearing in mind that the fish is quite bland. At this point the soup can be frozen or refrigerated for 3 days.

Wash the mussels under cold running water. Discard any that are open, and soak the others for 30 minutes in a large pan covered with cold water into which you have mixed 1 tablespoon salt. Drain them, scrub them and remove their beards by rubbing them together. Put them in a saucepan containing 1/2 inch (1.25 cm) of water and cook them over high heat, stirring once, for 4 minutes, or until the shells open. Discard any mussels that do not open.

1 pound (455g) scrod
 fillets, cut into serving
 portions
1 pound (455g) red
 snapper fillets, cut into
 serving portions
1/2 pound (225g) bay
 scallops

Divide the mussels among 8 serving dishes. Let any sand in their liquid settle to the bottom and ladle the broth carefully into another container. Add the liquid to the *bouillabaisse* if more liquid is required, or freeze it and reserve it for another use.

Heat the soup until it simmers, add the monkfish, and simmer the soup for 2 minutes. Add the scrod, red snapper, and reserved green leek pieces and simmer for 3 more minutes. Add the scallops, simmer the soup for 30 seconds, and correct the seasoning.

Ladle the soup and fish into the dishes and garnish with the reserved parsley, and a spoonful of *sauce rouille* if a strong garlic taste is desired. Pass the remaining sauce separately.

Makes 8 main-course servings.

Sauce Rouille

1 slice homemade or
 good quality bread
 (1 ounce, 30g), crusts
 removed
2 tablespoons soup
 liquid or clam broth
3 large garlic cloves,
 peeled
1 4-ounce (115g) jar
 pimientos, undrained
2 tablespoons parsley
 leaves
1/2 teaspoon dried basil
1/2 teaspoon salt
6 drops of Tabasco
1/3 cup (8 cl) olive oil
 (preferably French)

Soak the bread in the soup liquid or clam broth.

Metal Blade: With the machine running, mince the garlic by dropping it through the feed tube. Add the soaked bread, pimiento, parsley, basil, salt and Tabasco, and process the mixture for 1 minute, stopping the machine once to scrape down the sides of the bowl. With the machine running, drizzle the oil slowly through the feed tube in a thin, steady stream. Process the sauce for 1 minute longer, and transfer it to a sauce dish. Serve the sauce at room temperature.

Makes 1 cup (24 cl).

This soup is almost as quick to prepare as a canned one, but it tastes much better. The celery looks like noodles and provides a pleasing crunch.

2 large celery ribs (4 ounces, 115g), strings removed and cut into 1-inch (2.5 cm) pieces
5 cups (1.1 l) chicken broth
1 teaspoon dark soy sauce
1/2 teaspoon sesame oil
Salt
Cayenne
1/2 cup (12 cl) parsley leaves
1 large egg
1 teaspoon vegetable oil

Medium Shredding Disc: Stack the celery in the feed tube horizontally, and shred it, using light pressure. Transfer it to a 2-quart (1.9 l) saucepan and add the broth, soy sauce, and sesame oil. Simmer the mixture, uncovered, for 10 minutes. Add salt and cayenne to taste and remove the pan from the heat.

Metal Blade: Mince the parsley by turning the machine on and off. Remove it and set it aside.

Process the egg and oil for 3 seconds and drizzle the mixture into the soup. Let the egg set, then stir the soup gently to distribute the egg. Ladle the soup into heated bowls and garnish each serving with reserved minced parsley.

Makes 10 servings.

Gazpacho

For a lively brunch, make Gazpacho Bloody Marys by adding vodka to this peppery soup just before serving.

Soup

- 1/3 cup (8 cl) parsley leaves
- 3 large garlic cloves, peeled
- 1 small onion (2-1/2 ounces, 70g), peeled and quartered
- 2 large tomatoes (1 pound total, 455g), peeled, seeded and quartered
- 1 46-ounce (131 cl) can tomato juice
- 2 teaspoons ground coriander
- 1-1/2 teaspoons Worcestershire sauce
  Pinch of cayenne
  Salt
  Freshly ground pepper

Metal Blade: Mince the parsley by turning the machine on and off about 3 times. With the machine running, drop the garlic and onion through the feed tube. Add the tomatoes, 1/2 cup (12 cl) tomato juice, coriander, Worcestershire sauce and cayenne and purée the mixture until it is smooth, stopping the machine once to scrape down the sides of the bowl. Pour the soup into a pitcher. Add remaining tomato juice and salt and pepper to taste. Refrigerate the soup for several hours, or overnight.

Garnishes

- 1 large green pepper (6 ounces, 170g), seeded and cut to fit the feed tube
- 1 cucumber (7 ounces, 200g), unpeeled, cut in half vertically, seeded, and cut to fit the feed tube
- 8 scallions (4 ounces, 115g), including the green tops, cut into thirds

Transfer each vegetable to an individual serving dish after preparing it.

Medium Slicing Disc: Place the green pepper in the feed tube vertically and slice it, using light pressure.

Place the cucumber pieces in the feed tube and slice them, using medium pressure.

Place the scallions in the feed tube vertically and slice them, using light pressure.

Metal Blade: Now coarsely chop the pepper and cucumber slices by placing half the slices of each vegetable in the work bowl at a time, and turning the machine on and off until they are coarsely chopped.

Makes 10 to 12 servings.

Note: When fresh tomatoes are not at their peak of flavor, substitute 2 16-ounce (455g) cans of tomato wedges, including the liquid. First rinse the wedges and strain out their seeds.

Cooked cucumbers have a unique taste, and in this recipe they are complemented by leek and spinach.

3 large cucumbers (2 pounds total, 910g), peeled, halved lengthwise, seeded, and cut into lengths to fit the feed tube

1 large leek (1/2 pound, 225g), including the green top, split, washed, drained, and cut into lengths to fit the feed tube

1 quart (95 cl) chicken broth

1 very small cucumber or 1 small piece of cucumber (3 ounces, 85g), unpeeled, scored, and ends cut flat

1 cup uncooked spinach leaves (2 ounces, 55g), washed and drained

1 teaspoon dried dillweed, or 2 teaspoons fresh

1 teaspoon dried chervil
Salt
Freshly ground pepper

1/2 cup (12 cl) plain yogurt, sour cream, or Crème Fraîche (see Index)

Medium Slicing Disc: Slice the cucumbers and leek, using medium pressure. Transfer them to a saucepan with the chicken broth and simmer the mixture, uncovered, for 30 minutes. Put the small cucumber in the feed tube vertically and slice it, using medium pressure. Reserve the cucumber slices.

Metal Blade: Transfer the cooked vegetables to the work bowl with a slotted spoon. Add 1/2 cup (12 cl) of the liquid, and process the mixture until it is puréed. Leave the purée in the bowl and add the spinach. Combine them by turning the machine on and off until the spinach is finely chopped. Stir the mixture into the broth and add 1/2 the dillweed, chervil, salt and pepper. Ladle the soup into bowls and garnish each serving with a dollop of yogurt, sour cream, or Crème Fraîche, the reserved cucumber slices, and a sprinkling of dillweed.

Makes 8 servings.

Note: This soup can be frozen after the vegetables are puréed, before the spinach is added. Reheat it thoroughly and proceed with the remainder of the recipe.

Dilled Cucumber Soup

A tasty, year-round soup.

6 small zucchini
   (1 pound, 2 ounces
   total, 510g), trimmed
   and cut into lengths to
   fit the feed tube
2 teaspoons salt
1/4 cup (6 cl) parsley
   leaves
1 tablespoon chives,
   snipped
2 onions (10 ounces
   total, 285g), peeled
   and quartered
2 tablespoons oil
1 quart (95 cl) chicken
   broth
1 large tomato
   (6 ounces, 170g),
   peeled, seeded and
   quartered
1/2 teaspoon sugar
1/2 teaspoon dried
   oregano
1/2 teaspoon dried basil
2 teaspoons lemon juice
1/4 teaspoon freshly
   grated nutmeg
   Salt
   Freshly ground pepper

Medium Slicing Disc: Put the zucchini in the feed tube vertically and slice it, using medium pressure. Reserve 8 slices, wrapped in plastic, and transfer the remaining slices to a colander. Mix them with the salt and let them drain for 30 minutes. Wash off the salt and pat the zucchini dry with paper towels.

Metal Blade: Mince the parsley and chives by turning the machine on and off; reserve them. Mince the onions by turning the machine on and off.

Heat the oil in a kettle and cook the zucchini and onion, covered, over low heat for 10 minutes. Add the broth, cover and simmer the mixture for 20 minutes.

Chop the tomato coarsely by turning the machine on and off. Reserve it.

Metal Blade: Transfer the zucchini and onion to the work bowl with a slotted spoon and purée them, stopping the machine once to scrape down the sides of the bowl. Transfer the purée to the kettle. Add the reserved tomato, sugar, oregano, basil, lemon juice, nutmeg, salt and pepper, and cook the soup for 5 minutes. If the soup is too thick, thin it with additional broth, cream, or milk. Serve it hot or cold, garnished with the reserved zucchini slices, parsley, and chives.

Makes 8 servings.

Note: This soup can be frozen after it is puréed, before the tomato and seasonings are added. Reheat it thoroughly and proceed with the recipe.

A delicious old-fashioned soup that is prepared in a flash with a modern machine.

4 pounds (1.8 kg) center-cut beef shanks
Salt
Freshly ground pepper
2 tablespoons vegetable oil
2 onions (1/2 pound total, 225g), peeled and quartered
1 bay leaf
2 tablespoons red wine vinegar
2 large celery ribs including leaves (4 ounces total, 115g)
1 28-ounce (800g) can Italian-style plum tomatoes, including juice
1 small rutabaga (1 pound, 455g), peeled and cut into pieces to fit the feed tube
2 large carrots (6 ounces total, 170g), peeled and cut into lengths to fit the feed tube
4 ounces (115g) green beans, trimmed and cut into lengths to fit the feed tube
1/2 pound (225g) cabbage, cut into wedges to fit the feed tube
1 teaspoon dried dillweed
1 teaspoon dried basil
1/2 cup (12 cl) dry Sherry (optional)

Season the beef with the salt and pepper. Heat the oil in a 6-quart (5.7 l) kettle and add the beef in batches, browning it well on all sides.

Metal Blade: Chop the onions until they are finely minced by turning the machine on and off. Stir them into the last batch of meat during the last few minutes of browning. Return all the meat to the kettle, add water to cover, the bay leaf, vinegar and celery, and bring the liquid to a boil. Skim the froth from the top and simmer the mixture, covered, for 3 hours, skimming it occasionally as necessary. Strain the stock into a bowl and skim the fat carefully. Or refrigerate the stock until the fat solidifies and then remove it. Measure the stock, add water to make 6 cups (1.4 l), and return it to the kettle.

Drain the tomatoes, reserving their juices, and coarsely chop them by turning the machine on and off. Add the tomatoes and the reserved juices to the kettle.

French-Fry Disc, Julienne Disc, or Medium Slicing Disc: Put the rutabaga and carrots in the feed tube horizontally and cut them with the French-fry disc or julienne disc, using firm but not hard pressure. Or use the medium slicing disc and a double-slicing technique to cut them into julienne strips as follows. First cut them into slices, using firm pressure. Then remove the slices from the work bowl and insert as many slices as you can into the feed tube, wedging them tightly so they will hold. Slice them again, to make julienne strips. Repeat the process with any remaining slices. Add the rutabaga and carrots to the kettle and simmer the mixture for 10 to 20 minutes, or until the vegetables are almost tender but still crisp.

Thin Slicing Disc: Place the beans in the feed tube vertically and slice them, using medium pressure. Slice the cabbage, using firm pressure. Add the vegetables to the kettle.

Cut the meat into 3/4-inch (2 cm) cubes, add it to the kettle with the seasonings, and simmer the soup, uncovered, for 10 minutes, or until the beans and cabbage are still crisp but cooked through. Add the Sherry and correct the seasoning.

Makes 8 main-course or 12 first-course servings.

Note: This soup is best frozen after the addition of the rutabaga, carrots, meat, and herbs. Add the green beans and cabbage when it has been thoroughly reheated and cook it for 10 minutes longer.

Meats

Meats

Stir-Fried Beef with Bean Threads
Yogurt Beef Stroganoff
Meat Loaf with Lemon Slices
Pot Roast with Beer
Sliced Beef in Madeira Sauce
Oriental Hamburgers
Chili
Beef Tacos
Osso Bucco
Lamb Shish Kebab
Lamb à la Grecque
Turkish Meat Casserole, Vegetables and Rice
Boneless Leg of Lamb with Mushroom Stuffing
Roast Pork with Caramelized Apples

When it comes to meat cookery, I am definitely a fiscal conservative. So you'll find plenty of party dishes in this chapter — but no filet mignon or costly crown roasts. And you'll find plenty of easy, everyday entrées — but no ordinary hamburgers or dead-weight casseroles. For me, both kinds of meals present the same challenge: use imagination to stretch the meat, making it colorful and exciting. The right complement of seasonings, vegetables, fruits or sauce can make the distinction between humble and extravagant cuts of meat irrelevant.

That principle didn't originate in my kitchen, of course. Chinese, Middle Eastern, Mexican, Italian and French cooks have been practicing similar meat economies for centuries, with results so sublime that nobody belittles them as "budgetwise". Their ingenuity is reflected in the flavors and methods of many of my recipes, ranging from Chinese Stir-Fried Beef with Bean Threads to Turkish Casserole of Meat, Vegetables and Rice.

Economy is by no means my sole motive, however. I love the worldliness, the unsnobbish savvy of being able to serve Osso Bucco Milanese, Sliced Beef in Madeira Sauce and a great bowl of American Chili with equal ease and enthusiasm. It's the dining style of our times — exuberant, cosmopolitan and full of surprises! It pokes gentle fun at our expensive and not-altogether-healthy reverence for steaks; it puts wellnurtured peasant wisdom back in the kitchen.

Stir-Fried Beef with Bean Threads,
page 37.

The food processor makes it all possible for those of us who long ago gave up clumsy meat grinders and who never will master the cleaver speed of a Chinese chef. Processor power gives you marvelous flexibility as a consumer. You can buy whatever meat is on sale and decide whether you want to slice it elegantly or grind it into meatloaf when you are ready to cook it. And you don't have to measure cost savings against the time needed to prepare the meat. What especially pleases me is knowing exactly what goes into processor-chopped beef, lamb or pork and being able to control the fat content — to say nothing of the freshness and sanitary conditions. I also like having the option of serving the same lean chopped beef either as superb steak tartare or a satisfying hamburger.

There is yet another bonus built directly into correct food processor technique. Because meat, whether raw or cooked, should be semi-frozen before it is sliced, you can sear the meat well in advance of dinner and freeze it. Then you can partially thaw and slice it at your convenience and heat it with the sauce just before serving.

The results are fantastic! The presentation of beautifully rare, thin slices is worthy of a fine French restaurant. Try the Sliced Beef in Madeira Sauce or the Yogurt Beef Stroganoff and you'll see what I mean!

When I was asked, not long ago, to prepare dinner for Jean Banchet, the acclaimed chef-owner of Le Français in Wheeling, Illinois, I had to come up with an entrée that would be delicious and different yet completely unlike Banchet's celebrated *nouvelle cuisine*. I immediately thought of lamb, for its delicate flavor, with Middle Eastern overtones for a taste of intrigue. Result: Festive Lamb Shish Kebab and Pilaf with Currants — a resounding success. I highly recommend this recipe for those occasions when you want to savor something unusual and you have a bit of time, even in stages, to devote to the preparation. But I confess that when I have no time at all, I just marinate the meat for Lamb à la Grecque and count on the tantalizing grilled lamb aroma to save the occasion. My students swear by the recipe for Boneless Leg of Lamb with Mushroom Stuffing, a somewhat fancier party attraction that can be prepared up to the point of roasting a day in advance. This dish is so popular that I have included a Pimiento Stuffing variation for repeat performances.

Looking for something simple yet special? See what a piquant glaze and a sunny layer of lemon slices can do for a meatloaf. Enjoy the water chestnut crunch of Oriental Hamburgers. Whiz through an eye-catching assortment of garnishes for Beef Tacos. It doesn't take financial genius to figure out that a little machine strategy can yield enormous returns on your meat investment!

A dish as attractive as it is delicious.

Meat

2-1/2 pounds (1.2 kg) bottom round or flank steak

Marinade

1/2 cup (12 cl) dark soy sauce
1 tablespoon light soy sauce
1/2 cup (12 cl) dry Sherry
1/2 teaspoon MSG (optional)
2 teaspoons sugar

Vegetables

1-1/4 pounds (567g) bok choy, cut in pieces to fit the feed tube
2 medium red peppers (6 ounces total, 170g), seeded and cut into 2-inch (5 cm) squares
1 8-ounce (225g) can water chestnuts, drained
1 quart peanut oil
6 ounces (170g) bean threads (also known as cellophane noodles)
1-inch (2.5 cm) piece fresh ginger root, peeled
1 large garlic clove, peeled and split
2 tablespoons oyster sauce

Cut the beef into pieces of uniform size that will just fit into the feed tube. The pieces should be cut with the grain running lengthwise so the meat will be sliced against the grain.

Place the pieces of beef in a single layer on a foil-lined baking sheet. Freeze it until it is firm to the touch but easily pierced with the tip of a sharp knife.

Medium Slicing Disc: Put a piece of beef into the feed tube and slice it, using firm pressure. Continue until all the meat is sliced.

Put the slices into a 1-gallon plastic bag with all the marinade ingredients. Close the bag by tying it tightly and shake it to distribute the marinade evenly around the slices of beef. Refrigerate for at least 30 minutes or up to 2 hours.

Medium Slicing Disc: Slice the bok choy, using medium pressure. Wedge the red pepper pieces into the feed tube and slice them, using light pressure. Arrange the water chestnuts in the feed tube and slice them, using firm pressure.

Heat the oil in a wok or deep sauté pan until it registers 400°F. (205°C.). If you don't have an appropriate thermometer, test it by dropping in a bean thread. If it pops up immediately, the oil is at the correct temperature.

Deep-fry the bean threads, adding them in 2 batches, and turning them when they are puffed to cook quickly on the other side. Transfer them with a slotted spoon to paper towels and drain well. Break them into portions adequate for one serving and arrange them around the edge of a large serving platter. Remove all but 2 tablespoons of oil from the pan.

Drain the beef slices. Brown the ginger root and garlic in the oil remaining in the pan and discard them. Cook the slices of meat, stirring them constantly, until they reach the desired degree of doneness. Add them in 3 batches and set aside the first two batches as they are cooked. Add additional oil as necessary, but use as little as possible. When the last batch of meat is cooked, add the oyster sauce, bok choy, pepper, water chestnuts and the first two batches of cooked meat. Heat until thoroughly warm but do not cook it.

Heap the meat in the center of the platter and serve immediately.

Makes 8 servings.

An unusual, low-calorie version of an old favorite.

2-1/2 pounds (1.2 kg) top
round roast, cut into
cubes 3-3/4 by 2 by
1/2-inch (9.5 x 5 x 1.5
cm) to fit the feed tube
with the grain running
lengthwise so that it
will be sliced against
the grain
Salt
Freshly ground pepper
2 tablespoons butter
1 tablespoon oil
1/2 cup (12 cl) parsley
leaves
1 large garlic clove,
peeled
3 small onions (6 ounces
total, 170g), peeled
and cored
1-3/4 cups (42 cl) beef broth
3 tablespoons tomato
paste
1 tablespoon dried
dillweed
1 teaspoon salt
1/4 teaspoon freshly
ground pepper
1/4 teaspoon freshly
grated nutmeg
8 large mushrooms
(1/2 pound total, 225g),
trimmed and sides cut
flat
2 large carrots (6 ounces
total, 170g), unpeeled,
trimmed and cooked
1-1/3 cups (31 cl)
plain yogurt
Herbed Pasta (see
Index)

Season the meat with salt and pepper. Melt the butter and oil in a large skillet and brown the meat on all sides over moderately high heat. Cook to desired degree of doneness (preferably rare within and well browned outside). Transfer the meat to a foil-lined baking sheet, arranging it in 1 layer, and freeze it until it is firm but not frozen solid. To slice well in the food processor, it must be easily pierced with the tip of a sharp knife.

Metal Blade: Mince the parsley by turning the machine on and off about 10 times; remove it and reserve it. With the machine running, mince the garlic by dropping it through the feed tube. Leave it in the work bowl.

Medium Slicing Disc: Slice the onions, using medium pressure, and sauté it with the garlic in the same skillet used for the meat, adding more butter and oil if necessary. Add 1-1/4 cups (30 cl) of beef broth and simmer the mixture until it is reduced to 3/4 cup (18 cl). Add the tomato paste and the seasonings and remove the pan from the heat.

Put the flat sides of 2 or 3 mushrooms on the slicing disc, put on the work bowl cover, and stack mushrooms sideways in the feed tube. Slice the mushrooms, using light pressure, and repeat the process with the remaining mushrooms. In a small skillet simmer the mushrooms in 1/2 cup (12 cl) beef broth for 3 minutes and transfer them with a slotted spoon to a dish, reserving the broth. (If the Stroganoff is not to be served immediately, the mushrooms may be left in the broth and reheated.)

Arrange the meat pieces vertically in the feed tube, at least 2 pieces at a time, and slice them, using firm pressure.

Metal Blade: Purée the cooked carrots, adding a little broth if necessary.

Transfer the carrots to the larger skillet, which contains the onions. Heat the mixture thoroughly. Then stir in the yogurt, and heat the mixture again but do not let it boil. Correct the seasoning and add the meat. Heat the mixture thoroughly, but do not cook the meat further. Pour the reserved hot broth over hot, drained Herb Pasta. Toss the pasta and correct the seasoning. Transfer the pasta to a platter, ladle the Stroganoff over it and garnish the platter with mushrooms and the reserved parsley.

Makes 8 servings.

This meat loaf is marvelous when hot, but it's equally good cold — thinly sliced for sandwiches.

Meat Loaf

- 1/4 cup (6 cl) parsley leaves
- 1 small onion (2 ounces, 55g), peeled and quartered
- 2 thin slices of firm white bread (1-1/2 ounces, 43g), torn into pieces
- 2 pounds (910g) lean beef chuck, cut into 1-inch (2.5 cm) cubes
- 2 teaspoons seasoning salt
- 1/4 teaspoon freshly grated nutmeg
- 1 teaspoon salt
  Freshly ground pepper
- 1/2 cup (12 cl) plus 2 tablespoons spicy tomato-vegetable juice
- 1 large egg

Metal Blade: Put the parsley in the work bowl. Turn the machine on and drop the onion through the feed tube. With the machine still running, add the bread and process the mixture for 5 seconds. Transfer it to a bowl. Finely chop the beef in batches by turning the machine on and off until the meat is of the desired texture. Transfer the first batch of meat to a large bowl. Add the seasonings, tomato juice, egg and the bread mixture to the second batch of meat and process the mixture for 1 second. Add the mixture to the first batch of meat and combine gently but well. Shape the mixture into a freeform loaf in a small roasting pan.

Note: Make several meat loaves at a time, put them on foil-lined baking sheets, and freeze them, unbaked. When they are frozen wrap them tightly in foil. Let the frozen meat loaves thaw completely in the refrigerator. Glaze and garnish each loaf before baking as described below.

Glaze

- 1/4 cup (6 cl) ketchup
- 1 teaspoon dry mustard
- 1/2 teaspoon freshly grated nutmeg
- 1 tablespoon dark brown sugar
  Dash of Tabasco

Process the glaze ingredients to combine them well and spread the glaze on the meat loaf.

Garnish

- 1 small lemon, scored and ends cut flat

Thin Slicing Disc: Slice the lemon, using firm pressure, and arrange the slices over the loaf.

Preheat the oven to 350°F. (175°C.). Bake the meat loaf for 1 hour, pour off the fat, and transfer the loaf to a platter.

Makes 8 servings.

A hearty main dish that is superb with the mushroom stuffing, and — if you lack time to prepare the stuffing — very good without it.

Sauce

- 3 large Spanish onions (2 pounds total, 908g), peeled and quartered
- 2 tablespoons unsalted butter
- 2 tablespoons oil
- 1 tablespoon sugar
- 1 12-ounce (35 cl) can of beer
- 3 garlic cloves, peeled
- 1 large bay leaf
- 1/2 teaspoon dried thyme
- 1/2 to 1 cup (12 to 24 cl) beef broth
- 2 thin ribs celery (2 ounces total, 55g), with leaves

Medium Slicing Disc: Slice the onions, using medium pressure. Melt the butter and oil in a skillet and cook the onions over medium heat for about 25 minutes, or until they are well browned. Add the sugar and cook over high heat, stirring constantly, until the onions are deep brown. Add the beer, garlic, bay leaf, thyme and 1/2 cup (12 cl) of the broth. Mix well and transfer to a baking dish just large enough to hold the meat. Add the celery ribs and leaves.

Mushroom Stuffing

- 1 large garlic clove, peeled
- 2 large shallots (2 ounces total, 55g), peeled
- 12 large mushrooms (3/4 pound total, 340g), trimmed
- 2 tablespoons unsalted butter
- 2 tablespoons oil
- 2 slices firm white bread (2 ounces total, 55g), crusts removed and torn into pieces
- 1/4 cup (6 cl) parsley leaves
- 3 tablespoons currants
- 1/2 teaspoon dried dill weed
- 1 teaspoon salt
  Freshly ground pepper
- 1 large egg

Metal Blade: With the machine running, mince the garlic and shallots by dropping them through the feed tube. Leave them in the work bowl. Add the mushrooms and mince them by turning the machine on and off. Melt the butter and oil in a large skillet and sauté the mushroom mixture over medium-high heat for 5 minutes. Remove the skillet from the heat.

Put the bread and parsley in the work bowl and process for about 5 seconds. Add to the mushroom mixture, along with the currants, dill weed, salt and pepper.

Break the egg into the work bowl and process it for about 2 seconds. Fold it gently but thoroughly into the mushroom mixture and adjust the seasoning if necessary.

Meat _____

1 5 to 6-pound (2.3 to
   2.7 kg) brisket of beef,
   trimmed and covered
   with a 1/4-inch (.75 cm)
   layer of fat on the top
   side, slit to make a
   pocket for stuffing
1-1/2 teaspoons salt
   Freshly ground pepper

Preheat the oven to 325°F. (165°C.) and adjust the rack to the middle level.

Season the beef generously on all surfaces, including the pocket, with salt and pepper. Put the stuffing into the pocket and spread it evenly. Secure the stuffing in place by skewering the edges of the meat together at 1-inch (2.5 cm) intervals. Put the meat in the baking dish with the sauce. Roast it, uncovered, for 1 hour, or until it is well browned. Cover it and cook it for 2 or 3 hours longer, basting it occasionally, until the meat is fork tender. Remove it from the oven and transfer the meat to a cutting board.

Skim the fat from the sauce, or refrigerate the sauce until the fat solidifies on top, then remove it.

Metal Blade: Process the sauce for about 30 seconds, or until it becomes a smooth purée. If it is very thick, add the remaining beef broth. Adjust the seasoning, put it in a saucepan and heat it.

Slice the meat into 1/4-inch (3/4 cm) slices with a very sharp knife or an electric knife. Arrange the slices on a platter and spoon the sauce over them. Serve the remaining sauce separately.

Note: The meat can be cooked well before serving and reheated. Bring it to room temperature, wrap it in foil and place it in a 350°F. (175°C.) oven for about 30 minutes. Be careful not to overcook it.

Makes 10 servings.

This lovely beef dish is perfect for a dinner party. Although it can be prepared in advance and reheated when you are ready to serve it, the beef stays rare and juicy.

Meat _____

4 pounds (1.8 kg) top beef butt, trimmed
1 large garlic clove, peeled and split
Coarse Kosher salt
Freshly ground pepper
2 tablespoons unsalted butter
2 tablespoons oil

Cut the beef into pieces of uniform size that will just fit into the feed tube. The pieces should be cut with the grain running lengthwise so the meat will be sliced against the grain.

Rub the meat with garlic and season it with salt and pepper. Heat the butter and oil in a large skillet. When it is very hot, add the meat — a few pieces at a time — and sear it on all sides. Do not crowd pieces into the pan; to ensure even browning, they should not touch each other while they are cooking.

As they are cooked, transfer the pieces to a baking sheet lined with foil. Cool, then freeze on the foil-lined sheet.

If you plan to use it immediately, freeze it until it is firm to the touch, but easily pierced with the tip of a sharp knife.

If you plan to freeze it for later use, wrap it when frozen into double airtight bags. When you are ready to use it, allow it to thaw only partially, to the state where it is still firm to the touch but easily pierced with the tip of a sharp knife.

Medium or Thick Slicing Disc: Put a piece of meat in the feed tube and slice it, using firm pressure. Continue until all the meat is sliced. Arrange the slices in an ovenproof baking dish, and let the meat come to room temperature.

Madeira Sauce _____

1 medium garlic clove, peeled
3 large shallots (3 ounces total, 85g), peeled
2 tablespoons unsalted butter
1 cup (24 cl) Madeira wine
1 cup (24 cl) beef broth
2 teaspoons cornstarch
2 tablespoons Beaujolais wine
2 drops Kitchen Bouquet

Metal Blade: Mince the garlic and shallots by dropping them through the feed tube while the machine is running. Melt the butter in a skillet and sauté the garlic and shallots gently over medium heat for about 5 minutes, or until they are soft.

Add the Madeira and 3/4 cup (18 cl) of the broth and simmer until the mixture is reduced to 1 cup (24 cl). Dissolve the cornstarch in the remaining broth and whisk it into the Madeira mixture. Cook the sauce, stirring it occasionally, for about 5 minutes or until it is thick enough to coat a spoon lightly. Stir in the Beaujolais and the Kitchen Bouquet, adjust the seasoning and strain the sauce into a bowl. Let it cool.

Pour the sauce over the slices of beef. It can be heated immediately, or covered and refrigerated at this point. If you refrigerate it, let it come to room temperature before reheating.

Heat the meat in a preheated 350°F. (175°C.) oven for 18 to 20 minutes. Keep a close watch on it because you want to be sure to retain the beef in a rare state, not to overcook it.

Parsley sprigs
Tomato rose(s)
Cherry tomatoes

Arrange the meat on a serving platter and spoon over only enough sauce to moisten it. Garnish the platter with parsley, one or two tomato roses or cherry tomatoes. Serve the remaining Madeira Sauce separately, or serve it with the Béarnaise Sauce with Pimiento (see Index) or the Béarnaise Sauce with Tomato (see Index).

Variation _____

Prepare and slice the beef as indicated, but substitute Green Peppercorn Sauce (see Index) for the Madeira Sauce.

Makes 10 to 12 servings.

Oriental Hamburgers _____

1 large garlic clove, peeled
3 large scallions (3 ounces total, 85g), including the green tops, cut into 1-inch (2.5 cm) pieces
8-ounce (225g) can water chestnuts, drained
2 pounds (910g) lean beef, cut into 1-inch (2.5 cm) cubes
2 tablespoons dark soy sauce
1 teaspoon light soy sauce
3 tablespoons dry Sherry or water
Pinch of salt
3 tablespoons vegetable oil
Several drops of sesame oil

Metal Blade: With the machine running, mince the garlic by dropping it through the feed tube. Add the scallions and water chestnuts to the work bowl and chop them coarsely by turning the machine on and off. Transfer the mixture to a mixing bowl. Chop the meat in batches by turning the machine on and off until it is the consistency of hamburger. Add the meat to the mixing bowl. Add the soy sauces, Sherry, and salt and combine the mixture well with your hands. Form the mixture into 6 to 8 patties. Broil them on a grill, or sauté them in a skillet in the vegetable and sesame oils.

Makes 6 to 8 servings.

Keep a container of this hearty fare in your freezer for quick and satisfying meals.

2 large garlic cloves, peeled
2 large onions (10 ounces total, 285g), peeled and quartered
2 tablespoons oil
2 pounds (910g) lean beef chuck, cut into 1-inch (2.5 cm) cubes
28-ounce (800g) can whole tomatoes, including the juice
6-ounce (170g) can tomato paste
3 cups (70 cl) beef broth
15-ounce (425g) can red kidney beans, drained and rinsed
3 tablespoons chili powder
2 teaspoons ground cumin
1 teaspoon dried oregano
1 tablespoon salt
1/4 teaspoon freshly ground pepper

Metal Blade: With the machine running, mince the garlic by dropping it through the feed tube. Mince one onion by turning the machine on and off. Heat the oil in a large stainless steel saucepan and add the onions and garlic. Mince the remaining onion and add it to the pan; sauté the mixture over medium high heat for 10 minutes. Chop the meat in batches to medium coarseness by turning the machine on and off. Add it to the pan and brown it for 10 minutes. Pour the juice from the tomatoes into the pan.

Metal Blade or French-Fry Disc: Coarsely chop the tomatoes by turning the machine on and off about 5 times if you are using the metal blade, or by applying light pressure with the French-fry disc. Add them to the pan with all the remaining ingredients, and simmer the chili uncovered for 1 hour. Correct the seasoning and add water if the chili becomes too thick.

Makes about 9 cups.

Note: If you find the texture of whole kidney beans objectionable, use the metal blade to chop them to the desired texture before adding them to the meat.

Beef Tacos

A hit for all ages — especially the birthday party set, who can devour astonishing quantities of them.

Filling

2 large garlic cloves, peeled
2 onions (10 ounces total, 285g), peeled and quartered
2 tablespoons oil
3 pounds (1.4 kg) lean beef, cut into 1-inch (2.5 cm) cubes
2 tablespoons chili powder ("hot" if desired)
1 teaspoon ground cumin
1 tablespoon seasoning salt
Freshly ground pepper
15-ounce (425g) can tomato sauce
2 tablespoons tomato paste
2 to 3 tablespoons water

Metal Blade: With the machine running, mince the garlic by dropping it through the feed tube. Leave it in the work bowl. Chop the onions in 2 batches by turning the machine on and off about 6 times. In a 3-quart (285 cl) saucepan sauté the garlic and onions in the oil for 10 minutes over moderately high heat.

Chop the meat in batches, turning the machine on and off until the meat reaches the consistency of hamburger. Transfer it to the saucepan as it is chopped. Cook the meat mixture over moderately high heat for 10 minutes, then add the seasonings, tomato sauce, and tomato paste, combining the mixture well. Simmer the mixture, covered, for 1 hour. If the mixture becomes too thick, add the water. Correct the seasoning.

Makes 1-1/2 quarts (142 cl).

Note: This mixture can be made in advance, frozen and reheated.

Garnish

Choose several of these:
6 ounces (170g) Longhorn Cheddar cheese, chilled
1/2 head of iceberg lettuce (12 ounces, 340g), cut into wedges to fit the feed tube
12 scallions (6 ounces total, 170g), including the green tops, cut into thirds
1 large cucumber (11 ounces, 310g), unpeeled, split and seeded
1 large tomato (6 ounces, 170g), cored and quartered
Bottled taco sauce
20 packaged taco shells

Process each ingredient separately and place each one in an individual serving dish as it is processed.

Shredding Disc: Shred the cheese, using light pressure.

Medium Slicing Disc: Shred the lettuce, using light pressure. Stand the scallions in the feed tube and slice them, using light pressure. Slice the cucumber, using medium pressure, and leave it in the work bowl.

Metal Blade: Coarsely chop the cucumber by turning the machine on and off 4 times. Add the tomato and chop it by turning the machine on and off 4 times.

Heat the taco shells for 10 minutes in a preheated 350°F. (175°C.) oven. Spoon the filling into the shells. Arrange the tacos on a platter, and serve them with the garnishes and taco sauce, if desired.

Makes 20 tacos.

Prepare *Osso Bucco* a day in advance and give the flavors a chance to develop and blend. Veal shanks are the traditional choice for this dish; their marrow provides an essential element of its great appeal. If they are difficult to obtain, however, you can substitute lamb or chicken as described in the variation.

Meat

2/3 cup (3 ounces, 85g) all-purpose flour
1 tablespoon salt
1-1/2 teaspoons dried basil
1/2 teaspoon dried thyme
1/2 teaspoon freshly ground pepper
8 pounds (3.6 kg) veal hind shanks, cut into 2-inch (5 cm) rounds (16 pieces)
3 tablespoons unsalted butter
3 tablespoons oil

Sauce

1 large garlic clove, peeled
1 large onion (5 ounces, 140g), peeled and quartered
1-1/2 cups (35 cl) dry white wine or dry vermouth
2 28-ounce (83 cl) cans Italian plum tomatoes, drained
1/2 teaspoon sugar
1/2 to 1 cup (12 to 24 cl) beef broth
1 bay leaf
Salt
Freshly ground pepper

Preheat the oven to 350°F. (175°C.).

Metal Blade: Process the flour, salt, basil, thyme and pepper for 1 second. Put the mixture in a large bowl and coat the veal pieces with it on all sides. Heat the butter and oil over high heat in a large skillet and brown the veal pieces on all sides, adding them in several batches. Remove them to a dish with a slotted spoon and reserve the juices in the skillet.

Metal Blade: With the machine running, mince the garlic by dropping it through the feed tube. Add the onion and mince it by turning the machine on and off about 6 times. Heat the juices left in the skillet in which you cooked the veal and sauté the garlic and onions until soft. Add the wine and simmer until the liquid is reduced to about 1 cup (24 cl).

Metal Blade: Add the tomatoes to the work bowl in batches and chop them coarsely by turning the machine on and off. Add the sugar, 1/2 cup (12 cl) of the broth, the bay leaf, and salt and pepper to taste.

Arrange the veal shanks in a large ovenproof casserole, setting them upright in one layer so the marrow won't fall out during the cooking. Pour the wine mixture from the skillet over the veal. Add the chopped tomatoes, cover and cook for 2 to 3 hours, or until the veal is tender. Turn the veal pieces twice during the cooking, always rearranging them in upright positions. If the sauce is too thick, add the remaining beef broth. Adjust the seasoning.

Osso Bucco can be prepared in advance to this point and refrigerated for as long as 3 days, or frozen. To reheat it, bring it to room temperature, cover it and place it in an oven that has not been preheated. Set the oven at 350°F. (175°C.) and heat the veal thoroughly, but do not overcook it.

Gremolata

1 large garlic clove,
  peeled
Zest of 1 lemon and 1
  orange, removed with
  a zester or grater
1 cup (24 cl) parsley
  leaves

Metal Blade: With the machine running, mince the garlic by dropping it through the feed tube. Add the lemon and orange zest and the parsley leaves and mince them by turning the machine on and off about 10 times. Remove the mixture from the work bowl and reserve it. Wipe the bowl out with a paper towel.

Garnish

1 small lemon, scored
  and ends cut flat

Thin or Medium Slicing Disc: Slice the lemon, using firm pressure.

Assembly

Sprinkle half the *gremolata* over one side of the veal. Turn the veal over, taking care that the marrow stays in place, and re-arrange the pieces in upright positions. Sprinkle with the remaining *gremolata*. Arrange the lemon slices around the dish for garnish.

Makes 8 servings.

Variation

Use 8 pounds (3-1/2 kg) of lamb shanks, or two 3-pound frying chickens, cut into serving pieces. Brown them and cook them in the same way as the veal.

This festive dish is worthy of the most spectacular occasion. To make preparation easier, assemble the lamb slices and mushroom mixture a day ahead of serving.

Meat

4 pounds (1.8 kg) lamb from the leg, cut into 2-inch (5 cm) squares

Freeze the lamb on a foil-lined baking sheet until it is firm but not frozen solid. To slice well in the food processor, it should be firm, but easily pierced with the tip of a sharp knife.

Medium Slicing Disc: Put the meat in the feed tube with the grain running lengthwise so that the meat will be sliced against the grain. Slice it, using firm pressure.

Preheat the oven to 400°F. (205°C.) and adjust the rack to the middle level.

Mushroom Mixture

1 ounce (30g) dried Polish or Italian mushrooms
1/2 stick unsalted butter (2 ounces, 55g), cut into pieces
2 tablespoons oil
2 pounds (910g) small mushrooms, trimmed

Soak the dried mushrooms in warm water for 30 minutes. In a jelly-roll pan heat 2 tablespoons each of the butter and oil. Place the fresh mushrooms in the pan in 1 layer, and bake them for 15 minutes. Reduce the heat to 350°F. (175°C.) and continue baking for 20 minutes more, or until they shrivel slightly. Shake the pan once or twice during the cooking. Drain the dried mushrooms and in a small skillet sauté them in 2 tablespoons butter over medium high heat for 5 minutes.

Metal Blade: Mince all the mushrooms by turning the machine on and off until they are as fine as grains of rice.

Béchamel Sauce

2 tablespoons unsalted butter
2 tablespoons unbleach-ed all-purpose flour
1 cup (24 cl) milk
2 teaspoons Dijon-style mustard
1/2 teaspoon dried basil
1/2 teaspoon dried oregano
1/2 teaspoon dried savory
1/2 teaspoon salt
Freshly ground pepper
2 large egg yolks

Make a *roux* by melting the butter and stirring in the flour. Cook the *roux* over low heat for 5 minutes. Whisk in the milk and seasonings and cook the sauce until it is thickened and smooth. Remove the pan from the heat. Whisk 2 tablespoons of the sauce into the egg yolks, then whisk the egg yolk mixture back into the sauce.

Combine 2/3 cup (16 cl) of the sauce with the minced mushrooms and correct the seasoning. Reserve extra sauce for another use; it can be frozen.

Rub both sides of the meat slices with salt and pepper and spread a thin layer of the mushroom mixture on 1 side of 5 slices. Stack the slices and lay a sixth slice on top. Spread and stack the remaining slices in the same manner and refrigerate the resulting packets overnight, wrapped in plastic wrap.

Garlic Butter

1 garlic clove, peeled
1/2 stick unsalted butter (2 ounces, 55g), at room temperature

Metal Blade: Mince the garlic by dropping it through the feed tube with the machine running. Add the butter, salt and pepper and process for 2 seconds, or until it is well mixed. Transfer the butter to a small saucepan and melt it.

4 small lemons, scored
and ends cut flat

Medium Slicing Disc: Slice the lemons using firm pressure, and transfer them to a sheet of wax paper.

Sprinkle the tops of the meat packets with the salt and pepper and thread 2 packets alternately with lemon slices onto each skewer. Broil the meat over hot coals or close to the heat source, turning the skewers and brushing the meat with the garlic butter, melted, for about 8 minutes for meat that is pink inside and seared outside. Serve with Pilaf with Currants (see Index).

Makes 8 servings.

Lamb à la Grecque

Marinade

2 large garlic cloves,
peeled
1 onion (4 ounces, 115g),
peeled and halved
1 small lemon, scored
and ends cut flat
1/2 cup (12 cl) oil
(preferably safflower
with 1 tablespoon
olive oil)
1 cup (24 cl) dry red wine
2 teaspoons Dijon-style
mustard
2 teaspoons dried
oregano
1 teaspoon salt
Freshly ground pepper

Metal Blade: With the machine running, mince the garlic by dropping it through the feed tube. Leave it in the work bowl.

Medium Slicing Disc: Slice the onion, using firm pressure. Slice the lemon, using firm pressure. In a large bowl combine the slices with the remaining ingredients. Stir in the garlic mixture.

Meat

1 9-pound (4 kg) leg of
lamb, boned

Garnish

Lemon wedges
Parsley sprigs
Tomato rose

Put the lamb into the marinade and turn to coat it on all sides. Cover it and marinate it in the refrigerator overnight, turning it occasionally.

Let the lamb come to room temperature. Remove it from the marinade, and pat it dry with paper towels. Broil it on a grill or in the oven, searing — but not charring — both sides. Turn it frequently, basting it with the marinade each time. For pink lamb, broil it until an instant-reading thermometer registers 117°F. (47°C.) when inserted in the thickest part. The meat will continue to cook after it is removed from the heat. Let it rest for 20 to 30 minutes, covered with foil, before slicing it into thin diagonal slices. Simmer the remaining marinade in a saucepan for 10 minutes, strain it into a bowl, and correct the seasoning. Spoon this sauce over the lamb and garnish.

Makes 10 servings.

This dish was the sensation of a dinner party in Paris, where a distinguished Turkish woman taught me the recipe. Even with a food processor the preparation is time-consuming, but it is well worth it. To allow the flavors to develop, prepare the casserole a day before you plan to serve it.

3/4 cup (18 cl) long-grain rice
4 cups (95 cl) hot water
4 teaspoons salt
2 eggplants, (1 pound 10 ounces total, 740g), unpeeled, trimmed and cut into pieces to fit the feed tube
2 teaspoons salt
3 large green peppers (12 ounces total, 340g), cored and cut into 2-inch (5 cm) wide rectangles
4 large tomatoes (1-1/2 pounds total, 680g), cored and cut into wedges to fit the feed tube
1 large garlic clove, peeled
1-1/2 medium onions (1/2 pound total, 225g), peeled and quartered
1 pound (455g) lean round steak or chuck, cut into 1-inch (2.5 cm) cubes
1 pound (455g) lean lamb from the leg, cut into 1-inch (2.5 cm) cubes
2 teaspoons cinnamon
2 teaspoons salt
1/3 cup (8 cl) currants
1 teaspoon allspice
1 teaspoon salt
1/3 cup pine nuts, (2 ounces, 58g)
1 tablespoon oil
1/2 teaspoon sugar
1/2 cup (12 cl) water
1 tablespoon butter

Soak the rice for 30 minutes in the hot water to which you have added 4 teaspoons of salt.

Medium Slicing Disc: Slice the eggplant, using medium pressure. Transfer it to a colander and sprinkle it with 2 teaspoons salt. Toss the eggplant slices and let them drain for 30 minutes. Slice the green peppers, using medium pressure, and reserve them. Slice the tomatoes, using light pressure, and reserve them. Wipe out the work bowl with a paper towel.

Metal Blade: Mince the garlic by dropping it through the feed tube while the machine is running. Add the onion to the work bowl and mince it by turning the machine on and off. Transfer the garlic and onion to a skillet. Chop the beef and lamb finely by turning the machine on and off; add it to the skillet. Cook the mixture over moderate heat for 20 minutes. Stir in the cinnamon and salt and reserve the mixture.

Drain the rice and combine it with the currants, allspice, salt and pine nuts, lightly browned in 1 teaspoon oil, if desired.

Preheat the oven to 350°F. (175°C.) and fit a round of parchment paper into the bottom of a covered 5-quart (475 cl) ovenproof casserole.

Drain the eggplant, pat it dry with paper towels, and put it in a heated large skillet with 1 tablespoon oil. Cover the skillet and steam the eggplant over moderate heat for 5 minutes, shaking it from time to time to prevent it from sticking.

Assembly ――――――――――――― Arrange the green peppers in the casserole in a spoke design, placing a decoratively cut piece of green pepper in the
center. Arrange the tomatoes over the peppers and sprinkle
them with sugar. Add the meat mixture, press it into place,
and add half the eggplant, with its skin side against the outside of the casserole. Spoon in the rice mixture, smooth it,
and add the remaining eggplant, again with the skin against
the outside. Press the ingredients firmly into place, pour in
1/2 cup (12 cl) water, and dot the top with the butter.

Cover the casserole with parchment paper and its lid and
bake it for 1-1/4 hours. Remove it from the oven and let it stand
for 30 minutes. Carefully drain off any excess liquid. Serve
directly from the casserole or place a large platter over the
casserole and carefully invert the mixture onto the dish. Let
the mixture rest for 5 minutes, remove the casserole, and
serve the dish hot or at room temperature.

Makes 8 to 10 servings.

Note: After layering the ingredients in the casserole, you can
refrigerate the dish for a day, then bring it to room temperature before cooking as directed above. Or you can prepare
and cook it in advance, refrigerate it and bring it to room temperature before reheating it. Reheat by baking it, covered,
for 40 minutes, in a 350°F. (175°C.) oven that has not been preheated.

This dish holds together when it is inverted, but falls apart as
it is served. Use a large platter for easy serving.

This entrée is unquestionably one of the most popular party dishes I've ever taught. It can be prepared a day in advance and roasted just before your guests arrive. The lamb slices into most attractive servings.

Stuffing _____

1 large garlic clove, peeled
2 large shallots (2 ounces total, 55g), peeled
4 large mushrooms (4 ounces total, 115g), trimmed
2 tablespoons unsalted butter
2 tablespoons oil
1 slice firm white bread (1 ounce, 30g), torn into pieces
1/2 cup (12 cl) parsley leaves
1/2 pound (225g) lamb, cut into 1-inch (2.5 cm) cubes
1/4 cup (2 ounces, 58g), pistachio nuts
1 large egg
1 teaspoon salt
Freshly ground pepper

Metal Blade: With the machine running, mince the garlic and shallots by dropping them through the feed tube. Leave them in the work bowl. Add the mushrooms and mince them by turning the machine on and off.

In a large skillet, melt the butter and oil and sauté the mixture over moderately high heat for 5 minutes. Remove the pan from the heat.

Put the bread and parsley in the work bowl and mince them together by turning the machine on and off. Stir the mixture into the mushroom mixture.

Put the meat in the work bowl and chop it coarsely by turning the machine on and off. Add it to the mushroom/parsley mixture. Blanch the pistachio nuts for 30 seconds in a small saucepan of boiling water. Drain them and rub them vigorously in a towel to remove the skins. Add the nuts to the chopped meat mixture. Process the egg for 2 seconds and stir it gently into the stuffing mixture. Season the stuffing with salt and pepper. Sauté a small piece of stuffing, taste it and correct the seasoning if necessary.

Meat _____

1 7- to 8-pound (3.2 to 3.6 kg) leg of lamb, boned with bones reserved
Coarse Kosher salt
Freshly ground pepper
2 teaspoons of a mixture of dried thyme, oregano and savory in equal parts

Preheat the oven to 350°F. (175° C.) and adjust the rack to the middle level. Trim the lamb of any fell (outer skin) or excess fat, if necessary. Rub the inside with the salt and pepper. Spread the stuffing evenly over the lamb and roll it up lengthwise, tucking in any uneven pieces. Tie it with string, not too tightly. Season the surface with the herb mixture and additional salt and pepper, rubbing the herbs into the surface well. The lamb can be refrigerated at this point until the following day. Allow it to come to room temperature before cooking it.

Basting Sauce

1/4 cup (6 cl) oil
1/2 cup (12 cl) dry white wine or dry vermouth
1/2 teaspoon salt
1 tablespoon lemon juice

Combine the ingredients for the basting sauce in a small bowl.

Garnish

Parsley sprigs
Lemon wedges
Cherry tomatoes

Place the stuffed lamb roll and the reserved lamb bones in a roasting pan and roast for 1 hour. After the first 30 minutes, baste it occasionally with the sauce. Increase the temperature to 450°F. (230°C.) and roast the lamb for 15 to 20 minutes more for pink lamb, or until a meat thermometer registers 127°F. (53°C.). Let the meat rest for 30 minutes before slicing it. Transfer it to a platter and garnish the platter with the parsley, lemon wedges and cherry tomatoes.

Makes 10 servings.

Variation

Stuff the lamb with a colorful pimiento mixture such as the one served at the famed Taillevent restaurant in Paris.

Pimiento Stuffing

1 large garlic clove, peeled
1 leek including the green top (3 ounces, 85g), cut into 1-inch (2.5 cm) pieces
1 tablespoon butter
1 tablespoon oil
1 pound (455g) boneless veal, cut into 1-inch (2.5 cm) cubes
1/2 cup (12 cl) parsley leaves
1 large egg yolk
1/3 cup (8 cl) *Crème Fraîche* (see Index) or 1/4 cup (6 cl) heavy cream
1 teaspoon salt
Freshly ground pepper
4-ounce (115g) jar pimientos, drained and diced

Metal Blade: With the machine running, mince the garlic and leek by dropping them through the feed tube. Melt the butter and oil in a small skillet and sauté them over moderately high heat for 5 minutes.

Put the veal in the work bowl in batches and chop it by turning the machine on and off. Remove any unprocessed gristle with your fingers. Add the leek mixture, the parsley, egg yolk, cream, salt and pepper and process the mixture until it is smooth. Transfer the stuffing to a bowl and stir in the pimientos.

Stuff and roast the lamb as previously described.

Boneless Leg of Lamb with Mushroom Stuffing, with Sweet Pea Flan (see page 278)

Roast Pork with Caramelized Apples

Terrific everyday fare, this roast is enhanced by the accent of tart apples.

Meat

1 4-pound (1.8 kg)
 rolled loin of pork
1 tablespoon salt
1/2 teaspoon garlic
 powder (optional)
1/2 teaspoon Hungarian
 paprika
Freshly ground pepper

Preheat the oven to 425°F. (220°C.) and adjust the rack to the middle of the oven.

Wash the pork and pat it dry with paper towels. Mix the seasonings and rub them well into the roast. Roast the pork for 1 hour on a rack in a roasting pan lined with foil. Remove it from the pan and skim the fat from the pan juices.

Glaze

1 small onion (2 ounces,
 55g), peeled and
 halved
1 cup (24 cl) apple jelly
1 teaspoon dry mustard

Metal Blade: Mince the onion by turning the machine on and off. Add the jelly and mustard, and process the mixture for about 5 seconds.

Brush the glaze on the pork and roast the pork at 375°F. (190°C.) for 1 to 1-1/2 hours longer, or until an instant-reading thermometer registers 170°F. (75°C.).

Apples

5 large tart apples
 (2 pounds total, 910g),
 peeled, halved and
 cored
1/2 stick unsalted butter
 (2 ounces, 55g)
2/3 cups sugar
 (5-1/2 ounces, 155g)

Thirty minutes before the roast is done, prepare the apples.

Medium Slicing Disc: Slice the apples, using medium pressure. Melt the butter in a large skillet over moderately high heat. Add the sugar and apples, and cook them over moderate heat, lifting and turning them occasionally with a spatula, for 20 minutes, or until they caramelize. Keep the apples warm.

Transfer the roast to a platter; arrange the apples around it.

Makes 8 servings.

Poultry

Poultry

Chicken Patties Augusta
Chicken Provençal
Baked Chicken with Herbs and Onions
Orange Chicken Surprise
Chicken Breasts with Scallions and Pistachios
Stir-Fried Sesame Lemon Chicken
Moo Shu Chicken with Mandarin Pancakes
Roast Chicken with Broccoli
Turkey Tonnato
Herbed Barbecued Turkey
Barbecued Duck with Apricot Glaze
Roast Cornish Hens with Madeira Sauce

It sounds funny, but it's true: Chicken recipes have acquired a new sense of urgency in my classroom. As my students become increasingly concerned about cholesterol, chemicals and costs, they clamor for more and more ways to serve that old standby, chicken.

I couldn't be more delighted, for chicken is one of the most versatile and interesting ingredients to work with. Prepare it one way and it tastes just like delicate, top quality veal; try it another way and the aroma of a hearty goulash rises from the pot. In one guise, it's authentically Chinese; in another, it's pure French countryside. I love the fact that low-calorie chicken dishes never leave me feeling deprived. And I appreciate the fact that boneless chicken can be quickly sliced into enough morsels to feed an army!

So, let us count the ways . . .

First, a couple of techniques I learned in France that offer All-American convenience and time-savings: stuffing under the skin and high-temperature roasting. The inspiration for Orange Chicken Surprise, which has sliced oranges tucked under the skin and is roasted in Brown-'n' Bags®, came from three-star chef Alain Chapel. He used sliced truffles as the seasoning and a pig's bladder to protect the chicken, but the principle of an enclosure that will not, like aluminum foil, trap all of the moisture, is the same. The Orange Chicken Surprise, topped by a julienne of three vegetables, makes an exquisite presentation, but it can be served plain and unsauced as well, for the natural juices provide irresistible flavor.

Roast Cornish Hens with Madeira Sauce, page 74.

From the great Richard Olney, I borrowed the idea for Roast Chicken with Broccoli, another under-the-skin-stuffing recipe that results in an uncommonly moist bird. And bringing the same theme home to my own barbecue grill, I created a juicy self-basting turkey insulated with herb butter. All three of these recipes can be prepared to the roasting stage up to a day in advance and will only improve with the wait.

I was first introduced to the French practice of roasting poultry at high temperatures when I worked with Jean Delaveyne at his restaurant, Le Camélia, outside Paris. The chicken he roasted at 450°F. turned out superbly moist. After I arrived home, I used the same method with Rock Cornish Hens and found that the higher temperature makes an incredible difference. You can't tell that the hens have been frozen! Although it has little to do with the food processor, I teach the recipe and include it here because the hens go so well with vegetable purées and other elegant side dishes.

Delaveyne, who travels to Japan at least once a year, also shared his recipe for Chicken Breasts with Scallions and Pistachios. For me, the dish holds not only Oriental fascination but also a textural richness derived from combining whole and sliced chicken breasts. More traditionally Oriental are my recipes for Stir-Fried Lemon Chicken and Moo Shu Chicken. Wrap the Moo Shu Chicken in homemade Mandarin Pancakes and you'll create a sensation among Chinese food connoisseurs. Or wrap either stir-fry in lettuce leaves for a nouvelle-style low-calorie appetizer.

There's no reason to shy away from the stir-fried dishes for large parties, since everything up to the final assembly can be done well ahead of time. The same is true of the colorful, abundant Chicken Provencal and the hearty one-pot Baked Chicken with Herbs and Onions. I keep Chicken Patties Augusta in my freezer, ever-ready for instant hospitality. But the most nervous hosts and hostesses in my classes take special comfort in the recipes for Turkey Tonnato and Barbecued Duck with Apricot Glaze, which *must* be prepared in advance.

I have to add one triumphant postscript to this chapter: After years of dissatisfaction with the quality and prices of veal, I was thrilled to discover that sliced turkey breast surpasses the flavor of veal in the classic Italian tonnato sauce combination. And the mix of chopped lean beef and chicken in the Chicken Patties Augusta strikes this veal-lover's tastebuds as right on target!

Chicagoans will recognize this old-time regional favorite that has been revised for preparation with a modern machine. The patties taste more like veal than chicken. For last-minute cooking with a flair, make several recipes at a time and keep the patties in the freezer.

1 small onion (1-1/2 ounces, 42g), peeled
2 slices firm white bread (2 ounces total, 55g), crusts removed, quartered
4 ounces (115g) lean beef, chilled and cut into 1-inch (2.5 cm) pieces
1 pound (455g) skinned and boned chicken breasts, chilled and cut into 1-inch (2.5 cm) pieces
1/2 teaspoon Hungarian paprika
1 teaspoon salt
Freshly ground pepper
1/2 cup (12 cl) heavy cream, chilled
1/4 cup (6 cl) unbleached all-purpose flour
2 tablespoons unsalted butter
2 tablespoons oil

Metal Blade: Mince the onion by dropping it through the feed tube with the machine running. Add the bread to the work bowl and process the mixture for 1 minute. Add the beef and process for 30 seconds, then add the chicken and seasonings. Process the mixture for 1 minute, or until it is finely puréed. With the machine running, pour the cream through the feed tube. Process the mixture for 30 seconds. Transfer it to a bowl, cover it airtight and refrigerate it for at least 6 hours, or overnight. Divide the mixture into 6 portions and with lightly floured hands shape the portions into patties of uniform size. Heat the butter and oil in a large skillet over moderately high heat. Add the patties and reduce the heat to moderate. Cook for 15 to 20 minutes, or until the patties are well browned on both sides, and transfer them to a platter.

Makes 6 servings.

Variations

1. Serve the patties with Tomato Butter Sauce (see Index).

2. Serve the patties with a Shallot and Herb Butter made as follows.

Melt 1/2 stick butter over high heat in the same skillet in which the patties were cooked. Add 2 large minced shallots (2 ounces, 55g total), and 1 teaspoon of dried dillweed. Cook the mixture for 2 minutes. Add 1 teaspoon of red wine vinegar, 2 teaspoons of minced parsley, and salt and freshly ground pepper to taste. Spoon the butter over the patties, which have been kept warm while you were making the sauce.

Chicken Provencal

It is not quite accurate to say that it takes longer to read this recipe than to prepare it! Don't be put off by the list of ingredients. The food processor makes fast work of this colorful and zesty chicken dish.

Chicken

- 2 2-1/2-pound (1.1 kg) frying chickens, cut up
- 2 teaspoons salt
- 1/2 teaspoon freshly ground pepper
- 3 tablespoons unsalted butter
- 3 tablespoons oil, preferably French olive oil

Wash the chickens and pat them dry with paper towels. Season them with the salt and pepper. Melt the butter and oil in a large skillet over medium high heat. Brown 2 or 3 chicken pieces at a time — they will not brown if they are crowded into the pan. Transfer the pieces to a plate as they are browned and set them aside. Remove all but 2 tablespoons of the juices from the pan.

Sauce

- 1/2 cup (12 cl) parsley leaves
- 1 large garlic clove, peeled (optional)
- 1 large onion (5 ounces, 140g), peeled and quartered
- 2 tomatoes (8 ounces total, 225g), peeled, seeded and quartered
- 2 small green peppers (6 ounces total, 170g), seeded and cut into 3-inch (7.5 cm) squares
- 2 small red peppers (6 ounces total, 170g), seeded and cut into 3-inch (7.5 cm) squares
- 2 lemons, scored and ends cut flat
- 2 teaspoons dried oregano
- 1 teaspoon dried basil Pinch of saffron threads Pinch of cayenne
- 1/2 cup (12 cl) Calamata olives or ripe olives, pitted and drained
- 1/2 teaspoon sugar

Metal Blade: Mince the parsley by turning the machine on and off. Set it aside. With the machine running, mince the garlic by dropping it through the feed tube. Leave it in the work bowl, add the onion, and turn the machine on and off until it is minced. Add the garlic and onion to the skillet with the juices from the chicken. Sauté gently for about 10 minutes until the mixture is soft but not brown.

Chop the tomatoes coarsely by turning the machine on and off; leave them in the work bowl.

Medium Slicing Disc: Wedge the pepper squares into the feed tube and slice them into strips, using light pressure. Remove the tomato/pepper combination from the work bowl and set it aside.

Slice the lemons, using firm pressure, and reserve them for garnish.

Put 2/3 of the tomato/pepper combination into the skillet, along with herbs, olives, sugar, broth and wine. Mix well and adjust the seasonings, if necessary.

Add the dark-meat pieces of chicken and spoon the sauce over them. Cover and simmer for 15 minutes. Add the white-meat pieces of chicken and the remaining tomatoes and peppers. Cover and simmer for 20 minutes longer, or until the chicken is just cooked through. Do not overcook.

1/2 cup (12 cl) chicken
    broth
1/2 cup (12 cl) dry
    white wine
    Salt
    Freshly ground pepper

Adjust the seasoning and transfer to a platter or casserole dish. Garnish with reserved parsley and lemon slices.

Makes 6 servings.

Baked Chicken with Herbs and Onions _____

Here is a simple chicken dish that is a favorite of long standing in my house. The herbs can be varied, and sliced mushrooms make a savory addition. The herbed chicken and onion juices can be skimmed off and spooned over Egg Noodles (see Index) or mixed into rice.

1 3-pound (1.4kg) frying
    chicken, cut into 8
    pieces
1 teaspoon dried thyme
1 teaspoon dried basil
1/4 teaspoon garlic
    powder (optional)
1 tablespoon salt
    Freshly ground pepper
1/2 cup (12 cl) parsley
    leaves
2 large Spanish onions
    (1 pound total, 455g),
    peeled and quartered

Preheat the oven to 350°F. (175°C.) and adjust the rack to the middle level.

Wash the chicken pieces and dry them very well with paper towels. Combine all the other ingredients except the parsley and onions, and rub the mixture well onto all sides of the chicken.

Metal Blade: Mince the parsley by turning the machine on and off.

Medium Slicing Disc: Slice the onions, using medium pressure.

Put half the onion slices in an ovenproof baking dish large enough to hold all the chicken pieces.

Lay the seasoned chicken pieces over the onions and sprinkle with half of the parsley. Tuck the rest of the onion slices between the chicken pieces and cover the dish tightly with its lid or with foil.

Bake for 1 hour and 15 minutes at 350°F. (175°C.). Remove the cover and increase the oven temperature to 400°F. (205°C.). Bake 15 minutes longer or until the chicken is lightly browned. Sprinkle with the remaining parsley.

Makes 4 servings.

Leave the butter out of the sauce to make this unusually appealing dish a low-calorie treat as well as one that is low in cost. It's an adaptation of a recipe prepared by Alain Chapel at his restaurant in Mionnay, France. He uses truffles instead of orange slices to tuck under the skin.

2 3-pound (1.4 kg) whole frying chickens
3 seedless oranges, halved and ends cut flat, 1 scored with a stripper
1 tablespoon plus 1 teaspoon salt
1/4 teaspoon garlic powder (optional)
Freshly ground pepper
2 small onions (4 ounces total, 115g), peeled
2 large self-basting bags for oven cooking, such as Brown-n-Bags
2 tablespoons flour
1/2 cup (12 cl) frozen orange-juice concentrate, thawed
1/4 cup (6 cl) Cognac or ruby Port
1 large turnip (7 ounces, 200g), peeled and halved
1 leek (5 ounces, 140g), split, washed, trimmed and cut into 2-inch (5 cm) lengths
4 ounces (115g) green beans, cut into 2-inch (5 cm) lengths
Salt
Freshly ground pepper
1 tablespoon Cognac or ruby Port (optional)
1/2 stick unsalted butter (2 ounces, 55g), chilled and quartered (optional)
Parsley sprigs

Preheat the oven to 325°F. (175°C.) and adjust the rack to the middle of the oven.

Wash the fryers and pat them dry with paper towels. Place the chickens on their backs, and carefully separate the skin from the flesh with your hands. Start at the neck cavity, slipping your finger under the skin. Work around the breast toward the wings and down around the legs. Be careful not to tear the skin and not to break the attached skin at the center of the breastbone.

Medium Slicing Disc: Put the unscored oranges in the feed tube vertically and slice them, using firm pressure. Slice the scored orange in the same way and reserve the slices for garnish. Tuck 10 to 12 of the unscored slices in a single layer under the skin of each chicken, distributing them evenly and creating a design on the breast.

Mix the salt, garlic, and pepper in a dish and season the cavity and the surface of the chickens with the mixture. Put 1 onion and any remaining orange slices in each cavity.

Tie the legs together, clip the tips of the wings, and tuck the remaining segments under the wings.

Put 1 tablespoon flour in each self-basting bag and shake the bags to distribute the flour. Mix the orange concentrate and Cognac or Port in a small bowl and pour half the mixture in each bag. Put a chicken in each bag. Tie the bags close to the chicken and cut 6 half-inch (1.25 cm) slits in the top of each bag with scissors. Put the chickens in a roasting pan and roast them for 1 hour and 20 minutes, or until an instant-reading thermometer registers 170°F. (77°C.).

Julienne Disc or Thin Slicing Disc: Cut the turnip into julienne strips, using light pressure. If you do not have a julienne disc, use a double-slicing technique to cut them into julienne strips as follows.

First slice them, using firm pressure. Then remove the slices from the work bowl, and insert as many slices as you can into the feed tube, wedging them tightly so they will hold. Slice them again to obtain julienne strips. Repeat the process with any remaining slices.

Thin Slicing Disc: Split the white part of the leeks lengthwise several times and lay the leek pieces into the feed tube horizontally. Slice the leeks, using medium pressure; remove them and reserve them.

Put the beans in the feed tube horizontally and slice them, using medium pressure.

Blanch each vegetable separately in 4 quarts (380 cl) boiling water with 2 teaspoons salt; the turnips for 30 seconds, the leeks for 30 seconds, and the beans for 1 minute. Remove the vegetables immediately with a strainer or slotted spoon and put them under cold running water until they are completely cool. Drain them well. Season the vegetables with salt and pepper.

Open the chicken bags carefully and pour the juices into a saucepan. Skim off the fat and reduce the liquid over moderately high heat to 3/4 to 1 cup (18 to 24 cl). Add Cognac or Port, and whisk in 3 tablespoons of the butter, 1 piece at a time. Add salt and pepper to taste.

Reheat the vegetables quickly in the remaining butter. Arrange the chickens on a platter and spoon the sauce over them. Spread the vegetables on the chicken breasts, with the beans on top. Garnish the platter with the reserved orange slices and the parsley sprigs.

Makes 6 to 8 servings.

Variation _____

Use chicken breasts instead of whole chickens, tucking the orange slices under the skin and baking the breasts at 325°F. (175°C.) for 50 minutes.

Orange Chicken Surprise

Despite its oriental touches, this recipe is the creation of Jean Delaveyne, who served it in his restaurant, Le Camélia, located in the Paris suburb of Bougival. The original calls for rabbit, but chicken is used in this variation.

Chicken

8 large chicken breasts, split, skinned and boned (16 pieces total, 4 pounds, 1.8 kg meat)
2 to 3 teaspoons salt
1/2 teaspoon freshly ground pepper
1 tablespoon Hungarian paprika
1/4 teaspoon garlic powder (optional)
3 tablespoons sesame oil
2 tablespoons oil, preferably safflower

Halve 8 of the chicken pieces crosswise and freeze them on a foil-lined baking sheet until they are firm, but not frozen solid. To slice easily in the machine, they should be firm to the touch, but easily pierced with the tip of a sharp knife.

Medium Slicing Disc: Wedge the frozen chicken pieces in the feed tube vertically and slice them against the grain, using firm pressure. Put the slices in a plastic bag and reserve them in the freezer.

Combine the dry seasonings and mix them well. Sprinkle the 8 remaining unfrozen chicken pieces on one side with 1/4 of the seasoning mixture. In a large skillet, heat 1-1/2 tablespoons sesame oil and 1 tablespoon oil until it is hot. Put in the chicken, seasoned side down, and cook it over medium high heat for 3 minutes. Sprinkle 1/4 of the seasoning mixture on the top sides of the chicken pieces. Turn them and cook the chicken for 3 minutes longer, or until it feels just firm. Remove the chicken and set it aside.

Add the remaining oils to the skillet, put in half the frozen slices and stir-fry them over moderately high heat until they are just opaque. Remove the chicken as it is cooked and repeat the process with the remaining slices. Sprinkle with remaining seasoning mixture.

Sauce

2 cups (47 cl) beef broth
2 teaspoons cornstarch dissolved in 2 tablespoons cold beef broth
1/3 cup (8 cl) ruby Port
2 tablespoons oyster sauce

In a 1-quart (95 cl) saucepan, combine all the ingredients. Bring the mixture to a boil; simmer it gently for 10 minutes.

Garnish

8 large scallions
(8 ounces total, 225g),
including the green
tops, cut into thirds
1/3 cup (2-1/2 ounces, 75g)
shelled pistachio nuts

Medium Slicing Disc: Wedge the scallions in the feed tube vertically and slice them, using light pressure.

Assembly

Return all the chicken to the skillet, add the sauce, and cook the mixture over moderate heat for 2 minutes. Stir in 3/4 of the scallions and nuts, simmer the mixture for 1 minute, and transfer the breast halves to a platter, arranging them in a row. Spoon the sliced chicken mixture around them and garnish the platter with the remaining scallions and nuts. Serve the dish with Egg Noodles (see Index) tossed with 1/2 pound (225g) cooked, diced zucchini and 2 tablespoons butter.

Makes 8 servings.

An absolutely super, low-calorie entrée which is really quick to prepare if you freeze chicken in advance.

Meat _____

6 large chicken breasts, split, skinned and boned (3 pounds meat total, 1.4 kg)

You will have 12 chicken cutlets from the 6 chicken breasts. Cut each in half horizontally and arrange the pieces in one layer on a foil-lined baking sheet. Freeze partially until firm but not frozen solid. The meat should feel firm to the touch, but it should be easily pierced with the tip of a sharp knife.

Medium or Thick Slicing Disc: Wedge the chicken pieces into the feed tube so the slicing disc will cut against the grain. Slice, using firm pressure, and put in a 1-gallon plastic bag.

Marinade _____

**1/4 cup (6 cl) parsley leaves
Zest of 2 lemons, removed with a zester or grater
1 large garlic clove, peeled
1/2 inch (1.5 cm) piece of fresh ginger root, peeled and halved
2 tablespoons lemon juice
1/4 cup (6 cl) dry Sherry
1 teaspoon Oriental sesame oil
1 teaspoon safflower oil
2 teaspoons cornstarch
1/4 cup (6 cl) sesame seed
7 dried black Chinese mushrooms (optional)**

Metal Blade: Mince the parsley and lemon zest by turning the machine on and off. With the machine running, mince the garlic and ginger root by dropping them through the feed tube. Add the remaining marinade ingredients except the sesame seeds and mushrooms, and process for 2 seconds. Add the marinade to the bag containing the chicken and seal it tightly. Shake the bag to distribute the marinade evenly over the chicken slices and marinate in the refrigerator for 30 minutes to 4 hours.

Spread the sesame seeds on a baking sheet and brown them in a 350°F. (175°C.) oven for 15 minutes or until they are deep brown.

Soak the Chinese mushrooms in hot water to cover for 30 minutes. Drain thoroughy. Remove the stems and discard them or save them for use in soups.

Shredding Disc: Shred the drained mushrooms, using light pressure; reserve them.

Sauce

1/4 cup (6 cl) chicken stock
1/4 cup (6 cl) honey
1/4 cup (6 cl) dry Sherry
1/3 cup (8 cl) lemon juice
2 tablespoons light soy sauce
2 tablespoons dark soy sauce
1-1/2 teaspoons salt
Freshly ground pepper
3 small lemons, scored and ends cut flat

Assembly

2 tablespoons safflower oil
2 tablespoons Oriental sesame oil

Metal Blade: Put the stock, honey, Sherry, lemon juice, soy sauces, salt and pepper in the work bowl and process for 5 seconds. Remove and set aside.

Thin or Medium Slicing Disc: Slice the lemons, using firm pressure.

Remove the chicken slices from the marinade and pat them dry with paper towels. Heat a wok or skillet and add 1 tablespoon of each of the oils. Add half the chicken slices and cook them just until they lose their translucency and become opaque. Remove them and add the remaining oil and the rest of the chicken. Cook until it is opaque, then return the first batch of chicken to the pan along with the shredded mushrooms, toasted sesame seeds and sauce. Heat thoroughly. Stir in 2 of the sliced lemons and adjust the seasoning. Place the chicken in the center of a platter and surround it with Asparagus Fried Rice (see Index). Garnish the platter with the remaining lemon slices.

Makes 8 servings.

Note: This chicken makes an elegant picnic or hot-weather dish when served at room temperature. The marinade, which can be made 2 days in advance and refrigerated, is also good when brushed on broiled fish fillets.

Universally appealing whether the chicken is wrapped in bright green lettuce or in homemade Mandarin pancakes. Let your guests have fun wrapping their own.

2 large chicken breasts split, skinned and boned (1 pound meat total, 455g), halved horizontally
1 large egg white
1 teaspooon salt
1/2 teaspoon sugar
1/4 cup dried mushrooms (1/2 ounce, 15g)
12 scallions (6 ounces total, 170g), including the green tops, cut into 2-inch (5. cm) lengths
1/4 pound (115g) Chinese cabbage
3 large eggs
1/2 teaspoon salt
1/4 cup (6 cl) oil
1 inch (2.5 cm) piece of fresh ginger root
2 tablespoons dark soy sauce
1 tablespoon light soy sauce
1/2 teaspoon sugar
2 teaspoons dry Sherry
1 teaspoon Oriental sesame oil
16 Mandarin Pancakes (recipe follows) or 16 large Boston lettuce leaves

On a foil-lined baking sheet freeze the chicken until it is firm but not frozen solid. To slice well in the food processor, it should be firm to the touch but easily pierced with the tip of a sharp knife.

Medium Slicing Disc: Slice the chicken, using firm pressure. Combine the slices in a bowl with the egg white, salt and sugar. Soak the mushrooms for 30 minutes in hot water to cover and drain them. Remove the stems and discard them or save them for soup.

Put the scallions in the feed tube horizontally and slice them, using light pressure. Leave them in the work bowl.

Cut the cabbage into quarters and put it in the feed tube vertically. Slice it, using medium pressure, and leave it in the work bowl.

Medium Shredding Disc: Shred the mushrooms, using light pressure. Transfer the vegetables from the work bowl to a small mixing bowl.

Metal Blade: Process the eggs and salt for 4 seconds. Heat half the oil in a wok, add the eggs, and scramble them very lightly. Divide the eggs into chunks with a spatula and transfer them to a plate.

Add the remaining oil to the wok and brown the ginger root. Remove it with a slotted spoon and discard it. Add the chicken to the flavored oil and cook it until it is almost opaque, stirring constantly but gently. Add the remaining ingredients, except the eggs and sesame oil, and heat through but do not overcook. Fold in the eggs and sesame oil gently and transfer the mixture to a serving dish. Serve it with Mandarin Pancakes or Boston lettuce leaves, placing 2 to 3 tablespoons of the mixture in the center of each pancake or leaf and wrapping it into a neat packet.

Makes 8 servings.

Note: *Moo Shu* Chicken is also exceptionally good served as a salad at room temperature.

Mandarin Pancakes

Here's a chance for "one-upmanship" with homemade Mandarin pancakes. After experimenting with fifty pounds of flour, I was finally satisfied with my tender, thin pancakes — only to discover that they are available by the piece at many Chinese restaurants!

1-2/3 cups unbleached all-purpose flour (8-1/4 ounces, 240g)
1/3 cup cake flour, (1-1/2 ounces, 42g)
1/4 teaspoon salt
1 cup (24 cl) boiling water
2 tablespoons Oriental sesame oil or vegetable oil

Metal Blade: Put the flours and salt in the work bowl and pour the water through the feed tube while the machine is running. Process the dough until it forms a ball and transfer it to an airtight plastic bag. Let it rest at room temperature for 30 minutes to 1 hour.

Put the dough on a well-floured board, form it into a smooth 12-inch (30 cm) cylinder, and cut the cylinder into 4 equal pieces. Cut each piece into 8 eight pieces. Roll each piece into a ball, and flatten each ball into a 2-inch (5 cm) round. Brush one side of each round — including the edges — very generously with oil. Pair the rounds with the oiled sides together, and flatten them smoothly with the heel of your hand.

On the well-floured board roll each pair out into a flat thin pancake about 6 to 7 inches (15 to 18 cm) in diameter, rotating and turning the cakes as you roll them out. It may be necessary to stretch the cakes with your hands.

Brush a skillet lightly with oil and fry the pancake pairs over moderately low heat, turning them to cook both sides. Brown spots will appear on the surface and the pancakes will bubble and puff.

Remove the pancakes and separate them carefully. Stack them and wrap them in foil or a kitchen towel. Line a steamer with foil and steam the pancakes for about 8 minutes. Fold them into quarters and transfer them to a serving plate.

Makes 32 pancakes.

_____

In this delightful dish inspired by Richard Olney, broccoli and cheese purée stuffed under the skin keep the chicken marvelously moist.

1 large bunch of broccoli (1-1/2 pounds, 680g), stems peeled and split lengthwise
Salt
1 shallot (1 ounce, 30g), peeled
3 ounces (85g) imported Parmesan cheese, at room temperature, cut into 3 pieces
1/2 cup (12 cl) parsley leaves
1/4 cup (6 cl) low-fat ricotta cheese
2 large eggs
2 teaspoons mixed, dried herbs (thyme, oregano and savory)
Freshly ground pepper
2 3-pound (1.4kg) whole frying chickens
2 teaspoons oil (optional)

Plunge the broccoli into boiling water to which you have added 2 teaspoons of salt. Cook it for 2 minutes after the water returns to the boil. Transfer it to a colander and place it under cold running water until it is completely cool. Drain it well and wrap it in several layers of paper towels to absorb the excess moisture. Cut the broccoli into 1-inch (2.5 cm) pieces.

Metal Blade: Chop the broccoli coarsely, but do not purée it. This may have to be done in 2 batches, turning the machine on and off 4 to 6 times for each. Transfer the chopped broccoli to a bowl. Mince the shallot, Parmesan cheese and parsley, turning the machine on and off about 10 times. Add the ricotta, eggs, 1-1/2 teaspoons of the mixed herbs and salt and pepper, and process the mixture for 3 seconds. Add the mixture to the broccoli, combining it well with a rubber spatula. Correct the seasoning. The stuffing should be slightly overseasoned.

Wash the chickens and pat them dry with paper towels. Cut the tips from the wings. Remove the backbone by cutting down both sides of the bone with kitchen shears. Discard the bone. Lay each chicken flat on a board with its skin side up and press your hands down on the breast bone to flatten it. Be careful not to tear the skin. Starting at the neck opening, carefully separate the skin from the flesh with your fingers. Work your fingers over one side of the breast and over the thigh and leg areas. Repeat the process on the other side. After the separation has been started, a smooth, long-handled wooden spoon can help. Repeat the process with the other chicken.

Preheat the oven to 425°F. (220°C.) and adjust the rack to the middle of the oven.

Stuff one fourth of the broccoli mixture under the skin of 1 side of a chicken, working it from the neck and over the leg, pressing along the outside of the breast to distribute it evenly. Repeat the procedure on the other side, and with the other chicken. Bend the wing and breast section gently toward you, breaking the shoulder bones. With a small sharp knife, make incisions on both sides of the breast near the tail opening between the point of the breast and the leg. Lift the legs and fit them through these slits, pulling the skin over the tips of the legs. Repeat this procedure with the other chicken.

Rub the chickens with oil, if desired, and season them generously with the salt, pepper and the remaining herb mixture. Roast them skin side up in a large roasting pan for 20 minutes. Reduce the heat to 375°F. (190°C.) and roast them for 40 minutes longer, basting them occasionally with the pan juices. Cover them loosely with foil if they begin to brown too deeply.

Makes 8 servings.

Note: This recipe can be prepared in advance and refrigerated until roasting time. If they are cold when they are put in the oven, roast the chickens for 5 to 10 minutes longer at 375°F. (190°C.).

Turkey Tonnato

The turkey breast is sliced with speed and perfection in the food processor, which also prepares the sauce and garnishes.

Turkey

1 4-pound (1.8kg) boned and rolled turkey breast
1 tablespoon oil
1 large onion (5 ounces, 140g), peeled and quartered
2 medium carrots (5 ounces total, 140g), unpeeled, trimmed, and cut into chunks
2 large celery ribs (4 ounces total, 115g), including the leaves, cut into chunks

Preheat the oven to 325°F. (165°C.).

Rub the surface of the turkey with oil and roast it with the vegetables for 1-1/2 hours, or until an instant-reading thermometer registers 170°F. (77°C.). Let the turkey cool. Transfer it to a cutting board, reserving the juice, and cut it into the largest pieces that will fit the feed tube. Cut it so that it will be sliced against the grain. Freeze the turkey pieces on a foil-lined baking sheet until they are firm but not frozen solid. To slice well by machine, they should be firm to the touch but easily pierced with the tip of a sharp knife. Skim the fat from the pan.

Medium Slicing Disc: Slice the turkey, using firm pressure and arrange the slices on a platter. Reserve any unattractive slices for sandwich filling.

Tonnato
Tunafish Mayonnaise

1 small onion (1 ounce, 30g), peeled
1 large egg
1 teaspoon lemon juice
1 teaspoon red wine vinegar
1 teaspoon Dijon-style mustard
1 teaspoon salt
Freshly ground white pepper
1-1/2 cups (35 cl) oil (preferably safflower oil with 3 tablespoons olive oil)
1 7-ounce (200g) can Italian tuna in olive oil, undrained
3 flat anchovy fillets
3 tablespoons lemon juice
3 tablespoons capers, drained

Metal Blade: With the machine running, mince the onion by dropping it through the feed tube. Leave it in the work bowl and add the egg, lemon juice, vinegar, mustard, salt, pepper and 3 tablespoons of oil. Process the mixture for 10 seconds. With the machine running, drizzle the remaining oil through the feed tube in a thin stream, letting the mayonnaise thicken as it is added. Add the remaining sauce ingredients and combine them by turning the machine on and off about 4 times. Process the sauce for 10 seconds. Pour the sauce over the turkey slices and refrigerate the turkey, covered, for several hours, or overnight.

1/4 to 1/3 cup (6 to 8 cl)
    turkey broth from the
    cooking of the turkey,
    diluted with water if
    the flavor is too strong
1/2 cup (12 cl) parsley
    leaves

Garnish _____

1/2 cup (12 cl) parsley
    leaves
  1 large egg yolk,
    hard-boiled
1/2 large head of iceberg
    lettuce (9 ounces,
    255g), cut into wedges
    to fit the feed tube
  2 small lemons, scored
    and ends cut flat
  2 tablespoons large
    capers, drained
    Sliced tomatoes and
    onions with Basil
    Vinaigrette (see Index)

Metal Blade: Mince the parsley by turning the machine on and off, and reserve it. Rice the egg yolk by turning the machine on and off about 4 times, and reserve it. Wipe out the work bowl with a paper towel.

Medium Slicing Disc: Slice the lettuce, using medium pressure, and arrange the shreds on a platter. Slice the lemons, using firm pressure.

Transfer the turkey to the bed of lettuce with a spatula and spoon the sauce over it. Garnish the platter with the reserved parsley, the reserved egg yolk, and capers. Let the platter stand at room temperature for 20 minutes and arrange the lemon slices and sliced tomatoes and onions with Basil Vinaigrette around the edge of the platter.

Makes 10 servings.

Note: The *tonnato* sauce is also terrific with sliced, cold chicken breasts and veal, and — as if that weren't enough — it makes a good salad dressing as well as a wonderful dressing for mixed vegetables or a dip for *Crudités* (see Index.)

Whether the turkey is roasted on the grill or in the oven, this version will be juicy and flavorful.

Herb Butter

1 large garlic clove, peeled
1 small piece of onion (1 ounce, 30g), peeled
1-1/2 sticks unsalted butter (6 ounces, 170g), at room temperature and cut into 6 pieces
1 teaspoon dried oregano
2 teaspoons parsley leaves
1 teaspoon dried dillweed
1/2 teaspoon salt
Freshly ground pepper

Prepare 2 or 3 days before serving

Metal Blade: With the machine running, finely mince the garlic and onion by dropping them through the feed tube. Add the remaining ingredients and process the mixture for 10 seconds, or until it is well combined, stopping the machine once to scrape down the sides of the bowl. Refrigerate the mixture, covered airtight, for 2 or 3 days. The mixture also freezes well.

Turkey

1 12-pound (55kg) hen turkey
3 tablespoons peanut oil
2 tablespoons salt
Freshly ground pepper
Garlic powder

Wash the turkey and pat it dry with paper towels. Place it on its back and with your forefinger, separate the skin from the flesh starting at the neck opening and working over both sides of the breast and over the thigh and leg areas. Loosen the skin gently with your fingers and try not to tear it. You may carefully insert a small wooden spoon to help the process.

Spoon the herb butter under the skin, reserving 2 tablespoons. Work it from the neck opening toward the tail opening by pressing along the outside of the breast. Rub the peanut oil over the turkey.

Mix the seasonings in a small bowl and sprinkle them over the turkey. (The turkey can be cooked now, or it can be refrigerated for several hours. It should be brought to room temperature before being cooked.)

Roast the turkey over a hot fire, either on a spit or in a covered grill. Allow 11 minutes per pound, or roast until an instant-reading thermometer registers 185°F. (85°C.).

Brush on the remaining herb butter during the last few minutes of cooking and let the turkey rest, covered loosely with foil, for at least 30 minutes before carving. Transfer the turkey to a platter.

Makes 10 servings.

Whole or cut-up fryers or chicken breasts can be prepared the same way, but the cooking time will be shorter.

Spread the herb butter on bread and heat in the oven.

Barbecued Duck with Apricot Glaze _____

Prepare the duck a day ahead for this unusual barbecue that is sure to rate rave reviews. When the weather's not right for outdoor cooking, the ducks can be done in the oven instead.

Duck _____

2 3-1/2-pound (1.6kg) ducks, quartered
1 tablespoon salt
1/2 teaspoon freshly ground pepper
1 large garlic clove, peeled and halved (optional)

Season the ducks with salt and pepper and rub them with garlic, if desired. Prick the skin all over with a fork and roast the ducks for 1-1/2 hours, or until they are browned and all the fat has been released. Turn them twice during cooking and prick them occasionally.

Sauce _____

1 seedless eating orange, scored and halved (for garnish)
Zest of 1 orange, removed in strips with a vegetable peeler
1-1/2 cups (35 cl) apricot preserves
1/2 cup (12 cl) orange juice
1/4 cup (6 cl) water
2 tablespoons red wine vinegar
3 tablespoons Cognac
1 teaspoon salt
Watercress or parsley sprigs

Medium Slicing Disc: Slice the orange, using firm pressure. Wrap it in plastic and refrigerate it.

Metal Blade: Process the zest and apricot preserves until the mixture is puréed. Add the remaining ingredients and process the sauce for 1 minute. Pour the sauce over the ducks as soon as you pour all the fat off them. Refrigerate the ducks, overnight, covered.

Transfer them to a baking sheet, reserving the sauce, and let them come to room temperature. Cook on a barbecue grill over a medium fire until heated through, basting them with the reserved sauce and watching carefully to prevent the marinade from burning. (Or reheat them in a 350°F. (175°C.) oven, basting them with the sauce, for 30 minutes. If more intense color is desired, finish the cooking by placing them under a broiler for 2 to 3 minutes.) Cut the ducks into serving pieces and transfer the pieces to a platter. Brush them with any remaining sauce and garnish the platter with the orange slices and watercress or parsley sprigs.

Makes 4 to 6 servings.

Variation _____

For Barbecued Chicken, season two quartered 3-pound (1.4kg) chickens and roast them for 1 hour. Pour the apricot sauce over them. Proceed with the rest of the recipe in the same manner as for the ducks.

Note: The sauce is excellent for pork roasts and spareribs.

These Cornish hens make a splendid presentation when nestled on a bed of Leeks Braised in Cream and surrounded by a Julienne of Carrots and Celery Root. Although the Cornish hens are not themselves a food-processor recipe, they make a perfect foil for processed vegetables. The Madeira Sauce is an optional accompaniment.

Cornish Hens

6 Cornish game hens
(thawed in refrigerator
if frozen)
1-1/2 teaspoons Hungarian
paprika
Coarse salt
Freshly ground pepper
2 tablespoons unsalted
butter
2 tablespoons olive oil
Leeks Braised in
Cream (see Index)
Julienne of Carrots
and Celery Root (see
Index)

Preheat the oven to 450°F. (230°C.) and adjust the rack to the middle level.

Season the hens inside and out with the paprika, salt and pepper. Heat 1 tablespoon of butter and 1 tablespoon of oil in each of two large ovenproof skillets, over medium high heat.

Place the hens in the skillets, on their side, and sear quickly, turning them on the other side as soon as the first side is browned. Do not put the hens on their backs or breasts.

Transfer the skillets to the oven and bake the hens for 5 minutes. Turn them over and bake for 5 minutes longer. Turn them over again and bake 5 more minutes, then reduce the heat to 400°F. (205°C.) and bake for 30 minutes, turning them after 15 minutes.

Sauce

1/2 cup (12 cl) rich chicken
broth
2 large garlic cloves,
split
3 tablespoons Madeira
wine
Drop of Kitchen Bouquet
1 stick unsalted butter
(4 ounces, 115g),
chilled and cut into
8 pieces
Salt
Freshly ground pepper
Parsley or watercress
sprigs for garnish

Place the chicken broth in a small saucepan with the garlic and reduce it to 2 tablespoons over high heat. Remove the garlic. Add the Madeira and the Kitchen Bouquet and bring the mixture to a boil. Reduce it to 4 tablespoons and lower the heat. Keep it hot, but not boiling, and add the butter, one tablespoon at a time. Whisk the sauce until the butter just melts before adding another piece. Do not let this sauce boil.

Remove the hens to a heated platter and cover them loosely with foil to keep them warm as you remove one at a time to split them. Cut each one in half with kitchen shears, removing the back bone.

Assembly

Arrange them on a bed of Leeks Braised in Cream, overlapping the halves. Surround them with a Julienne of Carrots and Celery Root and spoon the Madeira Sauce sparingly over them. Garnish the platter with parsley or watercress sprigs and serve any remaining sauce separately.

Makes 6 to 8 servings.

Fish and Shellfish

Fish & Shellfish

Fish Fillets with Pimiento Sauce
Mustard Fish Fillets with Zucchini
Baked Fish with Lemon Herb Stuffing
Poached Fish with Cucumber Caper Sauce
Pike Fillets with Tomatoes and Mushrooms
Broiled Fish Fillets with Ginger and Lime Sauce
Baked Pike or Turbot, with Julienned Vegetables
Shrimp and Vegetable Mousse Mosaic
Shrimp and Chicken in Orange Shells
Crab Stir-Fry
Clam Pilaf
Stir-Fried Shrimp and Scallops
Lobster Fricassee Primavera
Poached Scallops with Tomato Vinaigrette

Until recently, people went to restaurants to eat Beef Wellington, pâtés and soufflés — dishes they were unable or unwilling to attempt at home. Now they snack at home on pâtés and serve up soufflés — and go out to feast on fish. I have worked in enough restaurants, however, to know that the exquisite delicacy of their specialties can easily be matched at home. So I think it's time to demystify fish!

Timing is probably the most important factor, but that shouldn't make you nervous. It is easier to judge whether fish is done than it is to guarantee rareness in meat. With meat, you use a thermometer, but with fish you just have to touch it. If the fish feels firm, it's done; once it flakes with a fork, it's overdone. I cannot stress this point too strongly; so I'll repeat it: Don't let fish cook until it flakes or it will be too dry. To learn to recognize firmness, first touch the raw fish; it will feel "soft". Then cook it for the minimum amount of time specified in the recipe and touch it again. If it still feels "soft", put it back for a few minutes; if it feels firm, but not "hard", it's done. Try it once and you'll understand exactly what I mean.

Fast and hot are the keys to fish cookery, or so I learned at La Marée, a great fish restaurant in Paris. It's easier to control timing and the fish will lose less moisture if you cook it at a high temperature. You'll notice that when I bake or oven-poach fish, I first bring the liquid to a boil on top of the stove to raise the temperature as quickly as possible. Don't be afraid to cook fast, whether you're broiling, sautéing or stir-frying; this tried-and-true restaurant trick will save you from having to hover over the stove, waiting to test for doneness while guests are waiting to dine.

Mustard Fish Fillets with Zucchini and Tomato, page 78.

Beautiful presentation is no less a part of the restaurant lure. And it's the easiest part of fish cookery, because the garnishes can be prepared ahead of time. A whole fish, baked or poached and garlanded with citrus slices or vegetables, never fails to arouse appetites when it makes its grand appearance. You'll find two versions in this chapter, including Baked Fish with Lemon-Herb Stuffing and Poached Fish with Cucumber-Caper Sauce, which can be done completely ahead of time and served cold. A bright stripe of tomatoes adorns the mousse-layered glory of Pike Fillets with Tomatoes and Mushrooms, a specialty at La Marée. A similar dash of color belies the utter simplicity of Fish Fillets with Pimiento Sauce. The recipes for Broiled Fish Fillets with Ginger and Lime Sauce, from Frédy Girardet's restaurant, dispels the fish mystique with almost breezy glamour, even in its low-calorie variation.

I always look for the freshest-looking fish at the market — moist fillets and clear-eyed whole fish with no "fishy" odor. Lately, there seem to be more varieties available and I use them interchangeably in many recipes. What luck to find firm, juicy grouper fillets — but no less lucky, from a cooking standpoint, to fall back on inexpensive monkfish or scrod. I rely on a good fish store and hope that you can, too. However, since I live in the Midwest and have had to make do at times with frozen fish, I don't rule out that alternative. In fact, sometimes individually flash-frozen fish fillets have promised more flavor than the sad array at the fresh-fish counter. If you buy frozen fish, don't let it defrost completely or it will lose too much moisture. Thaw it only two-thirds of the way through, preferably in the refrigerator, and proceed with the recipe.

It used to be that no banquet was complete without a separate fish course. But those days are long gone — thank goodness! Today's elegance is more likely to take the form of a gorgeous buffet attraction, Shrimp and Vegetable Mousse Mosaic, or the stunning presentation of Chicken and Shrimp in Orange Shells with Ginger Broccoli. Shellfish is always festive, but usually very expensive. So I try to "fool the market" with combinations that make the most of the costliest ingredient. I serve Poached Scallops with Tomato Vinaigrette with homemade pasta and plenty of vegetables for color contrast. Crab Stir-Fry with Clam Pilaf parlays minimal quantities of seafood into an opulent spread. And lobster? If you can't remember the last time you savored its sweetness, then you must peek at the sumptuous market-foolery of Lobster Fricassee Primavera.

Quick and easy, this dish is appropriate for special occasions as well as for everyday. It is an adaptation of a dish served by Frédy Girardet at his restaurant in Crissier, Switzerland.

Fish

4 6-ounce (170g) fish
   fillets, washed and
   patted dry
   Salt
   Freshly ground pepper
1-1/2 tablespoons unsalted
   butter
1-1/2 tablespoons oil

Season the fish generously. Heat the butter and oil in a large skillet over moderately high heat until it sizzles and sauté the fillets quickly on both sides, skin side last. Or place the fillets skin-side down on oiled foil, dot them with butter, and broil them 4 inches (10 cm) from the heat. Do not overcook. Fish cooked until it flakes with a fork is overcooked. Transfer the fish to a platter and keep it warm.

Pimiento Sauce

1/2 cup (12 cl) parsley
   leaves
4 large shallots
   (4 ounces total, 115g),
   peeled
1/2 stick unsalted butter
   (2 ounces, 55g)
1 3-3/4-ounce (106g) jar
   pimientos, drained
3 tablespoons water
1 teaspoon cider vinegar
   Dash cayenne pepper
1/2 teaspoon salt
   Freshly ground pepper

Metal Blade: Mince the parsley by turning the machine on and off, and reserve it. With the machine running, mince the shallots by dropping them through the feed tube. Remove them from the work bowl.

Sauté the shallots in a small skillet in the melted butter over moderately high heat for 2 minutes.

Metal Blade: Purée the pimiento. Add it to the shallots with the water and vinegar, and simmer the mixture for 2 minutes. Season the sauce, spoon it over the fish, and sprinkle the top with the reserved parsley.

Makes 4 servings.

This recipe is an adaptation of a specialty at La Marée in Paris. Select fillets of uniform size so they will cook evenly. If you are using tail pieces, you will need to double the amount of zucchini and mustard sauce.

Fish and Vegetables _____

4 small zucchini (1 pound total, 455g), unpeeled, trimmed, scored and cut into lengths to fit the feed tube
8 firm-textured fish fillets such as halibut, grouper, red snapper, walleyed pike, tilefish or monkfish (6 ounces each, 170g)
Salt
Freshly ground pepper
Parsley sprigs

Preheat the oven to 500°F. (260°C.) and adjust the rack to the lower third of the oven.

Medium Slicing Disc: Put the zucchini into the feed tube vertically and slice it, using medium pressure. Drop the slices into a saucepan containing 2 quarts (190 cl) boiling water with 2 teaspoons salt. Simmer them for 45 seconds after the water returns to a boil. Drain the zucchini slices and put them immediately into a bowl of ice water. Drain them again and pat them dry with paper towels.

Wash the fillets and pat them dry. Sprinkle them generously with salt and pepper, and put each fillet on a piece of heavy-duty foil large enough to wrap it tightly.

Mustard Sauce _____

2 garlic cloves, peeled
2 shallots, peeled
1/2 cup (12 cl) safflower oil
2-1/2 tablespoons Dijon-style mustard
1 tablespoon lemon juice
2 teaspoons dried basil
Salt
Freshly ground pepper
Freshly ground nutmeg
1/4 cup (6 cl) snipped chives

Metal Blade: Mince the garlic and shallots by dropping them through the feed tube while the machine is running. Add the oil, mustard, lemon juice and basil, and combine the mixture by turning the machine on and off. Divide the mixture into 8 equal parts and spread one part evenly over each fish fillet.

Arrange zucchini in 2 rows of overlapping slices over the mustard sauce. Sprinkle the zucchini with the salt, pepper, nutmeg and chives. Wrap each fillet with the foil to make an airtight packet and put the packets on a baking sheet. Bake for 5 to 10 minutes, depending on the thickness of the fillets, but take care not to overcook. Transfer the fillets to a platter and garnish them with the parsley sprigs.

Makes 8 servings.

Variation _____

When Italian tomatoes are in season, tomato slices may be alternated with or substituted for the zucchini for a colorful change.

Baked Fish with Lemon-Herb Stuffing _____

This light and fresh tasting stuffing can be spread on almost any sautéed or baked fish fillets during the last 2 minutes of cooking.

Stuffing

2 large garlic cloves, peeled
2 cups (47 cl) parsley leaves
1 tablespoon dried basil
1 tablespoon dried dill weed
1/4 cup (6 cl) lemon juice
1 stick unsalted butter (4 ounces, 115g), at room temperature and cut into 4 pieces
2 teaspoons salt
Freshly ground pepper

Metal Blade: With the machine running, mince the garlic by dropping it through the feed tube. Add the parsley and mince it by turning the machine on and off. Add the remaining stuffing ingredients and process for 10 seconds or until all the ingredients are well blended.

Fish

2 3-pound (1.4 kg) or 1 6-pound (2.7 kg) whole whitefish or red snapper, with head and tail intact
2 tablespoons lemon juice
2 teaspoons salt
Freshly ground black pepper
1/2 teaspoon dried thyme
1/2 teaspoon ground coriander
2 tablespoons unsalted butter
1/2 cup (12 cl) parsley leaves
1 very small lemon, scored and ends cut flat
1 medium tomato (4 ounces, 115g) peeled, cored and halved
1 small onion (3 ounces, 85g), peeled
6 whole cloves
1/4 cup (6 cl) dry vermouth
1/4 cup (6 cl) clam juice
Parsley sprigs for garnish
Dijon Hollandaise Sauce (see Index)

Preheat the oven to 500°F. (260°C.)

Wash the fish and pat it dry with paper towels. Rub the inside with half the lemon juice, salt, pepper, thyme and coriander and spread it with the Lemon-Herb Stuffing. Rub the outside with the remaining lemon juice and seasonings. Put the fish on an oiled baking dish large enough to hold it, and dot it with the butter, cut into small pieces.

Metal Blade: Mince the parsley by turning the machine on and off. Reserve it.

Medium Slicing Disc: Slice the lemon, using firm pressure; the tomato, using light pressure; and the onion, using medium pressure.

Cover the fish with the onion slices. Add the cloves, vermouth and clam juice and bring the liquid to a boil on top of the stove. Cover the pan loosely with buttered parchment paper, buttered side down. Bake the fish for 18 minutes, then add the lemon and tomato slices, arranging them decoratively on top. Cover the pan tightly with foil and bake for about 8 minutes longer or until the fish feels firm to the touch. Be careful not to overcook it. When it flakes with a fork, it's overcooked.

Transfer the fish to a serving platter and garnish it with the reserved parsley and parsley sprigs. Serve it with Dijon Hollandaise Sauce.

Makes 8 servings.

The orange and lemon slices eliminate any strong fish flavor as well as providing a welcome surprise when the fish is served.

Sauce

- 1 large egg yolk
- 1 tablespoon lemon juice
- 2 teaspoons Dijon-style mustard
- 1 teaspoon minced parsley
- 1 teaspoon snipped chives
- 1 teaspoon dried dillweed
- 1 teaspoon salt
  Freshly ground white pepper
- 1 teaspoon capers, drained
- 2/3 cup (16 cl) oil
- 1 large cucumber (8 ounces, 225g), peeled, split lengthwise, seeded and cut into 2-inch (5 cm) pieces
- 1/2 cup (12 cl) heavy cream
- 1 teaspoon capers, drained (optional)

Metal Blade: For greater ease in processing a small amount of food, raise the back of the machine about 2 inches (5 cm) by placing a book under it. Put the egg yolk, lemon juice, mustard, herbs, seasoning, capers and 2 tablespoons of oil in the work bowl and process for about 10 seconds. Drizzle the remaining oil through the feed tube in a thin steady stream while the machine is running. The sauce will thicken as the oil is added. Leave the sauce in the the work bowl.

Shredding Disc: Shred the cucumber onto the sauce, using medium pressure. Transfer the mixture to a bowl and combine with a spoon.

Whip the cream until it is stiff and fold it into the cucumber mixture. Fold in the additional capers, if desired, and add salt and pepper to taste. Refrigerate the sauce until serving time.

Poached Fish with Cucumber Caper Sauce

Fish

1 5-pound (2.2 kg)
whole white fish such
as whitefish, salmon
or trout – head and tail
intact – boned for
stuffing (about 4
pounds boned, 1.8 kg)
Coarse salt
Freshly ground pepper
1/2 cup (12 cl) parsley
leaves
3 tablespoons dried
dillweed
6 large shallots
(6 ounces total, 170g),
peeled
2 small lemons, ends cut
flat
1 small seedless
orange, ends cut flat
2 large garlic cloves,
peeled
1 teaspoon dried thyme
1/4 cup (6 cl) dry white
wine
1-1/4 cups (30 cl) Fish Stock
(see Index) or bottled
clam juice

Garnish

2 pickle-sized
cucumbers, scored
and ends cut flat
1 small red pepper, ends
cut flat and seeded, or
1 pimiento, sliced
Fresh dill or parsley
sprigs

Variations

Preheat the oven to 450°F.

Wash and dry the fish and season it generously inside and out with salt and pepper. If you do not have a fish poacher, fold a double layer of heavy-duty foil into a rectangular shape just large enough for the fish and 1-1/2 cups (35 cl) liquid when you have folded it up 2 inches (5 cm) from the end at all 4 sides. Put it in a large roasting pan. If you are using a poacher, put a piece of cheesecloth under the fish so that it can be lifted out easily.

Metal Blade: Mince the parsley and dillweed by turning the machine on and off about 10 times. Reserve 1 teaspoon for garnish and leave the rest in the work bowl. With the machine running, mince the shallots by dropping them through the feed tube. Reserve the mixture.

Medium Slicing Disc: Slice the lemons and the orange, using firm pressure. Stuff the fish with half the parsley/shallot mixture and a few lemon and orange slices. Put the fish in the poacher and arrange the remaining parsley mixture and citrus slices under it and on top of it. Add the garlic, thyme, wine and stock or clam juice. Bring the liquid to a boil over moderate heat. Cover the fish loosely with buttered parchment paper, buttered side down, and bake it for 40 to 45 minutes, or until it feels firm but not hard. (If the fish is smaller than specified the cooking time will be less. Test it after 30 minutes of baking.) Be careful not to over-cook the fish. Let it cool in the liquid.

Remove the skin from the top side of the fish and carefully transfer the fish to a platter. Spread the sauce thinly on the fish, leaving the head and tail uncovered. Slice the cucumbers with the thin slicing disc and the pepper with the medium slicing disc. Garnish the head and body with cucumber and pepper or pimiento slices and reserved parsley and dill. Garnish the platter with dill or parsley sprigs; serve the remaining sauce separately.

Makes 8 servings.

Note: For the best flavor, let the fish come to room temperature before serving. If it is to be served cold, it can even be cooked a day in advance, as can the sauce.

1. Serve the fish with Orange Mayonnaise (see Index).

2. Serve the fish hot, with its top skin removed, and spread it with a thin layer of Orange Hollandaise Sauce (see Index). Omit the vegetable garnishes, sprinkle with parsley, and serve the extra sauce separately.

Pike Fillets with Tomatoes and Mushrooms

A specialty at La Marée in Paris, this recipe is the creation of Gérard Rouillard. Thinly sliced mushrooms layered over a stripe of tomato sauce form a beautiful pattern on each fillet. The fish can be prepared in the morning and cooked just before serving but the Lemon Butter Sauce must be made at the last minute.

Fish and Vegetables

2-3/4 pounds (1.3 kg) pike fillets, skinned
1 tablespoon lemon juice
2/3 cup (16 cl) parsley leaves
6 large shallots (3 ounces, 85g), peeled
1 medium garlic clove, peeled
3 large tomatoes (1 pound, 455g total), skinned, seeded and quartered
1/4 teaspoon sugar
1 tablespoon tomato paste
1 teaspoon salt
Freshly ground pepper
14 large firm white mushrooms (1/2 pound, 225g), trimmed and sides cut flat
1 cup (24 cl) Fish Stock (see Index) or bottled clam juice
3 tablespoons dry white wine or dry vermouth

Cut the fillets into 8 equal pieces, slicing them at an angle. Arrange them in a dish and cover them with water to which you have added the lemon juice. Allow them to soak for 5 minutes, then drain them and pat them dry with paper towels.

Metal Blade: Mince the parsley by turning the machine on and off about 10 times; reserve it. With the machine running, mince the shallots by dropping them through the feed tube. Remove 2 tablespoons of the shallots and reserve them. With the machine running, mince the garlic by dropping it through the feed tube. Reserve the shallot and garlic mixture.

Chop the tomatoes coarsely by turning the machine on and off about 4 times. Remove 1/4 cup (6 cl) and reserve it. In a 1-quart (95 cl) saucepan, combine the remaining tomatoes, the sugar, tomato paste, salt and pepper and cook the mixture over moderately high heat for 20 minutes, or until thick.

Thin Slicing Disc: Arrange 2 or 3 mushrooms directly on the slicing disc, flat sides down. Replace the cover on the work bowl and fill the feed tube with mushrooms. Slice the mushrooms, using light pressure. Repeat the process with the remaining mushrooms, and reserve them.

Mousse

12 ounces (340g) pike
   fillets, skinned and cut
   into 2-inch (5 cm)
   pieces
1 large egg
1 large egg white
2 teaspoons lemon juice
3 tablespoons *Crème
   Fraîche* or *Fromage
   Blanc* or heavy cream
   (see Index)
1-1/2 teaspoons salt
1/2 teaspoon freshly
   grated nutmeg
2 drops Tabasco
   Freshly ground pepper

Lemon Butter Sauce

2 teaspoons lemon juice
2 sticks unsalted butter
   (8 ounces, 225g),
   chilled and cut into
   16 pieces
   Pinch cayenne
1 teaspoon salt
   Freshly ground white
   pepper

Metal Blade: Put the reserved shallots, the reserved parsley and the pike fillets into the work bowl and purée them. Add the egg and egg white and process the mixture for 20 seconds. Add the lemon juice, cream, salt, nutmeg, Tabasco and pepper and process the mixture for 30 seconds or until it is fluffy.

Preheat the oven to 425°F. (220°C.) and adjust the rack to the lower third of the oven.

Sprinkle the fillets lightly with salt, pepper and nutmeg. Divide the mousse into 8 parts and spread one part evenly over each fillet. Spoon tomato mixture down the center of the mousse in a stripe. Arrange overlapping slices of mushrooms on the tomato stripes.

Put the fillets in a buttered shallow 16- by 10-inch (41 x 25 cm) flameproof baking dish. If they are not to be cooked immediately, cover them tightly and refrigerate them.

Pour the stock or clam juice around the fillets, add the wine and the reserved shallot and garlic mixture, and bring the liquid to a boil over moderately high heat. Cover each fillet with a piece of buttered parchment paper, buttered side down and crumpled into a cup shape. Bake for 10 to 15 minutes, depending on the thickness of the fillets. Be careful not to overcook them. Transfer the fillets with a slotted spatula to a heated platter and keep them warm.

Strain the liquid into a small saucepan and reduce it over moderate heat to 1/4 cup (6 cl). Add the lemon juice to the reduced fish juices and whisk in the butter over moderately low heat, 1 piece at a time, adding a new piece only as the previous one is melted. Do not let the sauce boil. Stir in cayenne, salt, pepper and reserved 1/4 cup (6 cl) tomatoes. Ladle some of the sauce sparingly around the fish and serve the remaining sauce separately. Garnish the platter with the reserved parsley. parsley sprigs and a small tomato rose.

Makes 8 servings.

Note: To make *Fromage Blanc "Michel Guérard"*: Put the metal blade in the work bowl and process 15 ounces (425g) of skim-milk ricotta cheese with 1/4 cup (6 cl) of plain yogurt for 1 minute, or until the mixture is smooth. Stop the machine once to scrape down the sides of the bowl. *Fromage Blanc* will keep in the refrigerator, tightly covered, for at least 10 days.

Broiled Fish Fillets with Ginger and Lime Sauce _____

Fish _____

8 6-ounce (170g) fillets of salmon or trout, all the same shape
1 tablespoon oil
  Coarse Kosher salt
  Freshly ground black pepper

Wash the fillets and pat them dry with paper towels. Rub them with oil and season them generously with salt and pepper. Place them over hot coals or under an oven broiler, skin side toward the heat, and broil. Turn so the skin side is away from the heat. Brush the fish with the ginger butter. Cook until the fish is firm to the touch but not hard. Fish cooked until it flakes with a fork is overcooked. Place the fish fillets on a platter and garnish them with slices of lime. Spoon the lime sauce sparingly over them.

Makes 8 servings.

Ginger Butter _____

1 piece fresh ginger (1-1/2 ounces, 42g), peeled
1 teaspoon lime zest, removed with a zester
2 large shallots (1-1/2 ounces total, 42g), peeled
1/2 stick unsalted butter (2 ounces, 55g), at room temperature
1/4 teaspoon salt
1 teaspoon lime juice

Shredding Disc: Lay the ginger in the feed tube horizontally and shred it, using light pressure. Remove the shredding disc and insert the metal blade.

Metal Blade: Put the lime zest in the work bowl and turn the machine on. Mince the shallots by dropping them through the feed tube with the machine running. Add the butter, salt and lime juice and process until the mixture is smooth. Transfer the mixture to a small skillet and cook it over low heat for 5 minutes. The butter can be prepared in advance.

Garnish _____

1 lime, scored and cut flat at ends

Medium Slicing Disc: Slice the lime, using firm pressure.

Lime Sauce _____

2 tablespoons fresh lime juice
1/4 cup (6 cl) plus 3 tablespoons white Port wine
1-1/2 sticks unsalted butter (6 ounces, 170g), chilled and cut into tablespoon-size pieces
1/3 teaspoon salt

In a 1-quart (95 cl) saucepan, cook the lime juice and Port over medium-high heat until it is reduced to 1 tablespoon. Add the butter, piece by piece, shaking the pan and stirring until each piece melts before adding the next. Season and serve immediately, or keep the sauce warm for 1 to 2 hours in a container set in warm water.

Makes 2/3 cup (16 cl) sauce.

Variation ——————————

For a low calorie version of this fish, cook it "*en papillote*". Wash the fish and pat it dry, oil it and season it as described above. For each fillet, take a piece of parchment paper or foil much longer than the fish and cut it into a heart shape. Grease one half of the paper and sprinkle it with salt and pepper. Mix together all the ingredients for the Ginger Butter except the butter, and sprinkle 1-1/2 teaspoons of it on the greased half of the paper or foil. Lay the seasoned fillet over the ginger mixture and sprinkle on 1-1/2 teaspoons more of the mixture. Put a slice of lime on top. Fold the other half of the paper or foil over the fish so the edges meet. Start at one end to fold the edges over and crimp them to make an airtight seal. As you come to the other end, tear off the point of the paper to make a straight end. Blow into the parchment or foil package through this opening to make the package puff slightly.

Close the package immediately, making sure it is airtight. Place the packages side by side on a baking sheet. The packages can be prepared in the morning up to the point where they are puffed up with air, and kept refrigerated until cooking time. Just before baking, blow into them to puff them slightly.

Preheat the oven to 500°F. (260°C.) 15 minutes before baking, and adjust the rack to the middle level.

Cook the fish fillets for 5 to 10 minutes, depending on their thickness – a little less than 10 minutes per inch. Serve with Lime Sauce, if desired.

Makes 8 servings.

Baked Pike or Turbot, with Julienned Vegetables and Butter Sauce ⎯⎯⎯⎯

This is an adaptation of a dish served by Jacques Cagna at his restaurant of the same name in Paris. You can choose the low-calorie version, with only the pan juices as sauce, or you can opt for the more calorific Butter Sauce. Both versions are delicious.

Fish ⎯⎯⎯⎯⎯⎯⎯⎯⎯

3-1/2 pounds (1.5 kg) pike or turbot fillets, skinned
2 tablespoons lemon juice

Place the fillets with the lemon juice in enough cold water to cover. Leave them for 5 minutes, drain them and pat them dry with paper towels. Reserve 1/2 pound (225g) for the mousse. Cut the remaining fillets into 16 serving pieces, slicing them on an angle.

Mousse ⎯⎯⎯⎯⎯⎯⎯

1/4 cup (6 cl) parsley leaves
1 large egg
1 large egg white
3 tablespoons heavy cream, *Crème Fraîche* or *Fromage Blanc* (see Index)

Cut the reserved 1/2 pound (225g) fillets into 1-inch (2.5 cm) squares.

Metal Blade: Put the fish squares into the work bowl with the parsley leaves and process until puréed. Add the egg, egg white and cream and process for 30 seconds, stopping the machine once to scrape down the sides of the bowl.

Vegetables ⎯⎯⎯⎯⎯⎯

1 medium leek (4 ounces, 115g), including the green top, cut into 2-inch (5 cm) lengths
1 large carrot (3 ounces, 85g), peeled and cut into 2-inch (5 cm) lengths
2 teaspoons salt
1 small lemon, scored and cut flat at ends
1/4 teaspoon freshly grated nutmeg
1 teaspoon salt
Freshly ground pepper
1/2 cup (12 cl) Fish Stock (see Index) or clam juice
2 tablespoons dry white wine or dry Vermouth Butter Sauce (see Index)
Parsley sprigs for garnish

Thin Slicing Disc: Place the leeks in the feed tube horizontally and sliver them, using light pressure. Remove them from the work bowl.

Make julienne strips of the carrots by using a double-slicing technique. Put the carrots in the feed tube horizontally and slice them, using firm pressure. Remove the slices from the bowl and wedge them into the feed tube side by side. Slice them again, using firm pressure, to obtain julienne strips.

Blanch the leeks and carrots for 1 minute in 4 quarts of boiling water to which you have added 2 teaspoons of salt. Drain them immediately in a colander and hold it under cold running water until the vegetables are cold to the touch. These vegetables can be prepared to this point ahead of time and kept for 1 day in the refrigerator in cold water.

Slice the lemon, using firm pressure.

Assembly ————————

Preheat the oven to 425°F. (220°C.) and adjust the rack to the lower third of the oven.

Butter a 13- x 8-inch (33 x 20 cm) baking dish and arrange 8 fillets in it in a single layer. Sprinkle them with nutmeg, salt and pepper. Spread about 1/8 of the mousse evenly over each fillet. Place another fillet on top and sprinkle again with nutmeg, salt and pepper.

Drain the vegetables and put about 1/8 of them on top of each piece of fish. Cover each loosely with a cupped piece of parchment or foil and pour in the stock and wine, which should cover the bottom of the pan.

Bring the liquid to a boil on top of the stove, then bake in the preheated oven for about 10 minutes. The cooking time depends on the thickness of the fillets. Be careful not to overcook them.

Arrange the fillets on a platter and spoon over them the pan juices or Butter Sauce. Garnish the dish with lemon slices and parsley.

Makes 8 servings.

Shrimp and Vegetable Mousse Mosaic _____

Shrimp _____

2 tablespoons safflower
  or corn oil
1-1/2 pounds (680g) shelled,
  deveined, frozen
  shrimp, unthawed
1/4 cup (6 cl) Fish Stock
  (see Index) or clam juice
1/4 cup (6 cl) dry vermouth
2 envelopes unflavored
  gelatin

Shallot Mayonnaise _____

6 small shallots
  (1/2 ounce total, 15g),
  peeled
1 large egg
2 teaspoons fresh lemon
  juice
1 teaspoon red wine
  vinegar
1 teaspoon Dijon
  mustard
1/4 teaspoon Tabasco
1 teaspoon salt
  Freshly ground white
  pepper
1-1/2 cups (35 cl) oil,
  preferably safflower

Shrimp Mousse _____

2 cups (47 cl) cooked
  shrimp, from above
1 4-ounce (115g) jar
  pimientos, drained
1 teaspoon *poivre rose*
  (red peppercorns),
  optional
3/4 teaspoon salt
  Freshly ground white
  pepper
1/2 cup (12 cl) shallot
  mayonnaise, from
  above
1/4 cup (6 cl) dissolved
  gelatin, from above

Oil a 6-cup (1.4 l) fish mold or a soufflé dish or coat with non-stick vegetable oil spray.

Heat 1 tablespoon of the oil in a large skillet over medium high heat. Add the shrimp in batches, and cook them over medium-high heat, stirring constantly. Remove the shrimp as soon as they turn opaque. Do not overcook them. You should have about 4 cups (95 cl) of cooked shrimp; set it aside.

Combine the clam juice, dry vermouth and gelatin in a small bowl. When the liquid is absorbed by the gelatin, dissolve the gelatin completely by setting the bowl in hot water.

Metal Blade: With the machine running, mince the shallots by dropping them through the feed tube. Add the egg, lemon juice, vinegar, mustard, Tabasco sauce, salt, pepper and 3 tablespoons of the oil. Process for 8 seconds, or until the mixture is slightly thickened. With the machine running, drizzle the oil through the feed tube, allowing the mayonnaise to thicken as the oil is slowly added. Once the mayonnaise has thickened, the oil can be added more quickly. Adjust the seasoning and set aside. Do not wash the work bowl.

Metal Blade: Process 2 cups (47 cl) of the cooked shrimp until it is finely minced. Scrape down the sides of the work bowl and add the pimiento, *poivre rose*, salt, pepper and 1/4 cup (6 cl) of the shallot mayonnaise. Process 5 seconds. Add 1/4 cup (6 cl) of the gelatin mixture and process for 2 seconds. Pour the contents of the work bowl into the prepared mold and spread it evenly with a spatula. Refrigerate the mold while preparing the vegetable mixture.

Vegetable Mixture

8 ounces (225g) green beans, trimmed
1 can artichoke bottoms (7-1/2 ounces dry weight, 212g), rinsed in cold water
2 cups (47 cl) cooked shrimp, from above
1/2 cup (12 cl) frozen tiny peas, thawed
1 4-ounce (115g) jar pimientos, drained, cut into 1/4-inch (.65 cm) dice
3/4 teaspoon salt
Freshly ground white pepper
1-1/2 cups (35 cl) shallot mayonnaise, from above
1 teaspoon dried dill weed
1/3 cup (8 cl) parsley leaves
2 teaspoons fresh lemon juice
3 drops Tabasco
1/4 cup (6 cl) dissolved gelatin, from above
Watercress to garnish platter

Bring 2 quarts of water to a boil with 1 tablespoon of salt. Cook the green beans 4 to 5 minutes, or until tender-crisp, and drain them. Hold them under cold running water until they are completely cool. Wrap them in several layers of paper towels to remove as much moisture as possible. On a board, cut the beans into 1/4-inch (.65 cm) slices and the artichoke bottoms into 1/4-inch (.65 cm) dice. Cut the shrimp into 1/4-inch (.65 cm) slices. Place the sliced beans, artichoke bottoms, shrimp, peas and pimientos in a large mixing bowl. Season them with salt and pepper and mix well.

Metal Blade: Put the mayonnaise, dill weed, parsley, lemon juice and Tabasco sauce in the work bowl. Process for 5 seconds, or until the parsley is finely minced. Add 1/4 cup (6 cl) of the dissolved gelatin and process for 2 seconds. Add the mixture to the vegetables and shrimp in the mixing bowl. Mix well and adjust the seasoning. Spoon this mixture on top of the mousse, which should be somewhat firm. Cover the mold with plastic wrap and use your hands to press the mixture firmly but gently into place. Bang the mold on the counter to remove air pockets. Refrigerate 4 to 6 hours, or until firm.

Separate the mixture from the mold with a small flexible metal spatula. Invert the mold onto a large platter. It may be necessary to place a damp hot towel over the inverted mold for 2 to 4 minutes to loosen the mixture. When the mold is removed, garnish the platter with watercress.

Makes 12 servings.

This dish, with its orange and green colors, reminds me of the South Sea paintings of Gaugin. Combining chicken with shrimp makes this less expensive than the usual shellfish dishes, as well as more imaginative.

Chicken and Shrimp _____

- 1 medium onion (3 ounces, 85g), peeled
- 1 large carrot (4 ounces, 115g), scrubbed and cut into feed-tube lengths
- 1 rib celery with greens, cut into feed-tube lengths
- 3 large chicken breasts (3 pounds total, 1.5kg), split, skinned and boned (reserve the bones for stock and remove the tendons)
- 3 sprigs parsley
- 1 bay leaf
- 1 teaspoon salt
  Freshly ground white pepper
- 1-1/4 pounds (565g) medium shrimp in the shell (about 40), shells removed and reserved
- 4 large seedless oranges, halved and juiced (about 1-1/2 cups (35 cl) orange juice), shells reserved
- 2 tablespoons peanut or safflower oil
- 6 tablespoons unsalted butter, chilled and cut into 3 pieces
- 3 tablespoons Grand Marnier
- 1 large seedless orange, rind and pith removed, cut into segments
- 5 tablespoons snipped fresh chives

Medium Slicing Disc: Slice the onion, carrot and celery, and place them in a 1-1/2-quart (1.4l) saucepan with the chicken bones, parsley, bay leaf, salt and pepper. Cover with water and simmer for 30 minutes, covered. Strain the stock and return it to the saucepan. Bring the stock to a boil over medium-high heat; cook the boned chicken meat in it for 4 to 5 minutes, in 2 batches. Do not overcook the chicken. Lift the chicken out with a slotted spoon and place it in a single layer on a piece of foil on a cookie sheet. When the chicken is cool, freeze it for 2 to 3 hours until the meat is firm but can be easily pierced with the point of a sharp knife. (If frozen for a longer time, the chicken should be partially thawed before slicing, but it should remain firm.)

Wash the shrimp shells and add them to the broth. Boil until the liquid measures about 1/2 cup (12 cl). Strain out the shells and return the liquid to the saucepan with 1-1/2 cups (35 cl) of orange juice. Boil over high heat for about 20 minutes, or until the combined liquids are reduced to 1 cup (24 cl).

Meanwhile, split the shrimp lengthwise and clean them. Heat the oil in a large skillet over medium-high heat. Add the prepared shrimp in 2 batches and remove each shrimp just as it becomes opaque; do not overcook. Set the shrimp aside.

Medium Slicing Disc: Cut the partially frozen chicken pieces in half and place them in the feed tube vertically. Slice them, using firm pressure. (The recipe can be prepared in advance to this point.)

When the liquid is reduced to 1 cup (24 cl), pour it into a large skillet and heat it over medium heat. When it is hot, add the butter, shaking the pan constantly as it melts. When the sauce has thickened and starts to boil, add the Grand Marnier, shrimp and chicken. Heat through over medium-high heat, but do not overcook. Add the orange segments and 4 tablespoons of chives. This mixture can be carefully reheated on top of the stove at serving time, but must not be overcooked.

Broccoli

1 large bunch broccoli
(1-3/4 pounds, 800g),
flowerets trimmed,
stems peeled with a
vegetable peeler and
cut into feed-tube
lengths
1 tablespoon salt
6 tablespoons unsalted
butter
2 teaspoons peeled and
finely julienned fresh
ginger
1 teaspoon salt
Freshly grated nutmeg
Freshly ground black
pepper

Medium Slicing Disc: Place the stems in the feed tube verti-cally and slice them, using firm pressure. Bring 2 quarts (190 cl) of water to a boil with 1 tablespoon of salt. Cook the stems about 5 to 6 minutes, or until they are tender-crisp. Lift them out with a slotted spoon and place them in a bowl of ice water. When the stems are cool, drain them. Cook the flow-erets in the same water for 3 to 4 minutes and follow with the same cooling and draining procedure.

At serving time, melt the butter in a 2-quart (190 cl) saucepan over medium heat. Add the ginger and cook it for 2 minutes, but do not let it brown. Add the broccoli slices and flowerets and reheat them over high heat, shaking the pan to prevent them from burning. Season with salt, nutmeg and pepper.

Assembly

Divide the chicken and shrimp mixture among the 8 orange shells, placing an orange segment and at least 1 shrimp (pink side up) on top. Garnish sparingly with the remaining chives. Place the orange shells around the border of a 14-inch (36 cm) round platter. Fill the center with the reheated broccoli and ginger, with flowerets on top, flower side up.

Makes 8 servings.

A surprising combination that produces an exciting feast for the eye and the palate.

1 ounce (30g) Chinese black dried mushrooms
6 small zucchini (1-1/2 pounds total, 680g), unpeeled, scored and cut into feed-tube lengths
1 8-ounce (225g) can water chestnuts, drained
8 medium scallions (4 ounces total, 115g), including the green tops, cut into thirds
2 tablespoons peanut or safflower oil
2 large garlic cloves, peeled and split in half
1 teaspoon salt
1 pound king crab leg meat, tendons removed, cut into 1-inch chunks
3 tablespoons bottled oyster sauce
Clam Pilaf (recipe follows)

Put the mushrooms in a small bowl with hot water to cover. Let them soak for 20 minutes, or until they are soft. Drain them, cut out any tough stems and reserve those stems and the liquid for use in soup. Cut any large mushrooms in half with a kitchen shears.

Medium Slicing Disc: Place the zucchini in the feed tube vertically and slice them, using medium pressure. Set them aside. Slice the water chestnuts, using medium pressure, and set them aside. Place the scallions in the feed tube vertically and slice them, using light pressure.

Warm the oil in a wok or a skillet and add the garlic cloves. Cook over medium high heat until the garlic starts to brown, then remove the garlic pieces. Add the salt, and cook the zucchini over high heat for 5 minutes, lifting the slices often for uniform cooking. Do not cover. Add the crabmeat, water chestnuts and mushrooms. Cook 3 to 5 minutes more until all the ingredients are heated through.

To combine the ingredients, lift them carefully so that the crabmeat and zucchini slices do not break. Add the oyster sauce and cook 1 minute more, stirring the ingredients gently. Garnish with sliced scallions, and serve with Clam Pilaf.

Makes 6 to 8 servings.

Clam Pilaf

2 dozen Little Neck or
  cherrystone clams
1 cup (24 cl) dry white
  wine or dry Vermouth
1 cup (24 cl) water
1/2 cup (12 cl) parsley
  leaves
1 large clove garlic,
  peeled
1 medium onion
  (3 ounces, 85g) peeled
  and quartered
3 tablespoons unsalted
  butter
1-1/2 cups long-grain
  converted rice
  (9 ounces, 255g)
1 cup (24 cl) chicken
  broth
1/2 teaspoon salt
  Freshly ground black
  pepper
1/2 teaspoon powdered
  oregano

Wash the clams and discard any that are open. Place them in a 4-quart (3.8l) pot with the white wine or dry vermouth and water. Bring to a boil over high heat, cover and cook 8 to 10 minutes, or until the clams open. Stir them around once after 4 minutes to bring the cooked clams on the bottom of the pot to the top. When the clams are cooked, remove them from the heat and pour the liquid through a strainer lined with 2 thicknesses of wet cheese cloth. Measure out 2 cups of the strained liquid for cooking the rice.

Metal Blade: Mince the parsley leaves by turning the machine on and off, and set aside. With the machine running, mince the garlic and onion by dropping them through the feed tube.

In a 2-quart (1.9l) heavy saucepan, melt the butter over medium heat. Cook the minced garlic and onion for 10 minutes until soft but not colored. Add the rice, 2 cups of reserved clam liquid, 1 cup of chicken broth, salt and pepper. Bring to a boil and stir through once. Cover, turn down the heat and simmer for 15 minutes, or until the liquid is absorbed. Meanwhile, remove the clams from their shells. Use kitchen shears to cut the Little Necks in half or the cherrystones in quarters. The clams should measure 1 generous cup (24 cl).

When the rice is cooked, remove it from the heat and add the clams and oregano. Stir the mixture gently with a fork. Cover the pan for 10 minutes. Adjust the seasoning, add minced parsley, and serve immediately.

Makes 6 servings.

Easy, delicious and sensational in appearance.

1 medium garlic clove, peeled
1/2 -inch piece of fresh ginger root, peeled
4 tablespoons peanut or safflower oil
1/2 pound (225g) raw shrimp, semi-thawed, split lengthwise and cleaned
1/2 pound (225g) bay or sea scallops
1 large red pepper (6 ounces total, 170g), cut into 2-inch (5 cm) rectangles
1 8-ounce (225g) can water chestnuts, drained
8 medium scallions (4 ounces total, 115g), including the green tops, cut into thirds
1/2 teaspoon salt
1/2 pound (225g) fresh Chinese pea pods, strings removed
3 tablespoons bottled oyster sauce

Metal Blade: With the machine running, mince the garlic and ginger root by dropping them through the feed tube. In a wok or large sauté pan, cook the minced garlic and ginger in 2 tablespoons of oil over medium heat for 3 minutes, but do not let them brown. Add the prepared shrimp, and cook over high heat about 2 minutes, stirring constantly. Remove the shrimp as they become opaque, and set them aside. Do not overcook them. Cook the scallops in the same manner, and set them aside.

Medium Slicing Disc: Stand the red pepper pieces on their sides, and slice them into matchsticks, using light pressure. Slice the water chestnuts, using medium pressure. Place the scallions in the feed tube vertically, and slice them, using light pressure.

Add the salt and remaining oil to the pan, and stir-fry the pea pods over high heat for 3 minutes. Add the sliced vegetables and the shellfish, and stir-fry 1 minute. Add the oyster sauce and cook 1 minute more. Serve immediately with boiled or steamed rice.

Makes 4 servings.

Stir-Fried Shrimp and Scallops

This delicious lobster dish originated at the Restaurant Boyer in Reims where I trained in the kitchen. It is very economical for a lobster dish since only four lobsters are needed to make six to eight dinner servings.

4 lobsters (1-1/2 pounds each, 680g)
Salt
1 large celery root (8 ounces, 225g), peeled
2 medium turnips (8 ounces total, 225g), peeled
2 large carrots (10 ounces total, 285g), peeled and cut into 2-inch (5 cm) lengths
1/2 pound (225g) green beans, cut into 2-inch (5 cm) lengths
Butter Sauce (see Index)
4 tablespoons unsalted butter
Freshly ground black pepper
Parsley leaves

Prepare the lobsters. Ask your fish market to barely cook them, or boil them yourself, for about 15 minutes. Do not overcook them. When they are cool, shell them and cut them into 2-inch (5 cm) chunks. (You should have about 1-1/2 pounds (680g) of meat).

Boil 2 quarts (190 cl) of water with 1 tablespoon of salt.

Medium Slicing Disc: Cut the celery root into julienne strips by using this double-slicing technique with the slicing disc. Slice the celery root, using firm pressure. Remove the slices from the bowl and insert them back into the feed tube, wedging in as many as possible so they will hold. Slice them, using light pressure, to produce julienne strips.

As soon as the celery root is cut, add it to the boiling salted water, and let it cook for 1 minute after the water comes to a boil again. Lift the celery root out with a slotted spoon, and place it in a bowl of ice water. Drain it when it is cold, and set it aside. Keep the water boiling for the other vegetables.

Cut the turnips and carrots into julienne strips, using the same double slicing technique. Cook and chill the turnips and carrots in the same manner as you followed with the celery root. Set them aside. Place the green beans in the feed tube horizontally and slice them, using light pressure. Cook them for 30 seconds after the water comes to a second boil. Chill them as above, and set them aside.

One hour before serving, prepare the Butter Sauce and keep it warm. At serving time, put 2 spoonfuls of butter in each of two 8-inch (20 cm) skillets. Melt the butter over medium-high heat and add the vegetables to one skillet and the lobster to the other. When the contents of both skillets are heated through, season the food with salt and pepper and remove it from the heat.

Use a large serving platter or individual serving plates. Place the lobster chunks in the middle and arrange a mixture of vegetables over the lobster, placing them carefully with an eye to visual impact. Arrange a few lobster chunks on top, red side up. Spoon the Butter Sauce over the dish and garnish sparingly with a few parsley leaves.

Makes 6 to 8 main course servings.

Poached Scallops with Tomato Vinaigrette

These scallops are good as a main course or as an appetizer. The sauce should be prepared 3 days in advance so that the flavors will intensify and blend. Let the sauce come to room temperature or heat it ever so slightly before spooning it over the hot scallops. The sauce, which has an unusually fresh and vibrant taste, is also good on poached fish fillets.

Sauce

- 1 cup (24 cl) parsley leaves
- 1 large garlic clove, peeled
- 4 large shallots (4 ounces total, 115g), peeled
- 2 large tomatoes (3/4 pound total, 22g), ripe but firm, peeled, seeded and quartered
- 1/2 cup (12 cl) oil (preferably safflower with 2 tablespoons olive oil)
- 2 tablespoons lemon juice
- 1 teaspoon dried basil
- 1 teaspoon dried tarragon
- 1/4 teaspoon sugar
- 12 coriander seeds
- 1 teaspoon salt
  Freshly ground pepper

Metal Blade: Mince the parsley by turning the machine on and off; reserve it in the refrigerator in an airtight bag. Mince the garlic and shallots by dropping them through the feed tube while the machine is running. Leave them in the work bowl. Coarsely chop the tomatoes by turning the machine on and off. Add the remaining ingredients and combine by turning the machine on and off a few times. Transfer to an airtight container and refrigerate for 3 days before using. Stir occasionally and adjust the seasoning if required.

Scallops

- 2 pounds (1.8 kg) sea or bay scallops, rinsed and drained
- 3/4 cup (18 cl) Fish Stock (see Index) or clam juice

Add the fish stock or clam juice to a 1-quart stainless steel or enameled saucepan. Poach the scallops in batches, over medium high heat, cooking them just until they become opaque. Be careful not to overcook. As they are cooked, transfer the scallops with a slotted spoon to a dish and drain them well. Arrange them on 8 serving plates and spoon 1/4 cup (6 cl) of the fresh Tomato Vinaigrette over each serving. The vinaigrette should be at room temperature or heated to about 115°F. (46°C.). Garnish with reserved parsley.

Makes 8 servings.

Pasta and Rice

Pasta & Rice

Basic Pasta
Herb Pasta
Spinach Pasta
Pimiento Pasta
Egg Noodles
Fettuccine Alfredo
Pasta Primavera
Pasta with Scallion and Herbed Tomato Topping
Pasta with Scallion, Clam and Garlic Topping
Mushrooms and Zucchini with Pasta
Pesto Sauce
Italian Meat Sauce

Asparagus Fried Rice
Mushroom and Pimiento Risotto
Pilaf with Currants
Rice with Vegetables

Homemade pasta is the surest form of flattery I've found. It's sexy, romantic, traditional and worldly — depending on how and to whom you serve it. When I serve it to my kids, they're flattered that I know that they know the difference between a box of spaghetti and the real thing. When I serve it to globe-trotting friends, it triggers reveries and talk of Italy and France. And when I bring out a heaping platterful for holiday dinners, everyone assumes that I spend hours in the kitchen just for them.

In fact, it takes me less than an hour to prepare the noodles from dough to finished dish. And I would gladly do it every-day – just for myself! How else can you get to heaven for 500 calories or less? How else can you serve a meatless meal without anyone noticing the absence? But why go on! Once you've tasted homemade pasta, you begin to crave the incomparable indulgence. So, if you haven't done so already, do invest in one of the hand-cranked stainless steel pasta machines from Italy. You don't need an expensive fancy model, and I have given directions for rolling the dough by hand, but the most basic machine makes it possible to roll and cut perfect noodles without practice or previous experience.

Top left to bottom right: Spinach Pasta, page 100; Basic Pasta, page 99; Pimiento Pasta, page 101; Herb Pasta, page 100; Spinach Pasta; Basic Pasta; Pimiento Pasta.

Whichever way you choose to roll and cut the pasta, the food processor mixes and kneads excellent dough in seconds. It also encourages easy variations, such as Herb Pasta, Spinach Pasta and Pimiento Pasta. The spinach noodles come out a bright, fresh green because I don't cook the vegetable before I purée it. The pale orange Pimiento Pasta has a subtle tang that adds a wonderful dimension to seafood. Egg noodles are merely a two egg-yolk enrichment to the Basic Pasta recipe. All of these can be cut narrow or wide, served fresh or kept dry indefinitely, and used interchangeably with the sauce recipes.

Needless to say, they're marvelous in soups or noodle casseroles — or simply devoured straight-up, with butter and grated cheese.

I don't believe in any iron-clad rules about how and when to serve pasta. In Italy, it's a first-course ritual, but it's just as likely to show up, freshly made, as a side dish in France. Since I see no reason to exercise self-restraint with this economical, nutritious fare, I often serve pasta as a main course. The flourish of Pasta Primavera can carry a dinner party menu; so can the Parmesan-redolent richness of Fettucine Alfredo. Pasta with Scallions and Herbed Tomatoes is a divine way to combine appetizer and salad courses, and Pasta with Scallions, Clams and Garlic begs only for a bottle of wine to complete a late-night supper.

To say that all of the vegetable pasta toppings are colorful is to understate the case; so I'll say only that I like to offset the delicate noodles, whether pale gold or bright green, with crisp, vivid slivers and slices of the freshest and best. Don't let the market deter you from maximizing the effect; feel free to substitute an equal weight of one vegetable for another. And if you must substitute store-bought pasta, do look for a good imported Italian brand.

I use vegetables to accent rice just as I do pasta. The crunch of green beans and carrots highlights Rice with Vegetables whether you serve it hot, with meats, or cold, as a salad. Asparagus Fried Rice rounds out an entrée with minimal effort, whether it's Chinese in flavor or *ad hoc* scrambled eggs. Other quick expedients for lamb or beef menus are the Mushroom and Pimiento Risotto and the Pilaf with Currants (which isn't a rice dish at all but a delicious bulghur wheat alternative that deserved to be in this book somewhere!).

Some do-ahead tips for this chapter you probably already know: keep Italian Meat Sauce and Pesto pasta-ready in the freezer, and cook rice in advance for the vegetable combinations. But do you know that pasta and sauces reheat beautifully in the microwave oven? It's a tip I pass on for partying times!

1-3/4 cups unbleached
    all-purpose flour
    (8-3/4 ounces, 248g)
  3 large eggs
  1 teaspoon salt

Metal Blade: Put all the ingredients except 1/2 cup (12 cl) flour in the work bowl. Process until the dough forms a ball. The dough should not be wet. Add the remaining flour if necessary, 1 tablespoon at a time, and process the dough for 40 seconds, or until it is smooth. Wrap the dough in plastic and let it rest for 30 minutes.

On a well-floured board cut the dough into 8 pieces. Keep the unworked pieces covered with plastic wrap. With a pasta machine or by hand, roll out and stretch each piece into a rectangle 1/16 inch (.15 cm) thick, adding flour sparingly when necessary.

With a Pasta Machine: Set the rollers at the widest setting. Lightly flour 1 piece of dough and put it through the rollers once. Flour it lightly, fold it into thirds, and put it through the rollers a second time. Repeat the folding and rolling, lightly flouring the dough only when necessary, 6 or more times, or until the dough is very soft and smooth. Pull the dough gently to stretch it as it comes out of the machine.

Reset the rollers for the next thinner setting. Lightly flour the dough but do not fold it. Put the dough through the machine again, repeating the process on each remaining setting until the dough is as thin as desired, and brush off any excess flour. Repeat the entire process with the remaining pieces of dough. Let the dough rest on towels until it is taut but not dry.

Cut the pasta on the noodle or vermicelli setting. Separate the strands and let the pasta dry completely, stretched out on towels or over a rack.

Rolling by Hand: Roll each piece of dough into a rectangle as thin as desired, using flour when necessary. Brush off the excess flour with a soft pastry brush. Starting with a short end, roll up the dough jelly-roll fashion and with a sharp knife cut it into 1/4-inch (.60 cm) widths for noodles or 1/16-inch (.15 cm) widths for vermicelli. Separate the strands and let the pasta dry completely, stretched out on towels or over a rack.

Bring 6 quarts of water to a boil in a large kettle with 2 tablespoons of salt. Drop in the pasta, and cook it for 30 seconds after the water returns to a boil, or until it is *al dente* (firm to the bite). The pasta cooks very quickly if it is rolled thin and cooked fresh. Drain the pasta and serve it immediately.

Makes 6 servings.

Herb Pasta

1/4 cup (6 cl) parsley
    leaves
2 medium scallions
    (1 ounce total, 30g),
    including greens, cut
    into 1-inch (2.5 cm)
    pieces
2-1/4 cups unbleached all-
    purpose flour
    (11-1/2 ounces, 325g)
1 teaspoon salt
3 large eggs

Metal Blade: Put the parsley leaves and the scallions in the work bowl and mince them by turning the machine on and off about 6 times. Add 1-3/4 cups of the flour, the salt and the eggs, and process until the dough forms a ball. Stop the machine and touch the dough; it should not be wet. Add the remaining flour as needed — 1 tablespoon at a time — and process the dough for about 40 seconds, or until it is smooth. Wrap the dough in plastic and let it rest for 30 minutes.

On a well-floured board cut the dough into 8 pieces. Keep the unworked pieces covered with plastic. With a pasta machine or by hand, roll out and stretch each piece into a rectangular shape 1/16 inch (.15 cm) thick, adding flour sparingly when necessary.

Roll and cook the dough as directed in the recipe for Basic Pasta.

Makes 6 servings.

Spinach Pasta

This pasta, which becomes bright green when cooked, is superior in color and texture to the imported variety.

1 cup (2 ounces, 55g)
    spinach leaves and
    stems, washed and
    dried
3 large eggs
2-1/4 cups unbleached all-
    purpose flour
    (11-1/2 ounces, 325g)
1 teaspoon salt

Metal Blade: Put the spinach in the work bowl and mince it by turning the machine on and off about 4 times. Add the eggs and process the mixture for 10 seconds. Reserve 1/2 cup (2-1/2 ounces, 70g) of flour and add the remaining flour to the work bowl with the salt. Process until the dough forms a ball. Stop the machine and touch the dough; it should not be wet. Add the reserved flour as needed — 1 tablespoon at a time — and process the dough for about 40 seconds, or until it is smooth. Wrap the dough in plastic; let it rest for 30 minutes.

On a well-floured board cut the dough into 8 pieces. Keep the unworked pieces covered with plastic to prevent drying out. With a pasta machine or by hand, roll out and stretch each piece of dough into a rectangular shape 1/16 inch (.15 cm) thick, adding flour sparingly as necessary.

Roll and cook the dough as directed in the recipe for Basic Pasta.

Makes 8 servings.

Note: You can make Fresh Spinach Pasta weeks before cooking it. To preserve its color, freeze it as soon as it is dry.

Pimiento Pasta

4 ounce (115g) jar
  pimientos, undrained
1 large egg
2-1/4 cups unbleached all-
  purpose flour
  (11-1/4 ounces, 320g)
1/2 teaspoon salt

Metal Blade: Purée the pimientos with their juice for 5 seconds. Add the egg, 2 cups of flour and salt, and process 10 seconds. Add the remaining flour by the tablespoon until the dough leaves the sides of the work bowl but is still soft. Process the dough for 40 seconds or until it is smooth. Wrap it in plastic and let it rest for 30 minutes.

Cut the dough into 8 pieces on a well floured board. To prevent drying out, leave unworked pieces covered with plastic. With a pasta machine or by hand, roll out and stretch each piece into a rectangular shape 1/16 inch thick (.15 cm), flouring as necessary.

Roll and cook the dough as directed in the recipe for Basic Pasta.

Makes 8 servings.

Egg Noodles

A tender noodle recipe from the kitchen of Jean Delaveyne's Le Camélia restaurant in Bougival, France, a suburb of Paris.

1-1/2 cups unbleached
  all-purpose flour
  (7-1/2 ounces, 215g)
1 teaspoon salt
2 large eggs
2 large egg yolks
2 teaspoons oil

Metal Blade: Combine all the ingredients by turning the machine on and off. Process the dough until it forms a ball. Check the consistency of the dough; if it is too wet, add flour, 1 tablespoon at a time, processing after each addition. Process the dough for 40 seconds, or until it is smooth. Wrap the dough in plastic and let it rest for 30 minutes.

Put the dough on a well floured board and cut it into 8 pieces. With a pasta machine or by hand, roll it out and stretch each piece into a rectangular shape 1/16 inch (.15 cm) thick, using as little flour as possible.

Roll and cook the dough as directed in the recipe for Basic Pasta, but cook it for 1 minute after the water comes to a boil.

Makes 8 servings.

Fettuccine Alfredo

A splendid first course or brunch dish that's irresistible when made with homemade pasta.

4 ounces (115g) imported Parmesan cheese, at room temperature
1 pound (445g) Spinach Pasta (see Index) or Basic Pasta (see Index)
3 tablespoons unsalted butter
1 cup (24 cl) heavy cream, or 1 cup (24 cl) *Créme Fraîche* (see Index) with 2 tablespoons heavy cream
1/2 teaspoon freshly grated nutmeg
Freshly ground white pepper

Medium Shredding Disc: Shred the cheese, using light pressure. Cook the pasta in a large kettle in 6 quarts (5.7 l) of boiling water to which you have added 2 tablespoons of salt. Allow it to cook only until it is *al dente* (firm to the bite). Drain it and gently stir in the butter, cheese, cream and seasonings, in that order. Toss the pasta carefully and transfer it to a platter.

Makes 6 servings.

Pasta Primavera

This dish makes a lovely first course for all seasons.

1 carrot (3 ounces, 85g), trimmed, peeled and cut into 2-inch (5 cm) lengths
2 zucchini (1 pound total, 455g), trimmed and cut into 4-inch (10 cm) lengths
1 cup (24 cl) parsley leaves
2 garlic cloves, peeled
1 stick unsalted butter (4 ounces, 115g), softened and quartered
Salt
Freshly ground pepper
2/3 cup (16 cl) tiny frozen peas, thawed
2 teaspoons lemon juice
1 pound (455g) Spinach Pasta, or Basic Pasta (see Index)

Julienne Disc or Shredding Disc: Cut the carrot into julienne strips or shreds, using firm pressure. Reserve it.

Julienne Disc: Cut the zucchini into julienne strips. If you do not have a julienne disc, use the double-slicing technique to make julienne strips with the medium slicing disc, as follows.

Slice the zucchini, using medium pressure. Remove the slices and reinsert them in the feed tube, side by side, wedging them in tightly so they will hold. Slice them again, using medium pressure, to produce julienne strips. Repeat the process with the remaining slices. Wipe out the work bowl with a paper towel.

Metal Blade: Mince the parsley by turning the machine on and off. With the machine running, mince the garlic by dropping it through the feed tube. Add the softened butter, salt and pepper and process the mixture for 5 seconds, stopping the machine once to scrape down the sides of the bowl. Reserve half the mixture and melt the other half in a sauté pan. Add the zucchini, peas, salt, pepper and lemon juice and heat the mixture only until it is hot. Do not overcook it; the vegetables should stay crisp.

Toss the hot, drained pasta in a warm serving dish with the reserved herb butter and the carrot. Correct the seasoning and heap the zucchini mixture in the center of the dish.

Makes 8 servings.

Pasta with Scallion and Herbed Tomato Topping

A real dazzler when made with bright green Spinach Pasta (see Index), this hot-cold combination is refreshing at any time of year.

1/2 cup (12 cl) parsley
   leaves
1 large garlic clove,
   peeled
3 tablespoons oil
8 large scallions
   including the green
   tops (6 ounces total,
   170g), cut into thirds
1 teaspoon salt
   Freshly ground pepper
5 tomatoes, peeled and
   cored (1-1/4 pounds
   total, 570g)
1 teaspoon sugar
1 teaspoon dried basil
1/2 teaspoon dried
   oregano
   Salt
   Freshly ground pepper
1 pound (455g)
   homemade pasta,
   such as Spinach Pasta
   (see Index)
1/2 cup (12 cl) Calamata
   olives, drained
   (optional)

Metal Blade: Mince the parsley by turning the machine on and off; reserve it. With the machine running, mince the garlic by dropping it through the feed tube. Add the oil, but do not process the mixture. Leave it in the work bowl.

Medium Slicing Disc: Slice the scallions, using light pressure. Add the salt and pepper, remove the mixture and reserve it.

Slice the tomatoes, halving them vertically to fit the feed tube if necessary. Use light pressure. Transfer them to a flat platter. Mix the sugar, basil, oregano, salt and pepper and sprinkle the mixture over the tomatoes. Refrigerate for at least 30 minutes.

Assembly

Toss the reserved scallion mixture gently with the hot, drained pasta and correct the seasoning. Transfer the pasta to a shallow serving bowl, arrange the tomatoes around it and garnish with the reserved parsley and the olives.

Makes 8 servings.

Variation

Use 1-1/4 pounds (567g) of fresh Italian tomatoes instead of ordinary tomatoes. Cut their ends flat and slice them, using light pressure.

Pasta with Scallion, Clam and Garlic Topping

One of the best of the short-order recipes for last-minute cooking.

8 scallions including the greens (4 ounces total, 115g), cut into thirds

3 large garlic cloves, peeled

4 6-1/2-ounce (185g) cans minced clams, drained, juices reserved

1 stick unsalted butter (4 ounces, 115g), at room temperature

1/4 cup (6 cl) parsley leaves

3/4 pound (340g) Basic Pasta (see Index)

1 lemon, cut into 6 wedges

Medium Slicing Disc: Wedge the scallions into the feed tube vertically and slice them, using medium pressure. Remove them and reserve them.

Metal Blade: With the machine running, mince the garlic by dropping it through the feed tube. Leave a third of the garlic in the work bowl and put the rest in a 2-quart (1.9l) saucepan. Add the clams and 1 cup (25 cl) of the clam juices to the pan and simmer for 5 minutes. Add the clams to the reduced liquid and simmer for 5 more minutes. Whisk in 4 tablespoons of butter, 1 tablespoon at a time. Remove the pan from the heat and fold in the scallions. Keep the sauce warm.

To the garlic in the work bowl, add 4 tablespoons of butter, cut into 4 pieces, and the parsley. Combine them into a smooth garlic butter by turning the machine on and off about 8 times. Toss the garlic butter in a warm bowl with the cooked, drained pasta and spoon the clam sauce over it. Toss the mixture gently and garnish it with lemon wedges.

Makes 6 servings.

Mushrooms and Zucchini with Pasta (recipe opposite)

This can be served as a vegetable dish, without the pasta. Either way, it's quick and easy.

1/2 cup (12 cl) parsley
    leaves
  2 garlic cloves, peeled
1/2 stick unsalted butter
    (2 ounces, 55g)
  1 pound (455g)
    mushrooms, trimmed
  2 tablespoons lemon
    juice
  4 small zucchini
    (1 pound total, 455g),
    trimmed
  2 teaspoons dried basil
1-1/2 teaspoons salt
    Freshly ground pepper
  1 pound (455g) Basic
    Pasta, cooked (see
    Index)

Metal Blade: Mince the parsley by turning the machine on and off; reserve it. With the machine running, mince the garlic by dropping it through the feed tube. Reserve half of the garlic and cook the rest in a large skillet in 2 tablespoons butter, over medium heat.

French-Fry Disc, Julienne Disc or Medium Slicing Disc: Put the mushrooms in the feed tube horizontally and cut them, using light pressure. Add them to the skillet and toss them with the lemon juice. Put the zucchini in the feed tube vertically and cut it, using medium pressure.

If you do not have a French-Fry disc, slice the mushrooms with the medium slicing disc, using light pressure, and use the julienne disc for the zucchini, with light pressure.

If you do not have a julienne disc, slice the zucchini with the medium slicing disc, using medium pressure, and remove the slices from the work bowl. Reinsert the slices in the feed tube, side by side, wedging them in tightly so they will hold. Make julienne strips by slicing them again, using medium pressure. Repeat the process with the remaining slices.

Add the zucchini to the skillet and increase the heat to medium high. Add the seasonings and half the reserved parsley. Cover and cook for 3 minutes, or until the mixture is steamed through but the zucchini is still crisp. Put 2 tablespoons of butter and the reserved garlic in a large serving dish, add the drained hot pasta and toss it with the garlic and butter. Sprinkle the vegetable mixture on top or toss it well with the pasta. Correct the seasoning and add the reserved parsley.

Makes 6 to 8 servings.

Note: To serve this dish without the pasta, omit 1 garlic clove and reduce the parsley to 1/4 cup (6 cl) and the butter to 2 tablespoons.

Sensational on pasta or tossed with rice, this sauce is also marvelous on small boiled potatoes, green beans, broiled fish and poached skinned chicken breasts.

2 large garlic cloves, peeled
3 ounces (85g) imported Parmesan cheese, at room temperature, cut into 1-inch (2.5 cm) cubes
2 cups (47 cl) fresh basil leaves, or 2 cups (47 cl) Italian parsley leaves or spinach leaves with 2 tablespoons dried basil, firmly packed
1 teaspoon salt
1/4 cup pine nuts or walnuts (1 ounce, 30g)
1 cup (24 cl) oil, preferably 3/4 cup (18 cl) safflower oil and 1/4 cup (6 cl) olive oil

Metal Blade: With the machine running, mince the garlic by dropping it through the feed tube. Add the cheese and chop it by turning the machine on and off about 10 times. Add the basil, salt and nuts and mince them by turning the machine on and off about 8 times. With the machine running, drizzle the oil through the feed tube in a thin steady stream. Process the mixture until it is well blended and serve it over pasta.

Makes enough for 6 servings of pasta.

Note: This sauce keeps for months if covered with a thin coat of oil and refrigerated. It can also be frozen. Freeze it in plastic ice-cube trays, then transfer the frozen cubes to an airtight plastic bag. Defrost in amounts needed.

You can easily double this recipe and store half the sauce in the freezer, always on hand for short-order cooking.

2 large garlic cloves, peeled
2 onions (8 ounces total, 225g), peeled and quartered
2 tablespoons oil
2 carrots (4 ounces total, 115g), peeled, trimmed and cut into 1-inch (2.5 cm) pieces
2 small celery ribs (2 ounces total, 55g), strings removed, cut into 1-inch (2.5 cm) pieces
2 pounds (910g) beef chuck, cut into 1-inch (2.5 cm) cubes
1 tablespoon seasoning salt
Salt
Freshly ground pepper
1 28-ounce (800g) can Italian-style plum tomatoes, including the juice
1 small tomato (4 ounces, 115g), peeled, halved and seeded
1/2 teaspoon sugar
1/3 cup (8 cl) tomato paste
1-1/2 cups (35 cl) tomato sauce
1 teaspoon dried basil
1 teaspoon dried oregano
Freshly ground pepper

Metal Blade: With the machine running, mince the garlic by dropping it through the feed tube. Add the onions and mince them by turning the machine on and off about 12 times.

Heat the oil in a large stainless steel saucepan. Add the garlic and onions and cook them over medium heat for 20 minutes, or until they are soft.

Put the carrots and celery in the work bowl and mince them by turning the machine on and off. Add them to the garlic and onions in the skillet. Put the meat in the work bowl in 2 batches and chop it by turning the machine on and off. Add it to the vegetable mixture and cook for 10 minutes over medium-high heat, stirring every few minutes. Add the remaining ingredients and simmer the sauce gently for 1-1/2 hours to 2 hours, uncovered. Thin with more tomato sauce, if necessary, and correct the seasoning.

Makes enough sauce for about 1-1/2 pounds (680g) of pasta.

This is an "idea" dish – substitute other vegetables according to their availability and your taste, but keep them tender-crisp for an interesting texture.

1 cup (24 cl) parsley
  leaves
2 large shallots (1 ounce
  total, 30g), peeled
1 cup (24 cl) long-grain
  converted rice
2 cups (47 cl) water
2 tablespoons unsalted
  butter (1 ounce, 30g)
1-1/2 teaspoons salt
2 pounds (910g)
  asparagus, stems
  peeled with a
  vegetable peeler
8 scallions
  (4 ounces total, 115g)
  cut into thirds
  Salt
  Freshly ground white
  pepper
2-1/2 tablespoons peanut oil

Metal Blade: Mince the parsley by turning the machine on and off; reserve it. With the machine running, mince the shallots by dropping them through the feed tube. Transfer the shallots to a saucepan and add the rice, water, butter and salt. Bring the water to a boil and stir the mixture once. Cover it and simmer for 15 minutes, or until the liquid is absorbed. Let the mixture stand for 10 minutes longer, covered. Fluff the rice with a fork, let it cool, and refrigerate it.

Medium Slicing Disc: Cut 1-1/2-inch (3.8 cm) tips from the asparagus and reserve them. Wedge the asparagus stems in the feed tube vertically and slice them, using medium pressure. Drop the slices into a saucepan containing 1 quart (95 cl) of boiling water to which you have added 2 teaspoons of salt. Blanch them for 30 seconds after the water has returned to a boil. Drain the asparagus and put it under cold running water until it is completely cool. Blanch and cool the reserved tips in the same manner.

Put the scallions in the feed tube vertically and slice them, using medium pressure. Transfer them to a bowl and stir in the rice, asparagus slices, reserved parsley, salt and pepper. Heat 3 tablespoons of peanut oil in a skillet over medium-high heat. Add the rice mixture and heat it through, stirring gently. In another skillet heat the asparagus tips quickly in 1/2 tablespoon oil. Heap the rice in a serving dish and garnish it with the asparagus tips.

Makes 8 servings.

Note: Arrange the rice around a large platter and fill the center with Sesame Lemon Chicken (see Index). Garnish the platter with the asparagus tips.

Mushroom and Pimiento Risotto

18 large firm mushrooms
(3/4 pound total, 340g),
stems trimmed and
reserved

8 large shallots
(2 ounces total, 55g),
peeled

5 tablespoons unsalted
butter

2-1/2 cups (60 cl) chicken
stock

1-1/4 cups (30 cl) long-grain
converted rice

1/2 teaspoon salt

1 tablespoon fresh
lemon juice

1 4-ounce (115g) jar
pimientos, drained
and cut into 1/4-inch
(.60 cm) dice
Freshly ground black
pepper

Metal Blade: With the machine running, drop the mushroom stems and the shallots through the feed tube to mince them.

Melt 2 tablespoons of butter in a 2-quart (1.9 l) saucepan over medium-high heat. Sauté the mushroom stems and shallots for 5 minutes, or until they are soft but not brown. Add the stock, rice and salt and bring to a boil. Cover the rice and simmer gently for 15 minutes, or until the liquid is absorbed. Do not stir but check the liquid from time to time by tilting the pan and lifting the rice aside with a fork. Remove the rice from the heat and set it aside, covered, for an additional 10 minutes.

Medium Slicing Disc: Cut flat sides on 2 to 3 mushroom caps. Place them on their flat sides in the feed tube. Stack as many mushrooms as possible sideways in the feed tube and slice them, using light pressure. Repeat this procedure for all the remaining mushrooms.

Melt 3 tablespoons of butter with the lemon juice in a large skillet over medium-high heat. Sauté the mushrooms for 3 minutes. Combine the mushrooms and their juices and the diced pimientos with the rice, using a fork. Adjust the seasoning and add pepper.

This dish can be prepared in advance and reheated, covered, in a 325°F. (160°C.) oven for 60 minutes.

Makes 6 servings.

Pilaf with Currants

Great with lamb and beef.

1-1/2 cups shallots
(7 ounces, 200g), peeled

3 tablespoons butter

2 cups bulghur (cracked
wheat) (10 ounces,
285g)

2/3 cup dried currants
(3 ounces, 85g)

4-3/4 cups (112 cl) Chicken
Stock (see Index)

1-1/2 teaspoons salt
Freshly ground pepper

Metal Blade: With the machine running, mince the shallots by dropping them through the feed tube. Melt the butter in a 2-quart (190 cl) saucepan and sauté the shallots until they are soft. Stir in the bulghur, currants and stock. Cover and cook over low heat for 15 minutes. Add the salt and pepper, toss the mixture gently with a fork and transfer it to a serving dish.

Makes 8 servings.

Note: Reheat the pilaf on top of the stove, stirring it occasionally and adding a little stock or water if it sticks to the pan.

1 cup long-grain converted rice (6 ounces, 170g)
2 cups (47 cl) water
1/2 stick butter (2 ounces, 55g), quartered
1 teaspoon salt
1 cup (24 cl) parsley leaves
1 medium onion (5 ounces, 140g), peeled and quartered
4 ounces (115g) green beans, cut to fit the feed tube vertically
1 small carrot (2 ounces, 55g), peeled and cut into 2-inch (5 cm) lengths
1 teaspoon dried dillweed
1-1/2 to 2 teaspoons salt
Freshly ground pepper

Combine the rice, water, 2 tablespoons of butter and salt in a saucepan. Bring the water to a boil, cover the mixture and simmer it for 20 minutes, or until all the liquid is absorbed. Do not stir the mixture, but check the amount of liquid by tilting the pan and lifting the rice with a fork.

Metal Blade: Mince the parsley by turning the machine on and off, and reserve it. Mince the onion by turning the machine on and off. Melt the remaining 2 tablespoons of butter in a skillet and sauté the onion until it is soft.

Medium Slicing Disc: Wedge the beans into the feed tube vertically so they fit compactly. Slice them, using medium pressure, and reserve them.

French-Fry Disc: Put the carrots in the feed tube horizontally and cut them, using firm pressure. Remove the carrot pieces and align them on a cutting board. Cut them again, into slices the same size as the bean slices. If you do not have a French-fry disc, use a knife to cut the carrot into strips of the same width as the beans, then dice them. Add the beans and carrots to the skillet with the onions. Cover and steam the vegetables for 5 minutes, shaking the pan to prevent them from sticking. Stir the rice, dillweed, salt and pepper into this mixture. Transfer to a serving dish and garnish the dish with the reserved parsley.

Makes 6 servings.

Note: This can be made early in the day and reheated at serving time. Heat the mixture quickly over medium-high heat, stirring it gently. The dish makes a delicious rice salad, served at room temperature.

Variation

Add 1 cup (24 cl) thawed tiny peas, well drained.

Vegetables

Vegetables _____

Stir-Fried Broccoli, Celery and Water Chestnuts
Fennel with Red Onion
Buttered Cucumbers
Leeks Braised in Cream
Julienne of Carrot and Celery Root
Stir-Fried Summer Squash
Fennel-Stuffed Zucchini
Lacy Potato Pancakes
Potatoes Anna
Gratin of Turnip and Potato
Celery Root Purée
Walnut Crusted Yam Soufflé
Layered Spinach, Parsnip and Carrot Purée
Corn Pancakes à la Paris
Ratatouille
Spinach Supreme
Zucchini Flan
Fresh Spinach Cannelloni
Spinach Gnocchi

If I never used the food processor for anything but vegetables, I'd still consider it indispensable. The machine relieves the sameness of potatoes, the dullness of zucchini, the predictable look of broccoli. It allows me to enter the produce section of the supermarket with renewed interest every time, for even if carrots turn out to be the only good choice, I know the possibilities for preparing them are endless.

More than with any other food, the taste of vegetables depends on how they are cut. Every home cook knows that mashed potatoes and scalloped potatoes flavor a menu quite differently, even though the ingredients are virtually the same. And every French chef expresses a similar idea when he insists that a garnish of carrots and turnips be cut into a delicate julienne for one dish and a denser dice for another. The reasons have to do not only with texture but also with the amount of moisture, minerals, sugar and starch released from the vegetables as more cut surfaces are exposed. You can ponder the possibilities for hours with a knife and cutting board—or you can put them into action immediately with the food processor!

Lacy Potato Pancakes, page 117.

Consider carrots, for example. It takes no more time to cut them into a julienne and quickly blanch the thin strips than it does to cook and purée them. But taste the difference between crisp, orange-sauced Julienne of Carrot and Celery Root and the smooth, apple-lightened Carrot Purée. The contrast potential of spinach purée ranges from Spinach Ricotta Gnocchi, which are wonderful airy dumplings, to Fresh Spinach Cannelloni, a supreme crêpe casserole. Thin slicing transforms tough broccoli stalks into stir-fryable discs for Stir-Fried Broccoli, Celery and Water Chestnuts or Ginger Broccoli. Shredding turns bulky potatoes into Lacy Potato Pancakes. Puréeing creates yet another alternative to a whole vegetable in Corn Pancakes à la Paris.

If, at this point, you still don't feel comfortably in command of basic food processor techniques, vegetables alone should prod you into daily practice! For perfect, professional-looking slices, be sure to wield the pusher with the amount of pressure specified in the recipe. And don't hesitate to substitute an equal weight of one vegetable for another in any recipe. I think it's silly not to use whatever bounty or bargain the market offers or to limit a simple vegetable formula, such as a stir-fry, to one interpretation, so I have deliberately supplied weight measurements to allow you to make such substitutions easily.

Every vegetable looks more interesting to me nowadays. But it's been especially exciting to experiment with some of the less frequently served varieties. The slightly spicy, licorice taste of fennel provides a nice change of pace with chicken entrées. I either slice and stir-fry it as in Fennel with Red Onion or slice and chop it for tangy appeal in Fennel-Stuffed Zucchini. Celery Root can be a delightfully crunchy side dish when julienne-cut and blanched, or it can replace some of the starch and calories of potatoes, as in Celery Root Purée.

Sometimes less is definitely more appealing. I like to highlight the flavors of subtly seasoned fish or chicken with a crisp, pale accompaniment of Buttered Cucumbers. And I have found that the egg whites enfolded in Walnut Crusted Yam Soufflé bring welcome lightness to the holiday favorite. Sometimes the most pleasant respite of all is a vegetable, rather than a meat, main course. On such occasions, you'll appreciate the cheese enrichments offered for Spinach Ricotta Gnocchi, Ratatouille, Spinach Supreme and Fresh Spinach Cannelloni.

Vegetables should never be overcooked—nor should cooks be overwhelmed. That's my final word on the subject and you'll find it written into all the recipes in this chapter. Each one is broken down into steps that allow you to do partial preparation in advance and still finish with the freshest possible flavor at serving time.

Stir-Fried Broccoli, Celery and Water Chestnuts

Because this very attractive dish uses the broccoli stems as well as the flowerets, there is absolutely no waste.

1 large garlic clove, peeled
2 large bunches broccoli (2 pounds total, 910g) stems peeled with a vegetable peeler
2-1/2 teaspoons salt
1 small onion (3 ounces, 85g), peeled
2 celery ribs (4 ounces total, 115g), cut into thirds
10 water chestnuts, drained
3 tablespoons oil
2 tablespoons soy sauce

Metal Blade: With the machine running, mince the garlic by dropping it through the feed tube. Remove it and reserve it.

Cut the stems from the broccoli just below the flowerets and cut them into lengths to fit the feed tube.

Medium Slicing Disc: Put the broccoli stems in the feed tube vertically and slice them, using firm pressure. Blanch them for 1 minute in 2 quarts (190 cl) of boiling water to which you have added 2 teaspoons of salt. Transfer them to a colander with a slotted spoon and put them under cold running water until they are completely cool. Cook the flowerets for 2 minutes in the same water in which you cooked the stems.

Slice the onion, using firm pressure; remove it and reserve it. Slice the celery and water chestnuts, using medium pressure on the pusher.

Heat the oil in a wok or skillet and cook the garlic and onion over moderately high heat for 2 minutes. Add the remaining salt, stir in the broccoli and cook for 8 minutes. Add the celery, water chestnuts and soy sauce and cook for 2 minutes, or until the vegetables are thoroughly heated. Do not overcook them. Add salt and pepper to taste and transfer the mixture to a serving dish. Or let the mixture cool to room temperature and serve it as a relish on a lettuce leaf.

Makes 8 servings.

Fennel with Red Onion _____

This is one of my favorite vegetable dishes for serving with chicken.

2/3 cup (16 cl) parsley
    leaves
2 large fennel bulbs
    (2 pounds total, 910g)
    feathery greens
    trimmed and cut into
    pieces to fit the feed
    tube
4 small red onions
    (8 ounces total, 225g)
    peeled
2 tablespoons oil
2 tablespoons unsalted
    butter
1 teaspoon salt
    Freshly ground pepper

Metal Blade: Mince the parsley by turning the machine on and off, and reserve it.

Thin Slicing Disc: Place the fennel in the feed tube vertically and slice it, using firm pressure. Cook it for 1 minute in 4 quarts (380 cl) of boiling water to which you have added 1 tablespoon of salt. Drain it and transfer it to a colander. Put it under cold running water until it is completely cool and drain it well. Wrap the fennel in paper towels.

Slice the onions, using firm pressure, and separate the slices into rings.

Heat the oil and butter in a skillet or wok. Add the fennel and onions and cook over moderately high heat, stirring, for 2 minutes. Do not overcook, the fennel should remain crisp.

Add the salt and pepper, and mix in the reserved parsley. Transfer the mixture to a serving dish.

Makes 8 servings.

Variation _____

Substitute 2 pounds (910g) of celery and 1 teaspoon of fennel seed for the fennel.

Buttered Cucumbers _____

This light vegetable dish enhances a main dish of poultry or fish.

2 large cucumbers
    (18 ounces total, 505g),
    peeled
3 tablespoons unsalted
    butter (1-1/2 ounces, 45g)
    Salt
    Freshly ground pepper

Medium Slicing Disc: Halve the cucumbers lengthwise, seed them and cut them into sections that will fit in the feed tube when inserted vertically. Slice them, using medium pressure. Cook them for 1 minute in 6 quarts (570 cl) of boiling water to which you have added 2 tablespoons of salt. Transfer the slices to a colander and hold it under cold running water until the cucumber feels completely cool to the touch.

Melt the butter over moderately high heat in a saucepan with the seasonings and add the cucumber slices. Heat until thoroughly hot but still crisp, and adjust the seasoning.

Makes 8 servings.

Leeks Braised in Cream

A Frédy Girardet invention that is simply delicious and deliciously simple.

5 large leeks (2 pounds total, 910g), including the green tops, washed and cut into lengths to fit the feed tube
1/2 stick unsalted butter (2 ounces, 55g)
1/2 cup (12 cl) heavy cream
1 teaspoon salt
Freshly ground pepper

Medium Slicing Disc: Wedge the leeks into the feed tube vertically and slice them, using medium pressure.

Melt the butter in a 2-quart (190 cl) saucepan, add the leeks and cook them over moderate heat for 10 minutes, stirring occasionally. Do not brown them. Add the cream and cook the leeks uncovered over moderately high heat for 10 minutes, or until the mixture is thickened. Add the salt and pepper to taste and transfer the leeks to a serving dish. This dish can be reheated, but the leeks will lose their bright color.

Makes 6 to 8 servings.

Julienne of Carrot and Celery Root

A beautiful and savory combination, made easy with a food processor.

1/2 cup (12 cl) parsley leaves
1/2 pound (225g) celery root, peeled and cut into the largest pieces that will fit the feed tube
1 pound (455g) very large carrots, peeled and cut into 2-inch (5 cm) lengths
2 tablespoons orange juice
1/4 cup (6 cl) water
1/2 stick unsalted butter (2 ounces, 55g)
1 teaspoon dried dillweed
Salt
Freshly ground pepper

Metal Blade: Mince the parsley by turning the machine on and off; reserve it.

Julienne Disc or Medium Slicing Disc: Cut the celery root and carrots into julienne strips with the julienne disc, or by using this double-slicing technique with the slicing disc.

Slice the celery root, using firm pressure. Remove the slices from the bowl and insert them back into the feed tube side by side, wedging in as many as possible so they will hold. Slice them again to produce julienne strips. Repeat the procedure with the carrots.

Cook the julienned vegetables for 4 minutes in 4 quarts (380 cl) of boiling water to which you have added 2 teaspoons of salt. Transfer them to a colander and hold them under cold running water until they are completely cool.

Heat the orange juice, water and butter in a sauté pan or wok. Add the vegetables and heat them through. Add the dillweed and salt and pepper to taste. Transfer the vegetables to a serving dish, and sprinkle them with parsley.

Makes 8 servings.

Variation

Add 1 cup (24 cl) of thawed tiny frozen peas, during the final cooking of the vegetables.

Stir-Fried Summer Squash

This appealing dish has no seasonal limits as it can also be made with zucchini.

1 garlic clove, peeled
2 small soft-shelled yellow squash, or 2 small zucchini (7 ounces total, 220g)
8 large scallions (4 ounces total, 115 g), including the green tops, cut into thirds
1 large head bok choy, (1 pound, 455g), Chinese celery cabbage or a combination of the two
1/4 cup (6 cl) peanut oil
12 pea pods
3 tablespoons soy sauce

Metal Blade: Mince the garlic by dropping it through the feed tube with the machine running.

French-Fry or Medium Slicing Disc: Cut or slice the squash, using medium pressure.

Medium Slicing Disc: Put the scallions in the feed tube vertically and slice them, using light pressure. Slice the bok choy and/or celery cabbage, including the greens, using medium pressure. Heat the oil in a wok or skillet. Add the garlic and squash, cover and cook over moderately high heat for 3 minutes. Add the scallions, bok choy and/or celery cabbage and the pea pods to the squash. Heat the vegetables through, but do not overcook them. Stir, add the soy sauce, and transfer the vegetables, tender but still crisp, to a serving dish.

Fennel-Stuffed Zucchini

Especially well suited to accompany poultry and beef, this vegetable dish is crunchy and flavorful.

4 large zucchini (2 pounds total, 910g), trimmed but not peeled
1-1/2 teaspoons salt
1/2 cup (12 cl) parsley leaves
1 garlic clove, peeled
1 small onion (2 ounces, 55g), peeled, cored and quartered
1/2 stick unsalted butter, (2 ounces, 55g)
1 large fennel bulb (3/4 pound, 340g), greens trimmed and cut to fit the feed tube
1/2 teaspoon dried thyme
Salt
Freshly ground pepper

Split the zucchini lengthwise. Scoop out the centers with a melon ball cutter, leaving 1/4-inch (.75 cm) shells, and reserve the pulp. Sprinkle the shells with salt and place them upside down on paper towels. Allow to drain for 30 minutes.

Preheat the oven to 350°F. (175°C.) and adjust the rack to the middle level.

Metal Blade: Mince the parsley by turning the machine on and off about 8 times; reserve it. With the machine running, mince the garlic by dropping it through the feed tube. Mince the onion by turning the machine on and off. Melt the butter in a sauté pan and add the onion and garlic. Put the reserved zucchini pulp in the work bowl and chop it coarsely by turning the machine on and off. Add it to the saucepan.

Medium Slicing Disc: Slice the fennel, using medium pressure. Remove half the slices and insert the metal blade. Chop the fennel slices coarsely by turning the machine on and off and add them to the sauté pan. Repeat the process with the remaining fennel slices. Add the thyme, salt and pepper and sauté the mixture over moderate heat for 10 minutes or until it is heated through but still crisp. Stir in the reserved parsley and correct the seasoning.

Wipe out the shells with paper towels. Fill them with the fennel mixture and put them in a flat baking dish. Add enough water to measure 1/4 inch (.75 cm) and cover the zucchini with foil. Bake for 30 minutes. Remove the foil and bake the zucchini for 20 minutes longer, or until the shells are just *al dente* (firm to the bite). Halve each shell and transfer them to a serving plate.

Makes 8 servings.

Variation ——————

Substitute 6 large celery ribs (12 ounces total, 340g) and 1 teaspoon of fennel seeds for the fennel.

Lacy Potato Pancakes ——————————————

These crisp, thin potato pancakes are excellent accompaniments to almost any main dish. The variation with zucchini is served as a garnish for meats at Alain Chapel's restaurant in Mionnay, France.

3 large Idaho potatoes
(1-1/2 pounds total,
680g), unpeeled,
scrubbed and cut into
the largest pieces that
will fit the feed tube
1/2 teaspoon freshly
grated nutmeg
2 teaspoons salt
Freshly ground pepper
1/2 stick unsalted butter
(2 ounces, 55g), or more,
if necessary
1/4 cup (6 cl) oil or more if
necessary
Parsley sprigs

Medium Shredding or Fine Julienne Disc: Shred the potatoes, using firm pressure. Soak them in cold water to cover with 2 teaspoons salt until you are ready to use them. Drain them and wrap them in a kitchen towel to dry. Toss them in a bowl with the nutmeg, salt and pepper.

Heat 1 tablespoon each of the butter and oil in a heavy skillet. Put 2 tablespoons of the shredded potatoes in the skillet and pat them into a round shape. Brown one side well, turn the pancake, and brown the other side. Transfer the pancake to paper towels and repeat the procedure with the remaining potatoes, adding butter and oil as necessary. Arrange the pancakes on a platter, overlapping them. Garnish them with the parsley sprigs.

Makes 24 pancakes.

Variation ——————

For Potato Zucchini Pancakes, substitute 1/2 pound (225g) of shredded zucchini for 1 large potato (1/2 pound, 225g). Stir the zucchini into the potato and seasoning mixture.

Note: These pancakes can be made in advance and refrigerated or frozen. Reheat them by placing them in a single layer on a baking sheet and putting it in a cold oven. Set the oven temperature to 350°F. (175°C.) and heat the pancakes for 10 minutes.

A long-time winner made simple to prepare with a food processor.

8 Idaho potatoes (2 pounds, 10 ounces total, 1.2 kg), peeled and cut into uniform wedges to fit the feed tube
1/2 stick unsalted butter (2 ounces, 55g)
2 tablespoons vegetable oil
2-1/2 teaspoons salt
3/4 teaspoon freshly grated nutmeg
1/2 teaspoon freshly ground pepper
Parsley or watercress sprigs

Preheat the oven to 450°F. (230°C.) and adjust the rack to the middle level.

Thin Slicing Disc: Slice the potatoes, using firm pressure. Rinse them in several changes of cold water and drain them well. Spread the potatoes on 2 kitchen towels and roll them up jelly-roll fashion to dry completely.

Melt 1 tablespoon of butter with the 2 tablespoons oil in an 8-inch (20 cm) round cake pan. Arrange the potatoes in overlapping circles in 1 layer covering the entire bottom of the pan. Mix the salt, nutmeg and pepper, sprinkle 1/3 of the mixture over the potatoes. Dot the top with 1-1/2 tablespoons butter cut into pea-size pieces. Continue making layers of potatoes, seasoning and butter in the same manner until you have used all the potatoes. Put the pan over moderately high heat for 10 minutes or so, until the butter sizzles and the underside of the potatoes is browned.

Press the potatoes firmly in place with a metal spatula and cover them tightly with foil. Bake for 30 minutes. Remove the foil and bake for 15 minutes longer. Invert the potatoes onto a platter and garnish them with parsley or watercress sprigs.

Makes 6 to 8 servings.

Variation

For Potatoes and Onions Anna, thinly slice a large onion (4 ounces, 115g), and arrange all the slices over the bottom layer of potatoes. Repeat the potato layering and bake the dish as directed.

Served at Frédy Girardet's restaurant in Crissier, Switzerland, and a splendid complement to lamb, beef or chicken.

1 large garlic clove, peeled
1 large Spanish onion (10 ounces, 285g), peeled and quartered
3 tablespoons unsalted butter
1 large Idaho potato (1/2 pound, 225g), peeled
2 small white turnips (1/2 pound total, 225g), peeled
1/2 cup (12 cl) plus 2 tablespoons heavy cream
1/2 cup (12 cl) plus 2 tablespoons milk
1 teaspoon salt
Freshly ground pepper
Freshly grated nutmeg
3 tablespoons heavy cream

Metal Blade: Mince the garlic by dropping it through the feed tube while the machine is running; leave it in the bowl.

Medium Slicing Disc: Slice the onion, using medium pressure. Melt the butter in a 2-quart (190 cl) saucepan over medium heat and cook the garlic and onion for 5 minutes. Do not allow the mixture to brown.

Thin Slicing Disc: Slice the potato and the turnips, using firm pressure. Add them to the onion mixture with the cream, milk and seasonings, and cook the mixture, stirring frequently, for 25 minutes, or until the mixture is thick and the vegetables are almost tender.

Preheat the oven to 325°F. (160°C.).

Transfer the mixture to a buttered 9-inch (23 cm) gratin dish and smooth the surface. Spoon 3 tablespoons of cream over it, and bake it for 20 minutes. Place the dish about 4 inches (10 cm) from a moderate broiler and broil it for 5 minutes, or until it is lightly browned.

Makes 6 servings.

Note: This dish can be prepared in advance to the baking stage. Refrigerate it, wrapped airtight. Let it come to room temperature before cooking, or increase the cooking time by 8 to 10 minutes if you place it in the oven directly from the refrigerator.

Celery root, or celeriac, looks like potato when puréed, but it has a much more interesting flavor.

2 large celery roots (2-1/2 pounds total, 1.1 kg), peeled and cut into 3-inch (7.5 cm) pieces
2 large potatoes (1 pound total, 455g), peeled and cut into 3-inch (7.5 cm) pieces
1/4 cup (6 cl) parsley leaves
1/2 stick unsalted butter (2 ounces, 55g), at room temperature and halved
1-1/2 teaspoons salt
1/2 teaspoon freshly grated nutmeg
Freshly ground pepper

Plunge the celery root and potatoes into 2 quarts (190 cl) of boiling water to which you have added 2 tablespoons of salt. Boil them for 15 to 20 minutes, or until they are soft. Drain the vegetables well and cook them over low heat until "dry".

Preheat the oven to 300°F. (150°C.) and adjust the rack to the middle level.

Metal Blade: Mince the parsley by turning the machine on and off about 8 times; reserve it. Add the vegetables, butter and seasonings to the work bowl and purée the mixture, stopping the machine once to scrape down the sides of the bowl. Add all but 1 tablespoon of the reserved parsley and process the mixture for 2 seconds. Adjust seasoning. Spoon the purée into a buttered 5-cup (120 cl) baking dish (preferably glass) and smooth the top. Cover the purée with foil and bake it for 30 minutes. Uncover and sprinkle the reserved parsley on top.

Makes 8 to 10 servings.

Note: This dish can be prepared in advance and refrigerated overnight, covered. To reheat it, put it in a cold oven and bake it at 300°F. (150°C.) for 30 minutes.

Yam Soufflé with Walnuts

Perfect with roast chicken, turkey or duck, and a natural for winter holidays.

1 tablespoon white
   vinegar
1 tablespoon water
8 large egg whites
1 22-ounce (624g) can
   yams, drained
4 tablespoons unsalted
   butter at room
   temperature
1/4 cup (60 ml) dark corn
   syrup
1 tablespoon light
   brown sugar
1 tablespoon fresh
   lemon juice
1 tablespoon dry Sherry
3 tablespoons walnuts

Preheat the oven to 425°F. (220°C.) and adjust the rack to the middle level. Butter a 6-cup (14 dl) soufflé dish. Assemble all the ingredients and a 1-quart (9.5 dl) mixing bowl conveniently near the food processor. Put the vinegar and water in a small dish.

Metal Blade: Put the egg whites into a clean work bowl and turn the machine on. After 8 seconds, pour the vinegar and water through the feed tube while the machine is running. Process for about 2 minutes and 10 seconds, or until the egg whites are whipped and hold their shape. With a rubber spatula, gently transfer the egg whites to the mixing bowl. It is not necessary to wash the work bowl.

Put the remaining ingredients in the work bowl and process for about 1 minute, stopping once to scrape down the sides of the work bowl. Add 1/4 of the egg whites and process for 10 seconds, stopping once to scrape down the sides of the work bowl. Spoon the remaining egg whites onto the mixture in a ring and turn the machine on and off 3 times. Run a spatula around the sides of the work bowl, to loosen the mixture. Turn the machine on and off 6 more times, or until the ingredients are just mixed. Some streaks of egg white may be visible; do not overprocess.

With a rubber spatula, gently transfer the mixture to the prepared soufflé dish. Bake in the preheated oven for 22 minutes.

Makes 8 servings.

Note: This soufflé can be baked in a 6-1/2-cup (15 dl) mold and inverted onto a platter.

Spectacular looking together, any one of these vegetable purées could be served alone.

Spinach Purée _____

2 pounds (910g) spinach, including the stems, washed
1 large pear (6 ounces, 170g), peeled, cored and quartered
3 tablespoons unsalted butter at room temperature
1/2 teaspoon freshly grated nutmeg
1-1/2 teaspoons salt
Freshly ground pepper

Put the spinach in an enameled or stainless steel saucepan with only the water clinging to its leaves. Cook, uncovered, over moderately high heat until it is wilted, turning it once or twice with a wooden spoon. Transfer the spinach to a colander and hold it under cold running water until it is completely cool. Drain it well and wrap it in a cloth towel, squeezing out as much moisture as possible.

Metal Blade: Chop the pear coarsely by turning the machine on and off about 6 times and process it for 10 seconds. Add the spinach and remaining ingredients, combining them by turning the machine on and off about 6 times. Process the mixture for 1 minute, stopping the machine twice to scrape down the sides of the bowl. Correct the seasoning and transfer the purée to a buttered 2-quart (190 cl) baking dish, preferably of glass, spreading it evenly.

Parsnip Purée _____

12 large parsnips (1-1/2 pounds total, 680g), peeled, cooked until tender and drained
1/2 cup (12 cl) parsley leaves
2 tablespoons unsalted butter, at room temperature
1/2 teaspoon freshly grated nutmeg
1-1/2 teaspoons salt
Freshly ground pepper

Pat the parsnips dry with paper towels and cut them into 1-inch (2.5 cm) pieces.

Metal Blade: Mince the parsley by turning the machine on and off; reserve it. Combine the parsnips with the remaining ingredients, turning the machine on and off about 4 times. Then process the mixture for 1 minute, stopping the machine once to scrape down the sides of the bowl. Correct the seasoning, add all but 1 teaspoon of the minced parsley and process the mixture for 1 second. Spoon the purée over the spinach purée, spreading it evenly.

Preheat the oven to 350°F. (175°C.) and adjust the rack to the middle level.

Carrot Purée

12 large carrots (1-1/2
  pounds total, 680g),
  peeled, cooked until
  tender and drained
1 small apple (3 ounces,
  85g), peeled, cored
  and quartered
2 tablespoons unsalted
  butter, at room
  temperature
1/2 teaspoon freshly
  grated nutmeg
1-1/2 teaspoons salt
  Freshly ground white
  pepper

Pat the carrots dry with paper towels and cut them into 1-inch (2.5 cm) pieces.

Metal Blade: Chop the apple coarsely by turning the machine on and off about 6 times. Process for 10 seconds and add the carrots and the remaining ingredients (except the reserved parsley), combining them by turning the machine on and off about 6 times. Process the mixture for 1 minute, stopping the machine once to scrape down the sides of the bowl. Correct the seasoning and spoon the purée over the parsnip purée, spreading it evenly. Cover the dish with foil and bake it for 30 minutes. Sprinkle the top with the reserved parsley.

Makes 10 to 12 servings.

Note: This dish can be prepared a day in advance, covered tightly and refrigerated, and baked just before serving. Let it come to room temperature before baking or, if it is chilled, bake it for an additional 8 to 10 minutes.

Corn Pancakes à la Paris

At the two-star Jacques Cagna restaurant in Paris, these pancakes are served with meat and poultry dishes. Easy to make and popular, they are also truly Parisian, believe it or not. The French love dishes made with American corn.

1-1/2 cups (35 cl) cooked
  corn, cut from the cob
  or 12-ounce (340g) can
  kernel corn, drained
4 large eggs
1/2 cup unbleached
  all-purpose flour
  (2-1/2 ounces, 70g)
  Freshly grated nutmeg
1 scant teaspoon salt
  Freshly ground pepper
3 tablespoons vegetable
  oil
3 tablespoons unsalted
  butter

Metal Blade: Put the corn, eggs, flour, nutmeg, salt and pepper in the work bowl. Process for 40 seconds, or until the corn is puréed, stopping the machine once to scrape down the sides of the bowl.

Heat 1 tablespoon each of oil and butter in a skillet until it is hot. Pour in about 1-1/2 tablespoons of batter for each 2-inch (5 cm) pancake. Brown one side well, turn the pancake and brown the other side. Use the remaining batter to make additional pancakes in the same manner, adding equal parts of oil and butter to the skillet when necessary.

Makes 30 pancakes.

Note: These pancakes can be made in advance. To reheat, place them on a baking sheet in a single layer and place in a preheated 400°F. (205°C.) oven for 6 to 8 minutes.

_____

Ratatouille never had it so easy! The optional topping makes this version unusually delicious as well as more substantial.

2/3 cup (16 cl) parsley
    leaves
2 large garlic cloves,
    peeled
2 tomatoes (9 ounces
    total, 255g), peeled,
    seeded and quartered
1/2 teaspoon sugar
1 eggplant
    (1-1/4 pounds, 565g),
    unpeeled and cut into
    pieces to fit the feed
    tube horizontally
3 zucchini (1 pound
    total, 455g), unpeeled
    and cut into 2-inch
    (5 cm) lengths
1 tablespoon salt
1/3 cup (8 cl) olive oil or a
    mixture of olive oil and
    vegetable oil
1/2 teaspoon ground
    coriander
1 teaspoon dried thyme
2 large onions (8 ounces
    total, 225g), peeled
    and quartered
2 small green peppers
    (6 ounces total, 170g), cut
    flat at the ends, seeded,
    cored and left whole
3 tablespoons tomato
    sauce
    Salt
    Freshly ground pepper
1/2 teaspoon dried basil

Metal Blade: Mince the parsley by turning the machine on and off; reserve it. With the machine running, mince the garlic by dropping it through the feed tube. Add the tomatoes and chop them coarsely with the sugar by turning the machine on and off about 6 times; reserve them.

Medium Slicing Disc: Slice the eggplant, using medium pressure. Stack the zucchini in the feed tube horizontally and slice it, using medium pressure. Transfer both eggplant and zucchini to a colander and sprinkle it with the salt. Let it stand for 30 minutes. Pat the vegetables dry with paper towels. In a skillet sauté the vegetables in 3 tablespoons of the oil over high heat for 1 minute. Cover the skillet and let the mixture steam for 3 minutes, shaking the pan several times. Stir in the coriander and thyme and reserve the mixture.

Slice the onions, using firm pressure. Stand the peppers in the feed tube vertically and slice them, using light pressure. In a stainless steel skillet sauté the onions and peppers in the remaining oil over high heat until they are just soft. Stir in the garlic, tomatoes and tomato sauce and cook the mixture, covered, for 5 minutes. Uncover and cook until the juices have evaporated. Season with the salt, pepper and basil and all but 3 tablespoons of the reserved parsley.

Adjust the oven rack to the middle level and preheat the oven to 350°F. (175°C.)

Assembly _____

Spread 1/3 of the tomato mixture in the bottom of an oiled 1-1/2 quart (142 cl) casserole and cover it with half the eggplant and zucchini mixture. Sprinkle the top with salt and pepper. Add the remaining tomato mixture, spreading it evenly, and the remaining eggplant and zucchini mixture. Sprinkle with salt and pepper and bake for 40 minutes or until the top is bubbly. Pour off any excess juices and garnish the dish with the reserved parsley.

Serve cold or at room temperature.

Variation

4 ounces (115g) imported Parmesan cheese, at room temperature

4 ounces (115g) mozzarella cheese, chilled

2 large eggs

Spread the following topping over the vegetables, cook as described above and serve hot. Or bake the ratatouille in advance without the topping and spread it with topping just before reheating. The topping can be mixed in advance and refrigerated.

Metal Blade: Divide the Parmesan cheese into several pieces of equal size and put them in the work bowl. Grate them by turning the machine on and off several times and leave them in the bowl.

Shredding Disc: Shred the mozzarella cheese, using light pressure, and leave it in the bowl.

Metal Blade: Add the eggs and process for 2 seconds.

Ratatouille

Spinach Supreme

The food processor makes spinach easy to prepare, with little waste. I usually use the stems as well as the leaves.

Spinach Mixture

3 pounds (1.4kg) fresh spinach, including the stems, washed
2 large eggs
1 tablespoon lemon juice
1 teaspoon freshly grated nutmeg
Pinch of cinnamon
Salt (Use with caution; the cheese is salty.)
Freshly ground pepper
1/2 cup (12 cl) parsley leaves
1 small onion, (2 ounces, 55g), peeled and halved
2 tablespoons unsalted butter
3 ounces (55g) Feta cheese, chilled
3 ounces (55g) mozzarella cheese, chilled

In a stainless steel saucepan, cook the spinach uncovered over moderately high heat in just the water clinging to its leaves. Turn it with a wooden spoon until it is wilted. Transfer the spinach to a colander and hold it under cold running water until it is completely cool. Drain well and wrap in towels, squeezing out as much moisture as possible. Reserve it.

Metal Blade: Process the spinach mixture with the eggs, lemon juice, nutmeg and cinnamon for 10 seconds, or until the spinach is puréed. Stop the machine once to scrape down the sides of the bowl. Transfer it to a large mixing bowl. Add salt and pepper to taste and transfer the mixture to a buttered 5-cup (118 cl) baking dish.

Mince the parsley by turning the machine on and off; reserve it. Mince the onions in the same way. In a small skillet sauté the onion in the butter until it is softened and add it to the spinach in the mixing bowl.

Medium Slicing Disc: Slice the Feta cheese, using light pressure, and leave it in the bowl.

Shredding Disc: Shred the mozzarella, using light pressure. Add the cheeses to the mixing bowl, combining all the ingredients well with a wooden spoon.

Adjust the oven rack to the middle level and preheat the oven to 375°F. (190°C.).

Ricotta Topping

1 tablespoon unsalted butter
4 teaspoons flour
1 cup (24 cl) milk
1/2 teaspoon salt
1 large egg yolk
1/2 teaspoon freshly grated nutmeg
1/2 cup (12 cl) skim-milk ricotta cheese

Melt the butter in a small saucepan and stir in the flour. Cook the *roux* over low heat for 5 minutes. Whisk in the milk and cook until the sauce is thickened and smooth. Remove the pan from the heat.

Metal Blade: Blend the remaining ingredients by turning the machine on and off about 6 times. Add 1/4 of the sauce and blend the mixture, turning the machine on once. Add the remaining sauce and blend by turning the machine on and off 3 times. Correct the seasoning and spoon the topping over the spinach, smoothing the surface. Bake for 30 minutes and brown the top under a broiler for 2 minutes, if necessary. Sprinkle the dish with the reserved parsley.

Makes 8 servings.

Note: This dish can be prepared in advance, covered tightly and refrigerated. Let it come to room temperature before baking or bake for 8 to 10 minutes longer if it is chilled.

Variation _____

The spinach is also delicious without the ricotta topping. It can be topped with peeled and thinly sliced lemons or 2 ounces (55g) each of shredded Parmesan cheese at room temperature, and shredded mozzarella cheese.

Zucchini Flan _____

Essentially a quiche without a crust, this flan provides a fairly rich, yet light vegetable dish.

7 small zucchini (1-3/4 pounds total, 795g), trimmed, unpeeled and cut into lengths to fit the feed tube
1 teaspoon salt
2 tablespoons vegetable oil
2 ounces (55g) imported Parmesan cheese, at room temperature
1/2 cup (12 cl) parsley leaves
4 large eggs
3 ounces (85g) Feta cheese, quartered
1/4 teaspoon dried oregano
1/4 teaspoon salt
Freshly ground pepper

Medium Slicing Disc: Put the zucchini in the feed tube vertically and slice it, using medium pressure. Transfer it to a colander, sprinkle it with salt and toss it. Let it drain for 30 minutes. Press the zucchini gently and pat it dry with paper towels.

Preheat the oven to 375°F. (190°C.) and adjust the rack to the middle level.

Heat the oil in a large skillet and add the zucchini. Cover it and steam it, shaking the pan occasionally, for 2 to 3 minutes or until it is just heated through. Transfer the zucchini to a buttered 8- by 1-1/2-inch (3.75 cm) round baking dish.

Shredding Disc: Shred the Parmesan cheese, using light pressure; reserve it.

Metal Blade: Mince the parsley by turning the machine on and off; reserve it. Process the eggs for 45 seconds or until they thicken and become lemon colored. Add the reserved parsley and Parmesan cheese, Feta cheese and seasonings. Process the mixture by turning the machine on and off 7 or 8 times. Pour the mixture over the zucchini and bake the dish for 30 minutes, or until it is lightly browned.

Makes 6 to 8 servings.

Variation _____

This dish can be made with a combination of broccoli, spinach, mushrooms and onions, all precooked in the same manner as the zucchini.

Butter a 10 by 16-inch (25 x 41 cm) ovenproof dish or two 8 by 13-inch (20 x 33 cm) ovenproof dishes.

Savory Crêpes

2 large eggs
1 cup unbleached all-purpose flour (5 ounces, 142g)
1 tablespoon vegetable oil
1/2 teaspoon salt
1-1/3 cups milk
Butter for cooking crêpes

Metal Blade: Put the eggs, flour, oil and salt in the work bowl and blend them by turning the machine on and off about 4 times. With the machine running, pour the milk through the feed tube, processing until the mixture is smooth. Stop the machine once to scrape down the sides of the work bowl. Let the batter rest at least 1/2 hour, or overnight. Crêpe batter should be like heavy cream. Add extra liquid if needed.

Heat 1 teaspoon of butter in a 6 to 7-inch (15 to 18 cm) crêpe pan. When the pan is hot, add just enough batter to coat the bottom of the pan. Brown the crêpe on both sides. Continue until all the batter is used, adding butter to the pan as needed. As the crêpes are cooked, stack them and set them aside. Crêpes can be made in advance and refrigerated, or frozen in an airtight package with parchment or wax paper separating the crêpes.

Spinach Mixture

1-1/2 pounds fresh spinach, including stems, roots trimmed
1 cup (24 cl) cooked chicken, turkey, fish, ham or beef (optional)
1-1/2 ounces (43g) imported Parmesan cheese, at room temperature and cut into 1-inch (2.5 cm) cubes
1/2 cup (12 cl) parsley leaves
1 large clove garlic, peeled
3 large scallions (3 ounces total, 85g), including green tops, cut in thirds
2 large eggs
1 cup ricotta cheese, drained
1/4 teaspoon salt
Freshly ground black pepper
1/4 teaspoon freshly grated nutmeg

Wash the spinach well and cook it quickly over high heat in a stainless steel saucepan, with only the water clinging to its leaves. Stir it once or twice with a wooden spoon to accelerate the cooking. As soon as the spinach is wilted, refresh it in cold water. Drain it well and squeeze it dry in a towel. You should have about 2 cups of spinach.

Metal Blade: Chop the cooked meat by turning the machine on and off until the meat is coarsely chopped. Set it aside. Add the Parmesan cheese, parsley, garlic and scallions and process for 5 seconds. Add the spinach and eggs and process for 40 seconds or until the mixture is puréed. Add the ricotta and process for 20 seconds longer. Transfer the mixture to a mixing bowl. Stir in the chopped meat and season to taste with salt, pepper and nutmeg. Divide the spinach mixture among 16 crêpes and roll them up.

Tomato Mixture

1-1/2 ounces imported Parmesan cheese, at room temperature
4 medium tomatoes (1-1/4 pounds total, 567g), peeled, seeded and quartered
Pinch sugar
1 teaspoon dried basil

Metal Blade: Finely chop the Parmesan cheese by turning the machine on and off several times. Add the tomatoes, sugar and basil; chop them coarsely by turning the machine on and off. Set the mixture aside.

Mornay Sauce

2 ounces (55g) imported Parmesan cheese, at room temperature
2 ounces (55g) mozzarella cheese, chilled
6 tablespoons (3 ounces, 85g), unsalted butter
6 tablespoons unbleached all-purpose flour (2 ounces, 55g)
3 cups milk
Salt
Freshly ground white pepper
Freshly grated nutmeg

Metal Blade: Grate the Parmesan cheese by turning the machine on and off. Leave it in the bowl.

Shredding Disc: Shred the mozzarella, using light pressure. Set the cheeses aside. Cook the butter and flour over low heat for 3 minutes, stirring gently, to make a *roux*. Pour in the milk and stir constantly until the sauce is thick. Remove the sauce from the heat and allow it to cool slightly. Stir the cheeses gently into the cooled sauce with a wooden spoon. Adjust the seasoning with salt, white pepper and nutmeg.

Assembly

Preheat the oven to 375°F. (190°C.) and adjust the rack to the middle level.

These crêpes are best baked in a single layer. Spread the tomato mixture in the prepared dish(es). Place the filled crêpes, seam side down, over the tomatoes. Cover them with Mornay Sauce. The cannelloni can be prepared ahead to this point and refrigerated or frozen. Bake them in a preheated oven for 40 to 45 minutes, or until they are browned.

Makes 8 servings of 2 cannelloni per serving.

Variation

Add 1 teaspoon each of minced parsley and dried dill weed to the crêpe batter, for Herbed Crêpes.

Spinach Ricotta Gnocchi

These light and fluffy spinach dumplings can be prepared in advance and baked just before serving.

Spinach Mixture

2 pounds (910g) spinach, including the stems, washed
6 ounces (170g) imported Parmesan cheese, at room temperature
2 slices firm white bread (2 ounces total, 55g), crusts removed and torn into pieces
2 tablespoons unsalted butter, melted
2 scallions(1 ounce total, 30g), including the green tops, cut into 2-inch (5 cm) pieces
1/4 cup (6 cl) parsley leaves
1/2 cup (12 cl) skim-milk ricotta cheese, drained
1/3 cup unbleached all-purpose flour (1-3/4 ounces, 50g)
3 large egg whites
1 teaspoon dried basil
1/2 teaspoon dried oregano
1/2 to 1 teaspoon salt
6 to 8 cups (140 to 190 cl) chicken broth or water (with 1 tablespoon salt)

Mornay Sauce

3 tablespoons unsalted butter
3 tablespoons unbleached all-purpose flour
1-1/2 cups (35 cl) milk
Salt
Freshly ground white pepper
Freshly grated nutmeg

Put the spinach in a stainless steel saucepan with just the water clinging to its leaves. Cook it, uncovered, over moderately high heat until it is wilted, turning it once or twice with a wooden spoon. Transfer it to a colander and hold it under cold running water until it is completely cool. Drain it well. Wrap the spinach in towels, squeezing out as much moisture as possible.

Shredding Disc: Shred the Parmesan cheese, using light pressure. Remove and reserve 3/4 cup (18 cl); leave the rest in the work bowl.

Metal Blade: Add the bread to the cheese in the work bowl and process for about 5 seconds or until it is finely crumbed. Add the butter and process for 5 seconds. Add the scallions and turn the machine on and off to mince them. Add the spinach and parsley and process for 30 seconds, or until the spinach is puréed, stopping the machine once to scrape down the sides of the bowl. Add the ricotta, flour, egg whites, basil, oregano and salt. (Add salt judiciously; both the cheese and the broth are quite salty.) Combine by turning the machine on and off about 6 times and process for 30 seconds. Correct the seasoning and transfer to a mixing bowl. Refrigerate the mixture for 2 hours, or overnight.

Flour your hands lightly and shape 1-inch (2.5 cm) balls from 1 tablespoon measures of the mixture. Bring the broth or salted water to a boil in a large saucepan. Gently lower the gnocchi 12 to 14 at a time, into the liquid, and simmer them uncovered for 6 to 8 minutes, or until they puff slightly and rise to the surface. Do not overcook them. Transfer the gnocchi with a slotted spoon to a well-buttered 13- by 9-inch (33 x 23 cm) oval baking dish.

Melt the butter in a saucepan and stir in the flour. Cook this *roux* over low heat for 5 minutes. Whisk in the milk and cook until the sauce becomes thickened and smooth. Remove the pan from the heat and let the sauce cool slightly. Stir in half the reserved Parmesan cheese and add salt, pepper and nutmeg. Spoon the sauce over the gnocchi, leaving some green showing, and sprinkle the remaining cheese on top. Preheat the oven to 350°F. (175°C.) and bake the gnocchi for 18 minutes.

Makes about 40 gnocchi.

Salads and Dressings_____

Salads & Dressings _____

Italian Salad in Marinated Artichokes
Red Pepper and Water Chestnut Salad with Ginger
Orange, Avocado and Jerusalem Artichoke Salad
Sliced Chicken Salad with Olives, Cornichons
    and Capers
Carrot, Turnip and Zucchini Salad
Spinach Salad
White Bean and Vegetable Salad with Sausage
Greek Salad
Festive Coleslaw
Herbed Egg Salad Ring
Eggplant and Pepperoni Salad
Beet, Leek and Artichoke Salad
Broccoli, Mushroom and Bean Sprout Salad
Celery Root and Tomato Salad
Radish, Scallion and Swiss Cheese Salad
Eleven Layer Salad
Celery Root and Caper Salad, Lemon Mayonnaise
White Beans with Tuna
Mushroom, Watercress and Red Pepper Salad

Basic Vinaigrette
Ginger Vinaigrette
Tarragon Vinaigrette
Green Peppercorn Mustard Vinaigrette
Hot Salad Dressing
Bacon Dressing
Onion Dressing
Creamy Parsley Dressing
Oriental Salad Dressing
Honey Dressing

Front row: Tarragon Vinaigrette, page 153; Walnut Vinaigrette, page 152. Middle row: Ginger Vinaigrette, page 152; Green Peppercorn Vinaigrette, page 153; Olive Oil. Back row: Tarragon Vinegar; Basic Vinaigrette, page 152.

I refuse to get serious about salads! They are a passion, a hobby and an art form for me. They are exactly what they appear to be — bright, tempting and as fresh as a red-ripe tomato, a bouquet of watercress, a deep purple eggplant or a buttery avocado. Yet they are also a stern winter challenge, a continuous summer invitation, an important accompaniment to cold foods and an essential counterpoint to casseroles and stews. And, at their most enticing, they should look both spontaneous and carefully composed.

In these recipes, you'll find the serendipity of more seasons in the supermarket than I care to recount. A gray day in February turned up nothing more than two cabbages — one purple, the other green — and thus Festive Coleslaw made its first appearance. An opulent August harvest demanded a bowl big enough to hold a glorious Greek Salad. The Mushroom, Watercress and Red Pepper Salad composed itself as I stared at the vegetable bins; so did the Orange, Avocado and Jerusalem Artichoke Salad on a more blustery day. Carrot, Turnip and Zucchini Salad was also a cold-weather makeshift that outshone the supply of available greenery.

My experiences with great French chefs yielded other salad combinations that pleased me with their subtle wit. Picture a julienne of pickled ginger root over sweet red pepper and crisp water chestnuts — an Oriental-flavored triumph from Jean Delaveyne's Le Camelia restaurant. From Taillevent's chef Claude Déligne came two surprising expedients — Celery Root and Tomato Salad for a low-calorie diet, and Beet, Leek and Artichoke Salad (I added the artichokes!) for a workaday kitchen staff lunch.

The Italian genius for salads suggested three robust combinations that could be served as first courses or as luncheon entrées with cheeses and bread: Italian Salad in Marinated Artichokes, White Beans with Tuna, and White Bean Salad with Sausage and Vegetables. For formal luncheons, I would make a fabulous centerpiece of either the elegant yet boldly seasoned Sliced Chicken Salad with Olives, Cornichons and Capers or the vivid Herbed Egg Salad Ring with Beets, Mushrooms and Watercress.

Many meals call for nothing more complex than mixed greens tossed with a light, refreshing dressing. Only your market or garden can supply the "recipe" for the greens. Use what looks best and try to gather several kinds, including a bit of spinach, escarole, curly endive, red leaf lettuce or watercress as well as, or even instead of, the more sedate pale lettuces. Then match the flavor of the greens with a dressing from the selection at the end of this chapter. I would soften the tang of Chinese cabbage with Walnut Vinaigrette, complement the crunch of iceberg lettuce with Creamy Parsley Dressing, or bring out the zestiness of spinach with Hot Salad Dressing. If the greens are fresh and thoroughly dried after washing, you can hardly make a mistake. Wash, sort and dry the leaves well ahead of time, if you wish; then roll them in paper towels and store them in a plastic bag in the refrigerator for up to 24 hours. And when you can pick a bunch of dillweed, basil, chervil, tarragon or any other fresh herb, by all means substitute it for the dried herb and use twice the amount specified in the recipe.

Italian Salad in Marinated Artichokes

A salad with surprising and appealing taste combinations, which is wonderful as a first course. The julienned pepperoni is a delicious accent.

8 artichokes, stems trimmed at the base
1 lemon, halved
2 tablespoons salt
2 tablespoons lemon juice
1 cup (24 cl) Basic Vinaigrette (see Index)
1/2 cup (12 cl) parsley leaves
8 large mushrooms (1/2 pound total, 225g), trimmed and sides cut flat
1/2 fennel bulb (4 ounces, 115g), greens trimmed
10 large radishes (4-1/2 ounces, 130g total), washed and trimmed
2-inch (5 cm) piece of pepperoni, skinned and soft enough to be pierced with the point of a knife
8 cherry tomatoes

Cut 1/2 inch (1.25 cm) from the tips of the artichoke leaves with a kitchen shears and rub the cut edges with the lemon. Cook the artichokes with the salt and lemon juice, uncovered, in water to cover for 25 to 35 minutes, or until they are tender. Drain them upside down until they are cool enough to handle. Spread the outer leaves open and pull out the center core. Scrape the chokes with a grapefruit spoon. While the artichokes are still warm, marinate them in 1/2 cup (12 cl) Basic Vinaigrette. (The artichokes can be prepared a day in advance and refrigerated overnight, covered.)

Metal Blade: Mince the parsley by turning the machine on and off; reserve it.

Medium Slicing Disc: Stack the mushrooms sideways in the feed tube and slice them, using light pressure. Repeat the process with the remaining mushrooms.

Put the fennel in the feed tube vertically and slice it, using firm pressure. Leave it in the work bowl. Put the radishes in the feed tube and slice them, using firm pressure. Transfer the vegetables to a large bowl.

Make julienne strips of the pepperoni by using a double-slicing technique, as follows. Put the pepperoni in the feed tube vertically and slice it, using firm pressure. Remove the slices from the bowl. Reinsert the slices in the feed tube, wedging them in tightly so they will hold. Slice the pepperoni again, using medium pressure, to make julienne strips. Repeat the process with the remaining pepperoni slices. Add the pepperoni to the vegetable mixture, and gently toss all ingredients except the cherry tomatoes with 1/2 cup (12 cl) Basic Vinaigrette. (This salad should be prepared several hours in advance to allow the flavors to develop and blend.) Fill the centers of the artichokes with the salad and garnish each serving with cherry tomatoes.

Makes 8 servings.

Variations

1. Substitute 4 ounces (115g) celery and 1 teaspoon fennel seed for the fresh fennel.

2. Omit the artichokes, double the recipe to yield 8 servings, and heap the salad in a bowl lined with lettuce leaves.

Red Pepper and Water Chestnut Salad with Ginger

This salad, inspired by Jean Delaveyne of Le Camélia in Bougival, is given an intriguing oriental accent by the julienne of pickled fresh ginger.

Salad

- 4 heads Bibb lettuce (3/4 pound total, 340g), washed
- 2 bunches watercress, stems trimmed
- 2 large red peppers (1 pound total, 455g) cut into equal-size squares
- 1 8-ounce (225g) can water chestnuts, drained
- 2 teaspoons julienned Pickled Fresh Ginger Ginger Vinaigrette

Line a salad bowl with whole Bibb lettuce leaves. Tear the remaining leaves into bite-size pieces and put them in the bowl with the watercress leaves.

Medium Slicing Disc: Stand the red pepper squares in the feed tube, side by side, wedging in the last slice tightly. Cut them into matchsticks, using light pressure. Slice the water chestnuts, using medium pressure. Arrange both on the lettuce and watercress. Sprinkle the julienne of ginger over the salad and toss with Ginger Vinaigrette.

Make 8 servings.

Pickled Fresh Ginger

- 3 ounces (85g) ginger root, peeled
- 1/2 cup (12 cl) red wine vinegar
- 1/2 cup plus 2 tablespoons sugar (2-1/4 ounces, 62g)

Thin Slicing Disc: Slice the ginger, using medium pressure. Combine it with the vinegar and sugar in a small stainless steel or enameled saucepan. Bring the mixture to a boil. Remove the pan from the heat and let the mixture cool. Refrigerate it, covered airtight. (The mixture will keep several weeks.) Before serving, cut the ginger into fine julienne strips.

Ginger Vinaigrette

- 3/4 cup (18 cl) oil (preferably safflower with 1 tablespoon French olive oil)
- 1/4 cup (6 cl) red wine vinegar
- 1 teaspoon Dijon-style mustard
- 2 teaspoons liquid from Pickled Ginger
- 1 teaspoon salt Freshly ground pepper

Metal Blade: Process all the ingredients in the work bowl for 2 seconds. Refrigerate the dressing in an airtight jar.

Makes about 1 cup (24 cl).

Orange, Avocado and Jerusalem Artichoke Salad

A very easy salad to prepare, thanks to the food processor, and one that makes a stunning presentation. The Honey Dressing adds an unusual flavor.

1 pound (455g) spinach, washed and stems trimmed
1 small red onion (2 ounces, 55g), peeled
1 wedge red cabbage (2 ounces, 55g)
3 large Jerusalem artichokes (9 ounces total, 225g), unpeeled and well scrubbed
5 firm seedless eating oranges, cut flat at ends
1 large avocado (1/2 pound, 225g), firm but ripe, peeled, split vertically and pitted
2 teaspoons lemon juice
3/4 cup (18 cl) Honey Dressing (see Index).

Line a 5-quart (4.75 l) salad bowl with the spinach leaves. Tear the remaining spinach into bite-size pieces and put it in a large mixing bowl.

Medium Slicing Disc: Slice the onions, using medium pressure.

Thin Slicing Disc: Slice the cabbage, using firm pressure. Add the onions and the cabbage to the spinach in the mixing bowl.

Julienne Disc or Thin Slicing Disc: Put the artichokes in the feed tube vertically and process them, using firm pressure. If you do not have a julienne disc, make julienne strips by using a double-slicing technique with the slicing disc, as follows. Slice the artichokes, using firm pressure. Reinsert the slices in the feed tube side by side, wedging them in tightly so they will hold. Slice them again, to produce julienne strips. Add the artichokes to the mixing bowl and toss all the ingredients well. Place them in the spinach-lined bowl.

Remove the rind from the oranges carefully, as follows. Place the orange on a cutting board, and use a sharp knife to cut off slices of rind from top to bottom, conforming to the shape of the orange. Rotate the orange as you cut off each slice, turning it around until all the rind is removed. Be sure to cut away all the white pith.

Medium Slicing Disc: Place an orange in the feed tube, flat side down. Slice it, using light pressure. Continue slicing all the oranges in this way.

Arrange overlapping slices of orange in a circle on the spinach leaves, leaving a 1-inch (2.5 cm) border of green.

Put the avocado halves in the feed tube and slice them, using light pressure. Add lemon juice and toss gently. Arrange the avocado slices in an attractive pattern in the center of the salad bowl. Serve the Honey Dressing separately.

Makes 8 servings.

Variation _____ Omit the avocado and Jerusalem artichokes, and add another small red onion (2 ounces, 55g).

Sliced Chicken with Olives, Cornichons and Capers _____

This is an appropriate centerpiece for a formal lunch. It was inspired by the *Salade aux Truffes* that Alain Chapel created at his restaurant in Mionnay, France with lobster, duck and truffles. To cut down on last-minute preparation, cook the chicken in advance.

2 large chicken breasts and thighs (2-3/4 pounds total, 1.2 kg)
1 medium onion, peeled
1 large carrot, scrubbed
1 celery rib
3 sprigs parsley
1 bay leaf
2 teaspoons salt
Freshly ground white pepper
2/3 cup (16 cl) parsley leaves
3/4 cup (18 cl) Green Peppercorn Mustard Vinaigrette (see Index)
1/2 teaspoon salt
1 5-1/4-ounce (148g) can pitted colossal black olives, drained and cut flat at ends
12 cornichons, drained
3 tablespoons capers, drained
2 large heads Boston lettuce (1 pound total, 455g), washed and crisped
Salt
Freshly ground pepper
4 tablespoons snipped chives

Bone the chicken pieces, taking care to keep the meat in pieces as large as possible. Put the bones in a 1-1/2-quart (142 cl) saucepan with the onion, carrot, celery, parsley, bay leaf, salt and pepper. Add water to cover and simmer for 30 minutes, covered. Strain the broth into a bowl and adjust the seasoning if necessary. Let the broth cool and skim off the fat. Reserve 1/2 cup (12 cl) of the broth for the vinaigrette and bring the remaining broth to boil in a 1-1/2-quart (142 cl) saucepan. Add the meat from the thighs and cook over medium-high heat for 5 minutes, turning the chicken pieces once. Remove the thigh meat and add the breast meat. Cover the pan and cook for 5 minutes, turning the pieces once. Remove them from the saucepan.

Wrap the chicken meat in foil in individual pieces. Wrap carefully to make each packet airtight. Freeze the chicken for 2 to 3 hours, until it is firm to the touch but easily pierced with the tip of a sharp knife. (If you freeze the chicken longer, allow it to thaw partially, to the condition described, before attempting to slice it in the food processor.)

Metal Blade: Mince the parsley by turning the machine on and off.

Medium Slicing Disc: Cut each piece of semi-frozen chicken flat at one end. Insert the pieces in the feed tube vertically, putting in as many as will fit at one time. Slice the chicken, using firm pressure. You should have about 4 cups of sliced chicken.

Pour 1/4 cup (6 cl) of Green Peppercorn Mustard Vinaigrette over the chicken slices, add the salt and mix gently with your hands. Set aside until the chicken is completely thawed.

French-Fry Disc or Medium Slicing Disc: Stack the olives in the feed tube, flat side down, and process them, using light pressure. Leave them in the work bowl.

Medium Shredding Disc: Put the cornichons in the feed tube horizontally and shred them, using light pressure. Remove the cornichons and olives to a small mixing bowl and add the capers. Mix the three ingredients gently and set them aside.

Tear the lettuce into bite-size pieces and toss it gently in a large salad bowl with 1/2 cup (12 cl) of the Green Peppercorn Mustard Vinaigrette, the minced parsley and salt and pepper. Add the chicken, mix carefully and adjust the seasoning if necessary. Sprinkle the olive, cornichon and caper mixture over the surface and toss just enough to mix a little into the salad. Most should remain on the surface. Sprinkle snipped chives over the salad.

Makes 6 main-course or 8 first-course servings.

Variation _____

Substitute 2 lobster tails (11 ounces, 310g) for 1 chicken breast and 1 thigh. Shell the lobster tails and cut the meat from each in half horizontally. Select a saucepan just large enough to hold them. Bring 1 cup (24 cl) of clam juice or Fish Stock (see Index) to a simmer over medium-high heat and add the lobster meat.

Simmer the lobster, turning it every minute so it will cook evenly. Remove it from the broth as soon as it becomes opaque. (This will take about 3 minutes for lobster that is not frozen, about 5 minutes for lobster that is.) In the Green Peppercorn Mustard Vinaigrette used to dress the salad, substitute the broth used for cooking the lobster for the chicken broth.

Carrot, Turnip and Zucchini Salad _____

A food processor makes fast work of this refreshing medley.

1/2 cup (12 cl) parsley
    leaves
  5 large carrots
    (3/4 pound total, 340g),
    peeled and cut into
    2-inch (5 cm) lengths
  3 small zucchini
    (3/4 pound total, 340g),
    trimmed and cut into
    2-inch (5 cm) lengths
  4 small white turnips
    (3/4 pound total, 340g),
    peeled and cut into
    2-inch (5 cm) lengths
1/2 cup (12 cl) Basic
    Vinaigrette (see Index)
1/2 teaspoon salt
    Freshly ground pepper
    Lettuce leaves or Bibb
    lettuce cups

Metal Blade: Mince the parsley by turning the machine on and off; leave it in the work bowl.

Julienne Disc or Shredding Disc: Stack the carrots in the feed tube horizontally and process them, using firm but not hard pressure. Stack the zucchini in the feed tube horizontally and process it, using medium pressure. Stack the turnips in the feed tube and process, using firm but not hard pressure.

Transfer all these vegetables to a large salad bowl and add 1/2 cup (12 cl) Basic Vinaigrette and salt and pepper to taste. Cover and refrigerate. Let the salad come to room temperature before serving. Heap it on a platter lined with lettuce leaves or in individual bowls lined with Bibb lettuce cups.

Makes 6 servings.

Spinach Salad

A healthful version of a favorite.

2 pounds (910g) spinach, preferably the flat-leaf type, washed and stems trimmed
1 pound (455g) fresh bean sprouts, washed
2 small red onions (4 ounces total, 115g), peeled
8 large mushrooms (1/2 pound total, 225g), trimmed and cut flat on sides
2 large eggs, hard-boiled, chilled and peeled
6 slices bacon, crisply cooked, drained and broken into pieces
Hot Salad Dressing (see Index)

Line a large salad bowl with spinach leaves. Tear the remaining leaves into bite-size pieces and add them to the bowl. Top the spinach with the bean sprouts.

Medium Slicing Disc: Slice the onions, using firm pressure. Arrange the onion rings on the bean sprouts. Slice the mushrooms, using light pressure; spread them over the onions.

Metal Blade: Separate the eggs, putting the whites in the work bowl. Chop the whites coarsely by turning the machine on and off 2 or 3 times; reserve them. Rice the yolks finely by processing them for about 2 seconds; reserve them. Wipe out the work bowl with a paper towel, put in the bacon and chop it by turning the machine on and off about 6 times.

Arrange the egg whites and yolks separately on the salad in concentric circles and put the bacon in the center. Pour Hot Salad Dressing over the salad and toss gently but thoroughly.

Makes 8 servings.

Variation

Substitute Oriental Dressing, Sweet Sour Dressing, Bacon Dressing or Creamy Parsley Dressing (see Index for dressings) for the Hot Salad Dressing.

White Bean and Vegetable Salad with Sausage

This hearty mélange adds a new twist to the increasingly popular bean salads. Sausage brings a meaty strength as well as a spicy tang. The salad can be served warm or chilled.

Beans

2 cups dried small white navy beans (12 ounces, 340g)
1 onion (4 ounces, 115g), peeled and halved
2 large garlic cloves, peeled and halved
1 tablespoon salt
Freshly ground pepper

Soak the beans overnight in cold water to cover. Drain them and put them in a saucepan with cold water to cover. Add the onion, garlic, salt and pepper, and bring the water to a boil over moderately high heat. Cover and simmer for 50 minutes to 1 hour, or until the beans are just tender. Do not overcook them. Drain the beans and discard the onion and garlic.

Sausage and Vegetables —

- 1 pound (455g) fresh Italian sausage, mild or hot
- 1 cup (24 cl) parsley leaves
- 1 large garlic clove, peeled
- 1 large onion (5 ounces, 140g), peeled and quartered
- 5 tablespoons olive oil
- 4 small zucchini (1 pound total, 455g), trimmed and cut into lengths to fit the feed tube
- 1 small lemon, scored and ends cut flat
- 3 large celery ribs (6 ounces total, 170g), strings removed with a vegetable peeler and cut into lengths to fit the feed tube
- 1/3 cup (8 cl) red wine vinegar
- 1 tablespoon lemon juice
- 1 teaspoon dried basil
- 1 teaspoon dried thyme
- 1 teaspoon ground coriander
- 1/2 teaspoon dried oregano
  Pinch of cayenne
- 1 teaspoon salt
  Freshly ground pepper
- 1 4-ounce (115g) jar pimientos, drained and cut into 1/4-inch (.75 cm) dice
- 16 Calamata olives, drained
  Boston or red or green leaf lettuce, washed

Cook the sausage in a large skillet in 1/2 inch (1.25 cm) of water over moderately high heat. Turn it after 8 minutes. When the water evaporates, brown the sausage on all sides. Wrap it in foil, and freeze it for 2 hours, or until it is firm to the touch but easily pierced with the tip of a sharp knife. Cut the sausage into 2-inch (5 cm) segments.

Medium Slicing Disc: Put the sausage in the feed tube vertically and slice it, using firm pressure; reserve it.

Metal Blade: Mince the parsley by turning the machine on and off; reserve it. With the machine running, mince the garlic by dropping it through the feed tube. Add the onion and mince it by turning the machine on and off. Heat the oil in a large saucepan and cook the garlic and onion over medium heat for 10 minutes, but do not brown them.

French-Fry Disc: Put the zucchini in the feed tube vertically and process it, using medium pressure. Reserve it.

Medium Slicing Disc: Slice the lemon, using firm pressure. Remove the slices and reserve them.

Put the celery in the feed tube vertically and slice it, using medium pressure. Remove the slicing disc, insert the metal blade and mince the celery by turning the machine on and off about 6 times.

Add the zucchini to the onion mixture. Cover it and steam it over high heat for 3 minutes, shaking the pan occasionally to prevent sticking. Add all the remaining ingredients except the olives, lemon, lettuce and 2 tablespoons of the reserved parsley. Heat the mixture for 5 minutes and correct the seasoning. Remove pan from the heat; stir in half the olives.

Line a large salad bowl with the lettuce and spoon in the salad. Arrange the remaining olives on top and garnish the salad with the reserved parsley and a border of lemon slices. Serve the salad warm, at room temperature or chilled and accompany it with sliced tomatoes in Basil Vinaigrette (see Index) and crusty Italian bread.

Makes 12 servings.

All the vegetables in this salad can be processed quickly with the French-fry disc, and there is no need to rinse the work bowl in between. The herbs and cheese require little more than a few seconds of processing. What appears to be a formidable list of ingredients becomes reduced to a series of simple steps. A good companion for many foods, this salad goes especially well with Lamb à la Grecque or the Middle Eastern Pizza (see Index).

Herb-Cheese Mixture

1 cup (24 cl) parsley leaves
1 tablespoon dried dillweed
4 ounces (115g) Feta cheese, chilled

Metal Blade: Mince the parsley and dillweed by turning the machine on and off; leave them in the work bowl.

French-Fry Disc or Medium Slicing Disc: Process the Feta cheese, using light pressure; leave it in the work bowl.

Metal Blade: Chop the cheese and herbs coarsely by turning the machine on and off; reserve the mixture.

Vegetables

2 small zucchini (1/2 pound total, 225g), trimmed and cut into lengths to fit feed tube
1 small firm cucumber (6 ounces, 170g), or a piece of English cucumber (6 ounces, 170g), unpeeled and cut into lengths to fit the feed tube
1 large firm, ripe tomato (6 ounces, 170g), cored and halved vertically
1 small red onion (3 ounces, 85g), peeled
1 cup large radishes (4 ounces total, 115g), washed and trimmed
3 heads Bibb lettuce, washed
6 Calamata olives, drained

French-Fry Disc or Medium Slicing Disc: Put the zucchini in the feed tube vertically and process it, using medium pressure. If you do not have a French-fry disc, make julienne strips by using a double-slicing technique with the slicing disc, as follows. Slice the zucchini, using medium pressure. Remove the slices and reinsert them in the feed tube side by side, wedging them in tightly so they will hold. Slice the zucchini again, using medium pressure, to produce julienne strips. Repeat the process with the remaining zucchini slices and reserve the julienne strips.

Process the cucumber in the same manner.

French-Fry Disc or Metal Blade: Put the tomato in the feed tube horizontally and process it, using light pressure. If you do not have a French-Fry disc, chop the tomato with the metal blade, turning the machine on and off.

Put the onion in the feed tube vertically and process it, using firm pressure. Or chop it coarsely with the metal blade, turning the machine on and off.

French-Fry Disc or Medium Slicing Disc: Stack the radishes in the feed tube and process them with the French-Fry disc, using firm pressure. Or slice them, using firm pressure.

Dressing

1 tablespoon plus 1
teaspoon lemon juice
1/4 cup (6 cl) oil
1/2 teaspoon dried
oregano
Freshly ground pepper
2 tablespoons
dry-roasted sunflower
seeds (optional)
Salt

Mix the dressing ingredients in a small bowl. Place all the processed vegetables in a large bowl and toss gently with the dressing. Blend in the herb-cheese mixture but do not over-mix. Add salt and pepper to taste. Spoon the salad into 6 individual bowls or 1 large bowl lined with lettuce leaves. Garnish the salad with olives.

Makes 6 servings.

Festive Coleslaw

Two kinds of cabbage are used in this coleslaw; their contrasting colors contribute to its visual appeal.

1 cup (24 cl) parsley
leaves
1 small green pepper
(3 ounces, 85g), whole,
seeded and cut flat at
ends
1 small head green
cabbage (1 pound,
455g), cored and cut
into wedges to fit the
feed tube
3 celery ribs (4 ounces
total, 115g), including
the leaves, cut into
thirds
3 large cauliflower
flowerets (4 ounces
total, 115g)
8 large scallions
(1/2 pound total, 225g),
including the green
tops, cut into thirds
3/4 cup (18 cl) Tarragon
Vinaigrette (see Index)
Salt
Freshly ground pepper
1 small head red
cabbage (1 pound
total, 455g), cored and
cut into wedges to fit
the feed tube

Metal Blade: Mince the parsley by turning the machine on and off. Transfer all but 2 tablespoons to a large bowl; reserve the 2 tablespoons minced parsley.

Medium Slicing Disc: Put the green pepper in the feed tube vertically and slice it, using light pressure. Reserve it. Slice the green cabbage, using firm pressure. Remove half the cabbage from the bowl and insert the metal blade.

Metal Blade: Chop the cabbage with on and off turns and add it to the parsley in the bowl. Repeat the process with the remaining cabbage.

Medium Slicing Disc: Slice the celery, cauliflower and scallions and leave the mixture in the work bowl.

Metal Blade: Finely mince the vegetable mixture in the work bowl by turning the machine on and off about 10 times. Add it to the cabbage mixture. Toss the chopped vegetables with 2/3 cup (16 cl) Tarragon Vinaigrette and add salt and pepper to taste.

Process the red cabbage in the same manner as the green cabbage and toss it in a separate bowl with the remaining Tarragon Vinaigrette. Add salt and pepper to taste.

Put the green cabbage mixture in a large glass salad bowl and arrange the red cabbage around the edge. Garnish the center with overlapping green pepper slices and sprinkle the salad with the reserved parsley.

Makes 8 servings.

Herbed Egg Salad Ring

Especially appealing for an informal lunch of do-it-yourself sandwiches, as well as for cocktails or snacks. The gelatin is a culinary trick, a *truc*, as the French call it, which keeps the salad together so that it serves neatly, yet is still creamy and spreadable.

Egg Salad

- 1 cup (24 cl) parsley leaves
- 1 package unflavored gelatin (1 tablespoon)
- 1/2 cup (12 cl) cold water
- 8 large eggs, hard-boiled, chilled and peeled
- 6 scallions (3 ounces total, 85g), including the green tops, cut into 2-inch (5 cm) pieces
- 2 small parsnips (4 ounces total, 115g), uncooked, peeled and cut into 1-inch (2.5 cm) pieces
- 1 cucumber (4 ounces, 115g), unpeeled and seeded
- 1 small garlic clove, peeled
- 1-3/4 cups (41 cl) Basic Mayonnaise (see Index)
- 1 teaspoon Dijon-style mustard
- 1 teaspoon dried basil
- 1 teaspoon dried dillweed
- 1 teaspoon dried savory
- 1/8 teaspoon dried thyme
- 1/8 teaspoon curry powder
- 2 teaspoons salt
  Freshly ground pepper
  Leaf or Boston lettuce leaves, washed

Metal Blade: Mince the parsley by turning the machine on and off. Reserve 2 tablespoons of it and transfer the rest to a large bowl.

Soften the gelatin in a measuring cup in the cold water and dissolve it by setting the cup in a pan of hot water.

Chop the eggs coarsely by turning the machine on and off about 8 times and add them to the parsley. Chop the scallions and parsnips by turning the machine on and off until they are minced; add them to the parsley and eggs.

Medium Slicing Disc: Slice the cucumber, using medium pressure; leave it in the work bowl.

Metal Blade Disc: Chop the cucumber by turning the machine on and off 3 to 5 times and add it to the egg mixture. Wipe out the work bowl with a paper towel.

With the machine running, mince the garlic by dropping it through the feed tube. Add the mayonnaise, mustard and seasonings and process the mixture for 2 seconds. Add the gelatin and process for 1 second, then combine with the egg mixture in the mixing bowl. Add salt and pepper to taste and spoon the mixture into an oiled 4-cup (95 cl) ring mold. Bang the mold on the counter to distribute the mixture evenly and refrigerate it, covered with plastic wrap, for at least 4 hours, or until it is firm.

Julienned Beets _____

3 large beets (11 ounces total, 310g), unpeeled
1 recipe Dijon Vinaigrette (see Index)
Salt
Freshly ground pepper

Cook the beets in a saucepan in boiling water to cover for 15 to 18 minutes, or until they are crisply cooked. Peel them and cut them into uniform widths to fit the feed tube.

Julienne Disc, French-Fry Disc or Medium Slicing Disc: Cut the beets into julienne strips, using medium pressure, or cut them with the French-Fry disc. If you don't have either disc, cut them into julienne strips using a double-slicing technique with the thin or medium slicing disc as follows. Slice the beets, using firm pressure, and remove the slices from the bowl. Stand the slices in the feed tube side by side, wedging them in tightly so they will hold. Slice them again, using medium pressure. Repeat the process with the remaining slices. Transfer the beets to a plastic bag, add 1/2 cup (12 cl) Dijon Vinaigrette, and shake the bag gently. Add salt and pepper to taste, tie the bag airtight and refrigerate it until serving time.

Mushroom and Watercress _

10 mushrooms (5 ounces total, 140g), trimmed and cut flat on sides
1/4 cup (6 cl) Dijon Vinaigrette (see Index)
1/4 teaspoon sugar
1/4 teaspoon mustard seed
Small bunch of watercress, stems trimmed

Medium Slicing Disc: Stack the mushrooms sideways in the feed tube, flat side down. Slice them, using light pressure, and transfer them to a plastic bag. Repeat the process with any remaining mushrooms. Tie the bag airtight and refrigerate it until serving time. Combine the Dijon Vinaigrette with the sugar and mustard seed; set it aside.

Assembly _____

Separate the egg salad from the mold with a flexible knife and invert it onto a 14-inch (36 cm) round platter lined with lettuce leaves. Surround the ring with the beets. Mix the mushrooms gently, first with the prepared Vinaigrette and then with the watercress. Place this mixture in the center of the ring. Sprinkle reserved parsley over all and serve the salad with thin slices of Cumin Light Rye Bread or Caraway Pumpernickel Bread (see Index for both).

Makes 6 to 8 servings.

Eggplant and Pepperoni Salad

Possibly closer to a relish than a salad, this is a combination sure to please eggplant lovers.

1 cup (24 cl) parsley leaves

2 eggplants (2 pounds total, 910g), unpeeled and cut into wedges to fit the feed tube

1 tablespoon salt

1 large garlic clove, peeled

1 large Spanish onion (7 ounces, 200g), peeled and quartered

1/4 cup (6 cl) oil

6 large celery ribs (10 ounces total, 285g), strings removed with a vegetable peeler and cut into 4-inch (10cm) lengths

1 red pepper (4 ounces, 115g), cored and cut into 2-inch (5 cm) squares

3-inch (7.5 cm) piece of pepperoni, skinned, soft enough to be pierced with the point of a knife

1/4 cup (6 cl) red wine vinegar

1 tablespoon lemon juice

1/2 teaspoon dried basil

1/2 cup (12 cl) Calamata olives or large ripe olives, drained
Red leaf lettuce, Boston lettuce or spinach, washed and crisped

Metal Blade: Mince the parsley by turning the machine on and off; reserve it.

French-Fry Disc or Medium Slicing Disc: Process the eggplant, using medium pressure. If you do not have a French-Fry disc, slice the eggplant into julienne strips using a double-slicing technique with the medium slicing disc as follows. Slice the eggplant, using medium pressure. Remove the slices and stand them in the feed tube side by side, wedging in as many as possible so they will hold. Slice the eggplant again, using medium pressure, to make julienne strips. Repeat the process with the remaining slices.

Put the eggplant strips in a colander and sprinkle with salt. Toss and let stand for 30 minutes. Drain the eggplant well and pat it dry with paper towels.

Metal Blade: With the machine running, mince the garlic finely by dropping it through the feed tube. Mince the onion by turning the machine on and off. Heat 2 tablespoons oil in a large skillet and sauté the garlic and onion for 4 minutes, or until it is heated through.

Medium Slicing Disc: Slice the celery, using medium pressure. Leave it in the work bowl.

Wedge the red pepper squares into the feed tube and slice them into matchsticks, using light pressure. Transfer the celery and pepper to a large bowl.

Put the pepperoni in the feed tube vertically and slice it, using firm pressure.

Add 2 tablespoons of oil to the skillet containing the garlic and onion. Stir in the eggplant, cover, and cook over medium-high heat for 5 to 8 minutes, or until the eggplant is just heated through. Shake the pan several times to prevent the eggplant from sticking. Combine all the ingredients except the lettuce or spinach and 2 tablespoons of parsley in a large bowl. Add salt and pepper to taste and refrigerate the salad, covered with plastic wrap, for several hours or overnight. Let the salad come to room temperature before serving. Transfer it to a bowl generously lined with the greens, and garnish it with the 2 tablespoons of reserved parsley.

Makes 8 servings.

When I was training at the celebrated Taillevent restaurant in Paris, a beet and leek combination was served to the kitchen staff for lunch. We were all favorably impressed. The artichokes make the salad more festive.

4 medium beets
(1 pound total, 455g),
unpeeled
1/2 cup (12 cl) parsley
leaves
1 large leek (5 ounces,
140g), green ends cut
off, split and washed
1 10-ounce (285g)
package frozen
artichoke hearts,
cooked and drained
Mustard Dill
Vinaigrette (see Index)
Watercress leaves or
leaf lettuce

In a 1-1/2-quart (142 cl) saucepan cook the beets in water to cover for 20 minutes, or until they are 3/4 cooked and still crisp. Drain, cool and peel them; cut them into sections that will fit the feed tube.

Metal Blade: Mince the parsley by turning the machine on and off; reserve it.

French-Fry Disc or Medium Slicing Disc: Process the beets, using medium pressure. If you do not have a French-fry disc, cut the beets into julienne strips using a double-slicing technique with the medium slicing disc, as follows. Slice the beets, using medium pressure. Remove the slices from the work bowl and stand them in the feed tube, side by side, wedging in as many as possible so they will fit tightly. Slice the beets again, using medium pressure, to produce julienne strips. Repeat the process with the remaining slices. Transfer the slices to a plastic bag.

Medium Slicing Disc: Put the leek in the feed tube vertically and slice it, using medium pressure. Transfer it to a separate plastic bag.

Put the artichoke hearts in a separate plastic bag. Add 3 tablespoons of Mustard Dill Vinaigrette to each of the bags. Add salt and pepper to taste, tie the bags airtight and refrigerate them. Arrange watercress or lettuce leaves on a platter or on individual salad plates. Combine the beets and leek and place the mixture in the center of the greens. Garnish the mixture with artichoke hearts and reserved parsley.

Makes 8 servings.

Variation

Substitute 2 zucchini (14 ounces total, 400g) for the artichoke. Process them with the French-fry disc or cut them into julienne strips using the double-slicing technique with the medium slicing disc. Let the zucchini marinate separately and mix it gently with the other ingredients at serving time.

Broccoli, Mushroom and Bean Sprout Salad

This salad makes a good first course for Chinese dinners. The ingredients can be processed in advance, but to preserve the vibrant green of the broccoli, they must be combined only an hour before serving.

1 large bunch broccoli, (2 pounds, 910g), stems peeled with a vegetable peeler
16 large firm mushrooms (1 pound total, 455g), trimmed and cut flat on sides
1 tablespoon lemon juice
2 cups (47 cl) fresh bean sprouts
3/4 cup (18 cl) Oriental Dressing (see Index)
Spinach or leaf lettuce
1/4 cup (6 cl) pine nuts

Cut the broccoli flowerets from the stems and cut the stems crosswise in lengths to fit the feed tube.

Medium Slicing Disc: Put the broccoli stems in the feed tube vertically, and slice them, using medium pressure; reserve them. Stack the mushrooms sideways in the feed tube, flat sides down. Slice them, using light pressure. Repeat the process with any remaining mushrooms and transfer all the mushrooms to a mixing bowl. Toss with the lemon juice and reserve them.

Cook the broccoli stems in a large saucepan for 1 minute in 6 quarts (570 cl) of boiling water to which you have added 2 teaspoons of salt. Transfer them to a colander with a slotted spoon and hold them under cold running water until they are completely cool. Cook the broccoli flowerets in the same water for 2 minutes and cool them in the same way. Marinate the broccoli, mushrooms and bean sprouts in Oriental Dressing for 1 hour, no more. Arrange the salad in a bowl lined with spinach or leaf lettuce and sprinkle with pine nuts.

Makes 8 servings.

Variation

Substitute Bacon Dressing or Hot Salad Dressing (see Index for dressings).

Celery Root and Tomato Salad

Claude Deligne, chef at the Taillevent restaurant in Paris, created this salad at the request of a client on a *régime*, or special diet. The mixture can be prepared quickly in a food processor; uncooked parsnips can be substituted for the celery root.

9 ounces (255g) curly
endive or chicory,
washed and stems
trimmed
1/2 cup (12 cl) parsley
leaves
1-1/2 teaspoons dried basil
7 small very firm, ripe
tomatoes (1-1/2 pounds
total, 680g), cored
1 pound (455g) celery
root, peeled and cut
into uniform pieces to
fit the feed tube
2 tablespoons lemon
juice
2/3 cup (16 cl) Basil
Vinaigrette (see Index)

Cut the greens into 1/2-inch (1.25 cm) lengths and put them in a shallow glass salad bowl, 10 to 12 inches (25 to 30 cm) in diameter.

Metal Blade: Put the parsley and basil in the work bowl and mince them by turning the machine on and off. Reserve the mixture.

Medium Slicing Disc: Slice the tomatoes, using light pressure. Arrange overlapping slices in a circle on the greens, leaving a 1-inch (2.5 cm) border.

Julienne Disc or Thin Slicing Disc: Process the celery root, using firm pressure. If you do not have a julienne disc, make julienne strips by using a double-slicing technique as follows. Slice the celery root, using firm pressure. Remove the slices from the bowl and reinsert them in the feed tube, side by side, wedging them in tightly so they will hold. Slice them again, using firm pressure, to produce julienne strips. Repeat the process with the remaining slices. Toss the celery root in a bowl with the lemon juice. Arrange the celery root in a circle outside the circle of tomatoes and sprinkle the tomatoes with the reserved parsley and basil. Serve the salad with Basil Vinaigrette.

Makes 8 servings.

Radish, Scallion and Swiss Cheese Salad

This salad is especially good with cold cuts.

1/2 cup (12 cl) parsley
leaves
4 cups radishes (1 pound
total, 455g), washed
and trimmed
1/2 pound (225g) Swiss
cheese, chilled
4 large scallions
(4 ounces total, 115g),
including the green
tops, cut into thirds
1/2 cup (12 cl) Basic
Vinaigrette (see Index)
1 teaspoon Dijon-style
mustard
Salt
Freshly ground pepper
Lettuce leaves

Metal Blade: Mince the parsley by turning the machine on and off; reserve it.

Shredding Disc: Shred the radishes, using firm pressure. Shred the cheese, using light pressure.

Medium Slicing Disc: Put the scallions in the feed tube vertically and slice them, using light pressure. Put the Basic Vinaigrette into a large bowl and stir the mustard into it. Combine the vegetables and cheese with the reserved parsley, and toss with the Vinaigrette. Add salt and pepper to taste and heap the salad on a platter lined with the lettuce leaves.

Makes 6 servings.

Eleven-Layer Salad

An impressive looking and delicious creation. It must be made well ahead of serving time, but the result is well worth the effort.

Layers

- 1/2 large head of iceberg lettuce (7 ounces, 200g), cored and cut into wedges to fit the feed tube
- 1 cup (24 cl) parsley leaves
- 4 large eggs, hard-boiled, chilled and peeled
  Salt
  Freshly ground pepper
- 1 large red pepper (6 ounces, 170g), halved vertically and seeded
- 4 medium carrots (6 ounces, 170g), peeled and cut into lengths to fit the feed tube horizontally
- 1 5-3/4-ounce (163g) can colossal pitted ripe olives, drained and cut flat at ends
- 3/4 pound (340g) green beans, trimmed and cut into uniform lengths to fit feed tube
- 1 teaspoon dried dillweed
  Freshly ground pepper
- 1 cup large radishes (4 ounces, 155g), washed and trimmed
- 4 ounces (115g) sharp Cheddar cheese, chilled

As you process each ingredient, layer it in a 2-1/2-quart (236 cl) glass bowl or soufflé dish, making sure that the edges of each layer are neat and visible. Keep the ingredients and the work bowl dry, patting the ingredients with a paper towel and wiping out the bowl with towels when necessary.

Medium Slicing Disc: Put the lettuce wedges in the feed tube vertically and slice them, using light pressure. Arrange the lettuce in a layer in the glass bowl.

Metal Blade: Mince the parsley by turning the machine on and off. Reserve 2 tablespoons of it and arrange the rest over the lettuce. Chop the eggs by turning the machine on and off about 8 times and season them with the 1/2 teaspoon salt and pepper to taste. Arrange them over the parsley.

Medium Slicing Disc: Put the red pepper in the feed tube vertically and slice it, using medium pressure. Arrange it over the eggs.

Julienne Disc or Shredding Disc: Put the carrots in the feed tube horizontally and process them, using firm pressure. Arrange them over the red pepper.

Medium Slicing Disc: Stack the olives in the feed tube, flat ends down, and slice them, using light pressure. Arrange them over the carrots.

Fit the green beans tightly into the feed tube and slice them, using medium pressure. Plunge the beans into a saucepan containing 2 quarts (190 cl) boiling water and 2 teaspoons salt. Blanch them for 30 seconds after the water returns to a boil. Drain them in a colander and hold them under cold running water until they are completely cool. Pat them dry with paper towels. Arrange the beans over the olives, and sprinkle with dillweed, 1 teaspoon of salt and pepper to taste.

Put the radishes in the feed tube and slice them, using firm pressure. Arrange them over the beans.

Shredding Disc: Put the cheese in the feed tube and shred it, using light pressure. Arrange it over the radishes.

1/2 pound (225g) bacon,
crisply cooked,
drained and broken
into pieces
2 small red onions
(3-1/2 ounces total,
110g), peeled

Metal Blade: Put the bacon in the work bowl, chop it by turning the machine on and off, and arrange it over the cheese.

Medium Slicing Disc: Stack the onions in the feed tube and slice them, using firm pressure. Separate them into rings and arrange them over the bacon so that the red edge is visible through the sides of the bowl.

Green Salad Dressing _____

2 cups (47 cl) Basic
Mayonnaise (see
Index)
1/2 cup (12 cl) parsley
leaves
1 teaspoon dried basil
1 teaspoon dried
dillweed
2 tablespoons sugar
1/2 cup (12 cl) sour cream

Metal Blade: Process all the dressing ingredients in the work bowl for 5 seconds. Spoon 1/2 the dressing over the salad, smoothing it with a spatula. Put the remainder in a serving dish. Sprinkle the salad with the reserved parsley and wipe any dressing from the edges of the bowl. Cover the salad with plastic wrap and refrigerate it for at least 6 hours, or up to 12 hours.

Do not toss the salad. Serve it with 2 long-handled spoons so each person can reach down to the bottom and sample each layer. Pass the remaining dressing separately.

Makes 8 servings.

Celery Root and Caper Salad _____

1 large celery root
(1 pound, 455g) peeled
and cut into wedges to
fit the feed tube
Salt
1/2 cup (12 cl) parsley
leaves
1/2 cup (12 cl) Basic
Mayonnaise (see
Index)
2 tablespoons capers,
drained
1 teaspoon Dijon-style
mustard
1 teaspoon lemon juice
Freshly ground white
pepper
Lettuce leaves

Julienne Disc or Medium Shredding Disc: Process the celery root, using firm but not hard pressure. Plunge it into a saucepan of boiling water with 1 tablespoon of salt, and blanch it for 30 seconds. Drain the celery root and refresh it in a bowl of ice water. Drain it well. Wrap the celery root in a kitchen towel, squeezing out as much moisture as possible.

Metal Blade: Mince the parsley by turning the machine on and off. Leave it in the work bowl. Add the mayonnaise, capers, mustard and lemon juice and process the mixture for 1 second. Transfer it to a large mixing bowl and fold in the celery root. Add salt and pepper to taste and heap the salad on a platter lined with lettuce leaves. Garnish it with the reserved parsley.

Makes 6 servings.

For an unusual and tasty picnic or light supper, serve this salad with several robust cheeses, a loaf of crusty Italian bread, sliced tomatoes with Basil Vinaigrette (see Index) and a bottle of Chianti.

2/3 cup (16 cl) parsley leaves
8 large scallions, including the green tops (4 ounces total, 115g), cut into 1-inch (2.5cm) pieces
1 7-ounce (198g) can Italian tuna fish, packed in oil, not drained
2 15-ounce (425g) cans small white beans, drained
6 tablespoons olive oil
5 tablespoons lemon juice
2 tablespoons red wine vinegar
Salt
Freshly ground pepper
1 lemon, cut in wedges
Lettuce leaves

Metal Blade: Mince the parsley by turning the machine on and off. Remove 2 tablespoons of it and set it aside for garnish. Chop the scallions with the parsley in the work bowl, turning the machine on and off. Add the tuna fish with its oil. Turn the machine on and off twice, just to break the tuna coarsely. Put the tuna mixture in a large mixing bowl.

Put the beans in a sieve, rinse them with cold water and drain them well. Add them to the tuna with all the remaining ingredients except the reserved parsley and the lemon wedges. Mix gently and adjust the seasoning. Refrigerate overnight and bring to room temperature before serving. Heap the salad on a platter lined with lettuce. Garnish it with the reserved parsley and lemon wedges.

Makes 6 to 8 servings.

Mushroom, Watercress and Red Pepper Salad

A pleasing combination of vivid colors.

24 to 30 large mushrooms (1 pound total, 455g), trimmed and cut flat on sides
2 tablespoons lemon juice
2 large red peppers (1 pound total, 455g), cut into 2-inch (5. cm) squares
3/4 pound (340g) Boston lettuce, washed and cored
1 small bunch watercress, (3 ounces total, 85g), stems trimmed
3/4 cup (18 cl) Creamy Parsley Dressing (see Index)

Medium Slicing Disc: Stack the mushrooms sideways in the feed tube, flat sides down. Slice them, using light pressure. Repeat until all the mushrooms are sliced, and toss them with the lemon juice in a large bowl.

Stand the peppers in the feed tube side by side, wedging in the last square tightly. Slice them into matchsticks, using light pressure.

Tear the lettuce into bite-size pieces and combine it with the mushrooms, peppers and watercress in a salad bowl. Toss the salad with Creamy Parsley Dressing and add salt and pepper to taste.

Makes 8 servings.

Note: Substitute Basic Vinaigrette for the Creamy Parsley Dressing when using this salad in the Antipasto Platter (see Index for both).

Variations

1. Let the sliced mushrooms marinate in the refrigerator for 4 hours in 1/4 cup (6 cl) of Herb Vinaigrette (see Index). Put the mixed greens in a salad bowl, heap the mushrooms in the center and garnish the salad with red pepper strips and a finely chopped hard-boiled egg. Toss the salad with 1/4 cup (6 cl) Herb Vinaigrette before serving.

2. Substitute Oriental Dressing or Bacon Dressing (see Index for both) for the Creamy Parsley Dressing.

Basic Vinaigrette Dressing _____

3/4 cup (18 cl) oil
1/4 cup (6 cl) red wine
   vinegar
1 teaspoon salt
Freshly ground pepper

Metal Blade: Process the ingredients by turning the machine on and off about 3 times.

Makes 1 cup (24 cl).

Variations _____

1. Dijon Vinaigrette: With the machine running, mince 1 small garlic clove by dropping it through the feed tube. Add 1 to 2 teaspoons of Dijon-style mustard and basic ingredients.

2. Mustard Dill Vinaigrette: Add 1 teaspoon of Dijon-style mustard, 2 teaspoons of dried dillweed and 1 additional teaspoon of salt to the basic ingredients.

3. Basil Vinaigrette: Process 1 shallot, 1-1/2 teaspoons of dried basil and 1/2 teaspoon of sugar until the shallot is minced. Add the remaining ingredients.

4. Italian Vinaigrette: Add 1/4 cup (6 cl) of minced parsley, 2 minced garlic cloves and 1 teaspoon of Bavarian-style mustard to the basic ingredients.

5. Herb Vinaigrette: Add 1/3 cup (8 cl) of minced parsley, 1 teaspoon each of dried chervil and dried basil, 1/2 teaspoon of dried oregano and 1 teaspoon of Dijon-style mustard to the basic ingredients.

6. Walnut Vinaigrette: Process 1/3 cup (8 cl) of walnuts for 3 seconds and add 1 teaspoon of Dijon-style mustard. Add the remaining ingredients and process briefly.

Ginger Vinaigrette _____

The ginger adds a piquant flavor to this dressing, making it a slightly unusual accompaniment for any green salad.

3/4 cup (18 cl) oil
   (preferably safflower
   with 1 tablespoon
   French olive oil)
1/4 cup (6 cl) red wine
   vinegar
1 teaspoon Dijon-style
   mustard
2 teaspoons liquid from
   Pickled Ginger Root
   (see Index)
1 teaspoon salt
Freshly ground pepper

Metal Blade: Process all the ingredients in the work bowl for 2 seconds and refrigerate the dressing in an airtight jar.

Makes about 1 cup (24 cl).

Tarragon Vinaigrette

Especially good on coleslaw.

1/2 cup (12 cl) oil
1 tablespoon lemon juice
5 tablespoons tarragon vinegar
2 teaspoons sugar
1 teaspoon salt
1 teaspoon dried thyme
1 teaspoon dried tarragon
1 teaspoon dried basil
1 teaspoon celery seed
2 teaspoons dried dillweed
Freshly ground pepper

Metal Blade: Process all the ingredients in the work bowl for 5 seconds.

Makes 3/4 cup (18 cl).

Green Peppercorn Mustard Vinaigrette

An enhancement for cold chicken, beef and tongue — either in salads or as cold cuts.

1/2 cup (12 cl) chicken broth
1 tablespoon green peppercorn mustard
1 teaspoon dried tarragon
1 teaspoon dried thyme
2 tablespoons red wine vinegar
2 teaspoons lemon juice
1/2 cup (12 cl) safflower oil
1/4 cup (6 cl) olive oil
Salt
Freshly ground pepper

In a small saucepan reduce the chicken broth over high heat to 3 tablespoons. Let it cool.

Metal Blade: Process the reduced broth in the work bowl with the remaining ingredients for 5 seconds. Correct the seasoning if necessary and refrigerate the dressing in an airtight jar.

Makes about 1 cup (24 cl).

Variation

Substitute clam juice or fish stock for the chicken broth to make a superb dressing for seafood salads.

Hot Salad Dressing

For cooked and chilled vegetables such as cauliflower, broccoli and carrots, as well as for spinach or other leafy salads, this dressing provides the perfect enhancement.

2/3 cup (16 cl) safflower oil
1 teaspoon sesame oil
3 tablespoons honey
1/4 cup (6 cl) ketchup
1/4 cup (6 cl) cider vinegar
1 teaspoon dry mustard
1 teaspoon celery seed
1 teaspoon celery salt
1/2 teaspoon salt

Metal Blade: Process all the ingredients in the work bowl for 2 seconds. Transfer the mixture to a small saucepan and heat until it is very warm. Pour the dressing over a green salad and serve the salad immediately.

Makes about 1-1/2 cups (35 cl).

Bacon Dressing

A flavorful dressing that enhances any green or mixed vegetable salad.

1/4 cup (16 cl) parsley leaves
1 small piece (1/2 ounce, 15g) onion, peeled
4 strips bacon, crisply cooked, drained and broken into pieces
3/4 cup (18 cl) oil, preferably safflower
1/4 cup (6 cl) cider vinegar
Pinch sugar
1-1/2 teaspoons salt
1/2 teaspoon Hungarian paprika
Freshly ground black pepper

Metal Blade: Put the parsley in the work bowl. Turn the machine on and mince the onion and bacon by dropping them through the feed tube with the machine running. Add the remaining ingredients and combine by turning the machine on and off about 4 times.

Makes 1-1/4 cups (30 cl).

Onion Dressing

A piquant taste for full-flavored, ripe tomatoes or a crisp mixed salad.

1 small piece of fresh ginger root, peeled
1 small onion (2 ounces, 55g), peeled and halved
1/2 cup (12 cl) parsley leaves
1 tablespoon sugar
1 teaspoon salt
2 teaspoons dry mustard
2 teaspoons Hungarian paprika
2 teaspoons Worcestershire sauce
6 tablespoons cider vinegar
3/4 cup (18 cl) oil

Metal Blade: With the machine running, mince the ginger root and onion by dropping them through the feed tube. Scrape down the sides of the bowl with a spatula. Add the remaining ingredients, except the oil, and process for 2 seconds. Add the oil and combine by turning the machine on and off 2 or 3 times.

Makes about 1-1/4 cups.

Creamy Parsley Dressing

This popular dressing is especially nice on salads that include mixed vegetables.

1/4 cup (6 cl) parsley leaves
1 small onion (1 ounce, 30g), peeled
3/4 cup (18 cl) oil (preferably safflower with 1 tablespoon French olive oil)
2 tablespoons red wine vinegar
1 teaspoon salt
1/2 teaspoon freshly ground pepper
2 tablespoons sour cream, yogurt or heavy cream

Metal Blade: Put the parsley in the work bowl, turn on the machine and drop the onion through the feed tube to mince it. Process the mixture for about 6 seconds, then add remaining ingredients and process for 3 seconds. Refrigerate the dressing in an airtight jar.

Makes about 1 cup (24 cl).

Oriental Salad Dressing

Fairly low in calories, but you'd never guess it from the taste.

1/3 cup (8 cl) cider vinegar
1/4 cup (6 cl) safflower oil
1/4 cup (6 cl) water
2 teaspoons granulated sugar
2 teaspoons light soy sauce
2 teaspoons dark soy sauce
1/2 teaspoon ground ginger
Freshly ground pepper

Metal Blade: Process all the ingredients in the work bowl for 3 seconds.

Makes 1 cup (24 cl).

Honey Dressing

A sweet dressing that's great on fruit salads.

2 tablespoons parsley leaves
1 small onion (1 ounce, 30g), peeled
1/2 teaspoon dry mustard
1/2 teaspoon Hungarian paprika
3/4 teaspoon salt
1/2 teaspoon celery seed
3 tablespoons honey
3 tablespoons cider vinegar
1 tablespoon lemon juice
1/3 cup (8 cl) oil

Metal Blade: Mince the parsley by turning the machine on and off. With the machine running, mince the onion by dropping it through the feed tube. Add the remaining ingredients and process for about 5 seconds.

Makes about 3/4 cup (18 cl).

Breakfast and Brunch

Breakfast & Brunch

Apricot Buttermilk Pancakes
Strawberry Cheese Crêpes
Omelet with Onion Filling
Baked Eggs with Cheese, Spinach,
  Red Pepper and Ham
Sausage Patties
Glazed Ham Loaf
Piquant, Glazed Corn Beef
Cottage Cheese and Apple Pancakes

The great thing about breakfast and brunch is that nobody has ever succeeded in pinning them down. A post-party interlude of pasta and poached fish? Sounds like a heavenly breakfast to me. An early-morning gathering around pancakes and sausage? Sounds downright sociable. A Sunday afternoon spread of chicken patties and crêpes? Nothing better for a long lazy day!

So the purpose of this chapter is not to prescribe menus for everyday nutrition or Sunday entertaining but merely to present some dishes that would fit the bill of fare either way. All of them could be served for a light, informal supper, and many of the appetizers and entrées found elsewhere in this book perform beautifully at a brunch.

From a teaching standpoint, however, there are some very important lessons in this chapter: pancakes and crêpes, omelets and sausage. All are staples that you should be able to whip up in the food processor without giving a second thought to commercial products or fear of failure.

Since I sorely need a cup of coffee or two before I can bear to "rise and shine", you can be assured that the Apricot Buttermilk Pancakes and Cottage Cheese and Apple Pancakes are as quickly prepared as any mix. They're both great favorites in my household, and they're much better and cheaper than the absurdly priced "gourmet" pancake mixes on the market.

Baked Eggs with Cheese, Spinach,
Red Pepper and Ham, page 164.

As much as I love the sizzle and fabulous aroma of sausage patties in the morning, I wouldn't serve them at all if I had to depend on commercial pork mixtures: they are just too fatty and full of chemicals. The pleasure of sausage only re-entered my kitchen with the food processor, which makes meat-grinding effortless. Prepare the sausage rolls anytime and refrigerate, or pre-slice and freeze them for everyday use. You can vary the seasonings in the Sausage Patties recipe to taste, but I think you'll find that the basic proportion of lean pork to fat provides just the right juiciness.

Brunch time entertaining can literally save the day for busy people: a brunch can be whatever and whenever you want it to be. You can make all the preparations the night before or early in the morning. You can relax and socialize without worrying about dinner-service details. And it doesn't take much to make a brunch festive. The fragrance of home baked bread will set the tone; so will a pitcher of vodka-spiked Gazpacho Bloody Mary, for that matter.

For a truly sybaritic weekender, pop open a bottle of champagne and bring on some spectacular fare. The baked Eggs with Cheese, Spinach, Red Pepper and Ham is sensational! Baked like a cake, in a springform pan, it slices to reveal the spectrum of its six tempting layers. It is the brunch equivalent of a one-pot entrée and can be assembled up to a day in advance. Strawberry Cheese Crêpes is another dish that never fails to impress with its delicate ingenuity; yet either the crêpes alone or the whole recipe can be frozen for baking when guests arrive. Omelets with either Onion or Artichoke and Cheese Filling are another sure winner. They do require last-minute cooking, but you can hedge your timing by making the filling and an accompanying platter of Piquant Glazed Corned Beef well in advance.

Look to the Yeast Bread and Quick Bread chapters for the indispensable highlights of any brunch. Among the Desserts, you'll find a gorgeous centerpiece in the Fruit Lovers' Platter, as well as refreshing Zested Strawberries, Berries Supreme and Oranges Orientale. But don't stop there! Savor the simple luxury of an Onion Tart, Smoked Salmon Pâté or Oysters Midas. Substitute Chicken Patties Augusta for sausage or ham. Or vary the crêpe concept with Fresh Spinach Cannelloni. The Index guides you to these recipes in other chapters.

Personally, I could sit down to Fettuccine Alfredo or Poached Whole Fish with Caper Sauce at noon or midnight with equal pleasure. I think these dishes, and many others, well satisfy the single brunchtime requirement: keep it light, amusing and slightly unpredictable!

Apricot Buttermilk Pancakes

1 cup unbleached
  all-purpose flour
  (5 ounces, 140g)
1 teaspoon baking soda
2 tablespoons sugar
1/2 teaspoon double-
  acting baking powder
1/2 teaspoon salt
7 dried apricots (1 ounce
  total, 30g)
1/4 cup walnut pieces
  (1 ounce, 30g)
2 large eggs
2 cups (47 cl) buttermilk
1/4 cup (6 cl) oil
3 tablespoons unsalted
  butter for the skillet or
  griddle

Variation _____

Metal Blade: Place the dry ingredients in the work bowl with the apricots and nuts. Combine them by turning the machine on and off a couple of times, then process for 2 seconds, or until the apricots and nuts are finely minced.

Add the eggs, buttermilk and oil and process the mixture for 20 seconds, stopping the machine once to scrape down the sides of the bowl.

Spoon the batter onto a hot, buttered skillet or griddle to form pancakes about 2-1/2 inches (6.5 cm) in diameter. Turn the pancakes when they are golden on one side and brown them on the other side. Make additional pancakes with the remaining batter, adding more butter to the skillet or griddle as needed. Serve with Fresh Strawberry Sauce (see Index).

Makes about 48 2-1/2 inch (6.5 cm) pancakes, enough for 4 to 6 servings.

Omit the apricots and nuts for plain Buttermilk Pancakes.

Apricot Buttermilk Pancakes, with Sausage Patties (see page 163)

Sweet Crêpes

- 1 cup unbleached all-purpose flour (5 ounces, 140g)
- 2 tablespoons sugar
  Pinch of salt
- 2 large eggs
- 1 tablespoon oil
- 1 teaspoon vanilla extract
- 1/4 cup (6 cl) water
- 1/2 cup (12 cl) plus 3 tablespoons milk
  Butter

Metal Blade: In the work bowl blend the flour, sugar, salt, eggs and oil by turning the machine on and off about 4 times. With the machine running, add the liquids gradually through the feed tube. Process the batter until it is smooth and let it rest for 30 minutes, or overnight. It should be the consistency of heavy cream; if it is thicker, add liquid.

Heat 1 teaspoon butter until it is hot in a 6- to 7-inch (15 to 18 cm) crêpe pan. Add just enough batter to coat the bottom of the pan and brown the crêpe on both sides. Make additional crêpes in the same manner with the remaining batter, stacking them as they are cooked.

Filling

- 2 8-ounce (225g) packages farmer cheese or 16 ounces (455g) cottage cheese, drained
- 2 large eggs
- 2 teaspoons vanilla extract
- 1/2 teaspoon salt
- 1/4 cup (6 cl) sugar
- 1-1/2 cups (35 cl) whole fresh strawberries, hulled
- 2 tablespoons sugar

Metal Blade: Put the cheese, eggs, vanilla, salt and sugar in the work bowl and combine them by turning the machine on and off. Transfer the mixture to another bowl.

Medium Slicing Disc: Slice the strawberries, using light pressure. Toss them in a bowl with 2 tablespoons of sugar.

Berry Sauce

- 1 10-ounce (285g) package frozen raspberries, thawed
- 1-1/2 cups (35 cl) whole fresh strawberries
- 2 tablespoons sugar
- 2 tablespoons Grand Marnier (optional)

Metal Blade: Process the raspberries for 10 seconds. To remove the seeds, force them through a sieve into a bowl. Transfer the purée to the work bowl and add the remaining ingredients.

Process the sauce for 30 seconds, transfer it to a serving dish, and refrigerate it.

Vanilla Sour Cream

1 cup (24 cl) sour cream
3 tablespoons
  confectioners sugar
1-1/2 teaspoons vanilla
  extract

Assembly

Metal Blade: Process the sour cream, sugar and vanilla in the work bowl by turning the machine on and off about 8 times or until the mixture is thoroughly combined. Transfer the cream to a serving dish.

Preheat the oven to 375°F. (190°C.) and adjust the rack to the middle level.

Spoon 2 tablespoons of the cheese mixture onto a crêpe, spread 1 teaspoon of sliced strawberries over it, and roll up the crêpe. Fill and roll the remaining crêpes in the same manner. Arrange the crêpes seam side down in a buttered oval ovenproof dish and bake them for 25 minutes. Serve the Berry Sauce and Vanilla Sour Cream separately, spooning them over the crêpes.

Makes 20 crêpes.

Note: Unfilled crêpes can be made in advance and refrigerated or frozen. Stack them with parchment paper between and wrap them airtight, until you are ready to bake and serve them. If they are frozen, they should be thawed in the refrigerator overnight before being baked.

Omelet with Onion Filling

This delicious omelet is typical of those that are popular in the area around Lyon in France.

Onion Filling

1/4 cup (6 cl) parsley leaves
1 large Spanish onion (1/2 pound, 225g), peeled and quartered
2 tablespoons unsalted butter
1/2 teaspoon salt
Freshly ground pepper

Metal Blade: Mince the parsley by turning the machine on and off, and reserve it.

Medium Slicing Disc: Slice the onion, using medium pressure.

Melt the butter in a large skillet over medium low heat and cook the onion for about 30 minutes, or until it is soft but not browned. Season with salt and pepper.

Makes enough filling for 3 omelets.

Omelet

2 large eggs
1 tablespoon water
1/2 teaspoon salt
Freshly ground white pepper
3 tablespoons unsalted butter
1 to 2 teaspoons red wine vinegar

Metal Blade: Break the eggs into the work bowl containing the water, salt and pepper and process for 4 seconds.

Melt 2 tablespoons of the butter over high heat in a heavy 9- or 10-inch (23 or 25 cm) omelet pan. When it is bubbling but not brown, pour in the egg mixture. Immediately start to tilt the pan with your left hand while using your right hand to stir the egg mixture with the flat side of a fork. Do not scrape the bottom of the pan; just keep the eggs in motion.

When the bottom is set and the top still almost liquid, add the filling, which should be warm. Use 1/3 of the filling for one omelet. Place the filling on the half of the omelet nearest the handle of the pan. Insert a spatula under the filled part of the omelet and fold it towards the center. Tip the pan, holding the handle up and roll the omelet onto a heated serving plate.

Heat the remaining tablespoon of butter in the omelet pan until it is sizzling. Add the vinegar and drizzle it over the omelet. Sprinkle with parsley.

Variation

For Artichoke and Cheese Filling, partially thaw a 10-ounce (285g) package of frozen artichoke hearts and slice them in the food processor, using firm pressure. Sauté them in 2 tablespoons of unsalted butter for 10 minutes over medium heat. Remove from the heat and stir in: 1/4 cup (6 cl) of minced parsley leaves, 1-1/2 ounces (42g) of minced scallions and 4 ounces (115g) of shredded Monterey Jack cheese. Mix the ingredients well. Makes enough for 3 omelets.

Freshly made sausage seasoned with your own choice of herbs and spices is a breeze with a food processor. This recipe produces well flavored sausage, without chemicals.

2/3 cup (16 cl) parsley
    leaves
  1 small onion (1 ounce,
    30g), peeled
  2 pounds (910g) lean
    pork shoulder, cut into
    1-inch (2.5 cm) squares
12 ounces (340g) pork fat,
    cut into 1-inch (2.5 cm)
    squares
  2 teaspoons salt
1/4 teaspoon ground
    cloves
1/4 teaspoon freshly
    grated nutmeg
1/4 teaspoon cinnamon
1/4 teaspoon dried
    oregano
1/4 teaspoon dried basil
1/2 teaspoon freshly
    ground pepper
  2 tablespoons water
1/2 teaspoon liquid smoke
1/4 to 1/2 cup unbleached
    all-purpose flour
    (1-1/4 to 2-1/2 ounces,
    35 to 70g)

Metal Blade: Mince the parsley and onion by turning the machine on and off; reserve them. Mix the pork and fat in a bowl and divide the mixture into 3 batches. Put 1 batch in the work bowl and chop it by turning the machine on and off until it reaches the desired texture. Transfer it to a large bowl and repeat the process with the 2 remaining batches. Mix the seasonings, water and liquid smoke and use your hands to blend the mixture gently but thoroughly into the chopped meat along with the reserved parsley and onion.

Divide the mixture in 2 and form each half into an 8- by 4-inch (20 x 10 cm) log. Refrigerate the logs overnight, wrapped in foil. Cut each log into 8 slices and lightly flour each slice. Put the sausage into a cold skillet and cook it over moderately high heat, turning it once, for about 20 minutes or until the patties are cooked through.

Makes 16 patties.

Baked Eggs with Cheese, Spinach, Red Pepper and Ham

I first saw this layered creation as a carry-out Sunday lunch in a Lenôtre Charcuterie in Paris. It was really stunning, encased in a puff pastry crust. My version is made without the crust. The layers stay intact, so it works that way. One of my personal favorites, it is certainly a testimonial to the performance of a food processor. Although not a quick dish, it's all done in one work bowl and can be set up in advance.

Red Pepper

2 medium red peppers
(8 ounces total, 225g),
split in half vertically
1 tablespoon butter

Medium Slicing Disc: Slice the peppers, using medium pressure, and sauté them in 1 tablespoon of butter over moderate heat for 5 minutes, or until the liquid has completely evaporated.

Ham

2 large egg whites
1 tablespoon Dijon-style
mustard
1 pound (455g) lean
ham, cut into 1-inch
(2.5 cm) cubes

Metal Blade: Combine the egg whites and mustard by turning the machine on and off about 4 times. Add the pieces of ham and chop it by turning the machine on and off. The mixture should resemble coarsely chopped hamburger; set it aside. Wipe out the work bowl with a paper towel.

Spinach

2 pounds (910g) spinach,
including the stems,
trimmed, washed and
drained
3 large shallots
(3 ounces total, 85g),
peeled
2 large egg whites
3 tablespoons unsalted
butter, softened
3/4 teaspoon salt
Freshly ground pepper
Freshly ground nutmeg

Put the spinach in 2 large saucepans with just the water clinging to its leaves and cook it over high heat, turning it once or twice with a wooden spoon, until it wilts. Plunge it into cold water immediately to stop the cooking process. Drain it and wring it out in towels until it is completely dry. Mince the shallots by dropping them through the feed tube with the machine running. Add the spinach, egg whites, butter and seasonings, and process the mixture, stopping the machine once to scrape down the bowl. Set it aside.

Eggs and Cheese ─────────

- 1/2 pound (225g) Swiss cheese, chilled
- 3 slices firm white bread (3 ounces total, 85g), crusts trimmed, torn into pieces
- 3 large scallions (3 ounces total, 85g), including the green tops, cut into 1-inch (2.5 cm) pieces
- 1/2 cup (12 cl) parsley leaves
- 1 cup (24 cl) milk
- 3/4 cup (18 cl) water
- 12 large eggs
- 1-1/2 teaspoons salt Freshly ground pepper
- 1/2 stick unsalted butter (2 ounces, 55g)

Assembly ─────────

Variation ─────────

Shredding Disc: Shred the cheese, using light pressure, and set it aside.

Metal Blade: Process the bread, scallions and parsley for 5 seconds. Place the mixture in a bowl, add the milk and water, and let it soak for 5 minutes. Drain the bread crumbs and herbs and reserve the liquid. Put the eggs in the work bowl with half of the reserved liquid and seasonings and process for 10 seconds. Combine this mixture with the remaining liquid in a large mixing bowl.

Melt the butter in a large skillet and scramble the egg mixture until very soft, but not runny. Stir gently and continually to prevent large, hard lumps from forming. Remove the eggs from the heat and add the soaked bread crumbs and 3/4 of the shredded cheese. Mix thoroughly.

Butter an 8-inch (20 cm) springform pan. To facilitate transfer of the completed dish, line the bottom of the pan with a piece of buttered foil extending 1-inch (2.5 cm) up the sides.

Preheat the oven to 400°F. (205°C.) and adjust the rack to the middle level.

As each layer is placed in the springform pan, smooth it firmly with a spatula.

Place 1/2 of the egg mixture in the pan. Cover it with 1/2 of the spinach mixture, followed by all of the ham. Arrange red pepper slices evenly over the ham. For a beautiful presentation, make sure that the curves of the slices are placed around the outer edge of the pan. Follow the pepper layer with the remaining spinach and then the remaining eggs. Sprinkle the reserved cheese on top.

(This dish can be prepared a day in advance to this point and refrigerated. It should be brought to room temperature before baking.)

Bake in preheated oven for 30 minutes. Let the dish rest for 10 minutes before unmolding. Drain off any excess moisture, and cut in wedges to serve.

Makes 8 to 10 servings.

Pimientos, drained and dried, can be substituted for red peppers. Place a cake rack on a cookie sheet; arrange drained pimientos in a single layer on the cake rack. Place them in a 250°F. (120°C.) oven for 20 minutes to dry out.

Glazed Ham Loaf

This somewhat sweet ham loaf is as good for breakfast as it is for a light lunch or supper.

Preheat the oven to 450°F. (230°C.) and adjust the rack to the middle level.

Glaze

Mix all the glaze ingredients together.

1-1/4 cups dark brown sugar
(9 ounces, 255g),
lightly packed
2 teaspoons dry mustard
1/4 cup (6 cl) tarragon
vinegar
2 tablespoons Madeira
wine

Ham Loaf

1 cup (24 cl) parsley
leaves
4 small shallots
(2 ounces total, 55g),
peeled
1/2 pound (225g) lean
pork, cut into 1-inch
(2.5 cm) cubes
2 pounds (910g) cooked
lean ham, cut into
1-inch (2.5 cm) cubes
2/3 cup (16 cl) milk
1 large egg
1/2 teaspoon freshly
grated nutmeg
1 teaspoon dried thyme
2 tablespoons glaze
Freshly ground pepper

Metal Blade: Put the parsley in the work bowl and mince it by turning the machine on and off. Leave it in the work bowl. Mince the shallots by dropping them through the feed tube with the machine running. Add the pork, chop it finely by turning the machine on and off, and reserve the mixture. Coarsely chop the ham in 2 batches by turning the machine on and off. Put all the remaining ingredients and the pork mixture into the work bowl with the ham. Combine the mixture until it is well blended by turning the machine on and off.

Form the mixture into an oval loaf with your hands and brush it generously with the glaze. Bake in a 13- by 9-inch (33 x 23 cm) pan for 20 minutes. Reduce the heat to 300°F. (150°C.) and bake the loaf for 45 minutes, basting it several times with the glaze. Drain off the juices and brush the loaf generously with the remaining glaze. Serve it hot or cold. The loaf can be sliced very thin when it is chilled.

Makes 8 to 10 servings.

Piquant, Glazed Corn Beef

A superb brunch meat that goes well with any style of eggs.

Corned Beef

3-1/2 pounds (1.6 kg) corned beef
1 onion (4 ounces, 115g), peeled and quartered
1 large garlic clove, peeled
1 celery rib (1 ounce, 30g), with the leaves
1 bay leaf

In a large saucepan simmer the corned beef with the onion, garlic, celery and bay leaf, in enough water to cover, for 1 hour per pound of meat. To ensure firm slices from the food processor, you want the meat to be slightly undercooked. Remove the meat from the cooking liquid. Remove all the fat from the meat and cut the meat into the largest pieces that will fit the feed tube, with the grain running parallel to the tube so the meat will be sliced against the grain. Refrigerate the meat until it is well chilled or put it in the freezer until it is firm, but not frozen solid.

Preheat the oven to 350°F. (175°C.) and adjust the rack to the middle level.

Medium Slicing Disc: Slice the meat, using medium pressure, and arrange the slices in a 12-inch (30 cm) gratin dish.

Sauce

1/2 cup dark brown sugar (3-1/2 ounces, 100g), firmly packed
3 strips of orange zest, removed with a zester
3 tablespoons orange juice
1 teaspoon Dijon-style mustard
1 teaspoon white horseradish
2 teaspoons red wine vinegar
1 teaspoon dark soy sauce

Metal Blade: Process the brown sugar and orange zest until the zest is well minced. Combine the mixture with the remaining ingredients in a small saucepan. Bring the mixture to a boil and pour half over the meat. Cover the meat and bake it for 30 minutes, basting it occasionally with the remaining sauce. Remove the cover and bake for 15 minutes longer, or until the meat is tender and browned. Serve the dish with scrambled eggs, Omelets, or Onion Tart (see Index) for brunch or late supper.

Makes 6 to 8 servings.

This dish can be made in advance and reheated.

Cottage Cheese and Apple Pancakes

These are not from my classroom, but are high on my family's list of favorite breakfast treats. They can be made even more nutritious by the addition of 2 tablespoons of wheat germ.

1 large tart apple (7 ounces, 200g), peeled, cored and quartered
1-1/2 cups (35 cl) cottage cheese or skim-milk ricotta cheese
6 large eggs
1 tablespoon sugar (optional)
1/2 teaspoon cinnamon
1/4 teaspoon freshly grated nutmeg
1/2 cup (2-1/2 ounces, 70g) unbleached all-purpose flour
1/8 teaspoon salt
3 tablespoons unsalted butter, for the skillet or griddle

Shredding Disc: Shred the apple, using medium pressure. It should yield about 1-1/2 cups (35 cl) of shredded apple. Leave it in the work bowl.

Metal Blade: Add all the remaining ingredients except the butter to the work bowl and process for 30 seconds, stopping the machine once to scrape down the sides of the bowl. Do not overprocess.

Spoon the batter onto a hot, buttered skillet or griddle to form pancakes about 2-1/2 inches (6.5 cm) in diameter. Cook until golden on one side, turn and brown the other side. Make additional pancakes with the remaining batter, adding more butter to the skillet or griddle as needed. Serve with Fresh Strawberry Sauce (see Index).

Makes about 40 2-1/2-inch (6.5 cm) pancakes.

Variation

Omit the apple and nutmeg for plain Cottage Cheese Pancakes.

Yeast Breads

Yeast Breads

Caramel Nut Rolls
Yeast Ring with Streusel Topping
Currant Meringue Coffee Cake
Basic French Bread
Garlic Cheese Bread
Beer Bread
Caraway Pumpernickel Bread
Wheat Germ Bread with Spinach Filling
Cumin Light Rye Bread
Buttermilk Bread
Whole Wheat Bread
Whole Wheat Pita Bread
Mushroom, Green Pepper and Pepperoni Pizza
Middle Eastern Pizza

Over and over again, I hear my students talk about how they wish they had time to bake their own bread. My response is always the same: you can do it! Because you can mix and knead yeast dough effortlessly in the food processor, making bread no longer takes hours.

The first thing I ever made in the food processor was a pizza. It was the best homemade pizza I had ever tasted—and it took no more than 10 minutes to assemble. If you have anxieties about working with yeast dough, I suggest you start the same way. It is virtually impossible to make a mistake with pizza, and the quick exercise will provide a delicious meal as well as introducing the "feel" of a properly mixed, kneaded and risen dough.

It is logical to go from pizza to French bread, since the major difference is that the loaves require shaping and a second rising. But you can proceed just as readily to sweet yeast breads like Yeast Ring with Streusel Topping, Currant Meringue Coffee Cake or Caramel Nut Rolls. The batter for these only becomes firm enough to handle after it has been refrigerated for hours. So plan ahead; these coffee cakes are definitely worth it!

To learn the secrets of the best French bread, I went to a great Parisian *boulangerie* at 8 rue du Cherche Midi. There, the celebrated Lionel Poilâne let me work in his kitchen, with its 12th-century ovens; he also mixed and kneaded pounds of bread dough in the food processor. Poilâne is a wonderful teacher. He helped me develop the techniques I describe in this chapter for crusty yet soft-textured bread.

Here are bread-making basics and techniques:

Equipment. My recipes were developed for a standard machine with a 6-1/2-inch diameter bowl: 3 cups of flour and 1 cup of liquid (about 1-1/2 pounds of dough) or 3-3/4 cups of flour and 1-1/2 cups of liquid (about 1-3/4 pounds of dough). The special plastic dough kneading blades now available increase the capacity of your standard-size machine. If you have a larger capacity machine, with a 7-inch work bowl, you can process up to 6 cups of flour and 2-1/2 cups of liquid (about 3 pounds of dough) at a time.

Kneading bread dough tests the power of any food processor. Some motors can't handle whole batches at one time; if your machine begins to slow down, divide the dough in half, process the two parts separately and combine them by hand. Since kneading only takes 40 seconds at most, this shouldn't discourage you.

In addition to the food processor, you need a scale or dry measuring cups (measuring cups with handles but no pouring spout or lip), liquid measuring cups, measuring spoons, a large ceramic or glass bowl, a heavy rolling pin, a wire rack and a dry work surface. For flawless glazes, you need a feather brush. I strongly recommend unglazed quarry tiles; about six provide an adequate oven surface for bread pans. I prefer black steel pans, but other heavy pans can also be used. As with any baking, an oven thermometer is essential, given the enormous differences among thermostats.

Flour. Next to the food processor, the best thing that happened to bread in recent years was the appearance of high-gluten bread flour in supermarkets across the country. I use it in combination with other flours for ideal texture.

It is very important that you measure all flour accurately, either with a scale or with dry measuring cups. Weighing flour not only ensures accuracy but allows you to substitute an equal weight of one type of flour for another. You could substitute whole wheat flour in either of the pizza recipes, for example. To make it easier to transfer the flour from the scale to the work bowl, line the tray of the scale with a plastic bag and make sure the scale is set at zero before adding the flour. If you don't have a scale, use dry measuring cups and the "dip and sweep" method. Stir the flour lightly and dip the measuring cup into it. Then level off the top with a straight edge of a knife or a metal spatula.

All flour is slightly fickle. You can't predict exactly how much liquid it will absorb. That's why many recipes call for you to withhold some of the flour until checking the consistency of the dough to see if more flour is needed.

Yeast. Yeast has to be activated before it can "raise" the dough. It becomes active in warm (105-115°F) liquid; hot liquid will kill it. I recommend using an instant-reading thermometer; if you test with your finger, the liquid should feel warm but not hot. Stir yeast into warm water with sugar; within about 10 minutes, the mixture should foam, indicating that the yeast is active. This step, called "proofing the yeast" ensures that the yeast is alive and will work properly.

Mixing. To avoid leakage through the center shaft of the work bowl, pour yeast through the feed tube while the machine is running. Most bread dough, as it masses together, should have a sticky, but not wet, consistency. If your dough is too wet, add more flour, one tablespoon at a time, and process two seconds after each addition. Don't add so much flour that your dough becomes hard and dense.

Kneading. For conventional loaves, the dough is kneaded by 40 seconds of processing. It becomes a smooth, elastic and sticky mass that leaves the sides of the work bowl. No hand kneading is required.

Some of my breads are mixed and kneaded in one continuous process. The proportion of flour to liquid in these recipes is exact; no flour is reserved. This dough does not knead into a smooth ball. It is an elastic, spongy, wet dough that would be difficult, if not impossible, to knead by hand. This method produces superb sweet yeast breads and Beer Bread.

Rising. For the first rising, place the kneaded dough in a large, oiled, ceramic or glass bowl. Do not use a metal bowl; it will conduct heat too quickly. Rotate the dough until it is coated with oil. Cover the bowl with a damp towel. Since the dough needs a constant warm environment for uniform rising, I recommend placing it in the oven. Set the oven to the lowest temperature for two minutes, then turn it off before you place the dough inside. (A gas oven with a pilot light might not require preheating.) Cushion the bottom of the bowl with a pot holder or towel to insulate it from the oven rack. The dough will rise and double in an hour unless you are using grain flours, which will take about 1-1/2 hours. The second rising requires the same environment but takes place after the dough has been shaped.

Shaping. The shaping of various loaves is detailed in the recipes. You don't have to treat dough gently while shaping it. If it is sticky, toss it on a lightly floured board and work in just enough flour to make it easy to handle and roll. To shape it into a loaf, roll out the dough on the lightly floured board to a rectangle two inches shorter than the bread pan. Starting at any edge, tightly roll up the rectangle, pinch the ends and seam to seal them. Place the loaf seam-side down in a prepared bread pan.

Bread Pans. You can shape the dough to fit any bread pan, including *pain de mie* pans. You can also bake free-form loaves or rolls on baking sheets. (Rolls should be baked at 375°F for about 10 minutes less than a standard loaf.)

I prepare bread pans by greasing them with vegetable-oil spray, oil or butter, and sprinkling them with cornmeal to produce crisp bottoms and sides. The only exception is *pain de mie* pans, which should not be sprinkled with cornmeal.

Slashing. After the dough has risen the second time, the surface can be slashed in any pattern you wish. Use the metal blade of the food processor as a razor. Grasp the plastic part carefully, holding the metal blade at an angle.

Glazing. Breads can be baked without a glaze and will brown without any sheen. A country loaf can be baked with a floured surface. But if you prefer a glazed loaf, lightly brush off any excess flour from the surface with a soft hair bristle brush. Dip a feather brush into the glaze and apply it lightly to the surface of the bread, being careful not to let any excess glaze drip onto the pan. If you want to sprinkle a loaf with seeds or grains, glaze the surface to hold them in place.

Glaze recipe: 1 large egg and 1/2 teaspoon salt processed for 5 seconds works well for all breads that require a glaze. The mixture can be covered and refrigerated for about 12 days.

Baking. Place unglazed quarry tiles on the oven rack to provide a large enough surface for the bread pans. Fifteen minutes before baking, preheat the oven to the temperature specified in the recipe. Place the bread pans on the quarry tiles and bake for the amount of time specified. Remove the bread from the pan and rap the bottom with your knuckles. If it sounds hollow, it's done. For a crisper crust, turn off the oven and place the loaf, without the pan, directly on the tiles for an additional five minutes. Cool the loaves on wire racks.

Storage. Breads should be cooled completely on wire racks before storing. You can store loaves in airtight plastic bags at room temperature. Or you can freeze them on a cookie sheet and tightly double-wrap them, once they are frozen, for longer storage. I prefer to wrap the bread in foil and reheat it while it's still frozen; to do so, I place the bread in a cold oven and heat it at the same temperature at which it was baked.

This lesson may seem awfully long, but you only have to study it once. All procedures are detailed in the recipes and will become automatic after you bake a loaf or two. So let's get on with the reasons for all this talk—14 fabulous breads!

Caramel Nut Rolls

These rolls are unsurpassed in taste and texture, and they can be frozen successfully.

Sour Cream Dough

- 1 package active dry yeast
- 1 teaspoon sugar
- 1 cup (24 cl) sour cream, warmed to 105°F. to 115°F.
- 2 cups unbleached all-purpose flour (10 ounces, 285g)
- 1/2 teaspoon salt
- 1 stick unsalted butter (4 ounces, 115g), chilled and cut into 6 pieces
- 1 tablespoon sugar
- 3 large egg yolks

Mix the yeast, 1 teaspoon sugar and the sour cream and let the mixture stand for 10 minutes, or until it is foamy.

Metal Blade: Put the flour, salt, butter and sugar in the work bowl and blend them by turning the machine on and off about 4 times. Add the egg yolks and the yeast mixture, and blend, turning the machine on and off until the dough is just combined. Transfer the dough to a bowl and refrigerate it, covered with plastic wrap, for several hours, or until it is firm.

Topping

- 3/4 cup firmly packed light brown sugar (5-1/4 ounces, 148g)
- 3 tablespoons hot water
- 1/2 stick unsalted butter (2 ounces, 55g)
- 36 pecan halves

Bring the brown sugar and water to a boil in a saucepan. Add the butter and stir until the butter is melted. Spoon 1 teaspoon of the syrup into each of 36 very small muffin cups (each about 1-7/8-inch (4.5 cm) in diameter) and put 1 pecan half, rounded side down, in each cup.

Filling

- 1 cup walnuts or pecans (4 ounces, 115g)
- 1/2 cup (12 cl) firmly packed dark brown sugar (3-1/2 ounces)
- 1 teaspoon cinnamon
- 1/2 cup (12 cl) golden raisins (2 ounces, 55g)

Metal Blade: Chop the walnuts or pecans by turning the machine on and off. Mix them in a bowl with the brown sugar, cinnamon and raisins.

Assembly

- 1/2 stick unsalted butter (2 ounces, 55g), melted

Divide the dough into fourths, keeping the unworked dough in the refrigerator until ready to use it. Roll each part into a 9 by 3-inch (23 by 7.5 cm) rectangle on a well floured board. Brush each rectangle with 1 tablespoon of the butter and sprinkle it with 1/4 the filling mixture. Lightly press the mixture into the dough with a rolling pin.

Starting with a long side, roll up each rectangle jelly-roll fashion, pressing it gently while rolling and pinching the seam and the ends closed. Cut each roll into 9 slices, each about 3/4 inch (2 cm) thick. Put one slice in each muffin cup and brush the tops with the remaining melted butter. Cover the cups loosely with a damp towel and set them in an oven that has been preheated to its lowest temperature setting for 2 minutes and then turned off. Let the rolls rise for about 45 minutes, or until they have doubled in size. Remove them from the oven.

Adjust the oven rack to the upper part of the oven and preheat the oven to 375°F. (190°C.).

Put the muffin cups on a baking sheet and bake the rolls for 25 minutes. Invert the cups immediately onto the cookie sheet.

Makes 36 small rolls.

Note: The rolls can be frozen on a foil-lined baking sheet, wrapped airtight in double plastic bags, and stored in the freezer. Before serving, put the frozen rolls on a baking sheet and put them in a cold oven. Set the oven at 325°F. (160°C.) and bake the rolls for 15 minutes or until heated through.

Yeast Ring with Streusel Topping

This delicious bread is popular for breakfast.

Streusel

1/2 **stick unsalted butter
  (2 ounces, 55g), chilled
  and quartered**
1/2 **cup sugar
  (3-1/2 ounces, 100g)**
1/3 **cup unbleached
  all-purpose flour
  (1-2/3 ounces, 47g)**
1/4 **teaspoon cinnamon
  Pinch of salt**

Metal Blade: Put all the ingredients in the work bowl and quickly turn the machine on and off several times, until you have crumbs the size of small peas. Refrigerate the mixture.

Dough

- 1 cup (24 cl) warm milk (105°F. to 115°F., or 40° to 46°C.)
- 2 packages active dry yeast
- 2 teaspoons sugar
- 3 cups unbleached all-purpose flour (15 ounces, 425g)
- 1/2 teaspoon salt
- 1/3 cup sugar (2-1/2 ounces, 70g)
- 1-1/2 sticks unsalted butter (6 ounces, 170g), chilled and cut into 12 pieces
- 3 large egg yolks
- 1 teaspoon vanilla extract

Filling

- 3/4 cup golden raisins (3 ounces, 85g)
- 1/2 teaspoon cinnamon
- 1/4 cup sugar (1-3/4 ounces, 50g)

Pour the milk into a small bowl and stir in the yeast and sugar. Let the mixture stand for 10 minutes, or until it is foamy.

Metal Blade: Put the flour, salt, sugar and butter in the work bowl and combine by turning the machine on and off about 6 times. Add the yeast mixture, egg yolks and vanilla, and process for 20 to 30 seconds, or until the dough is thoroughly mixed. Transfer the dough to a bowl, cover it airtight and refrigerate it for 4 hours, or overnight.

To assemble, roll half the dough on a well-floured board into a 10- by 4-inch (25 cm by 10 cm) rectangle. Sprinkle 1/2 the raisins over it, and press them firmly into place with the rolling pin. Sprinkle 1/4 teaspoon cinnamon and 2 tablespoons sugar over the raisins. Beginning with a long side, roll up the dough, pinching the seams and ends together tightly. Put the dough in a well-buttered angel cake pan with a removable bottom. Fit it in, seam side down, and join the ends to make a circle around the center tube, pinching the ends together lightly. Roll, fill and shape the remaining dough in the same manner and put it seam side down on top of the first roll, pinching the ends to join them on the opposite side from the joining of the bottom roll.

Preheat the oven to its lowest temperature for 2 minutes and turn it off. Cover the pan with a damp kitchen towel and put it in the oven, cushioning the bottom with a potholder. Let the dough rise for 1-1/2 to 1-3/4 hours, or until it has almost doubled in bulk. Remove the pan from the oven.

Adjust the rack to the middle level and preheat the oven to 350°F. (175°C.).

Sprinkle the streusel topping over the dough and bake the ring for 55 to 60 minutes. Let it rest in the pan for 10 minutes, then remove the outer rim of the pan. Let the ring cool for 30 minutes. Carefully remove the center stem from the pan and let the yeast ring continue cooling on a wire rack.

Makes one yeast ring, 12 servings.

Easy, light and really delicious — an all-time winner with my students.

Dough

1/2 cup (12 cl) warm milk
(105°F. to 115°F., or 40°
to 46°C.)
2 packages active dry
yeast
1 tablespoon sugar
2 sticks unsalted butter
(1/2 pound, 225g), at
room temperature and
cut into 8 pieces
2 tablespoons sugar
3 large egg yolks
1 teaspoon dark rum
1 cup unbleached
all-purpose flour
(5 ounces, 140g)
3/4 cup cake flour
(3 ounces, 85g)
1/2 teaspoon salt

Put the milk in a small bowl and stir in the yeast and sugar. Let the mixture stand for 10 minutes, or until it is foamy.

Metal Blade: Put the yeast mixture, butter, sugar, egg yolks and rum in the work bowl and process for 10 seconds, or until the mixture is well blended. Stop the machine once to scrape down the sides of the bowl. Add the flours and salt and process the mixture for 5 seconds, again stopping the machine once to scrape down the sides of the bowl. Spoon the batter into a bowl, cover it tightly, and refrigerate it for several hours, or overnight.

Filling

2/3 cup walnut pieces
(2-2/3 ounces, 75g)
1/2 cup currants
(2 ounces, 55g)
1 tablespoon dark rum
3 large egg whites
Pinch of salt
1/4 teaspoon cream of
tartar
3/4 cup sugar
(5-1/4 ounces, 150g)

Metal Blade: Chop the walnuts coarsely by turning the machine on and off 6 to 8 times. Remove and reserve them. Put the currants in a small saucepan with the rum and soften them over moderate heat until the rum is absorbed.

Beat the egg whites with an electric mixer until they are frothy. Add the salt and cream of tartar and beat until the egg whites are stiff but not dry. With the mixer running, add the sugar gradually, 2 tablespoons at a time, allowing each addition to become incorporated before adding the next. Continue to beat the meringue for about 4 minutes longer, or until it is stiff and smooth.

Assembly

13 pecan halves
1 teaspoon cinnamon
1 tablespoon butter, melted

Arrange the pecans round side down in a well-buttered 12-cup (2.8L) *kugelhopf* or angel cake pan. Roll half the dough into a 10- by 4-inch (25 cm by 10 cm) rectangle on a heavily floured board. Brush away any excess flour. Sprinkle the dough with 1/2 teaspoon cinnamon, half the reserved walnuts and half the reserved currants. Lightly press the nuts and currants into the dough with the rolling pin. Spread half the meringue on the dough, leaving a 1/2-inch (1.25 cm) border on all sides. Beginning with a long side, roll up the dough, pinching the seams and ends together tightly. Put the dough around the tube of the pan, seam side up, and join the ends by pinching them together lightly. Roll, fill and shape the remaining dough in the same manner. Put it seam side up on top of the first roll, pinching it to join ends on the opposite side from the joining of the bottom roll.

Preheat the oven to its lowest temperature for 2 minutes and turn it off. Brush the top of the dough with the butter and cover the pan with a damp kitchen towel. Put it in the oven, cushioning the bottom with a potholder. Let the dough rise for 45 minutes, or until it has almost doubled in bulk. Remove it from the oven.

Adjust the rack to the middle level and preheat the oven to 350°F. (175°C.).

Bake the coffee cake for 45 to 50 minutes, or until it is very brown. Invert the cake immediately onto a wire rack and brush it with the warm glaze.

Glaze (optional)

1/4 cup (6 cl) raspberry preserves
1 teaspoon water
1 tablespoon dark rum

Heat the preserves and water in a small saucepan until the preserves are thinned. Strain the mixture into a bowl and stir in the rum.

Makes 10 to 12 servings.

Currant Meringue Coffee Cake

Basic French Bread

Be sure to read the refrigerator method at the end of this recipe. You can mix and knead several batches of bread dough, let the dough rise once, punch it down and refrigerate it for up to five days. After a busy day, you or someone in your family can pull off a pound of dough, shape it, let it rise – and voila! – three hours later, you have a superb, freshly baked loaf of bread.

Glaze

1 large egg
1/2 teaspoon salt

Metal Blade: Process the egg and salt for 2 seconds and reserve it. Do not clean the work bowl.

Bread

1 package active dry yeast
1 teaspoon sugar (optional)
1 cup (24 cl) plus 2 tablespoons warm water (105°F. to 115°F., 40°C. to 46°C.)
2 cups bread flour (10 ounces, 285g)
1 cup unbleached all-purpose flour (5 ounces, 140g)
1 teaspoon salt

Stir the yeast and sugar into the water in a small bowl and let the mixture stand for 10 minutes, or until it is foamy. (If you omit the sugar, the mixture will not foam.)

Metal Blade: Put the flours and salt in the work bowl and turn on the machine. With the machine running, add the yeast mixture through the feed tube. Process the mixture for 40 seconds, or until the dough is uniformly moist and elastic. If it is too wet add flour, 1 teaspoon at a time, processing after each addition until the dough is of the proper consistency. Transfer the dough to an oiled bowl and rotate it to coat the surface with the oil.

Preheat the oven to the lowest temperature for 2 minutes and turn it off. Cover the bowl with a damp towel and put it in the oven, cushioning the bottom with a potholder. Let the dough rise for 1 hour, or until it has doubled in bulk.

Assembly

Put the dough on a heavily floured board and work in enough flour so that it is easy to handle and no longer sticky. Divide it in half and roll one half into a rectangle. Starting at a long side, roll up the rectangle into an oblong loaf. Pinch the ends and seam tightly. Put the dough, seam side down, into an oiled double French bread pan sprinkled with cornmeal.

Roll and shape the remaining dough in the same manner. Cover the loaves with a damp towel and let them rise again, for 45 minutes, or until almost doubled, following the directions for the first rising. Remove the pan from the oven.

Adjust the oven rack to the middle level and preheat the oven to 425°F. (220°C.).

Use the metal blade of your processor to make several slashes in the tops of the loaves. Brush them with the reserved glaze, taking care not to drip the glaze on the pan. Bake the loaves for 28 minutes, or until they are deeply colored and sound hollow when rapped on the bottom. Remove the loaves from the pan and let them cool on a wire rack.

Makes 2 French loaves.

Note: This is the basic recipe. The type of flour can be varied, but always use 15 ounces (425g) flour to 1 cup (24cl) plus 2 tablespoons liquid.

Refrigerator Method

Mix and knead the dough, and allow it to rise to double its size. Punch it down and put it in a bowl or plastic bag large enough to allow for a second doubling in size. Put it in the refrigerator.

Remove the dough from the refrigerator and punch it down at least 2-1/2 hours before the bread is to be served. Divide the dough into 1-pound (455g) amounts for French baguettes or into 1-1/2-pound (680g) amounts for a 7-cup (166 cl) loaf pan. Roll the dough into a rectangle. Starting with a short side, roll it into an oblong loaf. Pinch the ends and seam tightly. Gently stretching the dough to fit the pans, place it into oiled pans; cover it with a damp towel. Let it rise in the same manner described in the basic recipe, for 1-1/2 to 2 hours, or until it has doubled in bulk. Slash the top and bake as directed in the basic recipe.

Variations

1. For bread that stays fresh longer and has a softer texture than the basic bread, decrease the water by 2 tablespoons and add 2 tablespoons of butter or margarine to the dough after you add the yeast mixture. Knead the dough as directed.

2. For Sesame Seed Bread, add 1/4 cup (6 cl) sesame seeds to the flour.

3. For Herb Bread, mince 2 tablespoons of parsley, 1 teaspoon of snipped chives, 1 large scallion (1 ounce, 30g), and 2 teaspoons of dried dillweed. Add them to the flour and reduce the liquid by 1 tablespoon.

4. For Wheat Germ Bread, add 1/4 cup (6 cl) wheat germ to the flour.

5. For Cheese Bread, use 2 ounces (55g) of chilled Cheddar, Swiss or mozzarella cheese, or 2 ounces (55g) of Parmesan cheese at room temperature. Shred it with the shredding disc, using light pressure, and add it to the flour.

Note: If your food processor will not handle 3 cups of flour, you can divide the recipe in half and mix and knead the dough in two batches. The chart titled Ingredients for Bread Dough gives the correct proportions of major ingredients in dough, according to the flour capacity of various processors.

Ingredients for Bread Dough

Flour Capacity	2 cups (10 ounces, 285g)	3 cups (15 ounces, 425g)	4 cups (20 ounces, 570g)	6 cups (30 ounces, 850g)
Yeast Mixture	3/4 cup (18 cl) water 1 package yeast 1 teaspoon sugar	1 cup (24 cl) plus 2 tablespoons water 1 package yeast 1 teaspoon sugar	1-1/2 cups (35 cl) water 1 package yeast 1 teaspoon sugar	2-1/4 cups (55 cl) water 1 package yeast 2 teaspoons sugar
Salt	1/2 teaspoon	1 teaspoon	1 teaspoon	2 teaspoons
Dough Weight	about 1 pound (.46kg)	about 1-1/2 pounds (.68kg)	about 2 pounds (.90kg)	about 3 pounds (1.4kg)

Garlic Cheese Bread

A zesty loaf that seems to appeal to everyone. It is particularly good with Italian dishes such as Turkey Tonnato and the Antipasto Platter (see Index).

Glaze

1 large egg
1/2 teaspoon salt

Metal Blade: Process the egg and salt for 2 seconds and reserve it. Do not clean the work bowl.

Dough

1 package active dry yeast
1 teaspoon sugar
1 cup (24 cl) warm water (105°F. to 115°F., 40°C. to 46°C.)
2 cups bread flour (10 ounces, 285g)
1 cup unbleached all-purpose flour (5 ounces, 140g)
1-1/4 teaspoons salt
1 large egg
2 tablespoons butter, at room temperature

Stir the yeast and sugar into the water in a small bowl and let the mixture stand for 10 minutes, or until it is foamy.

Metal Blade: Reserve 1/4 cup (6 cl) unbleached flour and put the remaining flours in the work bowl with the salt. With the machine running, add the yeast mixture and egg through the feed tube. Process the mixture until it forms a ball, add the butter, and process for 40 seconds – the dough should be moist and elastic. If it is too wet, add the remaining flour – 1 tablespoon at a time – and process the dough after each addition until it is of the proper consistency. Transfer the dough to an oiled bowl and rotate it to coat the surface with the oil.

Preheat the oven to the lowest temperature for 2 minutes and turn it off. Cover the bowl with a damp towel and put it in the oven, cushioning the bottom with a potholder. Let the dough rise for 1 hour, or until it has doubled in bulk. Punch down the dough and let it rise a second time for 40 minutes, or until it has doubled.

Filling

1 large garlic clove,
    peeled
1 large shallot (1 ounce,
    30g), peeled
3 ounces (85g) imported
    Parmesan cheese, at
    room temperature
3 ounces (85g)
    mozzarella cheese,
    chilled
1/4 cup (6 cl) parsley
    leaves
1 large egg

Metal Blade: With the machine running, mince the garlic and shallot by dropping them through the feed tube. Leave them in the work bowl.

Shredding Disc: Shred the Parmesan and mozzarella cheeses, using light pressure. Leave them in the work bowl.

Metal Blade: Put the parsley in the work bowl and mince it by turning the machine on and off about 8 times. Add the egg and process the mixture for 5 seconds.

Assembly

Put the dough on a lightly floured board and roll it out into a rectangle. Spoon the cheese mixture over it in dollops, leaving a 3/4-inch (2 cm) border on all sides. Pat the cheese mixture onto the dough and roll up the dough, beginning with a long end. Pinch the ends and seam tightly, and put the roll, seam side down, in an oiled Italian bread pan — or on an oiled baking sheet — sprinkled with cornmeal. Cover the dough with a damp towel and let it rise again, in the same manner as described for the first rising, for 45 minutes, or until it has almost doubled. Remove it from the oven.

Adjust the rack to the middle level and preheat the oven to 375°F. (190°C.).

Use the metal blade of your food processor to slash the top of the loaf, deep enough to expose the layers. Brush it with the reserved glaze, taking care not to drip the glaze on the pan. Bake for 30 to 35 minutes, or until it is brown, and sounds hollow when rapped on the bottom. Remove the loaf from the pan and let it cool on a wire rack. Serve the bread warm.

Makes 1 large Italian loaf.

Note: To reheat the bread, wrap it in foil, put it in a cold oven and heat it at 325°F. (160°C.) for 25 minutes.

Beer Bread

This dough is very wet, much like a batter; the bread has a great crust and a wonderful spongy texture. I learned the method and formula with Lionel Poilâne, 8 rue de Cherche Midi, Paris. We spent an entire day making bread dough in the food processor.

Glaze

1 large egg
1/2 teaspoon salt

Bread

1 package active dry
  yeast
1 teaspoon sugar
1/4 cup (6 cl) warm water
  (105°F. to 115°F.)
1-1/4 cups (30 cl) warm beer
  (105°F. to 115°F.)
2-1/4 cups bread flour
  (11-1/4 ounces, 320g)
1-1/3 cups unbleached
  all-purpose flour
  (6-2/3 ounces, 190g)
2 teaspoons salt

Metal Blade: Process the egg and salt for 2 seconds; remove it and reserve it. Do not clean the work bowl.

Stir the yeast and sugar into the water in a small bowl and let the mixture stand for 10 minutes, or until it is foamy. Heat the beer in a saucepan.

Metal Blade: Put the flours and salt in the work bowl and turn on the machine. With the machine running, add the yeast mixture and the warm beer through the feed tube. Process the mixture for 10 seconds (it will be wet and elastic). Transfer the dough to an oiled bowl, and rotate it to coat the entire surface with the oil.

Preheat the oven to the lowest temperature for 2 minutes and turn it off. Cover the bowl with a damp towel and put it in the oven, cushioning the bottom with a potholder. Let the dough rise for 1 hour, or until it has doubled in bulk.

Put the dough on a heavily floured board and work in enough flour so that it is easy to handle and no longer sticky. Divide the dough in half and roll into a rectangle. Starting from a short side, roll up the rectangle into an oblong loaf. Pinch the ends and the seam tightly, and put the dough seam side down into an oiled double French bread pan sprinkled with cornmeal. Roll and shape the remaining dough in the same manner and cover both loaves with a damp towel. Let them rise again for 45 minutes, or until almost doubled, following the directions for the first rising. Remove from oven.

Adjust the rack to the lower third of the oven and preheat the oven to 425°F. (220°C.).

Use the metal blade of your processor to make several slashes in the tops of the loaves. Brush them with the reserved glaze, taking care not to drip the glaze on the pan. Bake the loaves for 28 minutes, or until they are deeply colored and sound hollow when rapped on the bottom. Remove them from the pans and let them cool on a wire rack.

Makes 2 French loaves.

Caraway Pumpernickel Bread

This bread has a deep, rich flavor that is wonderful for sandwiches and toast. It's also good paired with Nova Scotia salmon and cream cheese or with *gravlax* and Whipped Scallion Cream Cheese (recipe follows).

Glaze

1 large egg
1/2 teaspoon salt

Metal Blade: Process the egg and salt for 2 seconds and reserve the mixture. Do not clean the work bowl.

Bread

1 package active dry yeast
1 teaspoon sugar
1 cup (24 cl) warm water (105°F. to 115°F., 40°C. to 46°C.)
1 tablespoon cocoa
1 teaspoon caraway seeds
2 teaspoons salt
2 tablespoons molasses
2 cups whole wheat flour (10 ounces, 285g)
1 cup bread flour (5 ounces, 140g)
2 tablespoons unsalted butter, at room temperature

Stir the yeast and sugar into the water in a small dish and let the mixture stand for 10 minutes, or until it is foamy.

Metal Blade: Put all the ingredients into the work bowl except 2 tablespoons of whole-wheat flour and the butter. With the machine running, add the yeast mixture through the feed tube. Process the mixture until it forms a ball, add the butter and process for 40 seconds – the dough should be moist and elastic. If it is too wet, add the remaining whole-wheat flour – 1 tablespoon at a time – and process the dough after each addition until it is moist. Transfer the dough to an oiled bowl and rotate it to coat the surface with the oil.

Preheat the oven to the lowest temperature for 2 minutes and turn it off. Cover the dough with a damp towel and put it in the oven, cushioning the bottom with a potholder. Let the dough rise for 1-1/2 hours, or until it has doubled in bulk.

Put the dough on a lightly floured board and work in enough flour so that it is easy to handle and no longer sticky. Divide it in half. Roll one half into a rectangle. Roll up the rectangle into an oblong loaf, and pinch the ends and seam tightly. Put the dough, seam side down, in an oiled double French bread pan sprinkled with cornmeal. Shape the remaining dough in the same manner. Cover the dough with a damp towel and let it rise again, in the same manner as described for the first rising, for 45 minutes, or until it has almost doubled. Remove it from the oven.

Adjust the rack to the middle level and preheat the oven to 350°F. (175°C.).

Use the metal blade of your food processor to slash the tops of the loaves. Brush them with the reserved glaze, taking care not to drip the glaze on the pan. Bake the loaves for 35 to 40 minutes, or until they are deeply colored and sound hollow when rapped on the bottom. Remove them from the pans and let them cool on a wire rack. Serve with sweet butter or Whipped Scallion Cream Cheese.

Makes 2 French loaves.

Whipped Scallion Cream Cheese

A quick, simple and appealing spread.

1 8-ounce (225g) package cream cheese, at room temperature, cut into 4 pieces
1 large scallion (1/2 ounce, 15g), including the green top, cut into 1-inch (2.5 cm) pieces
1/8 teaspoon Tabasco sauce

Metal Blade: Put all ingredients in the work bowl and process until well mixed. Spoon the mixture into a 1-1/2-cup (35 cl) crock or dish and wrap airtight. Refrigerate until ready to use. Let the spread soften slightly before serving.

Makes 1 cup (24 cl).

Wheat Germ Bread with Spinach Filling

The spinach filling provides an appetizing surprise when the bread is sliced, but the recipe also works well without it.

Glaze

1 large egg
1/2 teaspoon salt

Metal Blade: Process the egg and salt for 2 seconds and reserve it. Do not clean the work bowl.

Dough

1 package active dry yeast
2 teaspoons sugar
1-1/4 cups (30 cl) warm water (105°F. to 115°F., 40°C. to 46°C.)
2-1/4 cups bread flour (11-1/4 ounces, 320g)
1 cup unbleached all-purpose flour (5 ounces, 140g)
1/4 cup wheat germ (1 ounce, 30g)
1-1/2 teaspoons salt
2 tablespoons nonfat dry milk

Stir the yeast and sugar into the water in a small bowl and let the mixture stand for 10 minutes, or until it is foamy.

Metal Blade: Put the flours, wheat germ, salt and dry milk in the work bowl and turn on the machine. With the machine running, add the yeast mixture through the feed tube. Process the mixture for 40 seconds – the dough should be moist and elastic. If it is too wet, add flour 1 tablespoon at a time, and process the dough after each addition until it is of the proper consistency. Transfer the dough to an oiled bowl and rotate it to coat the entire surface with the oil. Preheat the oven to the lowest temperature for 2 minutes and turn it off. Cover the bowl with a damp towel and put it in the oven, cushioning the bottom with a potholder. Let the dough rise for 1 hour, or until it has doubled in bulk.

Filling ————————

10 ounces (285g) spinach, including the stems, washed and trimmed
2 large garlic cloves, peeled
1 small onion (1 ounce, 30g), peeled
1 shallot (1/2 ounce, 15g), peeled
1 tablespoon butter
1/4 cup (6 cl) parsley leaves
3/4 teaspoon salt
1/4 teaspoon freshly grated nutmeg
  Freshly ground pepper
1 large egg white

In a stainless steel saucepan cook the spinach over moderately high heat, in just the water clinging to its leaves. Turn it twice, or until it wilts. Transfer the spinach to a colander and hold it under cold running water until it is completely cool. Drain it well. Wrap the spinach in a towel, squeezing out as much moisture as possible.

Metal Blade: With the machine running, mince the garlic, onion and shallot by dropping them through the feed tube. Melt the butter in a skillet and cook the minced garlic, onions and shallots over moderate heat for 10 minutes, or until they are soft. Combine the spinach, parsley, seasonings and egg white in the work bowl. Then purée by turning the machine on and off about 10 times. Scrape down the sides of the bowl, add the onion mixture, and process for 3 seconds.

Assembly ————————

Remove the risen dough from the bowl, put it on a floured board and divide it in half. Roll one half into a 16- by 8-inch (41 cm by 20 cm) rectangle. Spread half the spinach filling on the rectangle, leaving a 1-inch (2.5 cm) border on all sides. Beginning with a long side, roll up the dough tightly. Pinch the ends and seam tightly and put the roll, seam side down, in an oiled double French bread pan – or on an oiled baking sheet – sprinkled with cornmeal. Repeat the process with the remaining dough and filling.

Cover the loaves with a damp towel and let them rise in the same way described for the first rising, for 45 minutes, or until they have almost doubled. Remove them from the oven.

Adjust the rack to the middle level and preheat the oven to 425°F. (220°C.).

Use the metal blade of your processor to make shallow slashes on the tops of the loaves. Brush the tops with the glaze, taking care not to drip the glaze on the pan. Bake the loaves for 30 minutes, or until they are deeply colored and sound hollow when rapped on the bottom. Remove the loaves from the pans and let them cool on a wire rack.

Makes 2 French loaves.

Cumin Light Rye Bread

This is my choice to accompany French cheeses. It has a mild but distinctive flavor that complements them all, especially those made from goats' milk.

Glaze

1 large egg
1/2 teaspoon salt

Metal Blade: Process the egg and salt for 2 seconds and reserve it. Do not clean the work bowl.

Bread

1 package active dry
  yeast
2 tablespoons honey
1 cup (24 cl) plus 2
  tablespoons warm
  water (105°F. to 115°F.,
  40°C. to 46°C.)
2-1/2 cups combined
  rye and enriched
  whole wheat flours
  (11-1/4 ounces, 320g)
1 cup bread flour
  (5 ounces, 140g)
1-1/2 teaspoons salt
1/4 teaspoon ground
  cumin
2 tablespoons oil

Stir the yeast and honey into the water in a small bowl and let the mixture stand for 10 minutes, or until it is foamy.

Metal Blade: Put the flours, salt and cumin in the work bowl. With the machine running, add the yeast mixture through the feed tube. Process the mixture until it forms a ball, add the oil, and process for 40 seconds – the dough should be moist and elastic. If it is too wet, add flour – 1 tablespoon at a time – and process the dough after each addition until it is of the proper consistency. Transfer the dough to an oiled bowl and rotate it to coat the surface with the oil.

Preheat the oven to the lowest temperature for 2 minutes and turn it off. Cover the dough with a damp towel and put it in the oven, cushioning the bottom with a potholder. Let the dough rise for 1 hour, or until it has doubled in bulk.

Put the dough on a heavily floured board and work in enough flour so that it is easy to handle and no longer sticky. Divide it in half. Roll one half into a rectangle and roll up the rectangle into an oblong loaf. Pinch the ends and seam tightly. Put the loaf, seam side down, into an oiled double French bread pan sprinkled with cornmeal. Shape the remaining dough in the same manner. Cover the loaves with a damp towel and let them rise again, in the same manner as described for the first rising, for 45 minutes, or until almost doubled. Remove them from the oven.

Adjust the rack to the middle level and preheat the oven to 425°F. (220°C.).

Use the metal blade of your food processor to slash the tops of the loaves. Brush them with the reserved glaze, taking care not to drip the glaze on the pan. Bake the loaves for 28 minutes, or until they are deeply colored and sound hollow when rapped on the bottom. Remove the loaves from the pans and let them cool on a wire rack.

Makes 2 French loaves.

Glaze

1 large egg
1/2 teaspoon salt

Bread

1 package active dry
  yeast
1 tablespoon sugar
1/2 cup (12 cl) plus 2
  tablespoons warm
  water (105°F. to 115°F.,
  40°C. to 46°C.)
2 cups bread flour
  (10 ounces, 285g)
1 cup unbleached all-
  purpose flour
  (5 ounces, 140g)
1-1/2 teaspoons salt
1/2 cup (12 cl) warm
  buttermilk (105°F. to
  115°F., 40°C. to 46°C.)

Metal Blade: Process the egg and salt for 2 seconds and reserve it. Do not clean the work bowl.

Stir the yeast and sugar into the water in a small bowl and let the mixture stand for 10 minutes, or until it is foamy.

Metal Blade: Put the flours and salt in the work bowl. With the machine running, add the yeast mixture and the buttermilk through the feed tube. Process for 40 seconds – the dough should be moist and elastic. If it is too wet, add the flour – 1 tablespoon at a time – and process after each addition until it is of the proper consistency. Transfer the dough to an oiled bowl and rotate it to coat the surface with the oil.

Preheat the oven to the lowest temperature for 2 minutes and turn it off. Cover the bowl with a damp towel and put it in the oven, cushioning the bottom with a potholder. Let the dough rise for 1 hour, or until it has doubled in bulk.

Put the dough on a heavily floured board and work in enough flour so that it is easy to handle and no longer sticky. Roll the dough into a rectangle. Beginning with a short end, roll up the rectangle and pinch the ends and seam tightly. Put the dough, seam side down, into an oiled 7-cup (166 cl) loaf pan sprinkled with cornmeal. Cover it with a damp towel and let it rise again, in the same manner as described for the first rising, for 45 minutes, or until it has almost doubled. Remove it from the oven.

Adjust the rack to the middle level and preheat the oven to 425°F. (220°C.).

Brush the top of the loaf with the glaze, taking care not to drip the glaze on the pan. Bake the loaf for 28 minutes, or until it is deeply colored and sounds hollow when rapped on the bottom. Remove the loaf from the pan and cool on a wire rack.

Makes 1 loaf.

Variation

For Buttermilk Chive Bread, add 2 tablespoons of snipped chives after the dough is kneaded, and process for 2 seconds.

Stone-ground whole wheat flour is coarser and heavier than many flours, but the proportions given here produce bread that is lighter than usual.

Glaze

1 large egg
1/2 teaspoon salt

Metal Blade: Process the egg and salt for 2 seconds and reserve it. Do not clean the work bowl.

Bread

1 package active dry
   yeast
1 tablespoon sugar
1 cup plus 2 tablespoons
   warm water (105°F. to
   115°F., 40°C. to 46°C.)
3/4 cup stone-ground
   whole-wheat flour
   (3-3/4 ounces, 106g)
2 cups bread flour
   (10 ounces, 285g)
1-1/2 teaspoons salt

Stir the yeast and sugar into the water in a small bowl and let the mixture stand for 10 minutes, or until it is foamy.

Metal Blade: Reserve 1/3 cup (8 cl) of the bread flour and put the remaining flours in the work bowl with the salt. With the machine running, add the yeast mixture through the feed tube. Process the mixture until it forms a ball, then process the dough for 40 seconds – the dough should be moist and elastic. If it is too wet, add flour – 1 tablespoon at a time – and process after each addition until it is of the proper consistency. Transfer the dough to an oiled bowl and rotate it to coat the surface with the oil. Preheat the oven to the lowest temperature for 2 minutes and turn it off. Cover the bowl with a damp towel and put it in the oven, cushioning the bottom with a potholder. Let the dough rise for 1 hour, or until it has doubled in bulk.

Put the dough on a lightly floured board and roll it into a rectangle. Beginning with a short end, roll up the dough. Pinch the ends and seam tightly and put the roll, seam side down, into an oiled 7-cup (166 cl) loaf pan sprinkled with cornmeal. Cover the loaf with a damp towel and let it rise again, in the same manner as described for the first rising, for 45 minutes, or until it is almost doubled. Remove it from the oven.

Adjust the rack to the middle level and preheat the oven to 375°F. (190°C.).

Brush the top of the bread with the reserved glaze, taking care not to drip the glaze on the pan. Bake the loaf for 35 minutes, or until it is deeply colored and sounds hollow when rapped on the bottom. Remove the loaf from the pan and let it cool on a wire rack.

Makes 1 loaf.

Variation

For a flavorful Whole Wheat Cheese Bread, add 2 ounces (55g) of shredded sharp Cheddar, Swiss or mozzarella cheese to the flour mixture.

Whole Wheat Pita Bread

A light pita bread that is far more delicate than its store-bought counterpart.

1 package active dry
   yeast
1 teaspoon sugar
1 cup (24 cl) plus 2
   tablespoons warm
   water (105°F. to 115°F.,
   40°C. to 46°C.)
2-1/4 cups bread flour
   (11-1/4 ounces, 320g)
1/3 cup stone-ground
   whole wheat flour
   (2 ounces, 55g)
1-1/2 teaspoons salt

Stir the yeast and sugar into water in a small bowl and let the mixture stand for 10 minutes, or until it is foamy.

Metal Blade: Put the flours and salt in the work bowl and process them for 2 seconds. With the machine running, add the yeast mixture through the feed tube. Process the mixture – the dough should be moist and elastic. If it is too wet, add bread flour – 1 tablespoon at a time – and process the dough after each addition until it is of the proper consistency. Transfer the dough to an oiled bowl and rotate it to coat the entire surface with the oil. Preheat the oven to the lowest temperature for 2 minutes and turn it off. Cover the bowl with a damp towel and put it in the oven, cushioning the bottom with a potholder. Let the dough rise for 1-1/2 hours, or until it has doubled in bulk.

Punch down the dough with floured hands and let it rise again for 30 minutes – it will not double.

Put the dough on a heavily floured board and work in enough flour so that it is easy to handle and no longer sticky. Divide it into 12 equal pieces. Roll each piece into a 5-inch (12.5 cm) round. Cover the rounds with plastic wrap and let them rest for 20 minutes.

Adjust the rack to the lower third of the oven and line it with unglazed quarry tiles. Preheat the oven to 500°F. (260°C.).

Put a large baking sheet in the oven to heat it. Oil it after it is heated, and gently place the 6 rounds of dough on it. Bake the rounds for 4 to 5 minutes, or until they are puffy. Transfer them to a wire rack to cool. Repeat the process with the remaining rounds of dough. When the bread rounds are almost cool, wrap each one airtight in foil. Reheat them, wrapped in foil, at 250°F. (175°C.) for 15 minutes.

Makes 12 pita rounds.

Variations

1. This dough makes a pleasing light loaf of bread. Follow the directions given in the recipe for Basic French Bread (see Index) for shaping, rising and baking.

2. For White Pita Bread, make these substitutions in ingredients, and proceed as directed for Whole Wheat Pita: 1-3/4 cups bread flour (9 ounces, 255g), 3/4 cup unbleached all-purpose flour (4 ounces, 115g) and 1 teaspoon salt.

Mushroom, Green Pepper and Pepperoni Pizza

My first encounter with a food processor was 7 years ago, and I was making a pizza. Hundreds of pizzas later I still marvel at how easy they are to prepare by machine. Once the ingredients are ready, it takes no more than 10 minutes – instead of being a Sunday afternoon project as before. For easy informal entertaining, make several pizzas in sequence and freeze them.

Basic Pizza Dough

- 1 package active dry yeast
- 1 teaspoon sugar
- 7/8 cup (21 cl) warm water (105°F. to 115°F.)
- 2-1/4 cups unbleached all-purpose flour (11-1/4 ounces, 320g)
- 1 teaspoon salt
- 1 tablespoon oil

Stir the yeast and sugar into the water in a small bowl and let the mixture stand for 10 minutes, or until it is foamy.

Metal Blade: Put the flour and salt in the work bowl and turn on the machine. With the machine running, pour the yeast mixture through the feed tube. Process until a ball of dough forms. Add the oil and process the dough for 40 seconds, or until it is smooth.

Transfer the dough to an oiled bowl and rotate it to coat the entire surface with oil. Preheat the oven to its lowest temperature for 2 minutes and turn it off. Cover the bowl with a damp towel and put it in the oven, cushioning the bottom with a pot holder. Let the dough rise for 1 hour, or until double in bulk.

Topping

- 12 ounces (340g) mozzarella cheese, chilled
- 1 ounce (30g) Parmesan cheese (optional), at room temperature
- 1 small green pepper (3 ounces, 85g), cored and whole
- 1 small onion (2 ounces, 55g), peeled
- 3 large mushrooms (3 ounces, 85g), trimmed and cut flat at ends
- 4- inch (10 cm) piece of pepperoni, peeled and halved
- 2 large tomatoes (12 ounces total, 340g), peeled, seeded and quartered
  Pinch of sugar

Shredding Disc: Shred the mozzarella, using light pressure. Reserve it. Shred the Parmesan, using light pressure. Reserve it.

Medium Slicing Disc: Put the green pepper in the feed tube vertically and slice it, using light pressure. Put the onion in the feed tube vertically and slice it, using medium pressure. Remove and reserve the mixture. Stack the mushrooms in the feed tube, flat side down, and slice them, using light pressure. Remove and reserve them. Slice the pepperoni, using firm pressure. Remove and reserve it.

Metal Blade: Coarsely chop the tomatoes, in batches if necessary, turning the machine on and off about 3 times. Combine them with the sugar and tomato paste in a bowl.

2 tablespoons tomato
   paste
1 teaspoon dried
   oregano
1/2 teaspoon salt
   Freshly ground black
   pepper

Assembly _____

Remove the dough from the oven when it has doubled in bulk and adjust the rack to the lower third of the oven. Preheat the oven to 425°F. (220°C.).

Roll the dough on a floured board into a large circle 1/4-inch (.60 cm) thick. Transfer it to a large oiled pizza pan or baking sheet and pinch up the edges to form a rim. Spread half the tomato mixture on the dough and arrange the reserved mozzarella cheese over it. Spoon on the remaining tomato mixture. Arrange the reserved pepper mixture and the mushrooms on the pizza and sprinkle it with the seasonings, reserving the pepperoni and Parmesan cheese.

Bake the pizza for 15 minutes, then add the reserved pepperoni and Parmesan cheese. Bake the pizza for about 10 minutes longer, or until the bottom of the crust is browned and the cheese is lightly browned. For a puffier crust, let the pizza stand for 30 minutes before you bake it.

Makes 3 or 4 main-course servings.

Note: To freeze the pizza, bake it about 18 minutes, remove it from the pan and let it cool completely on a wire rack. Freeze it and wrap it airtight. When ready to bake the pizza, place it on a pizza pan or baking sheet in a cold oven. Set the oven temperature at 425°F. (220°C.) and bake for 25 minutes.

Variations _____

1. Omit the tomatoes, sugar and tomato paste and substitute an 8-ounce can of tomato sauce.

2. Omit the pepperoni and substitute 1/2 pound (225g) of Italian seasoned beef. With the metal blade, chop 1/2 pound (225g) of lean beef, cut into 1-inch (2.5 cm) cubes, with 1 teaspoon of dried fennel seed and salt and 1/4 teaspoon garlic powder. Chop them by turning the machine on and off. Divide the mixture into balls the size of a tablespoon. After the pizza has baked for 10 minutes, distribute the meat balls and 1 ounce (30g) of shredded Parmesan cheese on top of it. Bake the pizza for 15 minutes longer, or until the crust is brown and the cheese is lightly browned.

Middle Eastern Pizza

Dough

- 1 teaspoon active dry yeast (1/2 package)
- 1 teaspoon sugar
- 1 cup (24 cl) warm water (105°F. to 115°F.)
- 2-1/2 cups unbleached all-purpose flour (12-1/2 ounces, 354g)
- 1 teaspoon salt
- 1 tablespoon sesame seeds

Stir the yeast and sugar into the water in a small bowl and let the mixture stand for 10 minutes, or until it is foamy.

Metal Blade: Put the flour and salt into the work bowl and turn the machine on. With the machine running, pour the yeast mixture through the feed tube. Process the dough for 40 seconds, or until it is smooth. If the dough is too wet, add flour, 1 tablespoon at a time, and process the dough after each addition until it is just moist. Transfer the dough to an oiled bowl and rotate it to coat the surface with the oil. Preheat the oven to the lowest temperature for 2 minutes and turn it off. Cover the bowl with a damp towel and put it in the oven, cushioning the bottom with a potholder. Let the dough rise for 1 hour, or until it has doubled in bulk.

Topping

- 1/4 cup (6 cl) parsley leaves
- 3 large garlic cloves, peeled
- 1 small onion (1 ounce, 30g), peeled
- 3 tablespoons oil
- 14 ounces (400g) lean lamb from the leg, cut into 1/2-inch (1.25 cm) cubes (beef can be substituted)
- 1-1/2 teaspoons dried oregano
- 1/8 teaspoon cinnamon
- 1-1/2 teaspoons salt
  Freshly ground pepper
- 8 scallions (6 ounces total, 170g), including tops, cut into thirds

Metal Blade: Mince the parsley by turning the machine on and off. Remove and reserve it. With the machine running, mince the garlic and onion by dropping them through the feed tube. Put the oil in a large skillet and cook the garlic and onion until they are soft.

Put the lamb and the seasoning in the work bowl and chop to the desired texture by turning the machine on and off. Add the lamb to the vegetables in the skillet and cook the mixture over moderately high heat for 5 minutes, or until it is lightly browned. Add salt and pepper to taste, and remove the skillet from the heat.

Medium Slicing Disc: Wedge the scallions into the feed tube vertically and slice them, using light pressure. Stir the scallions into the lamb mixture in the skillet.

Adjust the rack to the lower third of the oven, cover it with unglazed quarry tiles and preheat the oven to 450°F. (230°C.). Sprinkle the sesame seeds on an oiled 16-inch (41 cm) pizza pan or baking sheet.

Roll the dough into a 15-inch (38 cm) round on a floured board. If it refuses to stretch, let it rest for a few minutes and resume rolling. Put the dough on the prepared pan and pinch the edges to make a small rim. Spread the filling evenly on top, almost to the edge of the dough. Press the filling lightly into place and bake the pizza for 15 to 18 minutes, or until the bottom of the crust is slightly colored. Do not overbake. Sprinkle the pizza with the reserved parsley and serve it immediately with a Greek Salad (see Index).

Makes 4 main-course or 8 first-course servings.

Quick Breads

Quick Breads

Apricot Nut Bread
Apple Currant Bread
Quick Beer Bread
Blueberry Muffins
Zucchini Nut Bread
Basil Tomato Bread
Herbed Baking Powder Biscuits
Cornmeal Pie with Cheese Topping
Banana Bread
Pumpkin Apple Bundt Bread

Everyone has a different definition of quick breads. Some call them batter breads, in an attempt to distinguish them from yeast-risen loaves. Others label them sweet or fruity. But I find that only one quality holds true for all varieties: they disappear as quickly as they're baked!

Tenderness is the common denominator. Quick breads should be so moist and crumbly that whole loaves and batches just seem to melt away — tempting just one more piece, and then another! That's the standard I apply, and food processor versions always measure up.

The key to tenderness, I have found, is the sequence in which you process the ingredients. I'll give you the basic formula so you can adapt any of your family's favorites to preparation in the food processor. First, process the dry ingredients to blend them. If the recipe calls for nuts, add them with the dry ingredients and chop them. Remove this mixture from the work bowl and reserve it. Then process the sugar and eggs for one minute. This relatively long processing ensures lightness. Add the shortening, whether softened butter or oil, and process for another full minute, to maximize lightness. Quickly blend in the liquid; then return the flour mixture and process as briefly as possible, with a few on and off turns. There's no sifting and no washing of the work bowl.

When a recipe calls for fruits or vegetables to be shredded or chopped, I add them with a view to the most efficient use of a single work bowl. To convert your own recipe for banana or zucchini bread, just follow the same sequence given in my version, even if the proportions and flavorings are different. There is only one thing to watch out for. If your recipe calls for sifted flour and you want to avoid that unnecessary mess, you should reduce the flour quantity by one tablespoon per cup before proceeding with the siftless formula I have described.

Cornmeal Pie with Cheese Topping, page 202, and Chili, page 44.

As convenient and comforting as they are, quick breads should be "on call" everyday, for dinner as well as snacks and lunchboxes. You can perk up a routine menu with the Herbed Baking Powder Biscuits and turn soup into a meal with Quick Beer Bread. In my home, the moist Cornmeal Pie is an absolute must with chili and a great brunch treat with sausage or ham. When super-abundant tomatoes and basil beg to be combined, I love to surprise people with ginger-spiced Fresh Tomato Basil Bread. In autumn or winter, Pumpkin Apple Bundt Bread provides homey satisfaction.

All of the fruit loaves make welcome, inexpensive gifts. So even if the quick bread disappearing act in your household doesn't prompt you to make double batches, consider the bonus of having an extra loaf in the freezer, ready to wrap up and take visiting.

Apricot Nut Bread (recipe opposite), Pumpkin Apple Bundt Bread (see page 204) and Blueberry Muffins (see page 198)

Apricot Nut Bread

For brunch, tea or luncheon, this bread has an unusual tangy flavor. Make several recipes in sequence and freeze the extra loaves.

2-1/2 cups unbleached all-purpose flour (12-1/2 ounces)
1 teaspoon baking soda
1 teaspoon double-acting baking powder
1 teaspoon cream of tartar
1 teaspoon salt
1 cup walnut pieces (4 ounces, 115g)
1-1/2 cups dried apricots (1/2 pound, 225g)
1/2 cup (12 cl) boiling water
1/4 cup (6 cl) vegetable oil
1-1/2 cups sugar (10-1/2 ounces)
3 large eggs
1 cup (24 cl) orange juice
1 teaspoon vanilla extract

Preheat the oven to 350°F. (175°C.) and adjust the rack to the middle of the oven.

Metal Blade: Process the flour, baking soda, baking powder, cream of tartar, salt and walnuts in the work bowl for 45 seconds, or until the walnuts are coarsely chopped. Reserve the mixture. Chop the apricots coarsely with on and off turns, pour the water over them, and process them for 5 seconds. Add the oil and sugar, process the mixture for 1 minute, and add the eggs. Process the mixture for 1 minute, add the orange juice and vanilla, and process for 5 seconds. Blend in the reserved nut mixture by turning the machine on and off 4 to 6 times or until the flour just disappears. Do not overprocess the batter.

Divide the batter between 2 buttered and floured 5-cup (118 cl) loaf pans and bake for 45 to 50 minutes, or until well browned. Let the bread cool in the pans for 10 minutes and turn it out on a wire rack to cool completely. (This bread will keep in the refrigerator, wrapped airtight, for 3 days.)

Makes 2 loaves.

Apple Currant Bread

Currants combined with tart apples make this an especially flavorful fruit bread.

2 cups unbleached all-purpose flour (10 ounces, 285g)
1 teaspoon baking soda
1 tablespoon double-acting baking powder
1 teaspoon salt
1 teaspoon cinnamon
1/4 teaspoon freshly grated nutmeg
2/3 cup dried currants (3 ounces, 85g)
2 large tart apples (preferrably Granny Smiths), (10 ounces total, 285g), peeled, cored and quartered
2 teaspoons lemon zest, removed with zester
1-1/4 cups sugar (8-3/4 ounces, 248g)
3 large eggs
1 stick unsalted butter (4 ounces, 115g), at room temperature, cut into 4 pieces
1 tablespoon lemon juice
1 teaspoon vanilla

Adjust the oven rack to the middle level and preheat the oven to 350°F. (175°C.).

Metal Blade: Put the flour, baking soda, baking powder, salt, cinnamon, nutmeg and currants in the work bowl and process for about 2 seconds to blend. Reserve the mixture. Coarsely chop the apples with the lemon zest by turning the machine on and off. Process them for 3 seconds, or until they are puréed, stopping the machine once to scrape down the sides of the bowl. Add the sugar and process for 30 seconds. Add the eggs and process for 1 minute. Add the butter, lemon juice and vanilla and process for 1 minute. Add the flour mixture, combining it by turning the machine on and off 5 to 7 times, or until the flour has just disappeared. Do not overprocess.

Pour the batter into 2 well-greased and floured 4-1/4-cup (106 cl) bread pans or 1 well-greased and floured 8-cup (189 cl) bread pan and spread it evenly with a spatula. Bake the bread for 40 to 45 minutes, or until it is browned. Let it cool in the pan(s) for 10 minutes and turn it out on a rack to cool completely.

Makes 2 small loaves or 1 large loaf.

Quick Beer Bread

Whip up this bread to accompany stews and chicken fricassees, and serve it right out of the oven. It's great spread with sweet butter.

Preheat the oven to 350°F. (175°C.) and adjust the rack to the lower third.

Glaze

1 large egg
1/2 teaspoon salt

Metal Blade: Process the egg and salt for 4 seconds. Remove the mixture and reserve it.

Bread

3 cups unbleached all-purpose flour (15 ounces, 425g)
1 tablespoon plus 1 teaspoon double-acting baking powder
1/2 teaspoon baking soda
1-1/2 teaspoons salt
3 tablespoons light brown sugar
1 12-ounce (340g) can of beer, at room temperature

Put the flour, baking powder, baking soda, salt and brown sugar in the work bowl and process for 2 seconds. Add half the beer and combine by turning the machine on and off about 4 times. Add the remaining beer and process the batter, turning the machine on and off until it is just combined.

Transfer the batter to a well-greased 7-cup (166 cl) loaf pan. Brush the glaze on sparingly and bake the bread for 45 minutes, or until it is golden brown. Turn the bread out on a wire rack and let it rest for 10 minutes. Serve it warm.

Makes 1 loaf.

1-3/4 cups unbleached
all-purpose flour
(9 ounces, 255g)
1 tablespoon double-
acting baking powder
3/4 teaspoon salt
1 teaspoon cinnamon
1/4 cup sugar
(1-3/4 ounces, 50g)
1/4 cup light brown sugar
(1-3/4 ounces, 50g),
firmly packed
2 large eggs
1/2 stick unsalted butter
(2 ounces, 55g), at
room temperature
3/4 cup (18 cl) milk
1 teaspoon cider vinegar
2 cups (47 cl) fresh,
frozen, or canned
blueberries, well
drained
1 tablespoon powdered
sugar

Preheat the oven to 400°F. (205°C.).

Metal Blade: Put the flour, baking powder, salt and cinnamon in the work bowl and process it for 2 seconds. Reserve the mixture. Add the white and brown sugars and eggs and process for 1 minute. Add the butter and process the mixture for 1 minute. Mix the milk and vinegar and pour the mixture through the feed tube with the machine running. Blend in the reserved flour mixture by turning the machine on and off 3 or 4 times or until the flour just disappears. Do not overprocess the batter. Transfer the batter to a bowl and gently fold in the berries.

Pour the batter into 16 large well-buttered muffin cups. Bake for 15 to 18 minutes, or until the muffins are lightly browned.

Turn them out onto a wire rack and sift the powdered sugar over them.

Makes 16 large muffins.

Zucchini Nut Bread

1/2 cup walnut pieces
  (2 ounces, 55g)
2 cups unbleached
  all-purpose flour
  (10 ounces, 285g)
1 tablespoon double-
  acting baking powder
1/2 teaspoon baking soda
1 teaspoon salt
1 large zucchini
  (10 ounces, 285g),
  trimmed and cut into
  lengths to fit the feed
  tube
2 large eggs
2/3 cup (16 cl)
  vegetable oil
1 cup light brown sugar
  (7 ounces, 200g), firmly
  packed
2 teaspoons cinnamon
2 teaspoons vanilla
  extract

Preheat the oven to 350°F. (175°C.) and adjust the rack to the middle level.

Metal Blade: Put the walnuts, flour, baking powder, baking soda and salt in the work bowl and process for 10 seconds, or until the nuts are coarsely chopped. Remove the mixture and reserve it.

Shredding Disc: Put the zucchini in the feed tube vertically and shred it, using medium pressure. Leave it in the bowl.

Metal Blade: Add the eggs, oil, brown sugar, cinnamon and vanilla. Combine the mixture by turning the machine on and off about 4 times. Process it for 1 minute. Add the reserved nut and flour mixture and combine by turning the machine on and off 3 or 4 times, or just until the flour disappears.

Transfer the batter to a buttered and floured 8-cup (190 cl) loaf pan. Bake for 50 minutes to 1 hour, or until the bread is browned. Let the bread cool in the pan for 5 minutes and turn it out on a wire rack to cool completely.

Makes 1 loaf.

Variation

Substitute 2 cups (47 cl) of self-rising flour for the all-purpose flour and omit the baking powder and salt.

A "fruit" bread with a surprising and unusual flavor.

2 cups unbleached all-purpose flour (10 ounces, 285g)
1 teaspoon baking soda
1 tablespoon double-acting baking powder
1 teaspoon salt
1 small piece of ginger root, peeled
1/2 cup (12 cl) fresh basil leaves, closely packed, or 1/4 cup (6 cl) dried basil
1 scallion (1/2 ounce, 14g), including the green top, cut into 1-inch (2.5 cm) pieces
3 tomatoes (15 ounces total, 425g), seeded and quartered
1 tablespoon tomato paste
1-1/4 cups sugar (8-3/4 ounces, 248g)
3 large eggs
1 stick unsalted butter (4 ounces, 115g), at room temperature and quartered

Preheat the oven to 350°F. (175°C.) and adjust the rack to the middle level.

Metal Blade: Put the flour, baking soda, baking powder and salt in the work bowl and process for 2 seconds. Remove the mixture and reserve it. Process the ginger root, basil and scallion for 2 seconds. Add the tomatoes and tomato paste and process the mixture for 10 seconds, or until the tomatoes are puréed, stopping the machine once to scrape down the sides of the bowl. Add the sugar and process the mixture for 30 seconds. Add the eggs and process the mixture for 1 minute. Add the butter and process for 1 minute, or until the mixture is fluffy. Add the reserved flour mixture and combine the batter by quickly turning the machine on and off about 5 or 6 times or until the flour has just disappeared.

Spoon the batter into 2 well-greased and floured 4-1/2-cup (105 cl) loaf pans or one 8-inch (20 cm) loaf pan. Spread the batter evenly and bake the bread for 45 minutes, or until it is browned. Let the bread cool in the pan(s) for 10 minutes and turn it out on a wire rack to cool completely.

Makes 2 small loaves or 1 8-inch (20 cm) loaf.

Note: For a great combination, spread the bread with Whipped Scallion Cream Cheese (see Index).

A tender biscuit that can be prepared and cooked in a flash!

Preheat the oven to 450°F. (230°C.) and adjust the rack to the middle level.

Glaze _____

1 large egg
1/2 teaspoon salt

Metal Blade: Process the egg and salt for 4 seconds. Remove the mixture and reserve it.

Biscuits _____

1/3 cup (8 cl) parsley
   leaves
2 large scallions
   (2 ounces total, 55g),
   including the green
   tops, cut into 1-inch
   (2.5 cm) pieces
1 teaspoon dried
   dillweed
   Pinch of curry powder
2 cups unbleached
   all-purpose flour
   (10 ounces, 285g)
1 teaspoon salt
1 tablespoon double-
   acting baking powder
2 teaspoons sugar
6 tablespoons solid
   shortening or unsalted
   butter (3 ounces, 85g),
   chilled and cut into 6
   pieces
2 teaspoons Dijon-style
   mustard
2/3 cup (16 cl) milk

Put the parsley, scallions, dillweed and curry in the work bowl and combine by turning the machine on and off 10 or 12 times. Add the flour, salt, baking powder, sugar and shortening or butter and combine the mixture by turning the machine on and off 3 to 5 times, or until the shortening is the size of small peas. Stir the mustard into the milk in a measuring cup and pour the mixture quickly through the feed tube with the machine running. Stop the machine immediately when the dough is combined.

Turn the dough out on a well-floured board, and roll it out to a thickness of 1/2 inch (1.25 cm). Cut biscuits with a cutter of 2 inches (5 cm) in diameter. Transfer them to a greased baking sheet with a metal spatula, placing them so they almost touch for soft biscuits, or 1 inch (2.5 cm) apart for crustier biscuits. Brush the glaze on the biscuits, if desired, and bake them for 12 to 15 minutes, or until they are golden.

Makes about 20 biscuits.

Variation _____

Substitute 2 cups of self-rising flour for the all-purpose flour and omit the baking powder and salt.

This moist cornbread makes a perfect companion to chili.

2/3 cup unbleached
   all-purpose flour
   (3-1/2 ounces, 100g)
2/3 cup cornmeal
   (4 ounces, 115g)
3/4 teaspoon salt
  2 teaspoons double-
   acting baking powder
10 ounces (285g) longhorn
   Colby cheese, chilled
  2 large scallions
   (2 ounces total, 55g),
   including the green
   tops, cut into 2-inch
   (5 cm) lengths
  1 canned *jalapeno*
   pepper, split and
   seeded
  1 12-ounce (340g) can
   whole kernel yellow
   corn, drained, with
   liquid reserved
1/3 cup (8 cl) vegetable oil
  2 large eggs
1/2 cup (12 cl) plus 2
   tablespoons liquid (the
   reserved corn liquid
   plus milk)
  2 tablespoons sugar

Preheat the oven to 425°F. (220°C.) and adjust the rack to the middle level.

Metal Blade: Combine the flour, cornmeal, salt and baking powder in the work bowl and process for 10 seconds. Remove the mixture and reserve it.

Shredding Disc: Shred the cheese, using light pressure. Remove and reserve all but 4 tablespoons.

Metal Blade: Add the scallions and pepper to the work bowl and mince them by turning the machine on and off about 6 times. Add the corn, oil, eggs, liquid and sugar and process the mixture for 30 seconds. Blend in the reserved flour mixture, turning the machine on and off 3 or 4 times or until the flour just disappears. Do not overprocess the mixture.

Sprinkle a thin layer of the reserved cheese on the bottom and sides of a buttered 11-inch (28 cm) round pie plate or baking dish. Ladle the batter into the dish, and bake for 18 minutes. Remove the pie from the oven and sprinkle it with the remaining reserved cheese. Bake it for 4 minutes longer or until the cheese is melted. Let the pie cool for 10 minutes, then cut it into wedges to serve.

Makes 6 to 8 servings.

Note: This dish can be baked in advance without the cheese topping. To reheat before serving, sprinkle on the cheese and bake the pie in a 350°F. (175°C.) oven for 10 minutes, or until cheese is melted and the pie is warm.

Variations _____

1. Use 2/3 cup of self-rising flour and omit a scant 1/2 teaspoon salt and 1 teaspoon of the baking powder.

2. Substitute 2/3 cup of self-rising cornmeal and omit a scant 1/2 teaspoon salt and 1 teaspoon of the baking powder.

Banana Bread

Make several loaves in sequence by processing all the dry ingredients and nuts for each recipe first. You won't have to wash the work bowl between batches of batter for each loaf.

2 cups unbleached all-purpose flour (10 ounces, 285g)
1 teaspoon baking soda
1 teaspoon double-acting baking powder
1/2 teaspoon salt
1/2 cup walnut pieces (2 ounces, 55g)
2 large ripe bananas (13 ounces total, 370g), peeled and cut into 1-inch (2.5 cm) pieces
1 cup sugar (7 ounces, 200g)
3 large eggs
1 stick unsalted butter (4 ounces, 115g), at room temperature and quartered
1/2 cup (12 cl) buttermilk
2 teaspoons vanilla extract

Preheat the oven to 350°F. (175°C.) and adjust the rack to the middle level.

Metal Blade: Put the flour, baking soda, baking powder, salt and nuts in the work bowl and process for 10 seconds, or until the nuts are coarsely chopped. Remove the mixture and reserve it. Process the bananas for 1 minute, or until they are puréed. Add the sugar and eggs and process the mixture for 1 minute. Add the butter and process for 1 minute. With the machine running, pour the buttermilk and vanilla through the feed tube. Blend in the reserved nut mixture by turning the machine on and off 3 to 5 times, or until the flour just disappears. Do not overprocess the batter.

Pour the batter into a buttered and floured 7-cup (166 cl) loaf pan and bake for 1 hour, or until the bread is brown and a cake tester inserted in the center comes out clean. Turn the bread out on a wire rack and let it cool.

Makes 1 loaf.

2 cups unbleached
  all-purpose flour
  (10 ounces, 285g)
1 tablespoon double-
  acting baking powder
1/2 teaspoon baking soda
1/2 teaspoon salt
1/2 teaspoon cinnamon
1/2 teaspoon freshly
  grated nutmeg
1/4 teaspoon ground
  cloves
1/4 teaspoon ground
  ginger
1-1/2 cups sugar
  (10-1/2 ounces, 300g)
2 large eggs
1 stick plus 2 table-
  spoons unsalted butter
  (5 ounces, 140g),
  at room temperature
  and cut into 5 pieces
1 large tart apple, such
  as Granny Smith or
  Greening (8 ounces
  total, 225g), peeled,
  halved and cored
1 cup (24 cl) canned
  pumpkin purée
2 tablespoons
  confectioners sugar
  (optional)

Preheat the oven to 350°F. (175°C.) and adjust the rack to the middle level.

Metal Blade: Put the flour, baking powder, baking soda, salt, cinnamon, nutmeg, cloves and ginger in the work bowl. Process the mixture for 2 seconds; remove it and reserve it. Add the sugar and eggs and process for 1 minute. Add the butter and process the mixture for 1 minute, or until it is fluffy, stopping the machine once to scrape down the sides of the bowl. Leave the mixture in the bowl.

Shredding Disc: Shred the apple, using medium pressure. Leave them in the work bowl.

Metal Blade: Add the pumpkin and process the mixture for 2 seconds. Add the reserved flour mixture and blend the batter by turning the machine on and off 4 to 6 times or until the flour just disappears.

Transfer the batter to a well-buttered and floured 12-cup (2.8L) Bundt pan and bake it for 52 to 55 minutes, or until the bread begins to pull away from the sides of the pan. Let the bread rest in the pan for 5 minutes, then turn it out on a wire rack to cool it completely. (This bread freezes very well.) Sift confectioners sugar over the bread, if desired.

Makes 1 large bread.

Cakes, Frostings & Cookies

Cakes, Frostings & Cookies _____

Yellow Cake
Chocolate Layer Cake
Mocha Fudge Cake
Apple Bundt Cake
Carrot, Prune and Raisin Cake
Lemon Sponge Roll
Hazelnut Upside-Down Apple Cake
Orange Cake Ring
Glazed Almond Praline Cake
Walnut Torte with Chocolate Mousse
Gingerbread Cake

Vanilla Butter Frosting
Maple Walnut Butter Frosting
Orange Apricot Buttercream Frosting
Lemon Glaze
Lemon Cream
Cream Cheese Frosting
Mocha Frosting
Coffee Buttercream Frosting

Cinnamon Nut Cookies
Apricot Squares
Lacy Oatmeal and Wheat Germ Cookies
Crisp Chocolate Wafers
Curved Almond Wafers *(Tuiles)*
Fudge Brownies

Much as the food processor has brought certain foods into the fashion limelight—notably seafood mousses and vegetable purées—so it has also played an important role in preserving some wonderful traditions. Fluffy, high-rising layer cakes, sumptuously frosted and too moist to resist, are one part of the legacy. Old-fashioned homebaked cookies are another.

Nostalgia is not usually my style. If I had to go through all the sifting and creaming that produced the pride of another era or settle for the cotton texture of mixes, my kids would consider layer cakes an extinct species. But it amuses me to bake "from scratch" with the food processor, to throw everything into one bowl and then watch the batter rise majestically in the oven. It's such a marvelous trick—an impromptu celebration in less than half an hour!

Clockwise from top right: Chocolate Butter Frosting, page 221; Maple Walnut Butter Frosting, page 221; Crisp Chocolate Wafers, page 228; Curved Almond Wafers, page 229; Lacy Oatmeal Cookies, page 227; Orange Apricot Buttercream Frosting, page 222; Glazed Almond Praline Cake, page 216, with Zested Strawberries, page 233.

It also amuses me when people claim that it can't be done. Of course it can be done! You just have to know how to take advantage of processor power. If you follow the mixing sequence in my recipes, you can match the texture of the best hand-mixed cakes crumb for crumb. Instead of creaming the butter and sugar, I process the sugar and eggs before adding the butter. As with quick breads, the dry ingredients are added last, and the machine turned on and off a few times. Processing the sugar and eggs for a full minute before adding the butter ensures lightness; the briefest possible processing of the dry ingredients at the end ensures tenderness. So don't get carried away! Once you have added the dry ingredients, process the batter *only* until the flour disappears.

The cake formula is so fundamental and foolproof that it points up other machine talents. Chocolate, for example, doesn't have to be pre-melted. Lemon and orange zest are pulverized in no time; shredded apples and carrots are as easy to add as any other flavoring. I don't think I would even bother with the incredibly good Glazed Almond Praline Cake if I didn't have the machine to grind the praline. Chopping nuts is so effortless that I don't think twice about making the flourless Walnut Torte layers, even though the egg whites have to be beaten separately because there is no other leavening in a classic torte.

Although this chapter highlights machine-fluffy layer cakes and smooth, creamy frostings, it also shows my penchant for streamlining whenever possible. I like the one-pan convenience of Bundt cakes and the lighter look of fruit glazes or a simple sprinkling of powdered sugar. So you'll find that many of the recipes evade frostings in various ways: Apple Bundt Cake and Carrot, Prune and Raisin Cake with the baked-in moisture of fruit, Gingerbread Cake with dollops of a fantastic praline topping. The Lemon Sponge Roll has such a delicious raspberry pear filling that it doesn't really require the whipped cream garnish except for the most festive occasions. The Orange Cake Ring looks glorious when you fill its center with Zested Strawberries. One variation that especially pleases me is cake layers sandwiched with the intense fruitiness of Lemon or Orange Curd and frosted with either sweetened whipped cream or whipped cream and curd.

I can't imagine cookies ever going out of style! The elegant Curved Almond Wafers are a classic French accompaniment to sherbets; the Crisp Chocolate Wafers seem to have been invented just for ice cream. Lacy Oatmeal Wheat Germ Cookies are crisp and scrumptious with frozen or fruit desserts. The Cinnamon Nut Cookies are a big improvement over commercial ready-to-bake cookie dough rolls. And the quick Fudge Brownies should carry a warning—they have proved habit-forming in my household!

This cake is almost as simple as a mix, but much lighter. The variations are all worth trying.

2 cups cake flour
(8 ounces, 255g)
1 tablespoon double-acting baking powder
3/4 teaspoon salt
3/4 teaspoon baking soda
1-3/4 cups sugar
(12-1/2 ounces, 355g)
4 large eggs
1-1/2 sticks unsalted butter
(6 ounces, 170g), at room temperature and cut into 8 pieces
1 cup (24 cl) minus 1 tablespoon buttermilk
1 tablespoon vanilla extract

Preheat the oven to 375°F. (190°C.) and adjust the rack to the middle level.

Metal Blade: Put the flour, baking powder, salt and baking soda in the work bowl and process for 2 seconds. Reserve the mixture. Process the sugar and eggs for 1 minute, or until the mixture is thick and light colored. Add the butter and process the mixture for 1 minute, or until it is fluffy, stopping the machine once to scrape down the sides of the bowl. With the machine running, pour the buttermilk and vanilla through the feed tube. Remove the cover and add the reserved flour mixture. Blend the batter by turning the machine on and off 4 to 6 times, or until the flour just disappears. Do not overprocess it. Divide the batter among 3 buttered and floured 8-inch (20 cm) cake pans, or pour it into a buttered and floured 12-cup (2.8 l) Bundt pan, spreading it with a spatula. Bake layers for 30 minutes or a Bundt for 35 minutes, or until the cake is browned and a toothpick inserted in the center comes out clean. Let the cake rest in the pan(s) for 5 minutes, then invert onto a rack, and let cool. Frost with Chocolate Butter Frosting (see Index).

Makes 12 servings.

Variations _____

1. For a lemon flavor, process the zest of 1 lemon, removed with a vegetable peeler, with 1/4 cup (6 cl) sugar until the zest is as fine as the sugar and proceed with the recipe.

2. For Marble Cake, process 1/2 pound (225g) German Sweet or Maillard's chocolate, broken into pieces, for 2 minutes, or until it is finely minced. Reserve it and proceed with the recipe. Pour the batter into the layer pans, leaving 1/2 cup (12 cl) of batter in the work bowl. Add the reserved chocolate and 2 teaspoons of cocoa to the work bowl and process the mixture for 1 second. Spoon the chocolate batter in dollops over the batter in the pans and use a knife to cut it through the batter at 6 points. This will mix the chocolate in a marbled pattern. Bake as previously directed and frost with Chocolate Butter Frosting or Fudge Butter Frosting with Walnuts (see Index).

3. For Maple Walnut Cake, bake 3/4 cup (18 cl) of walnut pieces in a 350°F. (175°C.) oven for 20 minutes and let them cool. Process the nuts with the dry ingredients for 10 seconds, or until they are finely minced, and proceed with the recipe, substituting 1-1/2 teaspoons of maple flavoring for the vanilla extract. Frost with Maple Walnut Butter Frosting (see Index).

1/2 cup (12 cl) buttermilk
1 cup (24 cl) water
1/2 cup (12 cl) plus 2
  tablespoons cocoa
2 teaspoons vanilla
  extract
2 cups cake flour
  (8 ounces, 225g)
1 tablespoon double-
  acting baking powder
1/2 teaspoon baking soda
1/2 teaspoon salt
2 cups sugar (14 ounces,
  400g)
2 large eggs
1 stick unsalted butter
  (4 ounces, 115g), at
  room temperature and
  quartered

Butter 2 8-inch (20cm) round pans, line their bottoms with parchment paper and butter the paper. Coat the inside of the pans with flour. Preheat the oven to 350°F. (175°C.) and adjust the rack to the middle level. Combine the buttermilk, water, cocoa, and vanilla in a large measuring cup.

Metal Blade: Put the flour, baking powder, baking soda and salt in the work bowl and process for 2 seconds. Reserve the mixture. Process the sugar and eggs for 1 minute, stopping the machine once to scrape down the sides of the bowl. Add the butter, and process the mixture for 1 minute. With the machine running, pour the buttermilk mixture through the feed tube and process for 20 seconds. Add the reserved flour mixture and combine the batter by turning the machine on and off 5 or 6 times, or until the flour just disappears. Do not overprocess.

Divide the batter between the pans and bake for 30 minutes, or until a toothpick inserted in the center comes out clean. Let the layers cool in pans for 5 minutes, then invert them onto wire racks. Remove the pans and let the cake cool completely. Frost the top of one layer and set the other layer on top of it. Frost the top and sides with Fudge Butter Frosting, Vanilla Butter Frosting or Coffee Buttercream (see Index).

Makes 10 servings.

Mocha Fudge Cake

1 cup unbleached all-purpose flour (5 ounces, 140g)
1-1/2 teaspoons baking powder
1 teaspoon baking soda
1/2 teaspoon salt
5 large eggs, separated
1-3/4 cups sugar (12-1/2 ounces, 350g)
2 tablespoons water
1/2 cup plus 1 tablespoon cocoa (2-1/3 ounces, 67g)
1 tablespoon instant coffee powder
2 sticks unsalted butter (8 ounces, 225g) at room temperature, cut into 8 pieces
2 teaspoons pure vanilla extract
1/2 cup plus 2 table-spoons plain yogurt (8 ounces, 225g)

A rich moist cake that's pure temptation — and easy!

Preheat the oven to 375°F. (190°C.) and adjust the rack to the middle level. Generously butter a 12-cup (28 dl) Bundt pan with 2 tablespoons of soft butter and dust it with flour. In a 2-cup (4.7 dl) mixing bowl, combine the flour, baking powder, baking soda and salt with a spoon and set the mixture aside.

Assemble all the ingredients and a 1-quart (9.5 dl) mixing bowl conveniently near the food processor.

Metal Blade: Put the egg whites and 4 tablespoons of sugar in the work bowl and turn the machine on. After 8 seconds, pour the water through the feed tube while the machine is running. Process for about 2 minutes, or until the egg whites are whipped and hold their shape. With a rubber spatula, gently transfer the egg whites to the mixing bowl. It is not necessary to wash the work bowl.

Process the egg yolks, remaining sugar, cocoa and coffee for about 1 minute. Add the butter and process for about 1 minute, stopping once to scrape down the sides of the work bowl. Add the vanilla and yogurt and process for 5 seconds. Add the flour mixture and combine the batter by turning the machine on and off twice.

Spoon 1/4 of the egg white mixture onto the batter and turn the machine on and off twice. Run a spatula around the sides of the bowl, to loosen the mixture. Spoon the remaining egg whites onto the mixture in a ring. Turn the machine on and off 3 times. Run a spatula around the sides of the bowl and turn the machine on and off once more.

Pour the batter into the prepared pan and cut through it with a knife to remove any air pockets. Bake for 35 minutes, or until the cake begins to pull away from the sides of the pan and a toothpick inserted in the center comes out clean. Let the cake cool in the pan on a rack for 10 minutes. Then invert it onto a wire rack and remove the pan. Let the cake cool completely and frost it with Mocha Frosting (see Index).

Makes 12 servings.

_____

This cake is so moist that I like it best without frosting.

2 cups unbleached all-
    purpose flour
    (10 ounces, 285g)
2 teaspoons double-
    acting baking powder
2 teaspoons baking
    soda
1 teaspoon salt
1/2 teaspoon freshly
    grated nutmeg
1/2 teaspoon ground
    allspice
1 teaspoon cinnamon
3/4 cup walnut pieces
    (3 ounces, 85g)
3 large tart apples
    (1 pound total, 455g)
    preferably Granny
    Smiths, peeled,
    halved and cored
2 strips lemon zest,
    removed with a
    vegetable peeler
2 cups sugar (14 ounces,
    400g)
4 large eggs
1 cup (24 cl) vegetable
    oil
1 teaspoon vanilla
    extract
1/2 cup (12 cl) golden
    raisins

Preheat the oven to 325°F. (160°C.) and adjust the rack to the middle level.

Metal Blade: Put the flour, baking powder, baking soda, salt, spices, and walnuts in the work bowl and process for 8 seconds, or until the nuts are coarsely chopped. Reserve the mixture.

Shredding Disc: Shred the apples, using medium pressure. Reserve them.

Metal Blade: Process the lemon zest with 1/2 cup (3-1/2 ounces, 100g) sugar until it is as fine as the sugar. Add the remaining sugar and eggs, and process the mixture for 1 minute, or until it is thick and light colored. Add the oil and process the mixture for 30 seconds. Add the vanilla and the shredded apples and combine the mixture by turning the machine on and off about 4 times. Add the reserved flour mixture and the raisins and combine the batter by turning the machine on and off just until the flour disappears. Do not overprocess it.

Pour the batter into a well buttered and floured 12-cup (2.8l) Bundt pan and bake the cake for 55 minutes, or until a toothpick inserted in the center comes out clean. Let the cake cool in the pan for 10 minutes. Then invert it onto a wire rack, remove the pan and let it cool completely.

Makes 12 servings.

Note: This cake can be baked in 3 8-inch (20 cm) round pans and frosted with Cream Cheese Frosting, Vanilla Butter Frosting, or Maple Walnut Butter Frosting (see Index).

Carrot, Prune and Raisin Cake

This cake recipe was sent to me by a reader of my food-processor column in *Bon Appetit* magazine. It won the Best of Show award in the 1978 Texas State Fair. You'll know why when you make it!

2 cups unbleached all-purpose flour (10 ounces, 285g)
2 teaspoons baking soda
2 teaspoons double-acting baking powder
1 teaspoon salt
1/4 teaspoon nutmeg
1/4 teaspoon ground allspice
1 tablespoon cinnamon
7 large dried prunes, pitted
3/4 cup pecans (3 ounces, 85g)
5 medium carrots (9-1/2 ounces total, 270g) scrubbed and trimmed
4 large eggs
2 cups sugar (14 ounces, 400g)
1-1/2 cups (35 cl) oil
3/4 cup (18 cl) golden raisins
2 tablespoons confectioners sugar

Preheat the oven to 325°F. (160°C.) and adjust the rack to the middle level.

Metal Blade: Put the flour, baking soda, baking powder, salt and spices in the work bowl and process them for 2 seconds. Leave about 1 tablespoon of the mixture in the bowl; remove the rest and reserve it. Put the prunes in the work bowl and process for 10 seconds to chop them. Add the nuts and process for 5 seconds. Transfer the mixture to a larger bowl.

Shredding Disc: Shred the carrots, using firm pressure. You should have about 3 cups of shredded carrots. Add them to the prune mixture and combine them with a spoon.

Metal Blade: Put the eggs and sugar in the work bowl and process for 1 minute, or until the mixture is thick and light colored. With the machine running, pour the oil through the feed tube and process for 1 full minute, or until the mixture is fluffy, stopping the machine once to scrape down the sides of the bowl. Add the prune and carrot mixture and the raisins and process for 3 seconds. Add the dry ingredients and combine by turning the machine on and off 5 or 6 times, or only until the flour just disappears. Do not overprocess.

Pour the batter into a greased and floured 12-cup (2.8 l) Bundt pan and smooth the top with a spatula. Bake in a preheated oven for 55 minutes. Allow the cake to cool in the pan for 10 minutes. Then invert it onto a wire rack, remove the pan and let it cool completely. Sift confectioners sugar over it.

Note: This cake can be baked in 3 8-inch (20 cm) round pans and frosted with a double recipe of Cream Cheese Frosting (see Index).

A light dessert that is also light on calories if you leave out the whipped cream.

3/4 cup cake flour
(3 ounces, 85g)
1-1/2 teaspoons baking
powder
Pinch of salt
4 large egg whites
2 tablespoons fresh
lemon juice
Zest of 1 lemon,
removed with a zester
3/4 cup sugar
(5-1/4 ounces, 148g)
3 large egg yolks
1 tablespoon
confectioners sugar

Preheat the oven to 325°F. (165°C.) and adjust the rack to the middle level. Line an 11 by 17-inch (28 by 43 cm) jelly roll pan with waxed paper, extending the paper 2 inches (5 cm) beyond the edges of the pan. Butter the paper.

Sift the cake flour, baking powder and salt onto a piece of waxed paper and set the mixture aside. Assemble all the ingredients and a 1-quart (9.5 dl) mixing bowl conveniently near the food processor.

Metal Blade: Put the egg whites in a clean work bowl and turn the machine on. After 8 seconds, pour 2 teaspoons of the lemon juice through the feed tube while the machine is running. Process for about 1 minute and 30 seconds, or until the egg whites are whipped and hold their shape. With a rubber spatula, gently transfer the egg whites to the mixing bowl. It is not necessary to wash the work bowl.

Put the zest and sugar in the work bowl and process until the zest is minced as fine as the sugar. Add the egg yolks and remaining lemon juice and process for about 1 minute, stopping once to scrape down the sides of the work bowl. Spoon the flour on top of the egg yolk mixture in a ring and combine by turning the machine on and off twice. Spoon the egg whites onto the mixture in a ring. Turn the machine on and off twice. Run a spatula around the sides of the work bowl, to loosen the mixture. Turn the machine on and off once more. Some egg white may be visible; do not overprocess.

Spread the batter evenly in the prepared pan and bang the pan on the counter to remove any air pockets. Bake for 15 to 18 minutes, or until the sponge is barely golden. Sift 1 tablespoon of confectioners sugar over the cake, cover it with waxed paper and a damp towel and invert it. Let the cake cool for 20 minutes, peel off the top sheet of paper and invert the cake onto another towel.

Filling

1 10-ounce (285g)
package frozen
raspberries, thawed
and well drained
3 pears (1 pound total,
455g), peeled, cored
and quartered
1 teaspoon sugar

Metal Blade: Process the raspberries for 5 seconds and force the purée through a sieve into a bowl. Chop the pears with the sugar, turning the machine on and off until they are finely chopped. Transfer the pears to a saucepan and cook them over moderate heat for 10 minutes.

1 package unflavored
   gelatin
3 tablespoons orange
   juice
1 large egg white
1 teaspoon sugar

Sprinkle the gelatin over the orange juice in a small dish. When the gelatin is dissolved, stir the mixture into the pears. Remove the pan from the heat, stir in the raspberry purée, and transfer the mixture to a bowl.

In another bowl beat the egg white until soft peaks form. Add the sugar and continue beating until stiff but not dry. Fold 1/4 of the beaten egg white into the pear mixture. Fold in the remaining egg white and refrigerate the mixture until it is slightly thickened.

Remove the remaining paper from the cake and spread the cake with the filling. Roll it up, using the towel to lift it. Or roll up the cake unfilled in a slightly damp towel and let it rest for a few hours until it is filled.

Garnish _____

1 cup (24 cl) heavy
   cream, chilled
2 teaspoons sugar

Metal Blade: Chill the work bowl, add the cream and process until it is thick. Add the sugar and process for 3 seconds.

Transfer the filled sponge roll to a platter and use a spatula to spread it with the cream. Make a ridged pattern in the cream with a knife. Refrigerate the sponge roll until serving.

Makes 8 servings.

Variation _____

Fill the roll with Lemon Cream or Lemon Curd Filling (see Index for both).

Lemon Sponge Roll with Lemon Curd Filling

This cake, which comes from a winning recipe in my Machine Cuisine classes, is best when served warm.

3 tablespoons unsalted butter
1/2 cup sugar (3-1/2 ounces, 100g)
1/2 teaspoon cinnamon
1/2 teaspoon freshly grated nutmeg
2 tablespoons hazelnuts
1-1/2 cups minus 1 tablespoon unbleached all-purpose flour (7-1/2 ounces, 215g)
2 teaspoons double-acting baking powder
1 teaspoon baking soda
1/2 teaspoon salt
4 tart apples (1 pound, 4 ounces total, 567g), preferably Granny Smiths, peeled, halved and cored
1 cup sugar (7 ounces, 200g)
2 large eggs
1 stick unsalted butter (4 ounces, 115g), at room temperature and quartered
1/3 cup (8 cl) milk
2 tablespoons rum
2 teaspoons vanilla extract

Preheat the oven to 350°F. (175°C.) and adjust the rack to the middle level.

Melt the butter over low heat in an 8-inch (20 cm) round baking pan, 3 inches (7.5 cm) deep. Brush the butter onto the sides of the pan and sprinkle the bottom with the combined sugar, cinnamon and nutmeg.

Metal Blade: Finely mince the hazelnuts by processing them with 1/4 cup flour for 20 seconds. Add the remaining flour, baking powder, baking soda and salt, and process the mixture for 3 seconds. Remove the mixture and reserve it.

Medium Slicing Disc: Reserve 2 halves of the apples and put the remaining pieces in the feed tube horizontally. Slice them, using medium pressure. Make a circle of slices, rounded sides down, and overlapping around the edge of the pan. Fill in the center with another circle of apples and arrange the remaining slices evenly over this base, covering any openings between slices.

Metal Blade: Chop the reserved apple halves in the work bowl by turning the machine on and off about 8 times. Measure them to be sure you have 1 cup (24 cl), and return them to the work bowl. Add the sugar and eggs and process for 1 minute. Add the butter and process for 1 minute. Add the milk, rum and vanilla and process for 5 seconds. Add the nut mixture and combine it by turning the machine on and off 4 or 5 times, or until the flour just disappears. Do not overprocess.

Ladle the batter carefully over the apples, spreading it evenly with a spatula. Bake the cake for 1 hour and 10 to 20 minutes, or until a toothpick inserted in the center comes out clean. Let the cake cool in the pan for 5 minutes. Separate it from the pan by running a flexible knife around the sides.

Invert the pan onto a wire rack and leave the pan on it for 10 minutes. Lift the pan off carefully.

Makes 8 to 10 servings.

Note: You can reheat this cake by putting it on a foil-lined baking sheet in a cold oven and heating it at 300°F. (150°C.) for 15 to 20 minutes.

Fill the center with fresh fruit, and you have the perfect ending for a festive luncheon or dinner party.

Cake

1 cup plus 3 tablespoons unbleached all-purpose flour (6 ounces, 170g)
2 teaspoons double-acting baking powder
1/2 teaspoon salt
1/4 teaspoon baking soda
Zest of 2 oranges, removed with a vegetable peeler
1 cup sugar (7 ounces, 200g),
3 large eggs
1 stick unsalted butter (4 ounces, 115g), at room temperature and quartered
2/3 cup orange juice

Preheat oven to 375°F. (190°C.) and adjust the rack to the lower third. Spray a 6-1/2 cup (1.5l) ring mold generously with nonstick vegetable oil spray or butter it generously with 2 tablespoons of softened butter. Sprinkle it with flour.

Metal Blade: Put the flour, baking powder, salt, and baking soda in the work bowl and process for 2 seconds. Reserve the mixture. Process the zest with 1/4 cup sugar until it is as fine as the sugar. Add the remaining sugar and the eggs and process the mixture for 1 minute, or until it is thick and light colored. Add the butter and process the mixture until it is fluffy, stopping the machine once to scrape down the sides of the bowl. With the machine running, pour the orange juice through the feed tube. Add the reserved flour mixture, and combine the batter by turning the machine on and off 3 or 4 times, or until the flour just disappears. Do not overprocess.

Spoon the batter into the prepared ring and spread it with a spatula. Bake the cake for 25 minutes, or until the sides begin to pull away from the pan or a toothpick inserted in the center comes out clean. Let the cake cool in the pan for 5 minutes. Separate it from the pan by running a small flexible knife around the sides; invert it onto a wire rack. Remove the pan.

Glaze

1/4 cup (6 cl) apricot preserves
Zest of 1 lemon, removed with a zester
1 tablespoon lemon juice
1 tablespoon water
2 teaspoons dark rum

Combine the preserves, zest, lemon, juice and water in a saucepan and bring the mixture to a boil. Simmer it for 2 minutes. Force the mixture through a sieve into a bowl and stir in the rum. Brush the glaze on the warm cake. Fill the center of the cake with Zested Strawberries (see Index) or any fresh fruit in season.

Variations

1. Substitute Orange Frosting Glaze (see Index) for the Lemon Apricot Glaze.

2. Bake the cake in 2 thin 8-inch (20 cm) layers and frost it with Orange Curd Cream Filling (see Index). Or spread Orange Curd between the layers and frost with Vanilla Butter Frosting (see Index).

Glazed Almond Praline Cake

A delicate and festive cake that would be very time consuming without the aid of a food processor.

Cake

1 cup sugar
(7 ounces, 200g)
1/4 cup (6 cl) water
1 cup whole or slivered
blanched almonds
(4 ounces, 115g)
Scant 1/2 cup
unbleached all-
purpose flour
(2-1/2 ounces, 70g)
1-1/2 teaspoons double-
acting baking powder
1/2 teaspoon salt
4 large eggs
1 stick plus 2
tablespoons unsalted
butter (5 ounces, 140g),
at room temperature
and quartered
2 teaspoons dark rum

Generously butter a 6-cup (1.5l) ring mold and line the bottom with buttered parchment paper. Sprinkle the mold and the paper with flour. Adjust an oven rack to the middle level, but do not preheat the oven.

Combine the sugar and water in a heavy saucepan and cook over medium-high heat, stirring only until the sugar is dissolved. Bring the syrup to a boil and add the almonds. Cook the mixture until it turns a rich brown, shaking the pan but never stirring. Quickly pour the mixture onto a greased baking sheet and let it harden for 20 minutes.

Metal Blade: Put the flour, baking powder, and salt in the work bowl, and process for 2 seconds. Reserve the mixture. Break the almond praline into pieces and put it in the work bowl. Chop it coarsely by turning the machine on and off about 4 times, then process until it is finely ground. (Praline, tightly covered, can be stored in the refrigerator or freezer for several weeks.)

Add the eggs and process the mixture for 2 minutes, or until it is very creamy and smooth, stopping the machine once to scrape down the sides of the bowl. Add the butter and rum and process for 2 minutes. Add the reserved flour mixture and combine the batter by turning the machine on and off 3 or 4 times, until the flour just disappears. Do not overprocess.

Pour the batter into the prepared pan and bang the pan on the counter to distribute the batter evenly. Put it in the oven, set the temperature at 300°F. (150°C.) and bake the cake for 50 to 60 minutes, or until it begins to pull away from the sides of the pan. Let it cool in the pan for 5 minutes. Separate it from the pan by running a small, flexible knife around the sides. Invert the cake onto a wire rack and carefully remove the pan and the parchment paper.

Glaze

1/4 cup (6 cl) apricot
preserves
Zest of 1 orange,
removed with a zester
1 tablespoon water
1 tablespoon dark rum

Combine the apricot preserves, zest, and water in a saucepan and bring the mixture to a boil. Force it through a sieve into a bowl and stir in the rum. Brush the glaze on the warm cake. Transfer the cake to a platter and fill the center of the cake with Zested Strawberries (see Index). Use any extra strawberries to garnish the platter.

Makes 8 servings.

Note: The cake can be wrapped tightly and frozen before glazing. To reheat, put the unwrapped cake on a baking sheet in the lower third of a cold oven. Set the temperature to 300°F. (150°C.) and bake the cake for 25 minutes. Let the cake cool on a wire rack.

Variations _____

1. For stronger almond flavoring, add 1/2 teaspoon almond extract and 1 tablespoon of vanilla extract.

2. For a quicker version, without the praline, omit the 1/4 cup (6 cl) water and brown the almonds in a 325°F. (160°C.) oven for 15 minutes. Process the browned almonds and sugar for 1 minute, or until the nuts are as fine as sugar, and proceed with the recipe.

3. For Pineapple Upside-Down Cake, melt 4 tablespoons of unsalted butter in a large skillet and stir in 1/2 cup (12 cl) of firmly packed dark brown sugar. Add 2 cups (47 cl) of sliced fresh pineapple and cook the mixture over moderate heat for 25 minutes or until the pineapple is browned and carmelized on both sides. Arrange the pineapple in a decorative pattern on the bottom of a buttered 8-inch (20 cm) round 3-inch (7.5 cm) deep cake pan and bake according to the recipe. Let the cake cool in the pan for 10 minutes, then invert it carefully onto a serving plate. Serve it warm or at room temperature and pass whipped cream in a separate dish.

Walnut Torte

This torte can be spread with Chocolate Mousse as specified in the recipe, or it can be served on its own, spread with coffee or chocolate flavored whipped cream.

Torte

- **7 large eggs, separated**
- **1 cup sugar (7 ounces, 200g)**
- **1 tablespoon white vinegar**
- **2 cups walnuts (8 ounces, 225g)**
- **1 tablespoon instant freeze-dried coffee flakes**
- **2 tablespoons dark rum**
  Pinch of salt
  Chocolate Mousse (see Index)

Assembly

Preheat the oven to 350°F. (175°C.) and adjust the rack to the middle level. Butter two 8-inch (20 cm) round cake pans and line the bottoms with parchment paper. Butter the paper, sprinkle the inside of the pans with flour and shake out any excess. Assemble all the ingredients and a 1-quart (9.5 dl) mixing bowl conveniently near the food processor.

Metal Blade: Put the egg whites and 2 tablespoons of sugar into a clean work bowl and turn the machine on. After 8 seconds, pour the vinegar through the feed tube while the machine is running. Process for about 2 minutes and 10 seconds, or until the egg whites are whipped and hold their shape. With a rubber spatula, gently transfer the egg whites to the mixing bowl. It is not necessary to wash the work bowl.

Put the egg yolks, remaining sugar, walnuts, coffee, rum and salt in the work bowl and process for 1 minute, stopping once to scrape down the sides of the bowl. Add 1/4 of the egg whites and turn the machine on and off once. Run a spatula around the sides of the work bowl, to loosen the mixture. Add the remaining egg whites and turn the machine on and off 3 times, until the ingredients are just mixed.

Divide the batter evenly between the two pans and smooth the surface with a spatula. Bake in the preheated oven for 26 minutes, or until the cakes just begin to pull away from the inside of the pans. Transfer the pans to a cooling rack and let cakes cool in the pans, which they will shrink back into. Run a small knife around the inside of the pans to loosen the cakes and invert them onto the cooling rack.

Spread the top of one layer with 1/2 inch (1.25 cm) of Chocolate Mousse that has been refrigerated until of spreading consistency. Center the remaining layer on the first one and spread the top and sides with the mousse. The torte can be made and assembled up to 3 days in advance and refrigerated or frozen. Be sure to wrap it airtight after it is frozen and let it thaw in the refrigerator overnight before serving.

Makes 12 servings.

This mousse is excellent on its own, and it can also be used to spread and frost the Walnut Torte (see Index).

1/2 cup (1.2 dl) water
3/4 cup sugar
   (5-1/4 ounces, 150g)
8 large egg whites
1 tablespoon white
   vinegar
1 tablespoon water
4 ounces (115g)
   unsweetened
   chocolate, broken into
   pieces
4 ounces (115g) sweet
   chocolate, broken into
   pieces
2 teaspoons instant
   freeze-dried coffee
   flakes
7 large egg yolks
2 teaspoons pure
   vanilla extract

Put the water and 1/4 cup (50g) of sugar in a 1-quart (9.5 dl) saucepan over medium heat, bring it to a simmer and allow to simmer until you are ready to use it.

Assemble all the ingredients and a 1-quart (9.5 dl) mixing bowl conveniently near the food processor. Put the vinegar and water in a small dish.

Metal Blade: Put the egg whites and 1/4 cup (50g) of sugar into a clean work bowl and turn the machine on. After 8 seconds, pour the vinegar and water through the feed tube while the machine is running. Process for about 3 minutes, or until the egg whites are whipped and hold their shape. With a rubber spatula, gently transfer the mixture to the mixing bowl. It is not necessary to wash the work bowl.

Put the chocolate, coffee and remaining sugar in the work bowl and turn the machine on and off 6 times to chop the chocolate. Then process continuously until the chocolate is as fine as the sugar. Stop the machine once to scrape down the sides of the bowl. With the machine running, pour the simmering sugar syrup through the feed tube and process for about 30 seconds, until the chocolate is melted. Add the egg yolks and vanilla and turn the machine on and off 3 times. Spoon the egg whites onto the chocolate in a ring. Turn the machine on and off twice and run a spatula around the sides of the work bowl to loosen the mixture. Some streaks of egg white may be visible; do not overprocess.

With a rubber spatula, transfer the mousse to a 6-cup soufflé dish or 12 individual ramekins. Cover airtight with plastic wrap and refrigerate at least 4 hours before serving.

The Chocolate Mousse will keep in the refrigerator for several days, or can be wrapped airtight and frozen.

Makes 12 servings, or 6 cups (14 dl).

The walnut praline topping adds a festive air to this old favorite.

Gingerbread

- 3 cups unbleached all-purpose flour (15 ounces, 425g)
- 1 teaspoon baking soda
- 1 teaspoon ground ginger
- 1 teaspoon cinnamon
- 1/2 teaspoon ground cloves
- 1/2 teaspoon ground allspice
- 1/2 teaspoon salt
- 2 large eggs
- 1 cup firmly packed dark brown sugar (8 ounces, 225g)
- 2 sticks unsalted butter (1/2 pound, 225g), at room temperature and cut into 8 pieces
- 1 cup (24 cl) buttermilk
- 3/4 cup (18 cl) molasses

Preheat the oven to 350°F. (175°C.) and adjust the rack to the middle level.

Metal Blade: Put the flour, baking soda, ginger, cinnamon, cloves, allspice, and salt in the work bowl and process for 2 seconds. Reserve the mixture. Process the eggs and brown sugar for 1 minute, stopping the machine once to scrape down the sides of the bowl. Add the butter and process for 1 minute. Add the buttermilk and molasses and process for 10 seconds. Add the reserved flour mixture and combine the batter by turning the machine on and off 8 or 9 times, or until the flour just disappears. Do not overprocess.

Spread the batter evenly in a greased 13- by 9-inch (33 cm by 23 cm) baking pan and bake for 40 minutes. Serve warm or at room temperature. To reheat it, place it in a preheated 300°F. (150°C.) oven for 10 minutes.

Topping

- 3 tablespoons water
- 1/2 cup sugar (3-1/2 ounces, 100g)
- 1/3 cup walnut pieces (1-1/2 ounces, 45g)
- 1 cup (24 cl) heavy cream, chilled

Stir the water and sugar together in a heavy saucepan until the sugar is dissolved. Cover and cook over moderately high heat for 1 minute. Add the walnuts and cook the mixture, uncovered, until it turns a rich brown, shaking the pan but never stirring. Pour the praline onto a greased baking sheet and let it harden for 20 minutes.

Metal Blade: Break the walnut praline into pieces and put it in the work bowl. Process for 1 minute, or until it is as fine as sugar, and reserve it. (Praline can be covered tightly and stored for several weeks in the refrigerator or freezer.)

Process the cream in the work bowl until it is thick and smooth. Add 1/2 cup (12 cl) of the praline, and combine it by turning the machine on and off a couple of times.

Cut the gingerbread into squares. Serve with a dollop of the topping sprinkled with 1/2 teaspoon of the praline. It is also good topped with Lemon Cream or Lemon Curd Filling (see Index).

Makes 8 to 12 servings.

Vanilla Butter Frosting

3 cups confectioners
  sugar (12 ounces, 340g)
  Pinch salt
2 teaspoons vanilla
  extract
5 tablespoons unsalted
  butter (2-1/2 ounces,
  70g), at room
  temperature
4 to 5 tablespoons sour
  cream

Metal Blade: Put the sugar and salt in the work bowl and process for 5 seconds. Add the vanilla, butter and 4 tablespoons of the sour cream. Process for 5 seconds. Add the remaining sour cream, if necessary, to bring the frosting to spreading consistency.

Makes enough frosting for the top and sides of 2 8-inch (20 cm) layers.

Variations

1. For Chocolate Butter Frosting, add 1/4 cup (6 cl) of cocoa with the confectioners sugar.

2. For Chocolate Walnut Butter Frosting, follow the above variation and add 1/3 cup (8 cl) of walnut pieces with the cocoa and sugar. Process until the nuts are finely minced before proceeding with the recipe.

Maple Walnut Butter Frosting

1/3 cup walnut pieces
  (1-1/2 ounces, 45g)
3 cups confectioners
  sugar (12 ounces, 340g)
5 tablespoons unsalted
  butter (2-1/2 ounces,
  70g), at room
  temperature
  Pinch salt
3/4 teaspoon maple
  flavoring
4 to 5 tablespoons sour
  cream

Metal Blade: Process the nuts for 5 seconds, or until they are finely minced. Add the sugar and process for 5 seconds, to remove any lumps. Add the butter, salt and maple flavoring and process for 5 seconds. Add 4 tablespoons of sour cream and process until the frosting is smooth. Add the remaining sour cream, if necessary, to bring the frosting to spreading consistency.

Makes enough frosting for the top and sides of 2 8-inch (20 cm) layers.

1/2 cup dried apricots
   (3 ounces, 85g)
   Zest of 1 orange,
   removed with a zester
1-1/4 cups (30 cl) orange
   juice
1 cup sugar (7 ounces,
   200g)
1/4 cup unbleached all-
   purpose flour
   (1-1/4 ounces, 35g)
3/4 cup (18 cl) milk,
   approximately
3 large egg yolks
1 tablespoons Grand
   Marnier
2-1/2 sticks unsalted butter
   (10 ounces, 285g), at
   room temperature

Combine the apricots, orange zest and orange juice in a small saucepan and cook over medium heat until the fruit is soft and the juice is reduced to about 1/4 to 1/3 cup (6 to 8 cl). Strain and reserve the juice in a measuring cup.

Metal Blade: Put the apricots and orange zest into the work bowl with the sugar. Process until the mixture is smooth. Add the flour and process until the flour disappears.

Add enough milk to the orange juice to make 1 cup of liquid. With the machine running, pour liquid through the feed tube.

Transfer the contents of the work bowl to a heavy 2-quart (1.9l) stainless steel saucepan. Put the egg yolks in the work bowl; there is no need to wash the bowl. Cook the apricot mixture over low to medium heat, stirring constantly, until it starts to bubble. With the machine running, carefully pour the hot apricot mixture through the feed tube, scraping the saucepan with a spatula. Process for 30 seconds and add the Grand Marnier. Let the mixture cool to room temperature. When it is cool turn on the machine and add the butter, one piece at a time, waiting until each one is thoroughly incorporated before adding the next one. Refrigerate until of spreading consistency.

Makes enough frosting for the top and sides of 2 8-inch (20 cm) layers.

Lemon Glaze _____

1 cup confectioners
   sugar (4 ounces, 115g)
   Pinch salt
   Zest of 1 orange,
   removed with a zester
   Zest of 1 lemon,
   removed with a zester
2 tablespoons unsalted
   butter, (1 ounce, 30g),
   at room temperature
2 teaspoons lemon juice
1 teaspoon Grand
   Marnier

Metal Blade: Put the sugar, salt and fruit zests in the work bowl and process them for 5 seconds. Add the remaining ingredients and process for 5 seconds longer.

This glaze should be spread while a cake is still hot. It thins out on the cake.

Makes enough glaze for 1 ring cake.

Lemon Cream

Zest of 2 large lemons or of 1 lemon and 1 orange, removed with a zester
2/3 cup sugar (5 ounces, 140g)
1-1/2 cups (35 cl) whipping cream, chilled

Metal Blade: Put the zest and the sugar in the work bowl and process until the zest is minced as fine as the sugar. Leave 3 tablespoons of the zested sugar in the work bowl. Remove the rest and put it in an airtight plastic bag to refrigerate or freeze for another use.

Add the cream to the work bowl and process until thick, watching carefully to prevent overwhipping. The cream can be refrigerated up to 2 days before it is spread on a cake of your choice.

Makes 3 cups.

Cream Cheese Frosting

1 8-ounce (225g) package cream cheese, softened and quartered
2 tablespoons sour cream
1/2 cup confectioners sugar (2 ounces, 55g)
2 teaspoons vanilla extract

Metal Blade: Process all the ingredients until the frosting is creamy. The recipe can easily be doubled

Makes enough frosting for the top and sides of an 8-inch (20 cm) layer cake.

Mocha Frosting

2 tablespoons walnut pieces (1/2 ounce, 15g)
1/4 cup (6 cl) water
2 tablespoons unsalted butter (1 ounce, 30g)
1 teaspoon instant-coffee powder
3 ounces (85g) sweet cooking chocolate, broken into pieces
1 cup confectioners sugar (4 ounces, 115g)

Shredding Disc: Mince the nuts, using light pressure. Reserve them.

Heat the water, butter, and coffee in a small saucepan until the butter is melted and the mixture is hot.

Metal Blade: Process the chocolate for 30 seconds, or until it is powder. With the machine running, pour the hot butter mixture through the feed tube. Add the sugar and process for 5 seconds, stopping to scrape down the sides of the bowl with a rubber spatula.

Let the frosting stand for 15 to 25 minutes, or until it is thick. Drizzle it evenly over the cake. Sprinkle the reserved nuts over the frosting.

Makes enough frosting for a 12-inch (30 cm) Bundt or the top and sides of an 8-inch (20 cm) layer cake.

Coffee Buttercream

3 large egg yolks
2 tablespoons instant coffee
Pinch of salt
2/3 cup sugar (4-1/2 ounces, 128g)
1/4 cup unbleached all purpose flour (1-1/4 ounces, 35g)
3/4 cup (24 cl) milk
2 sticks unsalted butter (1/2 pound, 225g) chilled and cut into 8 pieces

Metal Blade: Process the egg yolks, coffee, salt and sugar for 1 minute, stopping once to scrape down the work bowl. Add the flour and process for 5 seconds. With the machine running, pour the milk through the feed tube and process 2 seconds.

Transfer the mixture to a heavy 1-quart (95 cl) saucepan and cook gently, stirring constantly, until it is as thick as cake batter. Allow to cool to room temperature, stirring occasionally.

Metal Blade: Process the butter until fluffy, stopping once to scrape down the work bowl. Add all the cooled mixture and the vanilla and process until thoroughly mixed, about 10 seconds.

Makes enough for top and sides of 2 8-inch (20 cm) layers.

Cinnamon Nut Cookies

Keep rolls of the dough for these crisp and delicately flavored cookies in the freezer to bake for unexpected guests.

Cookie Dough

2 sticks unsalted butter (1/2 pound, 225g), at room temperature and cut into 8 pieces
1 cup sugar (7 ounces, 200g)
1 tablespoon cinnamon
1/2 teaspoon salt
1 large egg yolk
1 cup unbleached all-purpose flour (5 ounces, 140g)
1 cup cake flour (4 ounces, 115g)

Metal Blade: Mix the butter, sugar, cinnamon and salt in the work bowl by turning the machine on and off. Process the mixture for 1-1/2 minutes, or until it is fluffy. Add the egg yolk and process for 30 seconds longer. Add the flours and turn the machine on and off to combine them, stopping as soon as the flour has almost disappeared.

Quarter the dough and on a lightly floured board roll each quarter into a log 2 inches (5 cm) in diameter. Refrigerate the logs, each wrapped separately in plastic wrap, until they are firm. The dough can also be frozen. Wipe out the work bowl with a paper towel.

Garnish

1/2 cup walnut pieces (2 ounces, 55g)

Metal Blade: Chop the walnuts by turning the machine on and off and reserve them.

Glaze

1 large egg
1/2 teaspoon salt

Metal Blade: Process the egg and salt for 2 seconds and reserve it.

Assembly

Preheat the oven to 350°F. (175°C.) and adjust the rack to the middle level. Sprinkle 2 well greased baking sheets with water and shake off the excess.

Slice the dough 1/4 inch (.60 cm) thick and put the slices on the baking sheets. Press them to the desired thinness with the heel of your hand. (This dough will not spread as it bakes.) Brush the slices with glaze and sprinkle them with the reserved nuts, pressing the nuts lightly in place with the back of a spoon. Bake the cookies for 8 to 10 minutes, or until they are lightly browned. Transfer them to wire racks to cool.

Makes about 50 cookies.

Quick, easy and delicious — a perfect accompaniment to fresh fruit desserts and sherbets.

1 stick unsalted butter (4 ounces, 115g), cut into 6 pieces
1 cup unbleached all-purpose flour (5 ounces, 140g)
1/4 cup confectioners sugar (1 ounce, 30g)
Pinch of salt
2/3 cup dried apricot halves (2-1/2 ounces, 70g), soaked in water and drained
Zest of 1 lemon, removed with a vegetable peeler
1 cup sugar (7 ounces, 200g)
2 large eggs
1/4 cup (6 cl) lemon juice
1/2 teaspoon double-acting baking powder
1/8 teaspoon salt

Preheat the oven to 350°F. (175°C.) and adjust the rack to the middle level.

Metal Blade: Combine the butter, flour, confectioners sugar and salt in the work bowl by turning the machine on and off until the mixture is uniformly moist. It may form a ball but this is not necessary. Do not overprocess it. Press the mixture into the bottom of a 9-inch (23 cm) square baking pan and bake it for 15 minutes.

Process the apricots, lemon zest and sugar in the work bowl by turning the machine on and off until the apricots are finely chopped; reserve the mixture. Add the eggs and process the mixture for 10 seconds, until they are light. Add the chopped apricots and the remaining ingredients and combine by turning the machine on and off about 6 times. Pour the mixture over the crust and bake for 25 minutes, or until it is well browned around the edges. Let it cool and cut it into 1-1/2-inch (4 cm) squares.

Makes 36 squares.

Apricot Squares, and Lacy Oatmeal and Wheat Germ Cookies (recipe opposite)

Lacy Oatmeal and Wheat Germ Cookies

This small quantity of dough produces a surprising number of lovely delicate cookies that make a fine complement to fruit and ice cream desserts.

3/4 cup walnut pieces
(3 ounces, 85g)
1-1/2 sticks unsalted butter
(6 ounces, 170g),
softened
1-1/2 cups light brown sugar
(12 ounces, 340g),
firmly packed
1 large egg
1 teaspoon vanilla
extract
1 teaspoon cinnamon
1/2 teaspoon salt
1 cup quick-cooking
rolled oats
(3 ounces, 30g)
1/4 cup wheat germ
(1 ounce, 30g)
2 tablespoons cake flour

Preheat the oven to 375°F. (190°C.) and adjust the rack to the middle level.

Metal Blade: Chop the walnuts coarsely by turning the machine on and off about 10 times; reserve them. Process the butter and sugar for 1 minute, or until the mixture is creamed and fluffy. Add the egg, vanilla, cinnamon and salt and process the mixture for 1 minute, stopping the machine once to scrape down the sides of the bowl. Add the rolled oats, wheat germ, flour and reserved nuts and combine the batter by turning the machine on and off a couple of times, or until the flour just disappears. Do not overprocess it. Scrape down the sides of the bowl once during processing.

Drop the batter by the scant teaspoonful well apart on well greased aluminum baking sheets that have been sprinkled with water. Do not use Teflon coated sheets. Place about 12 cookies on each 17- by 14-inch (43 by 36 cm) sheet. (These cookies must be spaced well apart because they spread while baking.) Bake the cookies for 6 to 8 minutes, or until they are browned. Let them rest on the baking sheets for 2 minutes, then transfer them carefully and quickly to wire racks with a metal spatula. If they cool before they are removed from the baking sheet, return the sheet to the oven for 1 minute. Let the cookies cool completely before storing them in an airtight container.

Makes 110 cookies.

Low in fat and high in satisfaction. The chocolate in these crisp confections is not melted, but minced as fine as sugar.

1/4 cup plus 1 tablespoon cake flour (1-1/4 ounces, 35g)
1/2 teaspoon double-acting baking powder
1/8 teaspoon salt
2 ounces (55g) un-sweetened chocolate, broken into pieces
2/3 cup light brown sugar (5 ounces, 140g), firmly packed
2 tablespoons unsalted butter, at room temperature
3 large egg whites
1 teaspoon vanilla extract
1 teaspoon dark rum

Preheat the oven to 400°F. (205°C.) and adjust the rack to the middle level. Butter a cookie sheet, sprinkle it with flour and discard any excess.

Metal Blade: Put the flour, baking powder and salt in the work bowl and process for 2 seconds to blend; remove it and set it aside. Chop the chocolate in the work bowl by turning the machine on and off about 3 times, then process it until it is as fine as sugar. Add the sugar and butter and process the mixture for 30 seconds, stopping the machine once to scrape down the sides of the bowl. Add the egg whites, vanilla and rum and process the mixture for 10 seconds. Add the processed dry ingredients and combine the batter by turning the machine on and off just until the flour disappears. Do not overprocess.

Use a teaspoon to drop the batter onto the prepared cookie sheet in 1-1/4-inch (3.25 cm) rounds, leaving 1 inch (2.5 cm) between each. Bake the cookies for 9 to 10 minutes, or until crisp. Transfer them to wire racks to cool. When the cookies are completely cool they can be frozen in plastic bags.

Makes 40 to 50 cookies.

Note: If the cookies become soggy in humid weather, put them on a cookie sheet in a single layer and recrisp them in a 350°F. (175°C.) oven for 6 to 8 minutes.

Curved Almond Wafers (Tuiles)

These crisp and delicate cookies get their name from the old-fashioned roof tiles on French *châteaux* – which they are shaped to resemble. Every step in their preparation – mixing, baking and forming into their characteristic shape – should be done quickly.

You should bake only one sheet at a time because the cookies must be transferred immediately after baking to a *tuile* pan, a narrow French bread pan, a rolling pin or a bottle to make them curved in shape.

1/3 cup sugar
   (2-1/2 ounces, 70g)
3 tablespoons unsalted butter, in 3 pieces and at room temperature
   Pinch salt
1 teaspoon vanilla extract or dark rum
3 large egg whites
3 tablespoons unbleached all-purpose flour
2 tablespoons cake flour
3/4 cup sliced blanched almonds (3 ounces, 85g)

Preheat the oven to 425°F. (220°C.) and adjust the rack to the middle level. Grease a cookie sheet, sprinkle it lightly with water and shake off the excess.

Metal Blade: Process the sugar and butter for 1 minute. Add the salt, flavoring and egg whites and process for 1 minute, or until the mixture is light and fluffy.

Add the flour and combine it by turning the machine on and off just until it disappears. Do not overprocess. Drop the batter by half-teaspoonfuls, well apart, on the prepared cookie sheet – these cookies spread in baking. Dip a fork in cold water and use it to spread each lump of batter into a neat 2-1/2-inch (6.5 cm) circle.

Sprinkle 3/4 teaspoon of almonds over each. Bake the cookies for 5 to 8 minutes, or until they are deep brown at their edges.

Remove the cookie sheet from the oven and allow the cookies to rest for 30 seconds. Turn them quickly with a spatula and return them to the oven for 2 minutes.

Remove the cookie sheet from the oven and transfer the cookies quickly with a spatula to a *tuile* pan, a narrow curved bread pan, a narrow rolling pin or a bottle. Place them almond-side down if using pans, almond-side up if using a rolling pin or bottle.

Let the cookies cool for about 10 minutes before stacking them carefully. Repeat the procedure until all the cookies are baked.

Makes about 50 cookies.

Fudge Brownies

These moist brownies, a long-standing family passion, are now quick and easy to make in the food processor. You don't even have to melt the chocolate!

1 cup walnut pieces
(4 ounces, 115g)
4 ounces (115g) un-
sweetened chocolate,
broken into pieces
1-1/4 cups sugar
(8-3/4 ounces, 248g)
1 stick unsalted butter
(4 ounces, 115g), at
room temperature and
quartered
4 large eggs
1/4 teaspoon salt
2 teaspoons vanilla
extract
2/3 cup unbleached
all-purpose flour
(3-1/2 ounces, 105g)

Preheat the oven to 325°F. (160°C.) and adjust the rack to the middle level. Grease a 9- or 10-inch (23 or 25 cm) square baking pan, coat it with flour and shake off the excess.

Metal Blade: Chop the walnuts coarsely by turning the machine on and off about 4 times; reserve them. Chop the chocolate coarsely by turning the machine on and off 6 to 10 times. Add the sugar and process for 1 minute, or until the chocolate is as fine as the sugar. Add the butter and process the mixture for 1 minute, or until it is well creamed. Add the eggs, salt and vanilla and process the mixture for 30 to 40 seconds, or until it is fluffy. Add the flour and the reserved nuts and combine the batter, turning the machine on and off 4 or 5 times but taking care not to overprocess.

Spoon the batter into prepared baking pan and spread it with a spatula. Bake for 22 to 25 minutes, or until a toothpick inserted in the corner comes out moist but clean and the batter has not yet begun to pull away from the sides of the pan. This timing will produce fudge-like brownies. Bake 3 to 5 minutes longer for firmer, cake-like brownies. Let the brownies cool in the pan on a rack and cut them into 1-1/2-inch (4 cm) squares.

Makes 36 brownies.

Desserts, Pastries and Sauces

Desserts, Pastries & Sauces _____

Zested Strawberries
Oranges Orientale
Berries Supreme
Fruit Lovers' Platter
Pineapple Meringue Surprise
Pineapple Sherbet
Raspberry and Apple Sherbet
Fresh Peach Frozen Yogurt
Biscuit Tortoni
Old-Fashioned Apple Crisp
Pear Soufflé
Caramelized Orange Custard
Lemon Saxon Pudding
Coffee Nut Mousse
Frozen Double Chocolate Mousse

Tartlets
Basic Pastry
Walnut Pastry
Rich Butter Pastry
Fresh Orange Tart
Apple Custard Tart
French Almond Tarts
Pear Tart
Upside-Down Caramelized Apples
Caramel-Glazed Puffs with Coffee Cream Filling

Lemon Curd
Lime Yogurt Topping
Danish Berry Sauce
Strawberry-Raspberry Sauce
Apricot Sauce
Fresh Peach Sauce
Vanilla Custard Sauce
Fresh Strawberry Syrup
Hazelnut Praline Sauce

Clockwise from top: Fresh Peach Frozen Yogurt, page 237, with Apricot Sauce, page 258; Raspberry and Apple Sherbet, page 236; Pineapple Sherbet, page 236, with Danish Berry Sauce, page 258; Fresh Peach Frozen Yogurt.

I think one of the best clues to personality is what a person chooses for dessert. When I meet someone who agonizes over a choice between Pear Soufflé or Coffee Nut Mousse, French Almond Tarts or Caramelized Cream Puffs, I know I have found a kindred soul. As you can tell from the recipes in this chapter, I love all desserts!

The food processor indulges my weakness, if you want to call it that. Biscuit Tortoni, Old-Fashioned Apple Crisp, Frozen Double Chocolate Mousse — all are just about done before I have time to reconsider. Fortunately, the machine also bolsters my calorie conscience by turning out gorgeous sliced fruit for the Fruit Lovers' Platter, quick sauces for berries and juicy pineapple, and marvelous weight-wise deceptions, like Fresh Peach Frozen Yogurt.

Fresh fruit sherbets are a subject for endless experimentation. I am still inventing new flavors, following the proportions of three cups of chilled fruit purée to one cup of chilled sugar syrup. Divided among six to eight servings, the 2/3 cup of sugar delivers far more than its calorie count in pleasure. The food processor blends smooth lovely sherbets without any need for an ice cream maker. Every time I make one I am reminded of the brilliant Chicago restaurateur Jovan Trboyevic, who quipped when he met me, "Ah, so you are the woman who was seduced by a machine!" He, I might add, contributed to the seduction — with the inspiring array of sherbets I sampled at his restaurant, Le Perroquet.

The machine has proved equally adept at duplicating delicate pastries. To guard against overworking the flour and shortening, a major cause of tough crusts, I have reversed the steps of classic pastry formulas. Instead of adding the liquid last and processing the dough until it forms a mass, I blend the liquid and shortening for 5 seconds, then quickly add the dry ingredients, and process only until the dough begins to work together. I never let the dough form a ball. The pastry turns out light and flaky — the perfect foil for Pear Tart, with its almond crunch, or the vanilla goodness of Apple Custard Tart, or any of your favorite fillings.

I choose desserts randomly and ravenously, taking equal pleasure in the richness of Caramelized Orange Custard on one occasion and the refinement of pineapple-apricot Tartlets on another. But those of you with sturdy preferences can head straight for the trustiest temptation, be it Frozen Double Chocolate Mousse for chocoholics or Pineapple Meringue Surprise for calorie-watchers who want the last laugh. And cheesecake-lovers should not feel left out, for I'll alert you to a secret: as the light yet luscious Lemon Saxon Pudding sits, it settles into the consistency of pure creamy bliss.

Zested Strawberries

Zest of 2 oranges,
removed with a zester
1/4 cup sugar
(1-3/4 ounces, 50g)
4 cups (95 cl) whole
strawberries, hulled
2 tablespoons dark rum
(optional)

Metal Blade: Put the zest and sugar in the work bowl and process until the zest is finely minced. Transfer the mixture to a large plastic bag. Add the strawberries and rum, and tie the bag tightly. Refrigerate for 4 hours, turning the bag occasionally. Transfer the berries to a serving dish and serve with Lemon Cream, Hazelnut Praline Cream, Vanilla Custard Sauce or Orange Custard Sauce. (See Index for sauces.)

Makes 6 servings.

Oranges Orientale

Zest of 2 oranges,
removed with a zester
3 tablespoons sugar
6 large, firm seedless
eating oranges, rind
and pith removed
2 tablespoons orange
juice
1 tablespoon Grand
Marnier

Metal Blade: Put the zest and sugar in the work bowl and process for 1 minute, or until the zest is as fine as the sugar. Reserve the mixture.

Medium Slicing Disc: Insert the oranges in the feed tube and slice them, using light pressure. Transfer the orange slices to a bowl and add the zest mixture, orange juice and Grand Marnier. Toss the orange slices gently, cover them and refrigerate for at least 1 hour, or overnight. Let the oranges stand at room temperature for at least 20 minutes before serving. Serve them with Strawberry Raspberry Sauce (see Index).

Makes 6 servings.

Berries Supreme

Mixed berries macerated in a Kirsch-flavored strawberry sauce make a delightful dessert — and with Hazelnut Praline Sauce, they are really memorable.

2 pints strawberries,
blueberries or
raspberries, or any
combination of the 3
Zest of 1 orange,
removed with a
vegetable peeler
1/4 cup sugar
(1-3/4 ounces, 50g)
1 pint (47 cl)
strawberries
2 tablespoons Kirsch

Wash the berries, let them dry and hull them. Put them in a serving bowl.

Metal Blade: Put the orange zest in the work bowl with the sugar and process until it is as fine as the sugar. Add 1 pint (47 cl) of strawberries and the Kirsch and purée the mixture until it is smooth, stopping the machine once to scrape down the sides of the bowl. Pour the purée over the berries and let them macerate in the refrigerator for several hours. Serve them with Hazelnut Praline Sauce (see Index).

Makes 8 servings.

1 large ripe but firm
   pineapple
   (3 to 4 pounds,
   1.4 to 1.8 kg)
2 firm seedless eating
   oranges (8 ounces
   total, 225g), cut flat at
   ends, scored and
   halved vertically
3/4 cup (18 cl) orange juice
3 tablespoons Kirsch
1 teaspoon lemon juice
3 cups (30 ounces, 850g)
   whole strawberries,
   hulled
1 large banana
   (6-1/2 ounces, 185g),
   peeled and cut into
   thirds
1 medium cantaloupe
   (2 pounds, 910g),
   quartered and rind
   removed
1 large Red Delicious
   apple (6-1/2 ounces,
   185g), unpeeled,
   halved and cored
2 cups (26 ounces, 738g)
   seedless grapes,
   blueberries or
   raspberries
   Lemon or other green
   leaves
6 whole large
   strawberries for
   garnish, unhulled

With a sharp knife carefully remove the green top of the pineapple where it joins the fruit, and reserve it. Quarter the pineapple lengthwise, remove the core and cut the flesh from each quarter from the shell, keeping the quarters in 1 piece and the shells intact. Cut the flesh from each quarter crosswise to fit the feed tube.

Medium Slicing Disc: Put the pineapple in the feed tube vertically and slice it, using medium pressure. Replace the slices in the shell. Slice the oranges, using firm pressure, and arrange 1 orange slice, rind side up, between each 2 slices of pineapple. Center each pineapple quarter on a piece of foil. In a measuring cup mix 1/4 cup (6 cl) orange juice, the Kirsch, and lemon juice (and sugar if the fruit is very tart). Spoon 2 tablespoons of the mixture over each pineapple quarter. Wrap foil tightly around fruit and refrigerate the packets.

Stack the strawberries in the feed tube and slice them, using light pressure. Slice the banana, using light pressure.

French-Fry Disc or Medium Slicing Disc: Put the cantaloupe in the feed tube vertically and cut it, using light pressure. Place the apple in the feed tube vertically and cut it, using medium pressure. Transfer the fruits to a bowl and add the remaining 1/2 cup (12 cl) orange juice and the grapes. Combine the mixture gently with your hands and refrigerate it, covered.

On a 14-inch (36 cm) round platter lined with lemon leaves or other green leaves, center the reserved pineapple top and arrange the pineapple quarters in spokes around it. Drain the mixed fruit, mound it in the spaces between the pineapple quarters. Garnish the platter with the whole strawberries.

Makes 10 to 12 servings.

Pineapple Meringue Surprise

A low-calorie spectacular — with fresh fruit and sherbet hidden under the meringue.

Fruit

- 1 large pineapple (3-1/2 pounds, 1.6 kg)
- 2 cups (47 cl) sliced mixed fruit such as strawberries, bananas, unpeeled Red Delicious apples, grapes, melon, oranges and grapefruit sections, and pomegranate seeds
- 2 tablespoons sugar, or to taste
- 2 tablespoons imported Kirsch or dark rum

Carefully split the pineapple lengthwise, cutting through the leaves, and cut the flesh from each half in 1 piece, leaving a 1/2-inch (1.25 cm) shell intact and not cutting through the skin. Remove and discard the core. Cut each half into equal lengths, and then into wedges to fit the feed tube. Cut the ends of each wedge flat.

Medium Slicing Disc: Slice the pineapple, using medium pressure. Slice the other fruit, using medium or light pressure, depending on the texture of each fruit. Place the slices in a large mixing bowl.

Metal Blade: Chop the odd bits and any imperfect slices of fruit coarsely by turning the machine on and off. Transfer the mixture to the bowl with the sliced fruits and add the sugar and liquor. Toss gently and chill the fruit for at least 1 hour, but not more than 4 hours.

Italian Meringue

- 3/4 cup sugar (5-1/4 ounces, 150g)
- 1/3 cup (8 cl) water
- 3 large egg whites, at room temperature
- 1/2 teaspoon vanilla extract

Cook the sugar and water in a small saucepan, stirring until the sugar is just dissolved. Bring the syrup to a boil and boil it steadily until it reaches the soft-ball stage or it registers 240°F. (116°C.) on a candy thermometer. As the temperature of the syrup approaches 200°F. (95°C.), beat the egg whites in an electric mixer until they are stiff but not dry. With the mixer running, add the sugar syrup in a slow steady stream and continue to beat the meringue for 5 minutes, or until it is cool and very thick. Stir in the vanilla and transfer the meringue to a pastry bag fitted with a medium star tip. (The meringue is best used immediately, but it can hold in the pastry bag, refrigerated, for as long as 2 hours.)

Preheat the oven to 425°F. (220°C.).

Garnish

- 1 pint (47 cl) homemade sherbet (see Index), well frozen
- Lemon leaves

Sprinkle the pineapple leaves with water and cover them with foil. Fill the shells with the fruit mixture and put scoops of sherbet over it. Pipe the meringue over each shell, covering the sherbet and fruit completely and sealing the edges of the meringue to the pineapple shells to prevent the heat from penetrating. Put the shells on baking sheet and bake them for 4 to 5 minutes, or until the meringue is lightly browned. Transfer them to a platter lined with lemon leaves. Remove the foil and serve the dessert immediately.

Makes 6 to 8 servings.

Pineapple Sherbet

2/3 cup sugar
  (4-1/2 ounces, 128g)
2/3 cup (16 cl) water
  1 pineapple (3-1/2 to
    4 pounds, 1.6 to 1.8 kg)
  5 tablespoons lime juice
  1 tablespoon dark rum
  1 large egg white

Combine the sugar and water in a saucepan and cook, stirring, over medium heat until the sugar dissolves. Remove the pan from the heat just before the syrup comes to a boil. Let it chill, cover it and refrigerate it.

Cut the pineapple in half lengthwise, cutting through the leaves. Scoop out the flesh, leaving the shell intact. Remove the core and cut the fruit into 1-inch (2.5 cm) chunks. Place the pineapple shells in large plastic bags and freeze them until you are ready to use them.

Metal Blade: Place the pineapple chunks in the work bowl and process them to a smooth purée. You should have about 2 cups (47 cl). Add lime juice and rum to the purée. Process for 10 seconds and refrigerate the purée until it is chilled. Mix the chilled purée with the chilled sugar syrup, place the mixture in a container, and allow it to partially freeze. If it freezes solid, let it thaw partially before proceeding with the recipe.

Metal Blade: Spoon the partially thawed pineapple mixture into the work bowl and turn the machine on and off about 8 times. Then process until it is completely blended, smooth and fluffy — about 2 minutes. With the machine running, add the egg white through the feed tube. Process for about 1 minute, then place in a container and freeze.

Before serving, let the sherbet soften slightly. Spoon it into the reserved pineapple shells and garnish it with sprigs of fresh mint. Serve it with Danish Berry Sauce (see Index).

Makes 6 to 8 servings.

Raspberry and Apple Sherbet

2/3 cup sugar
  (4-1/2 ounces, 128g)
2/3 cup (16 cl) water
  1 10-ounce (285g)
    package frozen
    raspberries, thawed
  2 large tart apples
    (14 ounces total, 400g),
    preferably Granny
    Smiths, peeled, cored
    and quartered
  2 tablespoons Calvados
    (apple brandy)

Combine the sugar and water in a saucepan and cook, stirring, over medium heat until the sugar dissolves. Remove the pan from the heat just before the syrup comes to a boil. Let it chill, cover it and refrigerate it.

Metal Blade: Put the raspberries in the work bowl and process them for one minute. Press them through a sieve to strain out the seeds. Set them aside. Put the apples in the work bowl and process them until they are puréed. Add the raspberry purée and the Calvados and process until the mixture is smooth. Refrigerate the mixture until it is chilled. Mix the chilled purée with the chilled sugar syrup, place the mixture in a container, and allow it to partially freeze. If it freezes solid, let it thaw partially before proceeding with the recipe.

Metal Blade: Spoon the partially thawed raspberry-apple mixture into the work bowl and turn the machine on and off about 8 times. Then process until it is completely blended, smooth and fluffy — about 2 minutes. Place it in a container and freeze it. Before serving, let the sherbet soften slightly. Serve it with Vanilla Custard Sauce (see Index).

Makes 6 to 8 servings.

Note: This recipe illustrates the basic formula for a fruit sherbet: 3 cups (70 cl) of chilled, puréed fruit to 1 cup (24 cl) of chilled sugar syrup. Flavorings may be added to intensify the taste of the fruit. Sometimes an egg white is added to stabilize the mixture and make it smoother. This technique is used in the recipe for Pineapple Sherbet.

The sugar syrup is made from equal quantities of sugar and water placed over medium-high heat and stirred until the sugar is dissolved and the liquid is almost at a boil. The syrup can be stored in the refrigerator almost indefinitely.

If a sherbet becomes rough and grainy in the freezer, let it thaw partially, then process it for about 2 minutes, or until it becomes smooth and fluffy.

Fresh Peach Frozen Yogurt

1/2 cup (1.2 dl) honey
2 large egg whites
2 teaspoons white vinegar
Zest of 1 orange and 1 lemon, removed with a zester
3 large peaches (1 pound total, 455g), unpeeled, halved and pitted
2 tablespoons fresh lemon juice
2-1/2 cups plain yogurt (27 ounces, 765g)

Assemble all the ingredients and a 1-quart (9.5 dl) mixing bowl conveniently near the food processor. Heat the honey in a small saucepan until it is hot.

Metal Blade: Put the egg whites into a clean work bowl and turn the machine on. After 8 seconds, pour the vinegar through the feed tube while the machine is running. Process for about 50 seconds, or until the egg whites are whipped and hold their shape. With the machine still running, pour the hot honey through the feed tube in a thin, steady stream, taking about 45 seconds to add it. Continue to process for 1-1/2 minutes longer. With a spatula, gently transfer the whites to the mixing bowl. It is not necessary to wash the work bowl.

Put the orange and lemon zest and the peaches in the work bowl and process for about 1 minute, stopping once to scrape down the sides of the bowl. Add the lemon juice and yogurt and process for 5 seconds. Spoon the egg whites onto the mixture in a ring and turn the machine on and off twice. Run a spatula around the sides of the work bowl, to loosen the mixture. Turn the machine on and off 2 or 3 more times, until the ingredients are just mixed. Do not overprocess. Pour the yogurt into a 2-quart (19 dl) container, cover and let freeze for at least 4 hours. Let soften slightly before serving. Serve with Apricot Sauce (see Index).

Makes 6 cups (14 dl).

Biscuit Tortoni

A richly flavored Italian dessert that is delicious when prepared in the traditional way, without fruit, but even better in this variation with fresh strawberries.

1/2 cup blanched slivered almonds (2 ounces, 55g)
1/2 cup plus 2 tablespoons sugar (4 ounces, 115g)
3 large egg whites
1 tablespoon white vinegar
1 pint (4.7 dl) whipping cream, chilled
4 teaspoons dry Sherry
1/4 teaspoon almond extract
1 cup strawberries (6 ounces, 170g)

Spread the almonds on a cookie sheet in a single layer and toast in a preheated 450°F. (230°C.) oven for 3 to 5 minutes, or until they are light brown. Assemble all the ingredients and a 1-quart (9.5 dl) mixing bowl near the food processor.

Metal Blade: Put the almonds and 1/4 cup sugar (50g) into the work bowl. Process until the almonds are finely chopped and set them aside. Wash the work bowl and the metal blade to remove from them all traces of oil from the nuts.

Put the egg whites and 1/4 cup sugar (50g) into the clean work bowl and turn the machine on. After 8 seconds, pour the vinegar through the feed tube while the machine is running. Process for about 1 minute and 45 seconds, or until the egg whites are whipped and hold their shape. With a rubber spatula, gently transfer the egg whites to the mixing bowl. It is not necessary to wash the work bowl.

With the machine running, pour the cream through the feed tube and process until it begins to thicken. Add the remaining 2 tablespoons of sugar, Sherry and almond extract. Process until completely whipped and thick. Spoon the egg whites onto the cream in a ring. Turn the machine on and off 3 times. Run a spatula around the sides of the work bowl, to loosen the mixture. Turn the machine on and off once more.

With a spatula, transfer the mixture to a mixing bowl and wipe out the work bowl with a paper towel.

Medium Slicing Disc: Slice the strawberries, using light pressure.

Layer 1/3 of the almond-sugar mixture evenly over the bottom of a 1-quart (9.5 dl) glass bowl or soufflé dish. Add 1/2 the cream mixture and smooth on an additional 1/3 of the almond-sugar mixture. Add the remaining cream mixture and spread the remaining almond-sugar mixture over the top. Arrange the strawberry slices in a decorative pattern on top. Cover the dish airtight and freeze the Biscuit Tortoni. Let it soften slightly — about 40 to 60 minutes at room temperature — before cutting it into serving slices, or scooping serving portions from the dish.

Makes 6 to 8 servings.

A winning dessert that can be prepared in minutes.

5 large tart apples
(2 pounds total, 907g),
preferably Granny
Smith, unpeeled,
halved and cored
1/2 cup sugar (3-1/2
ounces, 100g)
2 teaspoons cinnamon,
divided
1 teaspoon freshly
grated nutmeg
1/2 cup walnut or pecan
halves
(2 ounces, 55g)
3/4 cup unbleached
all-purpose flour
(3-3/4 ounces, 106g)
1/4 teaspoon salt
3/4 cup dark brown sugar
(6 ounces, 170g),
firmly packed
1 stick unsalted butter
(4 ounces, 115g),
chilled and quartered
1/4 cup rolled oats or
wheat germ
(1 ounce, 30g)

Preheat the oven to 350°F. (175°C.) and adjust the rack to the middle level. Butter an 11-inch (28 cm) pie plate or a 2-quart (1.91) soufflé dish.

Medium Slicing Disc: Put the apples in the feed tube horizontally and slice them, using medium pressure. Mix them with the sugar, 1 teaspoon cinnamon and 1/2 teaspoon nutmeg in a large bowl. (If the apples are sweet, decrease the sugar and add 1 teaspoon of lemon juice.) Layer the apples in the prepared dish.

Metal Blade: Put the nuts in the work bowl and chop them coarsely by turning the machine on and off. Add the flour, salt, brown sugar, butter, rolled oats and remaining cinnamon and nutmeg, and butter. Turn the machine on and off until the butter is about the size of small peas — it will take about 20 seconds. Spread this mixture over the apples, pressing it around the edges of the dish. Bake the dish in a preheated oven for 1 hour, or until it is brown and crispy. Serve it warm or at room temperature with Vanilla or Orange Custard Sauce (see Index), or vanilla ice cream, softened so that it can be spooned over the dessert.

Makes 6 to 8 servings.

Biscuit Tortoni (recipe opposite)

Another triumph of the Taillevent restaurant in Paris, this soufflé is made even there with canned pears.

1/3 cup plus 2 table-
spoons sugar
(2-1/2 ounces, 70g)
2 29-ounce (822g) cans
pear halves,
well drained on
paper towels
Zest of 1 orange, re-
moved with a zester
1/2 cup (12 cl) water
2 teaspoons cornstarch
1 tablespoon lemon
juice
8 large egg whites, at
room temperature
Pinch of salt
1/4 teaspoon cream of
tartar
1 tablespoon sugar
1/4 cup (6 cl) pear brandy
1 tablespoon
confectioners sugar
Orange Custard Sauce
(see Index)

Preheat the oven to 425°F. (220°C.) 15 minutes before baking. Adjust the rack to the lower third of the oven. Butter the insides and the edges of a 2-quart (190 cl) soufflé dish, put 2 tablespoons of sugar in the dish, and rotate it to coat it with sugar. Discard any excess sugar.

Metal Blade: Put all but 2 of the pear halves in the work bowl with the zest. You should have about 2 cups (47 cl). Process for 10 seconds, or until puréed. Place the purée in a saucepan over medium heat and cook it for about 30 minutes, or until it is thick and reduced to about 1-1/2 cups (35 cl). Cut the reserved pear halves into 1/4-inch (.75 cm) dice; reserve.

Combine the remaining sugar and water in a saucepan, bring to a boil, and boil for 5 minutes. Dissolve the cornstarch in the lemon juice and add it to the pear mixture with the sugar syrup. Heat the pear mixture, stirring it constantly, until it thickens to the consistency of marmalade. Transfer it to a large mixing bowl.

Beat the egg whites until they are foamy. Add the salt and cream of tartar and continue beating until the egg whites are firm but not dry. Fold in 1 tablespoon of sugar. Whisk 1/4 of the egg whites into the pear mixture and mix thoroughly. Fold the remaining whites gently into the pear mixture with a spatula. Fold in the pear brandy.

Spoon 1/2 of the soufflé mixture into the prepared dish. Sprinkle 2/3 of the diced pears evenly over the surface. Add the remaining soufflé mixture and spread it evenly with a spatula. The soufflé mixture should come to the top of the dish. Run your finger around the inside of the dish to make a groove. Sprinkle the remaining diced pears over the surface.

Immediately place the soufflé in the preheated oven and bake it for 16 to 17 minutes, or until it is well browned. Sieve confectioners sugar over its surface while it is still on the edge of the oven rack. Remove it from the oven and serve it at once with chilled Orange Custard Sauce. The soufflé will "hold" a few minutes in a turned-off oven with door slightly ajar.

Makes 8 servings.

Variation

For Apple Soufflé, use 3 large tart apples (18 ounces total, 510g). I prefer to use Granny Smiths. Peel them, core them, and cut them into quarters. Purée them and add 1/4 teaspoon each of cinnamon and freshly grated nutmeg. Cook the mixture in the same manner as the pear purée. The reduced apple purée will measure about 1-1/4 cups (30 cl). Proceed with the instructions given above, omitting the garnish of diced fruit and substituting Calvados for the pear brandy.

Caramelized Orange Custard

High in calories, and worth every one! The crackled caramel is a perfect foil for this delicately flavored custard.

3/4 cup light brown sugar (5-1/2 ounces, 156g), firmly packed
1/4 cup plus 2 tablespoons granulated sugar (2 ounces, 55g)
2 teaspoons orange zest, removed with a zester
8 large egg yolks
1/4 cup (6 cl) frozen orange-juice concentrate
4 cups (95 cl) heavy cream, hot but not boiling

Preheat the oven to 300°F. (150°C.) and adjust the rack to the middle level. Bring a large kettle of water to a boil.

Metal Blade: Put the brown sugar in the work bowl and process until it is finely ground. Reserve it in a plastic bag, tied airtight. Put the granulated sugar in the work bowl with the zest and process for 30 seconds, or until the zest is as fine as the sugar. Add the egg yolks and process the mixture for 1 minute, or until it is thick and light colored. Add the orange-juice concentrate and process the mixture for 30 seconds. With the machine running, pour half the cream through the feed tube. Transfer the mixture to a bowl and whisk in the remaining cream. Pour the mixture into a 5-cup (1.2l) baking dish, about 1-1/2 inches (3.8 cm) deep or into 8 to 10 1/2-cup (12 cl) ramekins.

Put the dish(es) in a large baking pan and pour boiling water into the pan to a depth of 1-1/2 inches (3.8 cm). Bake the custard for 1 hour, or until it is somewhat set — it will become more firm in the refrigerator. Remove it from the pan of water, and let it cool. Refrigerate the custard until it is completely chilled.

Preheat the broiler. Sprinkle the custard with the reserved brown sugar, and broil it 4 inches (10 cm) from the heat, until it is caramelized. Turn the dish(es) at least twice and watch carefully to prevent burning. Refrigerate the custard until serving.

Makes 8 to 10 servings.

This pudding, one of my favorite desserts, is almost as light as a soufflé. It puffs up, but does not collapse appreciably after it is unmolded.

1 cup (2.4 dl) milk
1 stick plus 1 tablespoon unsalted butter (4-1/2 ounces, 128g)
1 cup sugar (7 ounces, 200g)
Zest of 1 lemon, removed with a zester
7 large egg whites
1/2 cup minus 2 tablespoons unbleached all-purpose flour (2 ounces, 55g)
1/2 cup minus 2 tablespoons cornstarch (2 ounces, 55g)
1 tablespoon white vinegar
6 large egg yolks
1/2 cup (1.2 dl) fresh lemon juice
Pinch of salt

Preheat the oven to 350°F. (175°C.) and adjust the rack to the middle level. Generously butter a *kugelhopf* or Bundt pan. Sprinkle the inside with sugar and shake out any excess. Have ready a kettle of boiling water and a baking dish large enough to hold the pan.

Assemble all the ingredients and a 1-quart (9.5 dl) mixing bowl conveniently near the food processor. Put the milk, butter, 1/2 cup sugar (100g) and lemon zest in a heavy 1-quart (9.5 dl) saucepan and cook over medium heat until the butter is completely melted and the milk is simmering. Meanwhile, process the egg whites.

Metal Blade: Put the egg whites and the remaining sugar into a clean work bowl and turn the machine on. After 8 seconds, pour the vinegar through the feed tube while the machine is running. Process for about 2 minutes and 50 seconds, or until the egg whites are whipped and hold their shape. With a rubber spatula, gently transfer the mixture to the mixing bowl. It is not necessary to wash the work bowl.

Add the flour and cornstarch to the simmering milk, remove them from the heat and mix thoroughly with a wooden spoon. The batter will be lumpy. Transfer this mixture to the work bowl and process for 20 seconds. With the machine running, add the egg yolks through the feed tube and process for 20 seconds. Add the lemon juice and salt and process for 5 seconds. Add 1/4 of the egg whites and turn the machine on and off twice. Run a spatula around the sides of the work bowl, to loosen the mixture. Spoon the remaining egg whites onto the mixture in a ring. Turn the machine on and off 4 times, until the ingredients are just mixed. Some streaks of egg white may be visible; do not overprocess.

With a rubber spatula, transfer the mixture to the prepared pan. Place the pan into the baking dish and put it on the oven rack. Carefully pour in enough boiling water to come up 2 inches (5 cm) on the sides of the pan. Bake the pudding for 32 to 34 minutes, or until it is lightly colored and begins to pull away from the sides of the pan. Surface cracks may develop in cooking; they don't matter. Remove the pan from the oven and let it rest on a cooling rack for 10 minutes. Carefully separate the pudding from the pan with a small flexible knife. Put a serving platter over the pan and quickly invert the pudding onto the platter. Serve hot, at room temperature or chilled, with Strawberry-Raspberry Sauce or Apricot Sauce. (see Index).

Makes 10 to 12 servings.

Coffee Nut Mousse

2/3 cup walnut pieces
  (2-1/2 ounces, 71g)
1 package unflavored
  gelatin
1/4 cup (6 cl) cold water
3 scant tablespoons
  freeze-dried instant
  coffee
4 large egg yolks
1/2 cup sugar
  (3-1/2 ounces, 100g)
3 tablespoons dark rum
4 large egg whites
1-1/2 cups (35 cl) heavy
  cream

Make a 2-inch (5 cm) collar for a 4-cup (95 cl) soufflé dish by folding a strip of foil long enough to encircle the dish, oiling one side, and fitting the foil around the dish, oiled side in. Tie or tape the collar in place.

Fine Julienne Disc or Shredding Disc: Mince the walnuts, using medium pressure, and reserve them. Mix the gelatin and the instant coffee with the cold water in a small dish. Put the dish in a pan of hot water until the gelatin is dissolved.

Metal Blade: Put the egg yolks and sugar in the work bowl and process for 1 minute, or until thick. With the machine running, pour the gelatin mixture through the feed tube. Transfer the mixture to a saucepan and heat until it is slightly thickened, whisking it constantly. Do not overcook it. Let it cool slightly and stir in the rum. Transfer the mixture to a large bowl.

Beat the egg whites in an electric mixer until they are stiff but not dry. Stir 1/4 of the whites into the coffee mixture, then fold in the remaining whites carefully. Whip the cream in the electric mixer until it is stiff, and fold it carefully into the mixture. You may add the nuts now, reserving 2 tablespoons to sprinkle on top of the mousse, or you may sprinkle the nuts between layers of the mousse as you assemble it. Spoon the mousse into the prepared soufflé dish and refrigerate it for at least 6 hours. Remove the collar and serve with Crisp Chocolate Wafers (see Index).

Makes 6 servings.

Variation _____

Layer Crisp Chocolate Wafers between layers of mousse.

Frozen Double Chocolate Mousse

The same basic batter is treated in two ways for a dessert with an interesting contrast of textures.

9 large eggs, separated
1 cup sugar (7 ounces, 200g)
1 tablespoon white vinegar
Zest of 1/2 orange, removed with a vegetable peeler
12 ounces (340g) sweet cooking chocolate, preferably Maillards or German's, broken into pieces
1-1/2 sticks unsalted butter (6 ounces, 170g), melted and sizzling hot
1 tablespoon plus 2 teaspoons orange liqueur
Pinch of salt
2 cups (4.7 dl) whipping cream, chilled
1/4 cup confectioners sugar (1 ounce, 28g)

Preheat the oven to 350°F. (175°C.) and adjust the rack to the middle level. Butter an 8-inch (20 cm) springform pan. Assemble all the ingredients and a 2-quart (19 dl) mixing bowl conveniently near the food processor.

Metal Blade: Put the egg whites and 1/2 cup sugar (100g) into a clean work bowl and turn the machine on. After 8 seconds, pour the vinegar through the feed tube while the machine is running. Process for about 3 minutes, or until the egg whites are whipped and hold their shape. With a rubber spatula, gently transfer them to a mixing bowl. It is not necessary to wash the work bowl.

Put the orange zest, chocolate and remaining 1/2 cup sugar (100g) into the work bowl and chop the chocolate by turning the machine on and off 6 times. Then process continuously until the chocolate is as fine as the sugar. With the machine running, pour the hot butter through the feed tube and process for about 20 seconds, or until the chocolate is completely melted. Add the egg yolks and 1 tablespoon of orange liqueur and turn the machine on and off twice. Scrape down the sides of the bowl. Add 1/4 of the egg whites and turn the machine on and off twice. Spoon the remaining egg whites onto the chocolate mixture in a ring. Turn the machine on and off twice. Run a spatula around the sides of the work bowl, to loosen the mixture, and turn the machine on and off 2 more times. Some faded streaks of egg white may be visible; do not overprocess.

Pour 1/2 the mixture into the springform pan. Bake in the preheated oven for 28 minutes. Let the crust cool for 30 minutes.

With a spatula, transfer the remaining mixture to a mixing bowl and reserve it.

Metal Blade: Process 1 cup (2.4 dl) of the whipping cream until it is slightly thickened — about 20 seconds. Add 2 teaspoons of orange liqueur and 2 tablespoons of confectioners sugar and process until thick. Fold gently but thoroughly into the remaining uncooked chocolate mixture. Spread over the cooled baked shell. Refrigerate it for 6 hours. Whip the remaining cup (2.4 dl) of whipping cream with the remaining 2 tablespoons of confectioners sugar. Spread it over the surface of the dessert, or serve it separately.

Makes 10 to 12 servings.

Note: This dessert can be frozen. Wrap airtight after freezing. To serve, allow to thaw in refrigerator for 2 to 3 hours.

These shells are classically known as *puits d'amour*, which means "wells of love". The recipe originated in France about 1750, but I spotted them on the pastry tray at La Marée, one of France's truly great restaurants. When I worked there, I learned how to make them — with cream puff dough in place of the classical puff pastry.

Tartlets _____

2 teaspoons orange zest, removed with a zester
3 tablespoons sugar
1/3 cup (8 cl) milk
1/3 cup (8 cl) water
1/8 teaspoon salt
6 tablespoons unsalted butter (3 ounces, 85g)
2/3 cup unbleached all-purpose flour (3-1/2 ounces, 100g)
2 large eggs

Butter 36 mini-muffin cups 1-7/8 inches (4.5 cm) wide and 3/4 inches (1.8 cm) deep.

Metal Blade: Put the zest and sugar in the work bowl and process for 30 seconds, or until the zest is as fine as the sugar. Transfer the mixture to a 1 quart (95 cl) heavy stainless steel saucepan and add the milk, water, salt and butter. Cook over medium heat until the butter has melted and the liquid is boiling. Remove the pan from the heat. Add the flour and stir vigorously with a wooden spoon until the mixture leaves the sides of the pan. Return the pan to medium heat and cook for 2 minutes, stirring constantly. Remove the pan from the heat and let the mixture rest for 5 minutes.

Transfer the mixture to the work bowl. Add the eggs and process for 30 seconds, or until it is well combined, thick and shiny. The batter should hold its shape on a spoon. Cover the batter with plastic wrap and let it cool at room temperature for 30 minutes.

Preheat the oven to 400°F. (205°C.) and adjust the rack to the middle level.

Assembly _____

Put 1 teaspoon of batter in each of the mini-muffin cups. Dip your thumb in cold water and shape the dough evenly in each cup, smoothing the top edges. Put the pans on a cookie sheet and place them in the preheated oven. Reduce the heat to 375°F. (190°C.). Bake for 25 to 27 minutes, or until the tartlets are medium brown but not dark. Remove them from the cups and transfer them to wire racks to cool.

Filling _____

Pineapple Apricot Curd, Orange Curd or Lemon Curd (see Index)

A few hours before serving, put 1 heaping teaspoon of chilled filling in each puff shell. If the filling is too thick, process it with the metal blade for 1 or 2 seconds. If desired, pipe a rosette of sweetened whipped cream onto each tartlet from a pastry bag fitted with a medium star tip. Keep the tartlets in a cool place but do not refrigerate them.

Makes 36 Tartlets.

Pastry making with a food processor is foolproof, and, as you will see from the suggested variations, the range of possible flavorings is enormous. Prepare several recipes in sequence without washing the work bowl, and freeze them.

1 stick unsalted butter
    (4 ounces, 155g),
    chilled and cut into
    tablespoon-size pieces
1 large egg yolk
1/2 teaspoon salt
5 tablespoons cold
    water
1-1/2 cups unbleached
    all-purpose flour
    (7-1/2 ounces, 213g)

Metal Blade: Put the butter, egg yolk, salt and water in the work bowl. Combine them by turning the machine on and off 5 or 6 times, then process for 5 seconds. There may be small lumps of butter. Add the flour and process just until the mixture forms a mass of dough. Do not overprocess. Do not allow the dough to form a ball. Put the dough and any little scraps on the bottom of the bowl into a plastic bag. Work through the bag to press it together into a ball, then into a disc. Refrigerate the dough for at least 2 hours, or overnight, or freeze it.

Butter an 11-inch (28 cm) quiche pan with a removable bottom.

Roll the dough on a lightly floured surface to a circle about 1/8 inch (.30 cm) thick. Press it into place in the prepared quiche pan. Use kitchen shears to trim the dough, leaving a 1-inch (2.5 cm) overlap beyond the pan. Fold the overlap inside to form a double thickness on the sides. Press the dough firmly into place, pushing the crust up 1/4 inch (.60 cm) above the edge of the pan to allow for shrinkage in baking. Pinch the crust to form a decorative edge. Prick the bottom and sides with a fork and refrigerate the crust for 30 minutes, or until it is firm.

Preheat the oven to 400°F. (205°C.) 15 minutes before baking.

Line the pastry shell with parchment paper and fill it with uncooked beans or rice. Bake it for 12 minutes. Remove the paper and the beans or rice, prick the shell again and bake it for 6 minutes longer, or until it is lightly browned. Remove the shell from the pan and let it cool on a wire rack. If there are any cracks in the shell, repair them with scraps of leftover raw dough.

Makes an 11-inch (28 cm) tart shell.

Variations

1. For Parsley Pastry, mince 1/4 cup (6 cl) parsley leaves, leave them in the work bowl, and proceed with the recipe as described above.

2. For Chive Pastry, add 1 tablespoon of snipped chives during the last second of processing.

3. For Sweet Tart Pastry, add 2 tablespoons of sugar with the butter, egg yolk and salt.

4. For Orange Pastry, add 2 tablespoons of sugar and 1 teaspoon of grated orange zest with the butter, egg yolk and salt, and substitute chilled orange juice for the water.

5. For Lemon Pastry, substitute 1 tablespoon of solid shortening for 1 tablespoon of butter, reduce the salt to a pinch, add 2 tablespoons of sugar and 1 teaspoon of grated lemon zest with the butter, egg yolk and salt, and substitute 2 tablespoons of chilled lemon juice for 2 tablespoons of the water.

Walnut Pastry

1/4 cup walnuts
  (1 ounce, 30g)
1-1/2 cups unbleached
  all-purpose flour
  (7-1/2 ounces, 213g)
6 tablespoons unsalted
  butter (3 ounces, 85g),
  chilled and cut into 6
  pieces
2 tablespoons vegetable
  shortening (1 ounce,
  30g), chilled
1 large egg
1 tablespoon dark rum
2 tablespoons cold
  water
2 tablespoons sugar
  Pinch of salt

Metal Blade: Process the nuts with the flour until the nuts are finely minced — about 5 seconds. Set them aside. Add the remaining ingredients to the work bowl and combine them by turning the machine on and off about 4 times. Process for 8 seconds. There may be small lumps of butter. Add the nuts and flour and process just until the mixture forms a mass of dough. Do not overprocess. Do not allow the dough to form a ball. Put the dough and any scraps at the bottom of the work bowl into a plastic bag. Work through the plastic bag to form the dough into a ball, then shape it into a disc. Refrigerate the dough at least 2 hours, or overnight, or freeze it.

Roll, shape and bake the dough as directed in the recipe for Basic Pastry.

Walnut Pastry, with Apple Custard Tart (see page 250)

A fragile, tender, mouthwatering crust.

1-1/2 sticks unsalted butter
(6 ounces, 170g),
chilled and cut into
tablespoon-size pieces
1 large egg
2 tablespoons cold
water
Pinch of salt
1-3/4 cups unbleached
all-purpose flour
(9-1/2 ounces, 270g)

Metal Blade: Put all the ingredients but the flour in the work bowl. Combine them by turning the machine on and off about 6 times, then process for 5 seconds. There may be small lumps of butter. Add the flour and process just until the mixture forms a mass of dough. Do not overprocess. Do not allow the dough to form a ball. Put the dough and any little scraps on the bottom of the bowl into a plastic bag. Work through the bag to press it together into a ball, then into a disc. Refrigerate the dough at least 2 hours, or overnight, or freeze it.

Butter an 11-inch (28 cm) quiche pan with a removable bottom.

Roll the dough on a lightly floured surface to a circle about 1/8 inch (.30 cm) thick. Press it into place in the prepared quiche pan. Use kitchen shears to trim the dough, leaving a 1-inch (2.5 cm) overlap beyond the pan. Fold the overlap inside to form a double thickness on the sides. Press the dough firmly into place, pushing the crust up 1/4 inch (.60 cm) above the edge of the pan to allow for shrinkage in baking. Pinch the crust to form a decorative edge. Prick the bottom and sides with a fork and refrigerate the crust for 30 minutes, or until it is firm.

Preheat the oven to 400°F. (205°C.) 15 minutes before baking.

Line the pastry shell with parchment paper and fill it with uncooked beans or rice. Bake it for 12 minutes. Remove the paper and the beans or rice, prick the shell again and bake it for 12 minutes longer, or until it is lightly browned. Remove the shell from the pan and let it cool on a wire rack. If there are any cracks in the shell, repair them with scraps of leftover raw dough.

Makes an 11-inch (28 cm) tart shell.

Variation ——————

For Almond Pastry, mince 1/4 cup (1 ounce, 30g) of blanched almonds by turning the machine on and off to chop them, then processing until they are finely minced. Leave them in the bowl. Add all ingredients except the flour, substituting 1 tablespoon milk and 1 teaspoon vanilla extract for the water, and adding 1 tablespoon sugar and 1/2 teaspoon salt.

Filling

- 11-inch (28 cm) prebaked Lemon Pastry Shell (see Index)
- 3 seedless eating oranges, cut flat at ends, rind removed
- 1-1/2 sticks unsalted butter (6 ounces, 170g)
- 1 cup sugar (7 ounces, 198g)
- 1/2 cup (12 cl) frozen orange juice concentrate
- 6 large eggs
- 2 teaspoons lemon juice

Preheat the oven to 375°F (190°C.) and adjust the rack to the middle level.

Medium Slicing Disc: Insert the oranges in the feed tube vertically and slice them, using light pressure. Reserve them.

Metal Blade: Put the butter and sugar in the work bowl and process them for 1 to 1-1/2 minutes, stopping the machine once to scrape down the sides of the bowl. The mixture should be light and fluffy. Add the orange juice concentrate and process for 30 seconds. Add the eggs and process for 1-1/2 minutes, stopping the machine to scrape down the sides of the bowl as necessary. The mixture should be blended and smooth. Add lemon juice and process 5 seconds.

Heat a 1-quart (95 cl) heavy stainless steel saucepan over medium heat and add the mixture from the work bowl. Stir it constantly until the mixture just starts to boil. Remove the pan from the heat and let it cool completely, stirring it occasionally.

Makes 2-3/4 cups (65 cl) filling.

Pour the cool filling into the cool prebaked pastry shell and smooth it out with a spatula. Bake for 20 minutes in a preheated oven.

Glaze

- 1/2 cup (12 cl) apricot preserves
- 2 tablespoons Grand Marnier

Heat the apricot preserves in a small saucepan over medium heat. Press them through a sieve into a bowl and add the Grand Marnier. Brush 1/2 of the warm glaze on the tart filling and its rim. Arrange a single layer of the reserved orange slices in a concentric circle over the glazed filling and brush the slices with the reserved glaze. Serve the tart warm or at room temperature. If it has been refrigerated, allow it to come to room temperature before serving.

Makes 8 to 10 servings.

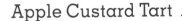

A French version of American apple pie, with vanilla ice cream flavor baked right in.

Prebaked 11-inch
(28 cm) Orange Pastry
Crust (see Index)
1 tablespoon unsalted
butter
8 Jonathan or Granny
Smith apples
(2 pounds total, 908g),
peeled, cored and
halved
1 tablespoon sugar for
Jonathan apples, or 3
tablespoons for
Granny Smith apples
1 teaspoon cinnamon
1 teaspoon freshly
grated nutmeg
3/4 cup (18 cl) heavy cream
2 tablespoons sugar
1 large egg plus 1 large
egg yolk
1 tablespoon vanilla
extract
1 tablespoon Calvados
or dark rum

Preheat the oven to 400°F. (205°C.) and adjust the rack to the middle level. Dot the pastry crust with little pieces of butter.

Medium Slicing Disc: Put the apples in the feed tube horizontally and slice them, using firm pressure. Separate the imperfect slices and put them on the crust. Arrange the remaining slices over them in concentric circles to create an attractive pattern. Combine the sugar, cinnamon and nutmeg in a dish, and sprinkle it over the apples. Bake for 35 minutes in the preheated oven.

Metal Blade: Combine the remaining ingredients by turning the machine on and off 4 times.

Pour this custard over the apples to within 1/8 inch of the top edge of the crust after the tart has baked for 35 minutes. Be careful not to overfill it. Bake for an additional 20 minutes. The center of the custard may appear wet but it will firm up as the tart stands. Serve the tart at room temperature.

Makes 8 servings.

French Almond Tarts

This superlative dessert was inspired by the renowned Taillevent restaurant in Paris.

Tart Shell

1 recipe Almond Pastry
dough (see Index)
chilled

Preheat the oven to 375°F. (135°C.) and adjust the rack to the middle level. Butter 24 3-inch (7.5 cm) tart pans.

Divide the dough into 6 pieces, keeping the unwanted pieces refrigerated until ready to use. Roll out one piece into a round about 1/8-inch (.30 cm) thick on a lightly floured board. Prick the dough in several places with a fork. Place 4 of the tart pans close to each other, so their rims touch. Lay the dough loosely over them and press the rolling pin over them to cut out rounds of dough to fit each pan. Press the dough gently but firmly into the tart pans. Repeat this procedure with the 5 remaining pieces of dough and the 20 remaining tart pans, working scraps of dough left from one portion of dough into the next. Refrigerate the shells 30 minutes before baking.

Put the shells on an aluminum baking sheet. Line each shell with parchment paper and weight them with dried beans or rice. Bake the shells for 10 minutes. Remove the paper and the weights, prick the shells again and bake them for 2 minutes longer or until they are lightly browned. Remove the tart shells from the pans and allow them to cool on a wire rack.

Almond Cream _____

Scant 1/2 cup (12 cl) blanched almonds, whole or broken
1/4 cup plus 2 tablespoons sugar (2-1/4 ounces, 64g)
Pinch salt
2 large eggs
1 stick plus 2 tablespoons unsalted butter, (5 ounces, 142g), at room temperature and cut into 5 pieces
1 teaspoon vanilla extract
2 teaspoons dark rum

Metal Blade: Process the almonds for 30 seconds or until they are finely ground. Add the sugar, salt and eggs and process the mixture for about 1 minute, or until it is fluffy. Add the butter, vanilla and rum and process for 30 seconds, or until all the ingredients are well combined. This mixture will keep for 3 days in the refrigerator, and it can be frozen.

Assembly _____

1/2 cup (12 cl) strawberry preserves
2 teaspoons confectioners sugar

Preheat the oven to 375°F. (190°C.). Return the tart shells to their pans. Spread a scant teaspoon of strawberry preserves on the bottom of each shell. Spread a generous tablespoon of almond filling in each shell. Put the pans on an aluminum baking sheet and bake for 15 minutes, or until they are browned. Transfer them to a wire rack to cool. Sieve confectioners sugar lightly over them and remove them from the pans before serving.

Makes 24 tarts.

Pear Tart

This dessert is best prepared beforehand and allowed to rest at least 3 hours so the juices will be absorbed.

Pastry

1 recipe Lemon Pastry Dough (see Index)

Prepare and prebake the pastry as specified in the recipe for Basic Pastry (see Index) in a buttered 11-inch (28 cm) quiche pan with a removable bottom. Cool the prebaked crust on a wire rack while you prepare the glaze and topping.

Glaze and Topping

1/4 cup (6 cl) blanched almonds
1/4 cup sugar (1-3/4 ounces, 50g)
1 tablespoon flour
1/2 cup apricot preserves (2-1/2 ounces, 70g)
2 tablespoons dark rum
8 large, firm but ripe pears, (3 pounds total, 1.4kg) preferably Anjou, peeled, halved lengthwise and cored

Metal Blade: Put the almonds, sugar and flour in the work bowl and process them until they are reduced to a powder. Set them aside. Process the preserves with the rum, transfer the mixture to a saucepan and keep warm over low heat. Brush the cooled pastry crust with glaze and reserve the remaining glaze. Spread the ground almond mixture evenly over the glazed crust.

Medium Slicing Disc: Stand 6 of the 8 prepared pears upright in the feed tube and slice them, using light pressure. Arrange the slices on the pastry shell in circular clusters, leaving a 2-inch space around the center cluster of pears.

Shredding Disc: Shred the 2 remaining pears and fill the spaces around the clusters of slices with the shreds.

Bake the tart in a preheated 400°F (205°C.) oven for 40 minutes. Remove the tart from the oven. Reheat the reserved glaze and brush it over the pears and the crust.

Makes 8 servings.

Upside-Down Caramelized Apples

Pastry

1 recipe Walnut Pastry (see Index), chilled

Grease a cookie sheet and preheat the oven to 375°F. (190°C). Adjust the rack to the middle level.

Divide the chilled dough in half. Roll out half of it on a lightly floured board until it is 1/8 inch (.60 cm) thick. Freeze the remaining half for another use. Place a 10-inch (25 cm) ovenproof skillet or a 10-inch (25 cm) tart pan without a removable bottom upside down on the dough. Use a pizza cutter to cut out a circle of dough the same size as the pan.

Place the circle of dough on the prepared cookie sheet and prick it in several places with a fork. Refrigerate it for 30 minutes.

Bake the pastry for 12 to 15 minutes, or until it is golden brown. Slide it off the cookie sheet onto a wire rack to cool. The pastry can be baked several hours in advance.

Set the oven to 400°F. (205°C).

Apples

- 6 large apples (3 pounds total, 1.4 kg), preferably Granny Smith, peeled, cored and halved
- 1 cup sugar (7 ounces, 200g)
- 1 stick unsalted butter (4 ounces, 115g)

Medium Slicing Disc: Put the apple halves in the feed tube horizontally and slice them, using firm pressure. Put the slices in a large mixing bowl and gently mix in 3/4 cup of sugar. Mix the sugar and apples with your hands to avoid breaking the slices. Melt the butter in the 10-inch (25 cm) skillet or the tart pan. If using the tart pan, first line it with foil. Add 1/4 cup of sugar. Cook the mixture over medium high heat until it is a light golden brown. Remove the pan from the heat and arrange the apple slices over it, round side down, overlapping each other in concentric circles. The slices should fit snugly, and cover the bottom of the pan completely. Place any remaining slices randomly over the bottom layer. Press the apples firmly into place with your hands or a flat spatula.

Bake the apples for 15 minutes in a preheated oven. Then place the pan over high heat on top of the stove, shaking the pan constantly until the liquid cooks down and is reduced to a depth of 1/8 inch (.60 cm) on the bottom of the pan. To avoid burning the apples, do not let the liquid reduce entirely. The underside of the apples should be brown. Check the progress of the browning occasionally by lifting the bottom edge with a spatula.

Remove the pan from the heat and carefully place the pre-baked crust on top. Cover the pan with a flat serving platter and invert the apples onto the platter carefully. If necessary, adjust the slices to reshape the dessert. If there is excess caramel sauce in the pan, spoon it over the apples. Serve the apples warm or at room temperature, with whipped cream. The dessert can also be made without the pastry crust.

Makes 6 servings.

The crackly caramel glaze on these cream puffs provides a sharp contrast with the smooth coffee cream filling. When served separately, the cream puffs make an elegantly simple dessert. Assembled as a Croquembouche, they are transformed into a stunning presentation.

Sprinkle 2 greased baking sheets with water and shake off the excess. Preheat the oven to 400°F (205°C) and adjust the rack to the middle level.

Glaze

1 large egg
1/2 teaspoon salt

Metal Blade: Put the eggs and salt in the work bowl and process for 2 seconds. Reserve the mixture.

Puff Dough

1 cup (24 cl) water
5 tablespoons unsalted butter (2-1/2 ounces, 71g)
1 tablespoon sugar
Pinch of salt
1 cup unbleached all-purpose flour (5 ounces, 142g)
4 large eggs

In a 1-quart (95 cl) saucepan cook the water, butter, sugar, and salt over medium-high heat until the butter is melted and the liquid is simmering. Remove the pan from the heat, and immediately beat in the flour with a wooden spoon. Continue beating until the mixture leaves the sides of the pan. Return the pan to medium heat and beat the mixture for 2 minutes with a wooden spoon. (A film should develop on the bottom of the pan.) Remove the pan from the heat and let the dough rest for 5 minutes.

Metal Blade: Put the dough in the work bowl and process for 5 seconds. Add the eggs and process for 1 minute, stopping the machine once to scrape down the sides of the bowl. The mixture should be thick and shiny, and it should hold its shape when it is lifted on a spoon.

Transfer the mixture to a pastry bag fitted with a 1/2-inch (1.5 cm) tip and pipe it into 1-1/4-inch (3.25 cm) rounds, spaced 1-1/2 inches (4 cm) apart on the baking sheet. With your finger or a feather brush, brush the rounds with the glaze. Do not let the glaze dribble onto the baking sheets. Push down any peaks and reshape the puffs if necessary. Bake the puffs for 25 to 30 minutes, or until they are golden and crisp. Turn off the oven, open the door, and let the puffs cool for 20 minutes with the oven door ajar.

Makes 40 puffs.

Cream Filling

2 cups (70 cl) milk
6 large egg yolks
2 teaspoons freeze-dried coffee (1/4 teaspoon less if powdered)
2/3 cup sugar (7 ounces, 200g)
1/2 cup unbleached all-purpose flour (2-1/2 ounces, 70g)
Pinch of salt
1 teaspoon vanilla extract

Bring milk to a boil in a saucepan; set aside and keep hot.

Metal Blade: Put the egg yolks, coffee and sugar in the work bowl and process them for 1 minute, stopping the machine once to scrape down the sides of the bowl. Add the flour and salt, and process the mixture for 5 seconds. With the machine running, pour 1 cup (24 cl) of the hot milk through the feed tube and transfer the mixture to the saucepan with the remaining milk. Mix it well as you add it. Bring the mixture to a boil over medium heat, whisking it constantly. Reduce the heat to low, and cook the mixture for 5 minutes or until it thickens, stirring it constantly. Transfer the custard to a bowl, stir in the vanilla. Cover the custard with plastic wrap and let it cool. The custard can be made several days in advance, and refrigerated or frozen.

Makes about 2 cups (47 cl), or enough for 40 puffs.

Caramel

1-1/2 cups sugar (10-1/2 ounces, 298g)
3 tablespoons water
3 tablespoons light corn syrup

Combine the sugar, water, and corn syrup in a heavy stainless steel saucepan. Bring the mixture to a boil over high heat, swirling the pan to dissolve the sugar. Cover the pan and continue cooking for 3 minutes. Uncover the mixture and continue to boil it until it is lightly colored and reaches the hard crack stage, or a candy thermometer registers 310° to 315°F (155° to 157°C.). Remove the pan from the heat and put it in a pan of simmering water over very low heat.

Assembly

Dip the tops of the puffs in the caramel, being careful not to touch the caramel. It is necessary to work quickly. Once the caramel has hardened on the puffs, fill them with pastry cream, using a pastry bag fitted with a 1/4-inch (.75 cm) tip. Press the tip into the base of each puff and pipe in some of the filling; do not overfill.

Variation

You can assemble the cream puffs into a spectacular Croquembouche. It takes effort, but is well worth it. Double the recipe for puff dough and make 80 puffs, as directed above. Puff shells for a Croquembouche must be completely dry. It is best to make them the day before and store them, uncovered, in a cool, dry place until ready to use them. If they are still not crisp, place them in a 375°F (190°C) oven for about 10 minutes before filling them.

Increase the filling recipe by 1/3. (Puffs for a Croquembouche need not be filled as much as those that are served separately.) Double the caramel recipe.

Glaze the puffs and fill them, as directed above. Generously butter a cone-shaped Croquembouche mold. Take a glazed cream puff and place it at the base of the mold, glazed side out. Take another cream puff, dip one side in caramel and, using the caramel as a glue, arrange it next to the first one. Do not allow the caramel to touch the mold. Continue dipping cream puffs in caramel, one by one, and arranging them, glazed side out, next to each other in a chain, with the caramel gluing them together. Arrange two rows of puffs, one on top of the other, pressing them lightly against the mold from time to time to ensure uniform shape. Let them cool for 5 minutes until the caramel is hard before building the next row.

When the first two rows are solidly set, continue building to the top of the mold, turning the mold as necessary. Press the puffs lightly against the mold from time to time. Be careful not to allow any caramel to touch the mold. Leave room at the top for a decoration like a flower or a final puff.

Let the Croquembouche dry at room temperature in a dry place for at least 1/2 hour, or until the caramel is very hard. Then pull the entire cone carefully off the mold. The Croquembouche is best when freshly made.

To serve, use two forks to pry off the cream puffs, beginning at the top. Allow 2 to 3 cream puffs per person.

Makes 20 to 25 servings.

Lemon Curd

This mixture is tart and very lemony, intentionally so as it is meant to provide a distinct flavor when used as a spread for cookies, a filling between cake layers, or as an ingredient in a topping.

Zest of 1 lemon, removed with a vegetable peeler
2/3 cup sugar (5 ounces, 140g)
5 large egg yolks
1/2 cup (12 cl) lemon juice
Pinch salt
1 stick (4 ounces, 115g) unsalted butter, melted and hot

Metal Blade: Mince the lemon zest with the sugar by turning the machine on and off. Process the mixture until the zest is as fine as the sugar. Add the egg yolks, lemon juice and salt and process for 10 seconds to blend. With the machine running, pour the hot melted butter through the feed tube.

Pour the mixture into a small stainless steel saucepan and cook over low heat, stirring constantly with a wooden spoon until it is thickened. Do not let the mixture boil at any time.

Cool the curd at room temperature, cover it and refrigerate it. It will keep for 2 or 3 months in a covered jar in the refrigerator. If it becomes too thick, process it for 1 to 2 seconds with the metal blade.

Makes 1-2/3 cups (40 cl).

Variations

1. For Orange Curd, use the zest of 1 large or 2 small oranges and 1/2 cup (12 cl) of frozen concentrated orange juice.

2. For Orange-Apricot Curd, soften 4 medium-sized dried apricots in orange juice and process with the orange zest.

3. For Pineapple-Apricot Curd, simmer 4 medium-sized apricots in 1/2 cup (12 cl) of boiling water until they are soft. Drain them and purée them with 1 4-ounce (115g) piece of fresh pineapple, cut into 1/4-inch (2.5 cm) pieces.

Lime Yogurt Topping

A refreshing way to use citrus zest and a great accent for all fresh fruit.

Zest of 2 limes, removed with a zester
1/4 cup sugar (1-3/4 ounces)
16 ounces (455g) plain yogurt

Metal Blade: Process the lime zest and sugar until the zest is as fine as sugar. Fold the mixture into the yogurt, adding more sugar, if desired.

Makes 2 cups (47 cl).

Variation

Substitute lemon or orange zest for the lime zest.

Danish Berry Sauce

This sauce is divine over sliced pineapples, poached pears, or apple desserts.

1/4 cup dried currants
   (1 ounce, 30g)
1/2 cup (12 cl) water
1 10-ounce (285g)
   package frozen
   raspberries, thawed
1 teaspoon cornstarch
2 tablespoons sugar

Cook the currants in the water over medium heat until the water is absorbed and the currants are soft.

Metal Blade: Process the raspberries for 1 minute, or until they are puréed. Strain the purée into a small bowl and return it to the work bowl with the currants, cornstarch and sugar. Process the mixture for 1 minute and transfer it to a small saucepan. Heat until the sauce thickens, then transfer it to a bowl and chill it, covered.

Makes about 1 cup (24 cl).

Strawberry-Raspberry Sauce

1 10-ounce (285g)
   package frozen
   raspberries, thawed
   and drained
1 pint (47 cl) fresh
   strawberries, hulled
1 tablespoon Kirsch

Metal Blade: Purée the raspberries for 1 minute, and press the purée through a strainer to remove the seeds. Return the purée to the work bowl with all but 4 of the strawberries, and the Kirsch. Process the mixture until it becomes a purée, stopping the machine once to scrape down the sides of the bowl.

Medium Slicing Disc: Slice the 4 reserved strawberries into the purée, using light pressure. Transfer the sauce to a bowl and serve it over ice cream, sherbets, fruits or berries.

Apricot Sauce

11 medium dried apricots
   (2-1/2 ounces total, 71g)
1-1/3 cups (31 cl) orange
   juice
1 teaspoon orange zest,
   removed with a zester
1 1-pound (455g) can
   apricot halves, well
   drained
2 tablespoons Kirsch

Put the dried apricots and the orange juice in a saucepan and cook over medium heat for 10 minutes, or until the apricots are soft.

Metal Blade: Put the softened dried apricots, the orange juice and the orange zest in the work bowl and process for about 1 minute, or until it becomes a smooth purée. Add the canned apricot halves and process the mixture for 30 seconds. Add the Kirsch and process until blended.

If the sauce is too thick, add orange juice to thin. Serve it warm or chilled over puddings, soufflés, ice creams, sherbets and mixed fruits. The sauce can be reheated and it freezes well.

Makes about 1-3/4 cups (41 cl).

Fresh Peach Sauce

This works equally well with nectarines or fresh apricots. Make serveral batches when the fruits are in season and freeze them.

2 teaspoons orange zest, removed with a zester
4 medium dried apricots (1 ounce total, 30g)
3 large ripe peaches (1 pound total, 455g), unpeeled, pitted and quartered
1 teaspoon lemon juice
1/2 cup or 2-1/2 ounces (70g) sugar
1 teaspoon Grand Marnier

Metal Blade: Process the orange zest and apricots for about 10 seconds. Add the peaches, lemon juice and sugar and process for 15 seconds, or until the mixture is completely smooth, stopping the machine once to scrape down the sides of the bowl. Add the Grand Marnier and process for 1 second longer. This sauce can be frozen.

Makes about 1-1/2 cups (35 cl).

Vanilla Custard Sauce

7 large egg yolks
1/2 cup sugar (3-1/2 ounces, 100g)
Pinch salt
2 cups (47 cl) milk, scalded
2 -inch (5 cm) piece of vanilla bean, split lengthwise

Metal Blade: Process the egg yolks, sugar and salt for 1 minute, or until the mixture is lightly colored and thick. With the machine running, pour 1 cup (24 cl) of hot milk slowly through the feed tube. Whisk this mixture gradually back into the remaining milk in the saucepan (which should not be aluminum). Add the vanilla bean, scraping all the seeds into the custard. Cook over moderate heat, stirring constantly until the cream thickens. Do not let it boil; the custard should lightly coat a spoon. Strain the custard into a metal bowl and set the bowl on ice or in cold water, to cool the custard quickly. Stir occasionally. When it is cool, chill the custard in the refrigerator, covered tightly.

Makes 2 cups (47 cl).

Variation ————

For Orange Custard Sauce, substitute the zest of 2 oranges, removed with a vegetable peeler, for the vanilla bean.

Fresh Strawberry Syrup

1-1/2 cups (35 cl) fresh
   strawberries, hulled
1/4 cup (6 cl) maple or
   pancake syrup

Metal Blade: Process strawberries until they are puréed — about 30 seconds — stopping the machine once to scrape down the sides of the work bowl. Add the syrup and process 10 seconds longer.

Note: The syrup maintains its bright red color if it is not heated. For a special taste, heat the Strawberry Syrup, and remove it from the heat before it boils. Blend in 2 tablespoons of unsalted butter. The color changes slightly, but the syrup has a delicious flavor. Serve immediately, while still hot.

Hazelnut Praline Sauce

An irresistible sauce that enhances many chocolate desserts and puddings as well as fresh berries.

3 tablespoons water
1/2 cup sugar (2-1/2
   ounces, 70g)
1/3 cup (1-1/2 ounces,50g)
   hazelnuts (or almonds)
1 cup (24 cl) or 5 ounces
   (140g) confectioners'
   sugar
2 large egg yolks
1 teaspoon vanilla
   extract
1 cup (24 cl) chilled
   heavy cream

Grease a baking sheet.

Combine the water and sugar in a heavy saucepan and cook over medium-high heat, stirring constantly, until the sugar is dissolved. Cover the mixture for 1 minute, uncover it and add the nuts. Shake the pan, but do not stir. Continue cooking vigorously until the mixture turns a rich brown. Turn it out immediately onto a well greased baking sheet and let it harden for about 20 minutes.

Metal Blade: Break the hardened praline into pieces and put them in the work bowl. Process until the praline is a fine powder. Remove it from the work bowl. This powder will keep for weeks in the refrigerator, or it can be frozen.

Process the confectioners sugar for about 2 seconds to "sift" it. Add the egg yolks and vanilla and process the mixture until it is very smooth — about 10 seconds.

Whip the cream with an electric mixer until it is stiff. Add the egg mixture and 3/4 cup (18 cl) of the crushed praline to the cream and fold gently with a spatula until blended. This sauce can be made 2 days in advance of serving and refrigerated in an airtight container. Try it on Berries Supreme, Zested Strawberries or Mocha Fudge Cake (see Index).

Makes 8 servings.

Basic Recipes

Basic Recipes

Fish Stock
Beef Stock
Chicken Stock
Veal Stock

Butter Sauce
Crème Fraîche
Hollandaise Sauce
Béarnaise Sauce
Green Peppercorn Sauce
Herbed Tomato Sauce
Madeira Wine Sauce (see Index)

Basic Mayonnaise
Scallop Mustard Mayonnaise
Basil Garlic Mayonnaise
Mushroom Mayonnaise
Walnut Mayonnaise
Ravigote Mayonnaise
Pimiento Mayonnaise

These are forethoughts and afterthoughts: basic recipes, like stocks and Crème Fraîche, that I make and keep on hand; simple formulas, such as Hollandaise Sauce, that are used as ingredients; and sauces I have referred to throughout this book as interesting ways to vary some of the dishes.

Except for flavored mayonnaises, which are a machine miracle, I don't use many sauces. Even fancy restaurants have turned away from heavy, complex preparations. So I certainly can't see why a home cook, working alone, should be expected to create extravagant blends. Moreover, I don't like to mask the flavors of foods; so when I make a sauce it's most likely to evolve from the pan juices or vegetables that are a natural part of the recipe. So what you will find here is a minimal repertoire of essentials: quickly processed Hollandaise and variations to enhance plain fish and vegetables any time; Béarnaise to do the same for grilled meat or fish; Green Peppercorn Sauce to complement beef; and Butter Sauce (Beurre Blanc) for fish and seafood. The Fresh Tomato Butter Sauce is the one I like best, not only because it is completely versatile but also because it tastes so fresh. You will not find any flour-thickened sauces or gravies here, because they don't suit my cooking style at all.

Clockwise from bottom left: Basic Mayonnaise, page 269; Walnut Mayonnaise, page 271; Pimiento Mayonnaise, page 272; Mushroom Mayonnaise, page 270; Basic Mayonnaise. Center: Ravigote Mayonnaise, page 272.

What does suit both my menus and my schedule perfectly is mayonnaise. Homemade mayonnaise is a light, delicate dip, accompaniment and salad ingredient that bears little resemblance to oversalted, slightly gelatinous commercial brands. With the food processor, you can make it in seconds and store it in the refrigerator for at least 10 days. There's no reason ever to buy another jarful! And there's every reason to get into the habit of making Basic Mayonnaise. For one thing, it makes tuna, chicken and egg salads taste wonderful. For another, it can be instantly enlivened with a dash of ground spice or chopped fresh herbs to serve as a dip with crudités. But what I find most exciting is that the food processor makes it possible to create spontaneous mayonnaise variations. When I wanted the perfect accent for a cold shellfish pâté, the machine created the flavor link by puréeing scallops for Scallop Mustard Mayonnaise. For a tomato salad, the perfect answer was Basil Garlic Mayonnaise. For cold roast beef, pickles and capers went into Ravigote Mayonnaise. And by first chopping the nuts for Walnut Mayonnaise and then neatly cutting up apples and celery, the machine made old-fashioned Waldorf Salad more appealing than I ever thought possible.

Meat and chicken stocks and Crème Fraîche are not food processor recipes. But I include them here because they are a logical extension of machine-easy techniques. Together, the food processor and homemade stocks give you access to the standard resources of a professional chef. Purchased broth and stock bases tend to be too salty and the cans get expensive when you want to make a large pot of soup. Sour cream can be substituted for Crème Fraîche, but it may curdle, as Crème Fraîche will not, and the flavor is not the same.

Professional chefs think constantly of cost efficiency in whatever they prepare. Working with them, I couldn't help adopting the same attitude. Nothing should be wasted, and in my kitchen nothing is. So in this chapter you'll find only the economy of homemade basics but also many ways to help you improvise quickly with leftovers and stray ingredients.

Fish Stock

3 bottles of clam juice (8 ounces each, 225g)
2 cups (47 cl) water
1/4 cup (6 cl) dry white wine
1 large leek (8 ounces, 225g), green tops included
2 medium onions (8 ounces total, 225g)
6 large mushrooms (8 ounces total, 225g)
1/2 teaspoon dried thyme
1 bay leaf

Place the liquids in a 6-quart (5.7 l) stainless steel pot.

Medium Slicing Disc: Slice the leek and onions, using medium pressure, and add them to the liquids in the pot.

French Fry Disc or Medium Slicing Disc: Cut or slice the mushrooms, and leave them in the work bowl. Insert the metal blade.

Metal Blade: Chop the mushrooms coarsely by turning the machine on and off. Add them to the pot with the thyme and bay leaf. Mix well with a wooden spoon. Bring the stock to a boil over medium-high heat and let it simmer steadily, uncovered, for 20 minutes. Strain it. This stock will keep for 3 days in the refrigerator, or it can be frozen and kept in airtight containers for several months.

Makes 6 cups (1.4 l).

Beef Stock

2 tablespoons oil
6 pounds (2.7 kg) beef shin bones
3 large carrots (14 ounces total, 400g), cut into 2-inch pieces
2 large celery ribs (6 ounces total, 170g), with leaves, cut into 2-inch pieces
2 large onions (12 ounces total, 340g) quartered
3 large cloves garlic, peeled
1 cup (24 cl) dry white wine or dry vermouth
1/2 teaspoon dried thyme
1 bay leaf
6 sprigs parsley
2 tablespoons tomato paste
2 teaspoons salt
Freshly ground black pepper

Preheat the oven to 550°F. (290°C.).

Pour the oil into a large roasting pan. Add the beef bones, carrots, celery, onions and garlic. Place the pan in the preheated oven for about 30 minutes, or until the meat is very brown and the onions are scorched. As the mixture browns, stir it a few times with a wooden spoon. Put the mixture into a large stock pot. Pour 1 cup (24 cl) of hot water into the roasting pan and dissolve the brown bits that cling to the bottom and sides. Pour this liquid into the pot.

Add 4 quarts (3.8 l) of water, wine, thyme, bay leaf, parsley, tomato paste, salt and pepper. Bring the mixture to a boil and skim the surface with a large spoon. Allow the stock to simmer for 4 hours, partially covered with the lid. Strain it through a sieve lined with a double thickness of cheesecloth which has been dipped into cold water and wrung out. This stock can be kept in the refrigerator for 3 days or it can be frozen in airtight containers.

Makes 8 cups (1.9 l).

Chicken Stock

Bones from 6 large
chicken breasts
2 medium onions
(8 ounces total, 225g),
peeled
1 large leek (8 ounces,
225g), cut into feed
tube lengths
2 small carrots (4 ounces
total, 115g), scrubbed
and cut into feed tube
lengths
8 parsley sprigs
2 medium celery ribs
(4 ounces total, 115g)
with leaves
1 teaspoon dried thyme
1 bay leaf
1 whole clove
Salt
Freshly ground black
pepper

Put the chicken bones in a 4-quart (3.8 l) pot.

Medium Slicing Disc: Slice the onions, leek and carrots, using medium pressure. Add them to the pot with the remaining ingredients. Add water just to cover the ingredients, and bring it to a boil. Simmer, uncovered, for 1-1/2 hours. Strain the stock and season it to taste. The fat can be skimmed off easily if you refrigerate the stock until the fat congeals on top. This stock will keep in the refrigerator for 3 days, or it can be frozen and kept in airtight containers for several months.

Makes about 5 cups (1.2 l).

Veal Stock

12 pounds (5.4kg) veal
bones, in 3 to 4-inch
(7.5 to 10 cm) pieces
3 tablespoons unsalted
butter
4 large onions (1 pound
total, 455g), peeled
and quartered
4 medium carrots (1/2
pound total, 225g)
peeled
3 large celery ribs (1/2
pound total, 225g)
8 medium mushrooms (6
ounces total, 170g)
4 garlic cloves,
unpeeled and halved
2 large tomatoes (12
ounces total, 340g),
halved
2-1/2 tablespoons tomato
paste
10 parsley sprigs

Preheat the oven to 425°F (160°C). Place the veal bones in a 16-quart (15 l) stockpot and cover them with water. Set the pot over medium-high heat. Melt the butter in a large flat roasting pan over medium heat; set it aside.

Metal Blade: Chop the onion in batches, turning the machine on and off. Transfer them to the roasting pan.

Medium Slicing Disc: Slice the carrots, celery and mushrooms and put them in the roasting pan.

Add the garlic to the pan and bake 50 minutes, turning the vegetables every 10 minutes. Add them to the stockpot. Pour 2 cups of water from the pot into the roasting pan and scrape the pan to dissolve all brown particles. Add liquid to the stockpot with the remaining ingredients.

Bring to a boil, reduce the heat and simmer, uncovered, about 12 hours. Skim occasionally, especially at first. Strain liquid into another pot and simmer 2 to 3 hours, skimming occasionally. Strain into containers.

Makes 6 to 7 cups (1.4 to 1.6 l).

Butter Sauce (*Beurre Blanc*)

2 large shallots
(2 ounces total, 55g),
peeled
1/4 cup (6 cl) white wine
vinegar
1/4 cup (6 cl) Fish Stock
(see Index)
2 sticks unsalted
butter (1/2 pound,
225g), chilled and cut
into tablespoons
Pinch of cayenne
Salt
Freshly ground pepper

Metal Blade: Mince the shallots by dropping them through the feed tube with the machine running. Add them to the vinegar and stock in a small saucepan. Cook over moderate heat until the liquid is reduced to 3 tablespoons. Whisk in the butter, 1 piece at a time, adding it quickly. Increase the heat when necessary to maintain a constant temperature, but do not let the sauce boil. The consistency of the sauce should be creamy and thick. Correct the seasoning and transfer the sauce to a serving dish. Serve it hot with hot fish or shellfish.

Makes 1 cup (24 cl).

Variation

After all the butter has been added and the sauce has thickened, add 1/4 cup (6 cl) of peeled, seeded and chopped tomato, 1 teaspoon lemon juice, and salt and pepper to taste. Serve the sauce over fish.

Note: You may reheat this sauce over moderate heat, but never let it boil. You can keep it warm for some time by placing the saucepan in a larger pan of warm water.

Crème Fraîche

1/2 pint (24 cl) sour cream
1 pint (47 cl) heavy
cream

Combine both types of cream in a heavy saucepan and heat very carefully over low heat until the mixture is barely warm. (If it becomes hot, the necessary fermentation would be prevented.)

Pour the mixture into a jar and cover it partially. Let it stand at room temperature until thickened, overnight or longer. Stir the mixture well, cover it tightly and refrigerate it. It will keep in the refrigerator for 2 weeks.

Makes 2 cups (47 cl).

Hollandaise Sauce

3 large egg yolks
1 tablespoon warm water
1/2 teaspoon dry mustard
1/2 teaspoon salt
1/2 teaspoon freshly ground white pepper
2 sticks unsalted butter (1/2 pound, 225g), bubbling hot
2 teaspoons lemon juice

Metal Blade: Process the egg yolks, water, mustard, salt and pepper for 10 seconds. With the machine running, pour the hot butter through the feed tube in a thin steady stream. The sauce will begin to thicken. Add more butter only when the previous addition has become incorporated into the egg yolks. If the butter becomes cool during this process, reheat it until it bubbles again. Add the lemon juice and salt and pepper to taste and transfer the sauce to a serving dish. Serve it with cooked vegetables and fish. The sauce may be kept warm in a pan of warm water.

Makes about 1-1/8 cups (27 cl).

Variations

1. Watercress Hollandaise: Blanch 1/4 cup (6 cl) watercress leaves for 30 seconds in 1 quart (95 cl) of boiling water to which you have added 1 teaspoon of salt. Drain the watercress and hold it under cold running water until it is completely cool. Wrap it in paper towels and wring out the excess moisture. Add the watercress to the sauce after the lemon juice and seasonings and process until the watercress is puréed. Serve the sauce over cooked vegetables, fish, shellfish and hot seafood pâtés and mousses. Makes 1-1/4 cups (30 cl).

2. Orange Hollandaise: Add 2 teaspoons of orange zest with the egg yolks. Increase the salt by 1/4 teaspoon and add 1 tablespoon of frozen orange-juice concentrate to the sauce at the end of processing. Correct the seasoning and serve the sauce over cooked asparagus or broccoli, or poached or broiled fish. Makes 1-1/3 cups (31 cl).

3. Dijon Hollandaise: Combine 1 large minced shallot (1 ounce, 30g), with 2 tablespoons of dry Sherry and cook the mixture over moderately high heat until the liquid has almost disappeared. Add this reduction to the egg yolks. Decrease the salt to 1/4 teaspoon, and add 1 teaspoon Dijon-style mustard to the sauce at the end of processing. Correct the seasoning and serve the sauce over broiled or poached fish. Makes 1-1/4 cups (30 cl).

4. Basil Hollandaise: Cook 1 tablespoon of minced parsley, 3 large minced shallots (3 ounces, 85g), 1 teaspoon of dried basil and 1/2 cup (12 cl) of dry red wine over moderately high heat until the liquid is reduced to 2 tablespoons. Add this reduction to the egg yolks and, at the end of processing, add 2 teaspoons of Dijon-style mustard and 1 teaspoon dried basil to the sauce. Process the sauce for 2 seconds and serve it over lamb and cooked vegetables. Makes 1-1/2 cups (35 cl).

Béarnaise Sauce

3 large shallots
    (3 ounces, 85g)
1/4 cup (6 cl) white
    tarragon vinegar
1/4 cup (6 cl) dry white
    wine
1 tablespoon plus 1
    teaspoon dried
    tarragon
3 large egg yolks
1 tablespoon warm
    water
1/2 teaspoon dry mustard
1 teaspoon salt
1/2 to 1 pound (255 to 455g)
    unsalted butter,
    bubbling hot
2 teaspoons lemon juice
1 tablespoon parsley
    leaves

Metal Blade: Mince the shallots by dropping them through the feed tube with the machine running. Simmer them in a saucepan with the vinegar, wine and 1 tablespoon of tarragon until the liquid is reduced to 2 tablespoons. Strain it into the work bowl and add the egg yolks, water, mustard and salt. Process the mixture for 1 minute, or until it is well combined and slightly thickened. With the machine running, pour 1/2 the hot melted butter through the feed tube in a thin steady stream. Add butter only when the previous amount has been incorporated into the egg yolks. Repeat the process with the remaining hot butter. Add the lemon juice and parsley and the remaining tarragon and process for 3 seconds. Add salt and pepper to taste, and transfer the sauce to a serving dish.

Makes 1-1/4 to 2-1/4 cups (30 to 53 cl).

Variations

1. Make Choron Sauce by cutting a peeled tomato shell into 1/4-inch (.60 cm) dice and using the diced tomato as a garnish for Béarnaise Sauce.

2. Dice a 2-ounce (55g) jar of pimientos and use the pimiento as a garnish for Béarnaise Sauce.

Note: Béarnaise Sauce can be made in advance and kept warm over hot, but not boiling, water. It can be made with 1/2 to 1 pound (225 to 455g) of butter, depending on the amount of sauce desired.

Fresh Asparagus with Hollandaise Sauce (recipe opposite)

Herb Tomato Butter Sauce

2 tablespoons parsley leaves
4 large shallots (4 ounces total, 115g), peeled
1 small garlic clove, peeled
4 large tomatoes (1-1/2 pounds total, 680g), peeled, seeded and quartered
3 tablespoons tomato paste
2 teaspoons sugar
1 teaspoon dry mustard
1 teaspoon dried basil
1 teaspoon dried oregano
1-1/2 teaspoons salt
Freshly ground pepper
1 stick plus 2 tablespoons unsalted butter (5 ounces, 140g), chilled and cut into tablespoons
3 tablespoons snipped chives

Metal Blade: Mince the parsley by turning the machine on and off; reserve it. With the machine running, mince the shallots and garlic by dropping them through the feed tube. Add the tomatoes to the work bowl and chop them coarsely by turning the machine on and off.

Transfer the mixture to a 1-quart (95 cl) saucepan and add the tomato paste, sugar, mustard, basil, oregano, salt and pepper. Cook the mixture over high heat for 8 to 10 minutes, or until the liquid has evaporated and the mixture is the texture of soft marmalade. Bring to a boil and whisk in 2 tablespoons of butter. When it is almost melted, whisk in 2 more tablespoons of butter. Repeat until all the butter is added. Do not let the sauce boil at any time. Correct the seasoning and transfer the sauce to a serving dish. Stir in the chives and sprinkle the sauce with the reserved parsley. Serve the sauce over fish, vegetable soufflés, chicken, sautéed veal, hash, rice or pasta.

Makes 1-1/2 cups (35 cl).

Green Peppercorn Sauce

A parsnip purée is used instead of flour to thicken this sauce and give it a delicate flavor.

1 cup (24 cl) Veal Stock (see Index)
1/3 cup (8 cl) dry white wine or dry vermouth
1 tablespoon Cognac
1/4 cup (6 cl) Crème Fraîche (see Index)
1 large parsnip (3 ounces, 85g), peeled, trimmed and cooked
2 teaspoons green peppercorns, drained
Salt
Freshly ground pepper

Simmer the stock, white wine or vermouth, and Cognac in a 1-quart (95 cl) saucepan until reduced to 1 cup (24 cl).

Metal Blade: Put the Crème Fraîche, parsnip, and 1 teaspoon of green peppercorns in the work bowl. Process until the mixture is smooth, stopping the machine once to scrape down the sides of the bowl. With the machine running, pour in the reduced liquid. Transfer the mixture to the saucepan, add salt and pepper to taste, and heat thoroughly. Transfer the sauce to a serving dish, sprinkle it with the remaining peppercorns, and serve it with beef.

Makes 1 cup (24 cl).

Basic Mayonnaise

1 large egg
1 teaspoon lemon juice
1 teaspoon red wine vinegar
1 teaspoon Dijon-style mustard
1 teaspoon salt
Freshly ground white pepper
1-1/2 cups (35 cl) oil (preferably safflower with 3 tablespoons French olive oil)

Metal Blade: Put the egg, lemon juice, vinegar, mustard, salt and pepper, and 3 tablespoons of oil in the work bowl and process for 8 seconds. With the machine running, drizzle the remaining oil through the feed tube in a thin steady stream. The mayonnaise will thicken as the oil is added. Add salt and pepper to taste and refrigerate the mayonnaise in an airtight jar. It can be stored in the refrigerator for at least 10 days.

Makes 1-3/4 cups (41 cl).

Variations

1. Watercress Mayonnaise: Add 1 cup (24 cl) of watercress leaves and stems to 1-1/2 cups (35 cl) of Basic Mayonnaise in the work bowl with the metal blade. Turn the machine on and off until the watercress is puréed.

2. Orange Mayonnaise: Add 2 teaspoons of orange zest, removed with a zester, 1 tablespoon plus 2 teaspoons of frozen orange juice concentrate and 1/2 teaspoon of salt to the egg and lemon juice. Proceed according to the recipe. If the mayonnaise is too thick, let the machine run while adding water through the feed tube, 1 teaspoon at a time, until the desired consistency is reached. Adjust the seasoning.

Scallop Mustard Mayonnaise

This sauce provides a delicate accent to cold shellfish and fish plates.

2 ounces (55g) scallops
1/2 cup (12 cl) reserved mussel cooking liquid, Fish Stock (see Index) or bottled clam juice
1 cup (24 cl) Basic Mayonnaise (see Index)
2 teaspoons lemon juice
1 teaspoon Dijon-style mustard
2 tablespoons heavy cream

In a very small saucepan cook the scallops over moderately high heat in the liquid for 3 minutes or until they just turn opaque. Drain the scallops, reserving and refrigerating the broth. Cool, then refrigerate them.

Metal Blade: Put the scallops, mayonnaise, lemon juice, mustard and cream in the work bowl and process for 5 seconds. With the machine running, add up to 1/4 cup (6 cl) of the reserved broth, 1 tablespoon at a time, until the sauce reaches the desired consistency. Refrigerate the sauce in an airtight container.

Makes about 1-1/4 cups (30 cl).

Basil Garlic Mayonnaise

A dollop of this mayonnaise enlivens the flavor of chilled, cooked green beans or a tomato salad.

1 large shallot
  (1/2 ounce, 15g),
  peeled
1 garlic clove, peeled
1/2 cup (12 cl) fresh basil
  leaves, firmly packed,
  or 1/4 cup (6 cl) dried
  basil, soaked in 1
  tablespoon water
1 large egg
1 teaspoon lemon juice
1 teaspoon red wine
  vinegar
1 teaspoon Dijon-style
  mustard
1 teaspoon salt
  Freshly ground pepper
1-1/2 cups (35 cl) oil
  (preferably safflower
  with 3 tablespoons
  French olive oil)
1 tablespoon water
  (optional)

Metal Blade: With the machine running, mince the shallot and garlic by dropping them through the feed tube. Add the basil and process for 2 seconds. Add the egg, lemon juice, vinegar, mustard, salt, pepper and 2 tablespoons oil. Process the mixture for 8 seconds or until it is thick. With the machine running, drizzle the remaining oil through the feed tube in a thin steady stream. The mayonnaise will thicken as the oil is added. If it becomes too thick, add water through the feed tube while the machine is running. Add salt and pepper to taste and refrigerate the mayonnaise in an airtight jar.

Makes 2 cups (47 cl).

Mushroom Mayonnaise

Delicious with cold meats, sliced tomatoes and potato salad, this mayonnaise is also a versatile spread for canapés.

8 large mushrooms with
  stems (1/2 pound, 225g)
1 large shallot, (1/2 ounce,
  15g), peeled
2 large egg yolks
1 teaspoon lemon juice
1 tablespoon white wine
  vinegar
1 teaspoon Dijon-style
  mustard
1-1/2 teaspoons salt
  Freshly ground pepper
1-1/3 cups (31 cl)
  safflower oil

Preheat the oven to 425°F. (220°C.) and adjust the rack to the middle level.

Arrange the mushrooms on a baking sheet and bake them for 10 minutes. Reduce the oven temperature to 350°F. (175°C.), and bake them for 15 to 35 minutes longer or until they are shriveled. (The exact time depends on their size and freshness.) Wrap the mushrooms in a paper towel and let them cool.

Metal Blade: With the machine running, mince the shallot by dropping it through the feed tube. Scrape down the sides of the bowl and add the mushrooms. Process the mixture for 5 seconds. Add the egg yolks, lemon juice, vinegar, mustard, salt, pepper and 2 tablespoons of the oil and process for 8 seconds, or until it thickens slightly. With the machine running, drizzle the remaining oil through the feed tube in a thin steady stream. The mayonnaise will thicken as it is added. Add salt and pepper to taste and refrigerate the mayonnaise in an airtight jar.

Makes 2 cups (47 cl).

Walnut Mayonnaise

Toss chopped celery and unpeeled, fragrant Jonathan apples, cut like French fries, in this mayonnaise for a modern, food processor version of Waldorf salad. The mayonnaise is delicious with chicken and turkey salads as well.

1 cup broken walnut
   pieces (4 ounces, 115g)
2 large eggs
1 teaspoon lemon juice
1 teaspoon cider vinegar
1/2 teaspoon ground
   ginger
1/2 teaspoon dry mustard
1/2 teaspoon salt
1/4 teaspoon freshly
   ground white pepper
1-1/2 cups (35 cl)
   safflower oil
1 to 2 teaspoons cold
   water (optional)

Bake the walnuts on a jelly-roll pan for 15 minutes at 350°F. (175°C.). Let them cool.

Metal Blade: Process the walnuts in the work bowl for 2 seconds, or until they are minced. Remove and reserve 1/2 cup (12 cl). Add to the work bowl the eggs, lemon juice, vinegar, ginger, mustard, salt, pepper and 2 tablespoons of the oil. Process the mixture for 8 seconds, or until it thickens. With the machine running, drizzle the remaining oil through the feed tube in a thin stream. The mayonnaise will thicken as the oil is added. If the mayonnaise is too thick after all the oil has been combined, let the machine run as you add water through the feed tube, 1 teaspoon at a time.

Put the reserved nuts on top of the mayonnaise and combine by turning the machine on and off about 4 times. Add salt and pepper to taste and refrigerate in an airtight jar.

Makes 2 cups (47 cl).

Artichoke Dill Mayonnaise

1 small shallot (1/2
   ounce, 15g), peeled
5 small artichoke hearts
   (4 ounces total, 115g)
2 large egg yolks
1 teaspoon lemon juice
1 teaspoon Dijon
   mustard
1 teaspoon dried dill
1/2 teaspoon Tabasco
1/2 teaspoon salt
   Freshly ground pepper
1-1/3 cups (31 cl)
   safflower oil

Metal Blade: With the machine running, drop the shallot through the feed tube to mince it finely. Wash the artichoke hearts and pat them dry. Add them to the work bowl and process for 2 seconds to purée them. Add the egg yolks, lemon juice, mustard, dill, Tabasco, salt, pepper and 2 tablespoons of oil. Process for 8 seconds, or until the mixture thickens. With the machine running, drizzle the remaining oil through the feed tube in a thin stream. The mayonnaise will thicken as the oil is added. Adjust the seasoning.

Makes 2 cups (47 cl).

Ravigote Mayonnaise

A perfect accompaniment to roast beef, cold cuts and fish.

1 teaspoon dried
  tarragon
1 tablespoon snipped
  chives
2 tablespoons parsley
  leaves
4 anchovy fillets,
  washed and patted dry
1 large *cornichon* or 1
  small piece of dill
  pickle (1 ounce, 30g)
2 teaspoons capers,
  drained
1 large egg
1 tablespoon lemon
  juice
1 teaspoon Dijon-style
  mustard
1/4 teaspoon salt
  Freshly ground pepper
1-1/2 cups (35 cl)
  safflower oil

Metal Blade: Put the tarragon, chives, parsley, anchovies, pickle and capers in the work bowl and process for 2 seconds. Add the egg, lemon juice, mustard, salt, pepper and 2 tablespoons oil. Process the mixture for 8 seconds, or until it thickens. With the machine running, drizzle the remaining oil through the feed tube in a thin stream. The mayonnaise will thicken as the oil is added. Add salt and pepper to taste and refrigerate the dressing in an airtight jar.

Makes 1-3/4 cups (41 cl).

Pimiento Mayonnaise

This is really more like a sauce than a mayonnaise. It's divine on poached fish at room temperature, or cold vegetable pâtés.

1 large shallot
  (1/2 ounce, 15g),
  peeled
1 5-1/2-ounce (155g) jar
  whole, sweet
  pimientos, well
  drained and patted dry
2 large egg yolks
1 teaspoon lemon juice
1 teaspoon white wine
  vinegar
1 teaspoon Dijon-style
  mustard
1-1/2 teaspoons salt
1/8 teaspoon freshly
  ground white pepper
1-1/3 cups (31 cl)
  safflower oil

Metal Blade: With the machine running, mince the shallot by dropping it through the feed tube. Process it until it is very fine. Scrape down the sides of the bowl, add the pimiento, and purée it. Add the egg yolks, lemon juice, vinegar, mustard, salt, pepper and 2 tablespoons of oil. Process the mixture for 8 seconds, or until it thickens. With the machine running, drizzle the remaining oil through the feed tube in a thin stream. The mayonnaise will thicken as the oil is added. Add salt and pepper to taste and refrigerate the dressing in an airtight jar.

Makes 2-1/4 cups (53 cl).

Recipes using Beaten Egg Whites

Beaten Egg Whites

Egg Timbales with Spinach
Pizza Puffs
Guacamole Mousse
Dilled Salmon and Caper Ring
Watercress Sauce
Sweet Pea Flans with Pepper and Lettuce
Southwestern Corn Roll with Cheese and Salsa
Fluffy Baked Omelet with Vegetables
Cheese Souffle
Fresh Spinach Souffle
Beer Batter
Pancakes "Comme Chez Soi"
Waffles with Fresh Strawberry Butter
Fresh Pineapple Sauce
Creamy Cheese Cake
Jamaican Banana Cake
Triple Layer Lemon Cake
Prune Whip
Glazed Chocolate Torte
Jacques Cagna's Chocolate Mousse Loaf
Raspberry Chiffon Pie
Apricot/Yogurt Bavarian Cream with Orange Slices
Fresh Strawberry Cake Roll
Maple Cake Roll with Maple Pecan Cream

Who says you can't beat egg whites in a food processor? At one time, just about everyone did. But since I discovered a way to do it, I've been developing recipes that prove it's as useful as it is possible. The selection in this chapter illustrates my technique. First, you process the egg whites in a clean work bowl. Then, while the machine is running, you pour through the feed tube a little water mixed with lemon juice or vinegar. Continue processing until the egg whites are whipped and hold their shape — about 1-1/4 to 2 minutes, depending on their number.

Although processor beaten egg whites don't increase in volume quite as much as those beaten with a whisk or electric mixer, the finished results are dramatic. We tested the cheese soufflé side by side with one prepared conventionally. The processor soufflé was lighter, fluffier *and* puffier.

The recipes in this chapter expand our culinary horizons. Mousses, tortes, fluffy omelets and sponge cakes all become simple, one work bowl preparations. As I apply my method to a wider range of dishes, I look forward with excitement to the recipes my fellow cooks will develop as they explore the possibilities of this new food processor technique.

Stages in preparing Chocolate Mousse, page 219.

These are lighter than most timbales because of the separately beaten egg whites, and thus perfect for a first course. The cheese must be ripe. If pine nuts are not available, they can be omitted without too much sacrifice in flavor.

1 10-ounce (284g) package fresh spinach
4 large shallots (2 ounces total, 56g), peeled
2 tablespoons olive oil
1/3 cup pine nuts (1-1/2 ounces, 43g), optional
3 large egg whites
1 tablespoon white vinegar
1 tablespoon water
1/2 cup (12 cl) whipping cream
4 large egg yolks
4 ounces (114g) ripe, well flavored goat's milk cheese, like Bucheron or Montrachet
1/4 teaspoon salt
Freshly ground nutmeg
Freshly ground pepper

Fifteen minutes before baking, preheat the oven to 350°F. (175°C.) and place the rack in the middle. Butter six 1/2-cup timbale or soufflé dishes and place them on a baking sheet.

Wash the spinach well and put it in a large non-aluminum pot with only the water clinging to its leaves. Cook just until it wilts. Transfer to a colander, hold under cold water until completely cool, and reserve 6 to 10 large leaves. Wrap the remaining spinach in a cloth towel, squeeze dry and reserve.

Metal Blade: With the machine running, drop the shallots through the feed tube and process until minced.

Heat the oil in a 10-inch (25 cm) skillet and brown the pine nuts lightly in the oil. Remove them with a slotted spoon and reserve. Add the shallots to the skillet and cook until soft, about 5 minutes. Stir in the spinach from the towel and cook until heated through, about 2 minutes.

Assemble all the ingredients and a 1-quart (95 cl) mixing bowl conveniently near the food processor. It is not necessary to wash the work bowl.

Metal Blade: Put the egg whites in the work bowl, turn the machine on and process for 8 seconds. With the machine running, pour the vinegar and water through the feed tube. Process until the egg whites are whipped and hold their shape, about 1-1/2 minutes. With a spatula, gently transfer the egg whites to the mixing bowl. Without cleaning the work bowl, add the cream and egg yolks and pulse twice. Add the contents from the skillet, the cheese, salt, nutmeg, pepper and reserved pine nuts and pulse 4 times. Spoon the egg whites onto the mixture in a ring and pulse once. Run a spatula around the sides of the work bowl to loosen the mixture and pulse once more. Some streaks of egg white may be visible; do not overprocess. Transfer to a mixing bowl.

Assembly

Pat the reserved spinach leaves dry. Line the bottom of each timbale mold or soufflé dish with leaves, covering the entire surface. Spoon the mixture into the molds, dividing it equally among them. Bake until just set, about 25 minutes. Cool 5 minutes, then reverse onto individual plates.

The timbales can be made up to 2 days in advance. Wrap them airtight and refrigerate until 30 minutes before serving. Reheat in the molds in a water bath on top of the stove for 30 minutes.

Makes 6 servings.

Pizza Puffs

Made with tiny rounds of bread, these are superb appetizers with cocktails. Substitute halves of English muffins for an easy and unusual lunch.

2 large egg whites
2 teaspoons red wine vinegar
1 small onion (2 ounces, 55g), peeled and cut in half
8 ounces (225g) Mozzarella cheese, chilled and cut into 1-inch (2.5 cm) cubes
1-1/2 ounce (42g) piece of pepperoni, peeled and halved
1/4 teaspoon salt
1/2 teaspoon dried oregano
1/2 teaspoon dried basil
1/3 cup (80 ml) Basic Mayonnaise (see Index)
48 1-1/2-inch (4 cm) rounds of a good homemade type bread or slices of *pain de mie*
1/3 cup (80 ml) tomato paste

Assemble all the ingredients and a 1-quart (9.5 dl) mixing bowl conveniently near the food processor.

Metal Blade: Put the egg whites into a clean work bowl and turn the machine on. After 8 seconds, pour the vinegar through the feed tube and process for 45 seconds, or until the egg whites are whipped and hold their shape. With a rubber spatula, gently transfer the egg whites to the mixing bowl. It is not necessary to wash the work bowl.

Put the onion, cheese, pepperoni, salt, oregano and basil in the work bowl and process for 10 seconds, stopping once to scrape down the sides of the bowl. Add the mayonnaise and process for 5 seconds. Add 1/4 of the egg whites and turn the machine on and off twice. Run a spatula around the sides of the work bowl, to loosen the mixture. Spoon the remaining egg whites onto the cheese mixture in a ring and turn the machine on and off 3 times. Run a spatula around the sides of the work bowl, to loosen the mixture. Turn the machine on once, until the ingredients are just mixed. Do not overprocess.

Assembly

Spread each bread round with about 1/4 teaspoon of tomato paste. Mound 2 teaspoons of the cheese mixture onto each round. Place the puffs on a baking sheet and broil 6 inches (15 cm) from the heat, for 3-1/2 to 4 minutes, or until they are puffy and golden brown.

Makes 8 appetizer servings.

Variation

For a quick lunch, substitute 4 split English muffins for the bread rounds. Spread each half with about 2 teaspoons of tomato paste and mound about 1/4 cup (60 ml) of the cheese mixture over it. Cook the same way as for the bread rounds; serves 3 or 4.

Snip corn tortillas into quarters, deep-fry them and serve in a basket. Add a dish of Salsa to the center of the mousse for a perfect first-course trio.

4 teaspoons unflavored gelatin (2 packages)
3/4 cup water
1 tablespoon wine vinegar
3 large egg whites
1 cup parsley leaves
1 medium onion (4 ounces, 115g), peeled and quartered
4 medium, ripe avocados (1-3/4 pounds total, 795g), peeled and cut into 1-inch (2.5 cm) pieces
1 tablespoon fresh lime juice
1 teaspoon Tabasco sauce
3/4 cup (1.8 dl) Basic Mayonnaise (see Index)
1-3/4 teaspoons salt
Freshly ground black pepper
1 teaspoon dried red chilies (optional)
Tortilla chips
Salsa (see Index to Egg White Recipes)

Lightly oil a 6 1/2-cup (15.4 dl) ring mold. Sprinkle the gelatin over 1/4 cup (60 ml) of water. When the water has been absorbed, dissolve the gelatin by setting the cup in a pan of hot water or placing it for 20 seconds in a microwave oven, set at the lowest temperature.

Assemble all the ingredients and a 1-quart (9.5 dl) mixing bowl conveniently near the food processor. Put the vinegar and 1 tablespoon of the water in a small dish.

Metal Blade: Put the egg whites into a clean work bowl and turn the machine on. After 8 seconds, pour the vinegar and water through the feed tube and process for 1 minute, or until the egg whites are whipped and hold their shape. With a rubber spatula, gently transfer the egg whites to the mixing bowl. It is not necessary to wash the work bowl.

Put the parsley and onion in the work bowl and turn the machine on and off until they are finely minced. Add the avocado pieces and process for 30 seconds, or until puréed, stopping once to scrape down the sides of the work bowl. Add the lime juice, Tabasco, mayonnaise, dissolved gelatin, remaining 7 tablespoons of water, salt, pepper, and chilies and process for 20 seconds, stopping once to scrape down the sides of the bowl. Spoon 1/2 the egg whites onto the avocado mixture in a ring and turn the machine on and off twice. Run a rubber spatula around the sides of the work bowl to loosen the mixture. Spoon on the remaining egg whites. Turn the machine on and off 4 more times, just until the ingredients are mixed. Some streaks of egg whites may still be visible; do not overprocess. With a rubber spatula, transfer the Avocado Mousse to the prepared ring mold. Cover airtight with plastic wrap and refrigerate at least 4 hours.

To serve, loosen the mousse from the ring mold with a small flexible knife and invert it onto a 12-inch (30 cm) serving platter. Fill the center with a small dish of Salsa and serve with tortilla chips.

Makes 6 cups (14 dl).

Dilled Salmon and Caper Ring

The light texture of this mousse comes from beaten egg whites and water — not from calorie laden heavy cream.

Ring

16 ounce (455g) can red salmon
4 teaspoons unflavored gelatin (2 packages)
1 tablespoon white vinegar
1 tablespoon water
4 large egg whites
1/2 cup (1.2 dl) parsley leaves
1 small onion (2 ounces, 55g), peeled and halved
2 celery ribs with greens (4 ounces total, 115g), peeled with a vegetable peeler, and cut into 1-inch (2.5 cm) pieces
1 tablespoon Worcestershire sauce
4 drops Tabasco sauce
1 tablespoon dried dill weed
Freshly ground black pepper
1 tablespoon fresh lemon juice
2 tablespoons water
3/4 cup (1.8 dl) Basic Mayonnaise (see Index)
2 tablespoons capers, drained

Garnish

1 bunch watercress, stems removed
1 English cucumber, unpeeled, scored and cut into feed-tube lengths
Watercress Sauce (recipe follows)

Oil a 6 1/2-cup (15.4 dl) ring mold. Measure 1/4 cup (60 ml) of the liquid from the salmon and sprinkle the gelatin over the liquid. When the liquid has been absorbed, dissolve the gelatin by setting the cup in a pan of hot water or placing it for 20 seconds in a microwave oven set at the lowest temperature. Set aside, and discard remaining liquid from salmon.

Remove the skin and bones from the salmon. Assemble all the ingredients and a 1-quart (9.5 dl) mixing bowl conveniently near the food processor. Put the vinegar and water in a small dish.

Metal Blade: Put the egg whites into a clean work bowl and turn the machine on. After 8 seconds, pour the vinegar and water through the feed tube and process for about 1 minute and 5 seconds, or until the egg whites are whipped and hold their shape. With a rubber spatula, gently transfer the egg whites to the mixing bowl. It is not necessary to wash the work bowl before proceeding.

Put the parsley, onion and celery in the work bowl and chop them finely by turning the machine on and off. Set aside. Add the salmon, Worcestershire sauce, Tabasco, dill weed and pepper, and process until puréed, stopping once to scrape down the sides of the work bowl. Add the lemon juice, gelatin mixture, water and mayonnaise and process until smooth and fluffy — about 30 seconds — stopping once to scrape down the sides of the work bowl. Add the capers. Spoon the reserved chopped vegetables onto the mixture in a ring, and spoon the egg whites onto the vegetables. Mix by turning the machine on and off 3 times. Run a spatula around the sides of the work bowl, to loosen the mixture, and turn the machine on and off 2 more times. Some streaks of egg whites may still be visible; do not overprocess.

With a rubber spatula, transfer the mixture into the prepared ring mold. Cover with plastic wrap and refrigerate at least 4 hours or overnight.

To serve, let the Dilled Salmon and Caper Ring rest on the counter for 20 minutes to remove the chill. With a small flexible spatula, separate the mousse carefully from the mold. Invert it onto a 12-inch (30 cm) round serving dish. Garnish the center with the watercress leaves and surround with cucumber slices, sliced with the Medium Slicing Disc, using medium pressure. Pass the Watercress Sauce separately.

Serves 8 to 10 for lunch.

Watercress Sauce

With egg whites to lighten it, this flavorful mayonnaise is transformed into a smooth, flowing sauce.

2 large eggs, separated
2 teaspoons red wine vinegar
1 large clove garlic, peeled
1 bunch watercress, cleaned, stems removed
1 teaspoon Dijon mustard
1 teaspoon red wine vinegar
1 teaspoon fresh lemon juice
1/2 teaspoon salt
  Freshly ground black pepper
1-1/2 cups (3.5 dl) safflower oil

Assemble all the ingredients and a 1-quart (9.5 dl) mixing bowl conveniently near the food processor.

Metal Blade: Put the egg whites into a clean work bowl and turn the machine on. After 8 seconds, pour 2 teaspoons of vinegar through the feed tube and process for 40 seconds, until the egg whites are whipped and hold their shape. With a rubber spatula, gently transfer the egg whites to the mixing bowl. Turn on the machine, drop the garlic through the feed tube and process until it is finely minced. Put the egg yolks, watercress, mustard, remaining vinegar, lemon juice, salt, pepper, and 3 tablespoons of oil in the work bowl and process for 8 seconds. With the machine running, drizzle the remaining oil through the feed tube in a thin, steady stream. The mayonnaise will thicken as the oil is added. If it is too thick, add water by the teaspoonful until the desired consistency is reached. Spoon the egg whites onto the mayonnaise in a ring and turn the machine on and off twice, just until the egg whites are mixed. Do not overprocess. Taste and adjust the seasoning.

Makes 2 cups (4.7 dl).

Sweet Pea Flans Garnished with Sautéed Peppers and Lettuce

The garnish of sweet-sour red peppers and lettuce complements the peas in flavor, color and texture. It's also a delicious vegetable offering on its own.

Flans

2 10-ounce (285g) packages frozen peas, thawed and drained on paper towels
1 tablespoon white vinegar
1 tablespoon water
3 large egg whites
2 teaspoons instant non-fat dry milk
1 teaspoon dried dill weed
1/2 teaspoon salt

Butter six 1/2-cup (1.2 dl) timbale molds or ovenproof dishes. Have ready a kettle of boiling water and a pan large enough to hold the molds. Preheat the oven to 350°F. (175°C.) and adjust the rack to the middle level.

Metal Blade: Process the peas for 20 seconds, stopping once to scrape down the sides of the bowl. Push the pea pulp through a strainer; you should have 1 cup (2.4 dl) of pea purée. Wipe the work bowl with paper towels to remove skins.

Assemble the remaining ingredients and a 1-quart (9.5 dl) mixing bowl conveniently near the food processor. Put the vinegar and water in a small dish. Put the egg whites in the work bowl and turn the machine on. After 8 seconds, pour the vinegar and water through the feed tube while the machine is running. Process for about 1 minute and 20 seconds, or until the egg whites are whipped and hold their shape.

With a rubber spatula, gently transfer the mixture to the mixing bowl. It is not necessary to wash the work bowl.

Put the pea purée back into the work bowl with the dry milk, dill weed and salt. Add 1/4 of the egg whites and turn the machine on and off twice. Run a spatula around the sides of the work bowl, to loosen the mixture. Spoon the remaining egg whites onto the pea mixture in a ring. Turn the machine on and off 3 times. Run a spatula around the sides of the work bowl, to loosen the mixture, and turn the machine on and off once more. Do not overprocess.

Divide the mixture equally among the 6 prepared dishes. Place the dishes in the baking pan, set it on the oven rack and pour in boiling water to come up 1 inch (2.5 cm) on the sides of the dishes. Bake 28 to 30 minutes, or until the surface feels firm. Prepare the garnish while the flans are cooking.

Garnish

1 large red pepper (6 ounces, 170g), cut into 2-inch (5 cm) rectangles
1 small head romaine lettuce (8 ounces total, 225g), cut into feed-tube lengths
4 tablespoons unsalted butter (2 ounces, 55g)
3 tablespoons red wine vinegar
1 tablespoon sugar
1/2 teaspoon salt
Freshly ground black pepper

Medium Slicing Disc: Stand the pepper pieces in the feed tube side by side, wedging in the last piece tightly. Cut them into matchsticks, using light pressure.

Thick or Medium Slicing Disc: Place the lettuce in the feed tube vertically and slice it, using light pressure.

Put the butter, vinegar, sugar and salt into an 8-inch (20 cm) skillet and cook for 3 minutes over medium high heat, until slightly thickened. Add the peppers and lettuce and cook until just heated through; do not overcook. Adjust the seasoning, adding freshly ground pepper.

Divide the garnish among 6 individual bread and butter plates and invert a Sweet Pea Flan onto each. Garnish the top of each flan with a red pepper strip and spoon over any sauce. Serve immediately. You could also use the flans to surround a roast on a platter.

The flans can be made up to 2 days in advance and reheated for 30 minutes in a water bath on top of the stove.

Makes 6 servings. See illustration on page 53.

Southwestern Corn Roll with Cheese and Salsa _____

Use as many hot peppers as you dare, in both the Corn Roll and the Salsa. For my palate, the hotter the better!

Corn Roll _____

- 3 tablespoons unsalted butter
- 3 tablespoons yellow cornmeal
- 1 tablespoon unbleached all-purpose flour
- 1 12 ounce (340g) can whole kernel yellow corn, drained, with liquid reserved
- 1 cup (2.4 dl) liquid (reserved corn liquid plus milk)
- 4 drops Tabasco sauce
- 1 teaspoon salt
- 1 tablespoon white vinegar
- 1 tablespoon water
- 8 large egg whites
- 1/2 cup (1.2 dl) parsley leaves
- 1 small onion (3 ounces, 85g), peeled and quartered
- 1-1/2 inch (3.8 cm) square of green pepper
- 1 fresh or canned green chili, drained
- 5 large egg yolks
- 12 ounces (340g) Longhorn Colby cheese, chilled, cut to fit feed tube

Preheat the oven to 350°F. (175°C.) and adjust the rack to the middle level. Line an 11- by 17-inch (28- by 43-cm) jelly roll pan with aluminum foil, extending it 2 inches (5 cm) beyond each end. Butter the foil, dust it lightly with flour and shake off any excess.

Melt the butter in a 1-quart (9.5 dl) saucepan and stir in the cornmeal and flour. Cook over low heat for 1 minute. Add the liquid, Tabasco and salt and whisk rapidly, taking care to reach the bottom and sides of the pan, until the mixture comes to a boil and thickens to a medium paste. Keep the mixture warm until needed.

Assemble all the ingredients and a 1-quart mixing bowl conveniently near the food processor. Put the vinegar and water in a small dish.

Metal Blade: Put the egg whites into a clean work bowl and turn the machine on. After 8 seconds, pour the vinegar and water through the feed tube while the machine is running. Process for about 1 minute and 55 seconds, or until the egg whites are whipped and hold their shape. With a rubber spatula, gently transfer the whites to the mixing bowl. It is not necessary to wash the work bowl before proceeding.

Put the parsley, onion, green pepper and chili in the work bowl and turn the machine on and off until they are finely chopped. Add the corn and process for 10 seconds, stopping once to scrape down the sides of the bowl. Add the warm cornmeal mixture and process for 5 seconds. Add the egg yolks and turn the machine on and off twice. Add 1/4 of the egg whites and turn the machine on and off 2 more times. Spoon the remaining egg whites onto the corn mixture in a ring and turn the machine on and off 3 times. Run a spatula around the sides of the work bowl, to loosen the mixture. Turn the machine on and off once more. Some streaks of egg white may still be visible; do not overprocess.

With a rubber spatula, transfer the mixture to the prepared jelly roll pan. Spread evenly with the spatula and bake in the preheated oven for 25 minutes, until it is brown and puffy. Small surface cracks may develop; they don't matter. While the roll is cooking, shred the cheese.

Shredding Disc: Shred the cheese, using light pressure.

Garnish

Salsa (recipe follows)
1 cup (2.4 dl) sour cream

After the corn roll has baked for 25 minutes, remove it to a cooling rack. Sprinkle the shredded cheese evenly over the surface, making sure the cheese extends all the way to the edges of the roll. Return it to the oven and bake 7 more minutes, just until the cheese is melted. Let the corn roll rest on a wire rack for 10 minutes before removing it from the pan. Lift it from the pan with the foil and rest it on the counter. Roll it up, with the aid of the foil, starting at a short side. Place it on a serving platter with the seam side down. Drain excess liquid from Salsa and garnish the top of the roll with Salsa. Or place a few spoonfuls of Salsa on a serving plate and place a slice of the roll over it. Serve with dollops of sour cream.

The Southwestern Corn Roll can be made up to 2 days in advance and refrigerated, wrapped airtight. To reheat it, place it in a cold oven, turn the oven to 350°F. (175°C.) and bake for 20 to 25 minutes, until it is heated through. Slices of corn roll can be heated for 45 seconds in a microwave oven set at the highest temperature.

Makes 8 to 10 servings.

Salsa

1/2 cup (1.2 dl) cilantro leaves
1 large garlic clove, peeled
1 medium onion (4 ounces, 115g), peeled and quartered
1 to 2 Serrano chilies, halved
2 medium tomatoes (12 ounces total, 340g), quartered
2/3 cup (1.5 dl) tomato sauce
1 teaspoon red wine vinegar
1/2 teaspoon salt
1/2 teaspoon sugar

Metal Blade: Put the cilantro in the work bowl. Turn on the machine, drop the garlic through the feed tube and process until it is finely minced. Add the onion, chilies and tomatoes and turn the machine on and off 5 or 6 times, just until the vegetables are coarsely chopped. Add the tomato sauce, vinegar, salt and sugar and turn the machine on and off twice to blend.

Makes about 2-1/2 cups (6 dl).

Note: If cilantro is not available, substitute 1/2 cup (1.2 dl) of parsley leaves; the taste will not be the same but the color will be. If Serrano chilies are not available, substitute 1 to 2 canned green chilies, drained.

Southwestern Corn Roll with Cheese and Salsa

Fluffy Baked Omelet with Vegetables _____

A garden of fresh vegetables nestles under fluffy baked eggs. For ease of preparation, it's all done in one dish and baked.

Fifteen minutes before baking, preheat the oven to 350°F. (175°C.) and set the rack at the middle level.

Vegetables _____

- 2/3 cup (20 ml) parsley leaves, loosely packed
- 1 large garlic clove, peeled
- 1 small onion (2 ounces, 55g), peeled and halved
- 4 tablespoons unsalted butter (2 ounces, 55g)
- 3/4 teaspoon salt Freshly ground black pepper
- 6 large scallions (3 ounces, 85g), including green tops, cut into thirds
- 1 medium red pepper (5 ounces, 140g), cut into 4 rectangles
- 3 large mushrooms (2 ounces, 55g), with stems trimmed and opposite ends cut flat
- 1 small zucchini (5 ounces, 140g), unpeeled and cut into feed-tube lengths
- 1 thick end of large carrot (2 ounces, 55g) peeled and cut into feed-tube width

Metal Blade: Mince the parsley by dropping it through the feed tube while the machine is running. Set it aside. With the machine running, drop the onion and garlic through the feed tube and process until finely minced. Melt the butter over medium heat in an oven-proof skillet or gratin dish with a 6-cup (14 dl) capacity. Brush the butter up on the sides of the pan. Add the minced onion, garlic, salt and pepper. Cook 5 minutes, or until vegetables are soft. While the onion and garlic are cooking, process the remaining vegetables as follows.

Medium Slicing Disc: Place the scallions in the feed tube vertically and slice them, using light pressure. Reserve 2 tablespoons for garnish. Leave the rest in the work bowl. Stand the red pepper pieces on their sides and slice them into matchsticks, using light pressure.

Medium or Thin Slicing Disc: Slice the mushrooms, using light pressure.

French Fry Disc: Stand the zucchini in the feed tube and process, using medium pressure.

Shredding or Julienne Disc: Put the carrot in the feed tube horizontally and process, using firm pressure.

Add these vegetables and all but 1 tablespoon of the reserved parsley to the skillet and cook for 7 minutes, or until they are just heated through. Shake the pan occasionally to mix the vegetables and to keep them from sticking. This can be done in advance, but the vegetables must be reheated when the egg mixture is added. Wipe out the work bowl thoroughly with paper towels.

Egg Mixture _____

- 1 tablespoon white vinegar
- 1 tablespoon water
- 7 large eggs, separated, at room temperature
- 1/2 cup (1.2 dl) milk minus 1 tablespoon

Combine the vinegar and water in a small dish. Assemble all the ingredients and a 1-quart bowl near the food processor.

Metal Blade: Put the egg whites in the work bowl and turn on the machine. After 8 seconds, pour the vinegar and water through the feed tube and process for 2-1/2 minutes, or until the egg whites are whipped and hold their shape. With a rubber spatula, transfer them gently to the mixing bowl. It is not necessary to wash the work bowl before proceeding.

Put the egg yolks, milk and seasonings into the work bowl and turn the machine on and off 3 times. Transfer the egg whites onto this mixture by large spoonfuls, arranging them

1 teaspoon dry mustard
6 drops Tabasco sauce
1 teaspoon seasoning salt
Freshly ground white pepper

in a ring around the inside of the work bowl. Turn on and off about 4 times, just until they are mixed. Some streaks of egg white may be visible; do not overprocess.

Transfer this egg mixture to the hot skillet. Gently lift up the vegetables with a spatula at 4 evenly spaced intervals to mix the ingredients. Garnish with the reserved scallions and parsley. Cover and cook for 5 minutes over medium heat to set the eggs. Remove the cover, transfer the pan to the preheated oven and bake for 25 minutes, or until the eggs are lightly browned on top. Remove from the oven and cut into 8 to 10 wedges. Serve immediately.

Makes 6 servings.

Cheese Soufflé

2 tablespoons unsalted butter
3 tablespoons unbleached all-purpose flour
3/4 cup (1.8 dl) milk
1 teaspoon Dijon mustard
3 drops Tabasco sauce
1/2 teaspoon salt
1 tablespoon white wine vinegar
1 tablespoon water
6 large egg whites
3 ounces (85g) white Cheddar cheese, chilled and cut into 3 pieces
3 ounces (85g) Monterey Jack cheese, chilled and cut into 3 pieces
4 large egg yolks

Preheat the oven to 375°F. (190°C.) and adjust the rack to the lower third level. Butter a 5 or 6-cup (12 to 14 dl) soufflé dish.

Melt the butter in a 1-quart (9.5 dl) saucepan and stir in the flour. Cook over low heat for 1 minute. Add the milk, mustard, Tabasco and salt. Whisk rapidly, taking care to reach all parts of the pan bottom, until the mixture comes to a boil and thickens to a medium paste. Keep warm until needed.

Assemble all the other ingredients and a 1-quart (9.5 dl) mixing bowl near the food processor. Put the vinegar and water in a small dish.

Metal Blade: Put the egg whites in the work bowl and turn on the machine. After 8 seconds, pour the vinegar and water mixture through the feed tube and process for 1-1/2 minutes, or until the egg whites are whipped and hold their shape. With a rubber spatula, transfer the whites gently to the mixing bowl. It is not necessary to wash the work bowl.

Put the cheese in the work bowl and process for 20 seconds, to chop it fine. Add the egg yolks and process for 5 seconds. Add the warm flour mixture and process 5 seconds. Spoon the egg whites onto the mixture by large spoonfuls. Turn the machine on and off twice. Run a spatula around the sides of the work bowl, to loosen the mixture. Turn the machine on and off 3 or 4 more times until the egg whites are just mixed. Some streaks of white may be visible; do not overprocess.

With a rubber spatula, gently transfer the mixture to the prepared soufflé dish. Bake the soufflé in the preheated oven for about 38 minutes, or until it is well browned.

Makes 4 servings.

12 ounces (340g) fresh
   spinach, including
   the stems, washed
3 tablespoons unsalted
   butter
3 tablespoons
   unbleached all-
   purpose flour
1 cup (2.4 dl) milk
1 teaspoon salt
1 teaspoon Dijon
   mustard
3 drops Tabasco sauce
   Freshly grated
   nutmeg
   Freshly ground black
   pepper
1 tablespoon white
   vinegar
1 tablespoon water
8 large egg whites
1 large garlic clove,
   peeled
1 small onion
   (2-1/2 ounces, 70g),
   peeled and halved
1/2 cup (1.2 dl) parsley
   leaves
2 ounces (55g) imported
   Parmesan cheese, at
   room temperature and
   in 2 pieces
5 large egg yolks

To retain the vibrant green of fresh spinach, run cold water over it when cooked and squeeze out all the moisture.

Preheat the oven to 375°F. (190°C.) and adjust the rack to the lower third. Butter a 6-1/2 cup (15.5 dl) soufflé dish.

Put the spinach in a non-aluminum pan with just the water clinging to its leaves. Cook over high heat until it is just wilted, turning it once or twice with a wooden spoon. Transfer it to a colander and hold it under cold running water until it is completely cool. Drain it well, wrap it in a dry cloth towel and squeeze out as much moisture as possible. (Often a second dry towel is required to release all the moisture.)

Melt the butter in a 1-quart (9.5 dl) saucepan and stir in the flour. Cook over low heat for about 1 minute. Pour in the milk and whisk rapidly, taking care to reach all parts of the pan. Add the salt, mustard, Tabasco, nutmeg and pepper and continue to cook until the mixture is a thick cream sauce. Keep warm until needed.

Assemble all the other ingredients and a 1-quart (9.5 dl) mixing bowl conveniently near the food processor. Put the vinegar and water in a small dish.

Metal Blade: Put the egg whites into a clean work bowl and turn the machine on. After 8 seconds, pour the vinegar and water mixture through the feed tube and process for about 1 minute and 45 seconds, or until the egg whites are whipped and hold their shape. With a rubber spatula, gently transfer the egg whites to the mixing bowl. It is not necessary to wash the work bowl before proceeding.

Put the garlic, onion, parsley and cheese in the work bowl and process for 15 seconds, until the ingredients are finely minced. Add the drained spinach and process for 5 seconds. Add the egg yolks and process for 5 more seconds. Add the warm flour mixture and process for 5 seconds, stopping once to scrape down the sides of the bowl.

Spoon the egg whites onto the mixture in a ring. Turn the machine on and off twice. Run a spatula around the sides of the work bowl, to loosen the mixture. Turn the machine on and off 3 more times, until the egg whites are just mixed. Some streaks of egg white may still be visible; do not overprocess.

With a rubber spatula, gently transfer the mixture to the prepared soufflé dish. Bake in the preheated oven for 38 to 40 minutes, until the soufflé is puffed and well browned.

Makes 6 to 8 servings.

This basic recipe for beer batter, which is used at Alain Chapel's restaurant in Mionnay, France, always produces a crisp, light coating.

1 tablespoon white
   vinegar
1 tablespoon water
2 large eggs, separated
1-1/4 cups (3 dl) beer
1-1/2 tablespoons
   vegetable oil
1-1/2 cups unbleached all
   purpose flour
   (7-1/2 ounces, 215g)
1 teaspoon salt
1/8 teaspoon sugar

Assemble all the ingredients and a 1-quart (9.5 dl) mixing bowl conveniently near the food processor. Put the vinegar and water in a small dish.

Metal Blade: Put the egg whites into a clean work bowl and turn the machine on. After 8 seconds, pour the vinegar and water through the feed tube and process for 1 minute, or until the egg whites are whipped and hold their shape. With a rubber spatula, gently transfer the mixture to the mixing bowl. It is not necessary to wash the work bowl.

Put the egg yolks, beer and oil in the work bowl and process for 5 seconds. Add the flour, salt and sugar, and turn the machine on and off 6 times, until the ingredients are combined. Add 1/4 of the egg whites and process for 5 seconds. Run a spatula around the sides of the work bowl, to loosen the mixture. Spoon the remaining egg whites on top of the batter in a ring and turn the machine on and off twice, until the egg whites are just mixed. Do not overprocess. Transfer the batter to a bowl, cover with damp paper towels and refrigerate for 2 hours. Mix the batter with a spoon before using.

The Beer Batter can be used to fry shrimp, fish filets or sliced vegetables. Fry in hot oil (350°F., 175°C.) until brown and crispy. Drain on paper towels and serve immediately.

Makes 4 cups (9.5 dl) of batter.

Fresh Spinach Soufflé (recipe opposite)

Pancakes "Comme Chez Soi"

This recipe, given to me by Chef Pierre Wynants of the Comme Chez Soi restaurant in Brussels, produces a light and fluffy pancake, which he serves with a sprinkling of brown sugar.

2 large eggs, separated
2 tablespoons sugar
1 tablespoon water
1 cup plus 2 tablespoons ricotta cheese (10 ounces, 285g)
1-1/2 tablespoons plain yogurt
1/4 cup (60 ml) milk
1/2 cup unbleached all-purpose flour (2-1/2 ounces, 70g)
Pinch of salt
Unsalted butter for frying

Assemble all the ingredients and a 1-quart (9.5 dl) mixing bowl conveniently near the food processor.

Metal Blade: Put the egg whites and sugar into a clean work bowl and turn the machine on. After 8 seconds, pour the water through the feed tube and process for 2 minutes, or until the egg whites are whipped and hold their shape. With a rubber spatula, gently transfer the mixture to the mixing bowl. It is not necessary to wash the work bowl before proceeding.

Put the ricotta cheese and yogurt in the work bowl and process for 1 minute, or until completely smooth, stopping once to scrape down the sides of the bowl. Add the egg yolks, milk, flour and salt and process for 15 seconds, stopping once to scrape down the sides of the bowl. Spoon the egg whites onto the mixture in a ring. Turn the machine on and off twice. Run a spatula around the sides of the work bowl, to loosen the mixture. Turn the machine on and off 2 or 3 times, just until the batter is mixed. Do not overprocess; the batter should have the consistency of softly whipped cream.

Spoon the batter onto a hot buttered griddle or skillet in 2-1/2 inch (6 cm) rounds. Cook until the edges of the pancake are well set and the top is bubbly. Turn and brown the other side. Make additional pancakes with the remaining batter, adding more butter to the griddle, as needed.

Serve the pancakes sprinkled with light or dark brown sugar or spread them with tart jam or Fresh Strawberry Butter (see Index).

Makes 30 2-1/2 inch (6 cm) pancakes.

Waffles with Fresh Strawberry Butter ───────────────────

Crisp, delicate waffles are welcome additions to the breakfast table — especially with Fresh Strawberry Butter!

1-1/4 cups unbleached
all-purpose flour
(6-1/4 ounces, 180g)
2 teaspoons baking
powder
1/2 teaspoon baking soda
1/2 teaspoon salt
2 tablespoons sugar
1 tablespoon white
vinegar
1 tablespoon water
3 large eggs, separated
6 tablespoons butter
(3 ounces, 85g),
melted
1-1/3 cups (3 dl) milk

Measure all the dry ingredients and the sugar into a bowl and stir until all lumps have disappeared. Put the vinegar and water in a small dish. Assemble all the other ingredients and a 1-quart (9.5 dl) mixing bowl near the food processor.

Metal Blade: Put the egg whites into a clean work bowl and turn the machine on. After 8 seconds, pour the vinegar and water through the feed tube and process for about 1 minute and 10 seconds, or until the egg whites are whipped and hold their shape. With a rubber spatula, gently transfer the mixture to the mixing bowl. It is not necessary to wash the work bowl before proceeding.

Put the egg yolks, butter and milk into the work bowl and process for 5 seconds. Add dry ingredients and sugar and mix by turning the machine on and off about 4 times. Scrape down the sides of the bowl. Spoon the egg whites onto the mixture in a ring, and turn the machine on and off twice. Run a spatula around the sides of the work bowl and turn the machine on and off once more.

To cook the waffles, follow the instructions of the waffle iron's manufacturer. To make pancakes with this batter, spoon it onto a hot buttered griddle or skillet in 4-inch (10 cm) rounds. Cook until the edges of the pancake are well set and the top is bubbly. Turn and brown the other side. Make additional pancakes with the remaining batter, adding more butter to the griddle, as needed. Serve the waffles or pancakes with Fresh Strawberry Butter.

Makes 6 cups of batter, enough for 6 to 8 waffles or about 30 4-inch (10 cm) pancakes.

Fresh Strawberry Butter ───────────────────────────

1 cup strawberries
(about 6-1/2 ounces,
185g), hulled
3/4 cup confectioners
sugar (3 ounces, 85g)
1 stick unsalted butter
(4 ounces, 112g), at
room temperature, cut
into 4 pieces

Metal Blade: Process the strawberries until puréed, stopping the machine once to scrape down the sides of the bowl. Add the sugar and butter and process 2 or 3 minutes, or until the mixture is smooth, fluffy and bright pink. (The long processing is necessary to blend the mixture thoroughly.) Spoon into a 1-1/2 cup (3.5 dl) crock, wrap airtight and refrigerate. This mixture can also be frozen. Let the butter stand at room temperature for 2 hours before serving or soften slightly, but do not melt, in a microwave oven.

Makes about 1-1/4 cups (3 dl).

Fresh Pineapple Sauce

3 × 1-inch (7.5 × 2.5 cm) piece of fresh pineapple (3 ounces, 85g), halved

1/2 cup plus 2 tablespoons sugar (4 ounces, 115g), divided

2 tablespoons fresh lemon juice

3 large eggs, separated

1 tablespoon white vinegar

Metal Blade: Put the pineapple and 6 tablespoons of sugar in the work bowl and process for 30 seconds, until the pineapple is puréed. Add the lemon juice and process 5 seconds. Transfer the mixture to a 1-quart (9.5 dl) saucepan. It is not necessary to wash the work bowl. Whisk the egg yolks into the pineapple and bring the mixture to a boil over medium heat, whisking constantly until it is opaque and thick enough to coat a spoon. Transfer to a small dish and refrigerate until completely cool.

Metal Blade: Put the egg whites and the remaining 1/4 cup (1-3/4 ounces, 50g) of sugar into the work bowl and turn the machine on. After 8 seconds, pour the vinegar through the feed tube and process for 3 minutes, until the eggs are whipped and hold their shape. With a rubber spatula, gently transfer them to the mixing bowl.

Put the pineapple mixture into the work bowl and process for 10 seconds. Spoon the egg whites onto the mixture in a ring and turn the machine on and off 3 times. Run a rubber spatula around the sides of the bowl, to loosen the mixture. Turn the machine on and off once more, until the ingredients are just mixed. Some streaks of egg whites may be visible; do not overprocess.

Serve the Pineapple Sauce in a separate dish with Zested Strawberries (see Index), Fruit Lovers' Platter (see Index), or any sliced fresh fruit.

Makes 2 cups (4.7 dl).

Creamy Cheese Cake

This quick preparation of a favorite American dessert has a strawberry sauce more elegant than the usual fruit topping.

Preheat the oven to 225°F. (110°C.) and adjust the rack to the middle level. Place a cookie sheet on the rack. Butter a 9-inch (23 cm) springform pan.

Crust

45 vanilla wafers
    (7 ounces, 198g)
1 stick unsalted butter
    (4 ounces, 115g),
    melted
3 tablespoons sugar
1 teaspoon cinnamon
1/2 teaspoon freshly
    grated nutmeg

Metal Blade: Put the cookies in the work bowl and turn the machine on and off about 8 times to chop them coarsely, then process continuously until they are finely and uniformly chopped. Add the remaining crust ingredients and process for 10 seconds. Press the crumbs into the bottom of the prepared springform pan and 2 inches up on the sides. Wash and dry the work bowl.

Assemble all the ingredients and a 1-quart (9.5 dl) mixing bowl conveniently near the food processor.

Filling

4 large eggs, separated
1 tablespoon white
    vinegar
3/4 cup sugar
    (5-1/4 ounces, 148g)
2 8-ounce (225g)
    packages cream
    cheese at room
    temperature, cut into
    6 pieces
1 cup whipping cream,
    chilled
1/2 teaspoon lemon zest
1 tablespoon
    unbleached
    all-purpose flour
1/4 teaspoon salt
2 teaspoons pure
    vanilla extract
    Strawberry-Raspberry
    Sauce (see Index)

Metal Blade: Put the egg whites into a clean work bowl and turn the machine on. After 8 seconds, pour the vinegar through the feed tube and process for about 1 minute and 15 seconds, or until the egg whites are whipped and hold their shape. With a rubber spatula, gently transfer the egg whites to the mixing bowl. It is not necessary to wash the work bowl.

Put the egg yolks and sugar into the work bowl and process for 1 minute, stopping once to scrape down the sides of the bowl. Add the cream cheese and process for 30 seconds, stopping once to scrape down the sides of the bowl. Add the cream, lemon zest, flour, salt and vanilla and process for 10 seconds. Spoon the egg whites onto the mixture in a ring. Turn the machine on and off twice, then run a spatula around the sides of the bowl, to loosen the mixture. Turn the machine on and off 3 more times, until the egg whites are just mixed in. Some streaks of egg white may be visible; do not overprocess.

With a rubber spatula, transfer the mixture to the crust. Put the pan onto the preheated cookie sheet in the oven and bake for 2 hours. Turn the oven off and leave the cheese cake in for 1 more hour, with the door closed. Remove it and let it cool completely on a rack. Cover airtight and refrigerate. Let it come to room temperature before serving.

Serve with Strawberry-Raspberry Sauce.

Makes 10 to 12 servings.

Jamaican Banana Cake

This cake is most successful when made with overripe bananas. The frosting idea came from Michel Colin, head chef at Frédy Girardet's restaurant in Crisser, Switzerland. He made it to celebrate his daughter's third birthday.

Cake

1-3/4 cups cake flour
(7 ounces, 198g)
2 teaspoons baking powder
3/4 teaspoon salt
1/2 teaspoon baking soda
1/2 teaspoon allspice
1/4 teaspoon freshly grated nutmeg
3 large egg whites
1 tablespoon white vinegar
2 medium-sized ripe bananas (12 ounces total, 340g), peeled and cut into 8 pieces
2 large egg yolks
1-1/2 cups sugar
(10-1/2 ounces, 298g)
1 stick unsalted butter (4 ounces, 115g) at room temperature, in 4 pieces
5 tablespoons buttermilk
1 tablespoon dark rum

Butter two 8-inch (20 cm) round layer cake pans and line the bottoms with waxed paper. Butter the paper. Preheat the oven to 350°F. (175°C.) and adjust the rack to the middle level. Sift the dry ingredients together.

Assemble all the ingredients and a 1-quart (9.5 dl) mixing bowl conveniently near the food processor.

Metal Blade: Put the egg whites and 1/4 cup of sugar (50g) into a clean work bowl and turn the machine on. After 8 seconds, pour the vinegar through the feed tube while the machine is running. Process for 50 seconds, or until the whites are whipped and hold their shape. With a rubber spatula, transfer them gently to the mixing bowl. It is not necessary to wash the work bowl.

Put the banana pieces in the work bowl and process to a smooth purée, stopping once to scrape down the sides of the bowl. You should have 1 cup (2.4 dl) of purée.

Put the egg yolks and remaining sugar in the work bowl and process for 1 minute, stopping once to scrape down the bowl. Add the butter and process for 1 minute, stopping once to scrape down the sides of the bowl. With the machine running, pour the buttermilk and rum through the feed tube and process for 5 seconds. Add the dry ingredients in a ring around the bowl. Turn the machine on and off twice. Spoon the egg whites onto the batter and turn the machine on and off twice. Run a spatula around the sides of the work bowl, to loosen the mixture. Turn the machine on and off 2 more times, until the batter is just mixed; do not overprocess.

With a rubber spatula, transfer the batter to the prepared pans and spread it evenly. Bake in the preheated oven for 30 minutes, or until a toothpick inserted in the center comes out clean. Let the layers cool for 10 minutes in the pans, then invert them onto a wire rack and remove the pans. Let them cool completely. Frost the top of one layer with Banana Buttercream Frosting and set the other layer on top of it. Frost the top and sides with the remaining frosting.

Makes 8 to 10 servings.

Banana Buttercream Frosting

       3 cups confectioners sugar (12 ounces, 340g)
       1 medium-sized ripe banana (6 ounces, 170g), peeled and cut into 4 pieces
 2-1/2 tablespoons unsalted butter at room temperature
         Pinch of salt
       1 tablespoon dark rum

Metal Blade: Process the confectioners sugar for 5 seconds to remove the lumps. Add the rest of the ingredients and process until smooth, stopping the machine once to scrape down the sides of the bowl.

Makes 1-1/2 cups (3.5 dl).

Jamaican Banana Cake

Triple Layer Lemon Cake

This velvety confection, filled with tangy lemon curd and frosted with lemon-flavored whipped cream, should satisfy even the most ardent lemon lover.

Cake

1-3/4 cups cake flour (7 ounces, 198g)
2 teaspoons baking powder
3/4 teaspoon baking soda
3/4 teaspoon salt
3 large eggs, separated
1-1/4 cups sugar (8-3/4 ounces, 248g)
2 tablespoons water
1-1/2 sticks unsalted butter (6 ounces, 170g) at room temperature, cut into 6 pieces
Zest of 1 lemon
1/4 cup (60 ml) orange juice
2 tablespoons fresh lemon juice
1-1/2 teaspoons lemon extract
3/4 cup (1.8 dl) sour cream
Lemon Curd Filling (see Index)
Whipped Cream Topping (recipe follows)

Butter three 8-inch (20 cm) round cake pans. Line the bottoms with waxed paper and butter the paper.

Preheat the oven to 350°F. (175°C.) and adjust 2 oven racks close to the middle level.

Stir the dry ingredients together in a mixing bowl. Assemble all the other ingredients and a 1-quart (9.5 dl) mixing bowl conveniently near the food processor.

Metal Blade: Put the egg whites and 1/4 cup (1-3/4 ounces, 50g) of sugar into a clean work bowl and turn the machine on. After 8 seconds, pour the water through the feed tube and process for 2 minutes, or until the egg whites are whipped and hold their shape. With a rubber spatula, gently transfer the mixture to the mixing bowl. It is not necessary to wash the work bowl.

Process the egg yolks and remaining sugar for 1 minute. Add the butter and zest and process for 1 minute, stopping once to scrape down the sides of the work bowl. Add the orange and lemon juices and extract and process for 10 seconds. Add the sour cream and process for 5 seconds. Add the dry ingredients, arranging them in a ring around the work bowl. Spoon the egg whites onto the dry ingredients in a ring. Turn the machine on and off twice. Run a spatula around the sides of the work bowl, to loosen the mixture. Turn the machine on and off 2 or 3 times, just until the batter is mixed. Some streaks of egg white may still be visible; do not overprocess.

With a rubber spatula, transfer the batter evenly into the prepared pans. Tap the pans gently on the counter several times to remove any air pockets. Bake the cakes in the preheated oven for 20 minutes, or until a toothpick inserted in the center comes out clean. Set the pans on cake racks for 10 minutes, then loosen each cake around the edge with a sharp knife and invert onto the rack to cool completely.

Set one layer on a serving platter. Spread evenly with 1/2 to 2/3 cup (1.2 to 1.6 dl) of the Lemon Curd Filling. Top with the second layer and spread with an equal amount of filling. Add the top layer and cover the top and sides of the cake with Whipped Cream Topping. Refrigerate until 30 minutes before serving.

Makes 12 servings.

Whipped Cream Topping

4 tablespoons instant non-fat dry milk
1/2 cup confectioners sugar (2 ounces, 56g), sifted
2 cups (4.7 dl) whipping cream, chilled
1 teaspoon lemon extract

Metal Blade: Put the dry milk and sugar in the work bowl and turn the machine on. Pour the whipping cream through the feed tube and process for 1 minute, or until it thickens. Add the lemon extract and process for 5 seconds.

Makes 2 cups (4.7 dl).

Prune Whip

1-1/2 cups pitted prunes (8 ounces, 226g)
Zest of 1 orange
1/3 cup (80 ml) Ruby Port
1/3 cup (80 ml) water
4 large egg whites
1/4 cup sugar (1-3/4 ounces, 50g)
1 tablespoon white vinegar
1 tablespoon water
1 teaspoon fresh lemon juice

Lightly butter a 1-quart (9.5 dl) soufflé dish. Have ready a kettle of boiling water and a baking dish large enough to hold the soufflé dish.

Cook the prunes, orange zest, Port and water in a 1-quart (9.5 dl) saucepan over medium heat for 15 minutes, or until all the liquid has evaporated. Let them cool.

Preheat the oven to 350°F. (175°C.) and adjust the rack to the middle level.

Metal Blade: Put the egg whites and sugar into the work bowl and turn the machine on. After 8 seconds, pour the vinegar and water through the feed tube while the machine is running, and process for 2 minutes, or until the egg whites are whipped and hold their shape. With a rubber spatula, gently transfer the egg whites to the mixing bowl. It is not necessary to wash the work bowl.

Process the prunes and lemon juice for about 1 minute, stopping once to scrape down the sides of the work bowl. Add 1/4 of the egg whites, and turn the machine on and off twice. Run a spatula around the sides of the work bowl, to loosen the mixture. Spoon the remaining egg whites onto the mixture in a ring. Turn the machine on and off 5 times. Some streaks of egg white may be visible; do not overprocess.

With a rubber spatula, gently transfer the mixture to the prepared soufflé dish. Place the soufflé dish in the baking pan and set the pan on the oven rack. Pour enough boiling water into the pan to come up 2 inches (5 cm) on the side of the soufflé dish. Bake 10 minutes, or until the surface feels firm. Remove the soufflé dish from the water bath and cool. Refrigerate at least 6 hours or overnight, covered airtight. Serve with Vanilla Cream Sauce (see Index).

Makes 4 cups (9.5 dl), or 8 servings.

Glazed Chocolate Torte

This decadently rich torte is made in a flash and it actually improves when refrigerated for one or two days. If you freeze it, be sure to glaze it on the day you plan to serve it.

Torte

- 1 tablespoon white vinegar
- 1 tablespoon water
- 7 large eggs, separated
- 3/4 slice firm, good quality bread, crust removed (1/2 ounce, 14g) — makes about 5 tablespoons crumbs
- 2 cups walnuts, pecans or almonds (8 ounces total, 225g)
- 6 ounces (170g) sweet chocolate, preferably Maillard or German's, broken into 8 pieces
- 1 cup sugar (7 ounces, 198g)
- 1 tablespoon baking powder
  Pinch of salt
- 1 stick unsalted butter (4 ounces, 115g) at room temperature, cut into 8 pieces
- 1 tablespoon pure vanilla extract or dark rum

Butter a 9-inch (23 cm) springform pan and cut a circle of parchment paper to fit the bottom. Butter the parchment paper. Preheat the oven to 350°F. (175°C.) and adjust the rack to the middle level.

Mix the vinegar and water in a small bowl. Assemble all the ingredients and a 1-quart (9.5 dl) mixing bowl conveniently near the food processor.

Metal Blade: Put the egg whites into a clean work bowl and turn the machine on. After 8 seconds, pour the water and vinegar through the feed tube while the machine is running. Process for about 1 minute and 30 seconds, or until the whites are whipped and hold their shape. With a rubber spatula, gently transfer the mixture to the mixing bowl. It is not necessary to wash the work bowl.

Put the bread, nuts, chocolate, sugar, baking powder and salt in the work bowl. Turn the machine on and off 4 times, then process for 1 minute, or until all of the ingredients are finely chopped. Scatter the butter over this mixture and process for 30 seconds, stopping once to scrape down the sides of the bowl. Add the egg yolks and vanilla and process only until all the ingredients are combined. Add 1/3 of the egg whites and turn the machine on and off 3 times. Run a spatula thoroughly around the sides of the bowl, to loosen the mixture. Spoon the remaining egg whites onto the mixture in a ring. Turn the machine on and off 2 or 3 more times, until the ingredients are just mixed. Some streaks of egg white may still be visible; do not overprocess.

With a rubber spatula, gently transfer the batter into the prepared pan, and bake in the preheated oven for 60 minutes, or until a toothpick inserted in the center comes out clean. Let the torte cool in the pan on a wire rack. To remove it from the pan, carefully run a thin sharp knife around its sides, separating the cake from the pan. This cake improves with refrigeration and freezes well, unglazed.

Glaze

- **2 tablespoons unsalted butter**
- **2 tablespoons water**
- **3 ounces (85g) sweet chocolate as above, broken into pieces**
- **1/4 cup confectioners sugar (1 ounce, 28g)**
- **2 teaspoons pure vanilla extract or dark rum**

Melt the butter and water in a small saucepan. Keep it bubbling hot until you are ready to use it. Put the chocolate and confectioners sugar in the work bowl and turn the machine on and off 3 times to chop the chocolate, then process continuously until it is finely minced. With the machine running, pour the hot water and butter through the feed tube and process until the chocolate is melted. Add vanilla or rum and process for 5 more seconds. Refrigerate the glaze just until it begins to thicken, then spread on sides and top of cake.

Makes 10 to 12 servings.

Glazed Chocolate Torte

Jacques Cagna's Chocolate Mousse Loaf

Can a dessert be sinful? Don't decide until you try this one!

Mousse

1-1/2 cups walnuts
(6 ounces, 170g)
1 tablespoon white
vinegar
1 tablespoon water
1-1/2 sticks unsalted butter
(6 ounces, 170g),
melted and sizzling
hot
6 large egg whites
12 ounces (340g)
semi-sweet chocolate,
broken into pieces
3 tablespoons cocoa
1/3 cup sugar
(2-1/3 ounces, 65g)
Pinch of salt
4 large egg yolks

Generously butter the bottom and sides of a 1-quart (9.5 dl) glass loaf pan. Line the bottom with parchment paper and butter the paper.

Shredding Disc: Process the walnuts, using medium pressure. Spread 1 cup (113g) of walnuts over the bottom and 2 inches (5 cm) up the sides of the prepared pan, pressing them into place. Reserve the remaining nuts. Wash and dry the work bowl.

Mix the vinegar and water in a small dish. Keep the butter hot on the stove, and assemble all the other ingredients and a 1-quart (9.5 dl) mixing bowl near the food processor.

Metal Blade: Put the egg whites into a clean work bowl and turn on the machine. After 8 seconds, pour the vinegar and water mixture through the feed tube while the machine is running. Process for about 1 minute and 45 seconds, or until the egg whites are whipped and hold their shape. With a rubber spatula, gently transfer the mixture to the mixing bowl. It is not necessary to wash the work bowl.

Put the chocolate, cocoa, sugar and salt into the work bowl. Turn the machine on and off 4 times to chop the chocolate coarsely, then process for 1 minute or until the chocolate is finely chopped. With the machine running, pour the hot butter through the feed tube and process for 1 minute, until the chocolate is completely melted. Stop the machine once to scrape down the sides of the bowl. Add the egg yolks and process for 10 seconds. Spoon the egg whites onto the chocolate mixture in a ring. Turn the machine on and off twice. Run a spatula around the sides of the work bowl, to loosen the mixture. Turn the machine on and off 3 more times until the ingredients are mixed. Some streaks of egg white may still be visible; do not overprocess.

With a rubber spatula, transfer the mousse to the prepared pan. Cover with plastic wrap and refrigerate for 3 hours, or until well chilled.

Carefully separate the mousse from the pan, using a thin sharp knife or a flexible spatula. Invert the mousse onto a serving platter and remove the pan. Press the remaining walnuts into the mousse, covering any bare spots. Let the loaf set at room temperature for 1/2 hour before serving.

Serve with Vanilla Cream Sauce.

Makes 8 to 10 servings.

Note: The mousse can be prepared up to 1 month in advance, covered airtight and frozen. Let thaw, covered, for 24 hours in the refrigerator.

Vanilla Cream Sauce _____

- 1 2-inch (5 cm) piece of vanilla bean
- 1 cup (2.4 dl) milk
- 3 large egg yolks
- 3 tablespoons sugar
- 2 tablespoons instant non-fat dry milk
- 1/4 cup confectioners sugar (1-1/2 ounces, 42g), sifted
- 1 cup (2.4 dl) whipping cream, chilled

Split the vanilla bean, scrape out the seeds and add the bean and the seeds to the milk in a 1-quart (9.5 dl) non-aluminum saucepan. Scald the milk and remove the bean from it just before using.

Metal Blade: Put the egg yolks and sugar in the work bowl and process for 1 minute, stopping once to scrape down the sides of the bowl. With the machine running, pour the hot milk through the feed tube and process for 10 seconds. Transfer the mixture back to the saucepan and cook over low heat, stirring constantly, until the custard is thick enough to coat a spoon. Remove the pan from the heat and place it in a pan of ice water to cool. Then refrigerate it until completely chilled.

Put the dry milk and confectioners sugar in the work bowl and turn the machine on. Pour the cream through the feed tube and process for about 1 minute, or until it is thick. Gently fold the whipped cream into the chilled custard sauce.

Makes 2 cups (4.7 dl).

Jacques Cagna's Chocolate Mousse Loaf

Raspberry Chiffon Pie

Chiffon pie is a dessert I never expected to make in the food processor. After four months and at least fifty attempts, I came up with this winner.

Crumb Crust

45 vanilla wafers
(7 ounces, 198g)
1 stick unsalted butter
(4 ounces, 115g),
melted
3 tablespoons sugar
1 teaspoon cinnamon
1/4 teaspoon freshly
grated nutmeg

Raspberry Filling

2 10-ounce (285g)
packages frozen
raspberries, thawed
2 tablespoons fresh
lemon juice
1 tablespoon unflavored
gelatin (1-1/2
packages)
4 large egg yolks
5 large egg whites
6 tablespoons sugar
1 tablespoon white
vinegar
1 cup whipping cream,
chilled

Lightly butter a 6-cup (14 dl) pie plate. (I prefer a "deep dish" type for this pie.) Preheat the oven to 350°F. (175°C.) and adjust the rack to the middle level.

Metal Blade: Put the cookies in the work bowl and chop them coarsely by turning the machine on and off about 8 times, then process continuously until they are finely and uniformly chopped. Add the remaining crust ingredients and process for 10 seconds. Transfer the contents of the work bowl into the prepared pie plate. Using your fingers, press the crumbs firmly into place on the bottom and sides of the plate. Bring the crumb crust all the way up to the edge of the plate and press firmly. (I use a round tumbler to press the crumbs firmly into the corner and up the sides of the dish.)

Bake the crust in a preheated oven for 6 minutes. If there is any slippage of the crust, work it back into place with your fingers while it is still warm. Cool the crust completely before filling it.

Still using the metal blade, process the raspberries and their syrup for 40 seconds. Transfer the mixture to a strainer and press the seeds to remove all the liquid. Discard the seeds. Place the mixture in a 4-cup (9.5 dl) liquid measure; it should measure about 2 cups (4.7 dl) plus 2 tablespoons of puréed raspberries. It is not necessary to clean the work bowl before proceeding.

Place the raspberries and lemon juice in a 1-quart (9.5 dl) non-aluminum saucepan. Sprinkle the gelatin over the surface and stir. After 1 minute, add the egg yolks and whisk them vigorously. Cook the mixture gently over medium heat until it thickens and coats a spoon. This will occur when it reaches about 175°F. (80°C.) Transfer to a shallow metal pan and place in the freezer for about 45 minutes, or until the mixture is hard.

Still using the metal blade, put the egg whites and sugar into the work bowl and turn the machine on. After 8 seconds, pour the vinegar through the feed tube while the machine is running. Process for 2 minutes, or until the egg whites are whipped and hold their shape. With a rubber spatula, gently transfer the egg whites to a mixing bowl. It is not necessary to wash the work bowl.

Turn on the machine and pour the cream slowly through the feed tube while the machine is running. Process for 1 minute, or until it is thick. Do not overprocess. Transfer the cream to a mixing bowl. Put the raspberry mixture in the work bowl and process for 2 minutes, or until it is smooth and fluffy, stopping twice to scrape down the sides of the bowl. Spoon the cream onto the raspberry mixture and combine by turning the machine on and off about 4 times. Add 1/4 of the egg whites and turn the machine on and off twice. Spoon the remaining egg whites onto the mixture in a ring. Turn the machine on and off twice. Run a spatula around the sides of the work bowl, to thoroughly loosen the mixture. Turn the machine on and off 3 more times, until the ingredients are just mixed. Some streaks of egg white may still be visible; do not overprocess.

With a rubber spatula, gently transfer the mixture into the cooled crust, mounding it in the center. Refrigerate for at least 2 hours, and garnish with whipped cream.

Whipped Cream Garnish

2 tablespoons instant non-fat dry milk
2 tablespoons confectioners sugar
1 cup (2.4 dl) whipping cream, chilled
1 tablespoon Kirsch

Metal Blade: Put the dry milk and confectioners sugar into the bowl and turn the machine on. Pour the cream slowly through the feed tube while the machine is running. Process for 1 minute, or until it is thick. Add the Kirsch and process for 5 seconds. Spoon the cream into a pastry bag fitted with a medium star tip and decorate the pie.

Makes 6 to 8 servings.

Raspberry Chiffon Pie

One of my first breakthrough recipes using egg whites beaten in the food processor. The intense orange flavor contributes a spark of freshness appropriate at a variety of meals from brunch to late supper.

Bavarian Cream _____

- 1/2 cup large dried apricots, (about 15 or 3-1/4 ounces, 100g)
- 1/2 cup (1.2 dl) frozen orange juice concentrate, thawed
- 1 tablespoon unflavored gelatin (1-1/2 packages)
- 1/4 cup (1.2 dl) cold water
- 4 large egg whites
- 3/4 cup plus 2 tablespoons sugar (6-1/4 ounces total, 185g)
- 2 tablespoons fresh lemon juice
- 2 8-ounce (225g) containers plain yogurt

Lightly oil a 6-1/2 cup (15 dl) ring mold. If possible, soak the apricots in the orange juice overnight in a covered container. Gently heat the apricots in the juice until almost completely soft. (If they remain firm, the dessert will have more texture.) It may be necessary to push the apricots down into the juice from time to time. Remove them from the heat and reserve.

Sprinkle the gelatin over the water. When the water has been absorbed, dissolve the gelatin by setting the cup in a pan of hot water, or placing it for 20 seconds in a microwave oven set at the lowest temperature. Reserve the gelatin.

Metal Blade: Assemble all the ingredients and a 1-quart (9.5 dl) mixing bowl conveniently near the food processor. Put the egg whites and 2 tablespoons of the sugar into a clean work bowl and turn the machine on. After 8 seconds, pour in the lemon juice and process for 45 seconds, or until the egg whites are whipped and hold their shape. With a rubber spatula, transfer them gently to the mixing bowl. It is not necessary to wash the work bowl.

Put the apricots and orange juice in the work bowl with the remaining 3/4 cup (5-1/4 ounces, 148g) sugar and process for 1 minute, stopping once to scrape down the sides of the bowl. Process 1 minute more. Add the dissolved gelatin and process 10 seconds more. (Be sure to use all the gelatin; if it has started to set, warm it slightly and stir.) Add 1/2 cup (5-1/2 ounces, 150g) of yogurt and process for 3 seconds. Scrape down the sides of the bowl. Add the remaining yogurt around the work bowl in a ring and spoon the egg whites onto the yogurt in large spoonfuls. Turn the machine on and off twice. Carefully scrape down any spatter inside the bowl. Turn on and off 3 to 5 more times, until the ingredients are just mixed. Some streaks of egg white may be visible; do not overprocess.

With a rubber spatula, transfer the Bavarian Cream to the prepared ring mold. Cover it with plastic wrap and refrigerate at least 4 hours.

Garnish

3 firm seedless navel oranges, with ends cut flat and rind scored or removed
2 8-ounce (225g) containers plain yogurt

Medium or Thick Slicing Disc: Slice the oranges, using firm pressure if you scored the rind, or very light pressure if you removed it. Wrap the slices in plastic and refrigerate until serving time.

Assembly

Invert the Bavarian Cream onto a flat 12-inch (30 cm) round platter. Fan the orange slices around the edge of the platter. Put the yogurt into a serving dish that fits in the center of the Bavarian Cream.

Makes 8 to 12 servings.

Apricot/Yogurt Bavarian Cream with Orange Slices

Fresh Strawberry Cake Roll

All the delights of a light strawberry shortcake served up in a sponge cake roll.

Cake

3/4 **cup cake flour (3 ounces, 85g)**
1-1/2 **teaspoons baking powder**
Pinch of salt
3 **large eggs, separated**
1 **tablespoon white vinegar**
3 **tablespoons water**
1 **tablespoon orange juice concentrate**
3/4 **cup sugar (5-1/4 ounces, 150g)**
1 **tablespoon confectioners sugar**

Line an 11- by 17-inch (28- by 43-cm) jelly-roll pan with waxed paper, extending it 2 inches (5 cm) beyond the edges of the pan. Butter the paper, dust it lightly with flour and shake off any excess.

Preheat the oven to 375°F. (190°C.) and adjust the rack to the middle level. Sift the cake flour, baking powder and salt together, and set aside. Assemble all the ingredients and a 1-quart (9.5 dl) mixing bowl near the food processor.

Metal Blade: Put the egg whites into a clean work bowl. Turn on the machine. After 8 seconds, pour in the vinegar and 1 tablespoon of water and process for about 1 minute and 10 seconds, or until the egg whites are whipped and hold their shape. With a rubber spatula, transfer them gently to the mixing bowl. It is not necessary to wash the work bowl.

Process the egg yolks, remaining 2 tablespoons of water, orange juice concentrate and sugar for 1 minute. Add the flour mixture in a ring. Transfer the egg whites onto the flour by large spoonfuls. Turn the machine on and off twice; stop the machine and scrape down the sides of the bowl. Turn the machine on and off 2 or 3 more times, just until the batter is mixed. Some egg whites may be visible; do not overprocess.

With a rubber spatula, transfer the batter to the prepared pan and spread it evenly. Lightly tap the pan on the counter to remove any air pockets. Bake the cake 10 or 12 minutes, just until it is lightly browned. Remove it from the oven and sift confectioners sugar evenly over the top. Cover the cake with a piece of waxed paper, then with a damp towel. Carefully turn the cake over to invert it onto the towel. Let the cake stand until cool, about 30 minutes. Carefully peel off the top sheet of waxed paper. Cover the cake with a piece of foil and turn it over again to invert it onto the foil.

Filling

1 **pint (about 13 ounces, 368g) large fresh strawberries, hulled**
1 **to 2 tablespoons sugar (depending on sweetness of berries)**
2 **tablespoons Grand Marnier liqueur**

Thick or Medium Slicing Disc: Reserve 6 large, perfect strawberries for garnish. Slice the remaining strawberries, using light pressure. Place them in a small mixing bowl with the sugar and Grand Marnier. Leave for 20 minutes, then drain off any excess juices.

Combine the gelatin and water in a 1-cup (235 cm) measure. When the water has been absorbed, dissolve the gelatin by setting the cup in a pan of hot water or placing it for 20 seconds in a microwave oven at the lowest setting. Set aside.

Whipped Cream

1 package unflavored gelatin
1/4 cup (60 ml) cold water
2 cups (4.8 dl) heavy cream
1/3 cup sugar (2-1/2 ounces, 70g)
1 tablespoon Grand Marnier liqueur
1 teaspoon pure vanilla extract

Assembly

1/2 cup (1.2 dl) raspberry jelly, melted

Variation

Whip the cream until stiff, gradually adding the sugar. Stir in the Grand Marnier and vanilla. Add the dissolved gelatin to the whipped cream and fold it in gently but thoroughly. Set aside 1-1/2 cups (3.5 dl) of the whipped cream to be used for frosting the cake roll.

Spread the raspberry jelly evenly over the surface of the cake. Fold the well-drained strawberries into the remaining 1-1/2 cups (3.5 dl) of whipped cream. Starting at the short end of the roll, about 3 inches (7.5 cm) in from the end, spread 1/3 of the strawberry-cream mixture in a 3-inch (7.5 cm) band. Start to roll up the cake gently, making one complete turn. Spread another 1/3 of the strawberry cream in a 3-inch (7.5 cm) band and roll the cake one more complete turn. Repeat with the remaining strawberry cream and finish rolling the cake. Carefully slide the roll on to a serving platter, seam side down. Spread the remaining whipped cream mixture over the entire roll with a flexible spatula, making small decorative peaks. Cut the reserved strawberries in half and garnish the cake with them.

To make a sponge cake layer, bake the same batter in a 9-inch (23 cm) round layer cake pan. Butter the pan, line it with waxed paper and butter the paper. Lightly dust the bottom and sides with flour. Bake on the middle rack of a preheated 350°F. (175°C.) oven for 32 to 35 minutes. Let cool completely on a wire rack. Loosen the cake completely around the edge with a sharp flexible knife and invert it onto a serving plate.

Maple Cake Roll with Maple Pecan Cream

I am passionately fond of maple flavor, and it is perfect in this moist, light dessert.

Maple Pecan Cream

1/3 cup confectioners sugar (1-1/3 ounces, 37g)
1/3 cup pecans (1-1/3 ounces, 37g)
1-1/2 cups (3.5 dl) whipping cream, chilled
2 teaspoons imitation maple flavor
Pinch of salt

Metal Blade: Process the sugar and pecans until the pecans are finely chopped. Transfer to a 1-quart (9.5 dl) mixing bowl and set aside. Turn on the machine, pour the cream through the feed tube and process until thick. Do not overprocess. Add the flavoring and salt and process for 5 seconds. Fold the cream into the pecan mixture. Wash and dry the work bowl. (This can be prepared 1 day in advance and refrigerated in an airtight container.)

Preheat the oven to 325°F. (165°C.) and adjust the rack to the middle level.

Cake

- 1/2 cup cake flour
  (2 ounces, 58g)
- 1 teaspoon baking
  powder
- 1/8 teaspoon salt
- 1 tablespoon white
  vinegar
- 1 tablespoon water
- 4 large eggs, separated
- 3/4 cup sugar
  (5-1/4 ounces, 150g)
- 1/2 cup pecans (2 ounces,
  58g)
- 2 teaspoons imitation
  maple flavor
- 1 tablespoon
  confectioners sugar
- 8 pecan halves

Line an 11- by 17-inch (28- by 43-cm) jelly-roll pan with waxed paper, extending it 2 inches (5 cm) beyond the edges of the pan. Butter the paper, dust it lightly with flour and shake off excess.

Stir the flour, baking powder and salt together in a bowl.

Assemble all the other ingredients and a 1-quart (9.5 dl) mixing bowl conveniently near the food processor. Put the vinegar and water in a small dish.

Metal Blade: Put the egg whites in a clean work bowl and turn the machine on. After 8 seconds, pour the vinegar and water mixture through the feed tube and process for about 1 minute and 45 seconds, or until the egg whites are whipped and hold their shape. With a rubber spatula, transfer the egg whites gently to the mixing bowl. It is not necessary to wash the work bowl before proceeding.

Add the egg yolks, sugar, pecans and flavoring and process for 1 minute, stopping the machine once to scrape down the sides of the work bowl. Add the dry ingredients, arranging them in a ring around the bowl. Spoon the egg whites onto the flour in a ring. Turn the machine on and off twice, then run a spatula around the sides of the bowl, to loosen the mixture. Turn the machine on and off 2 or 3 times, until the batter is just mixed. Some streaks of egg white may still be visible; do not overprocess.

With a rubber spatula, transfer the batter to the prepared pan, spreading it evenly. Tap the pan gently on the counter several times to remove any air pockets.

Bake the cake in the preheated oven for 14 to 15 minutes, or until it is just lightly browned; do not overbake. Remove it from the oven and sift confectioners sugar evenly over the top. Cover the cake with a sheet of waxed paper and then with a damp towel. Carefully turn the cake over to invert it onto the towel. Let it rest on a rack until cool, about 20 minutes. Carefully peel off the top sheet of waxed paper. Cover the cake with a piece of aluminum foil and turn it over again to invert it onto the foil. The foil will help you roll the cake.

Spread 2/3 of the Maple Pecan Cream over the cake. Use the foil to roll it up, starting with the long side for a long, narrow roll, which I prefer. If you like a thicker, short roll, start with the short side. Transfer to a serving platter, seam side down. Frost the surface with the remaining Maple Pecan Cream, garnish with the pecan halves, and refrigerate until ready to serve. Slice diagonally.

Makes 8 to 10 servings.

Index